FIFTH EDITION

JUST ENOUGH UNIX

Paul K. Andersen

New Mexico State University
Las Cruces, New Mexico

Higher Education

Boston   Burr Ridge, IL   Dubuque, IA   Madison, WI   New York   San Francisco   St. Louis
Bangkok   Bogotá   Caracas   Kuala Lumpur   Lisbon   London   Madrid   Mexico City
Milan   Montreal   New Delhi   Santiago   Seoul   Singapore   Sydney   Taipei   Toronto

The McGraw·Hill Companies

JUST ENOUGH UNIX, FIFTH EDITION

1 2 3 4 5 6 7 8 9 0 QPF/QPF 0 9 8 7 6 5 4

ISBN 0–07–295297–0

Publisher: *Elizabeth A. Jones*
Sponsoring Editor: *Kelly H. Lowery*
Developmental Editor: *Michelle L. Flomenhoft*
Marketing Manager: *Dawn R. Bercier*
Project Manager: *Peggy S. Lucas*
Senior Production Supervisor: *Kara Kudronowicz*
Media Technology Producer: *Eric A. Weber*
Senior Designer: *David W. Hash*
Cover Designer: *Crystal Kadlec*
(USE) Cover Images: front cover: *NASA/NSSDC, infrared image of Saturn taken by HST's NICMOS instruments;* back cover: *NASA/NSSDC, stellar formation in NGC 3603*
Supplement Producer: *Brenda A. Ernzen*
Typeface: *10/12 MinionPro*
Printer: *Quebecor World Fairfield, PA*

Library of Congress Cataloging-in-Publication Data

Andersen, Paul K.
   Just enough UNIX / Paul K. Andersen.—5th ed.
      p.   cm.
   Includes index.
   ISBN 0–07–295297–0 (hc. : alk. paper)
   1. Operating systems (Computers). 2. UNIX (Computer file). I.Title.

QA76.76.O63A48 2006
005.4'32—dc22   2004020676
                                                            CIP

www.mhhe.com

TABLE OF CONTENTS

PREFACE

What is UNIX?

UNIX is an operating system (OS), software that manages the hardware and software resources of a computer. UNIX is one of the most widely used operating systems in industry, government, and education. It is especially popular in academia: according to AT&T, where UNIX was developed, every major university in the United States now has at least one computer system running under UNIX.

Which Version of UNIX?

Although UNIX originated at the AT&T Bell Laboratories, much of its subsequent development has occurred in academia, most notably at the University of California, Berkeley. Computer manufacturers, too, have gotten into the act, producing their own variations on the UNIX theme. Examples include AIX, from IBM; OS X, from Apple Computer; HP-UX, from Hewlett-Packard; and Solaris, from Sun Microsystems. Then there are various UNIX work-alikes—systems that look and behave like UNIX—the best known of these being Linux.

From the user's standpoint, these versions of UNIX are quite similar. Most can trace their ancestry to either AT&T UNIX or Berkeley UNIX; some are amalgams of both. This book presents features that are found on almost all UNIX systems, with special emphasis on those that are common to AT&T System V and Berkeley System Distribution (BSD) 4.3 UNIX.

Who Should Read This Book?

This book is intended for anyone who wants to acquire a working knowledge of UNIX without having to become a UNIX expert. It is especially appropriate for students of science, engineering, or business who are taking their first computer programming course.

What Does This Book Cover?

This book covers the basics of the UNIX operating system. It has nine main parts:

I   INTRODUCTION TO UNIX

II   UNIX FILE SYSTEM

III   UNIX SHELLS

IV   TEXT EDITORS

V   NETWORKS

VI   COMPUTER SECURITY

VII   STARTUP FILES

VIII SCRIPTING LANGUAGES

IX   PROGRAMMING LANGUAGES

INTRODUCTION. In Part I, you will find an overview of the UNIX operating system, and you will learn what you will need to start using it. Three different approaches are presented: traditional (command-line) UNIX; the X Window System with Motif; and the Common Desktop Environment (CDE).

UNIX FILE SYSTEM. UNIX organizes information in collections called files. You will learn how to create, name, rename, copy, and delete files in Part II. You will also learn how UNIX keeps track of your files.

UNIX SHELLS. The part of UNIX that interprets user commands and passes them on to the computer is called a shell. Many different shells have been written for UNIX; the most prevalent are the Bourne Shell (sh), the Korn Shell (ksh), the C Shell (csh), the TC Shell (tcsh), and the Bourne-Again Shell (bash). These shells are considered in Part III.

TEXT EDITORS. You can create or modify UNIX files using a utility program called an editor. The most popular UNIX editors are vi ("vee-eye"), emacs, pico, and CDE Text Editor, which are discussed in Part IV.

NETWORKS. The recent growth of the Internet and World Wide Web around the world has been phenomenal. UNIX systems are a considerable part of this development. Internet and Web tools are presented in Part V.

COMPUTER SECURITY. The unauthorized use—or misuse—of computer resources can be costly. Computer security involves authentication, access control, and encryption, which are discussed in Part VI.

STARTUP FILES. One of the great advantages of the UNIX operating system is its flexibility. A startup file contains commands for the shell to execute when it begins running. Startup files are examined in Part VII.

SCRIPTING LANGUAGES. As an alternative to conventional programming languages, UNIX systems offer a variety of scripting languages. These are typically interpreted languages that are ideal for rapid development of software. Scripting using the shell, awk, and Perl is described in Part VIII.

PROGRAMMING UNDER UNIX. Most UNIX systems include the programming languages C, C++, Fortran, and Java. Many also include Pascal and other languages such as BASIC, Lisp, and COBOL. UNIX also offers a selection of software tools that are used in programming. UNIX programming is discussed in Part IX, with emphasis on C, C++, and Java.

What is New in the Fifth Edition

Several new chapters have been added; other chapters have been revised extensively. The following new topics are covered:

- Computer security (Chapter 24);

- Using Secure Shell (Chapters 25 and 26)

- Using Gnu Privacy Guard (Chapter 27);

- Scripting languages (Chapter 32);

- Scripting with awk (Chapter 34);

- Scripting with Perl (Chapter 36); and

- Formatted Output (Appendix E).

Chapters on network news, Internet browsers, and Fortran programming have been deleted from this edition.

How to Use This Book

Anyone who is just starting with UNIX should read straight through Parts I, II, III, and IV. The remaining parts may be read in any order.

Each part of this book begins with a chapter explaining the material without requiring the use of the computer. Other chapters are called "tutorials." These are intended to be read at the computer terminal. You should plan to spend about an hour at the terminal to cover each tutorial.

At the end of each section, you will find some short exercises. To derive the maximum benefit from this text, be sure to work through all of the exercises.

Acknowledgments

Many persons helped in the preparation of this edition. The following reviewers read the manuscript at various stages in its development and provided helpful comments and suggestions:

Marvin Bishop, Manhattan College

Robert M. Cubert, University of Florida

Timothy A. Davis, Clemson University

Jie Hu, St. Cloud State University

Nisar Hundewale, Georgia State University

Mark S. Hutchenreuther, California Polytechnic State University

John Koch, Wilkes University

Jeffery Korn, New York University

Robert W. Kramer, Youngstown State University

Curtis Larsen, Dixie State College

Stephen P. Leach, Florida State University

Sigurd L. Lillevik, University of Portland

Larry Morell, Arkansas Tech University

T.N. Nagabhushan, Sri Jayachamarajendra College of Engineering

William Nico, California State University, Hayward

Riccardo Pucella, Cornell University

Charles Robert Putnam, California State University, Northridge

Hara P. Satpathy, Barry University

Thomas N. Scanlan, University of Wisconsin, Platteville

Iren Valova, University of Massachusetts

Jeff Wolfe, Pennsylvania State University

This book could not have been produced without the invaluable assistance of Dr. M. G. Scarbrough, colleague and friend.

PART I
INTRODUCTION TO UNIX

INTRODUCTION TO UNIX

Mention *computer*, and many people are apt to think of *hardware*—the physical device, consisting of circuit boards, a central processing unit (CPU), memory chips, and so on. Equally important, however, is the software—the programs that tell the hardware what to do. Without software, a computer is just a box with wires attached to it.

The operating system is an especially important kind of software that manages the resources of the computer. This chapter provides a brief overview of computer hardware and software, with emphasis on the UNIX operating system.

1.1 Computer Hardware

Computers come in a bewildering range of shapes, sizes, and types. Despite their differences, almost all have four essential components (see Figure 1–1):

■ **Central processing unit (CPU).** The CPU performs calculations and manipulates data. It is the "brain" of the computer.

■ **Main memory (primary memory, internal memory, RAM).** This is the place where the CPU looks for instructions and data to process. Main memory—also called *random-access memory* or *RAM*—is fast but limited in how much it can hold.

■ **Mass storage (external memory, secondary memory).** Information that is not immediately needed by the computer is placed in mass storage or secondary memory, which is usually slower than main memory but can hold much more. The most common mass storage devices are magnetic disks.

■ **Input/output devices.** Input/output (I/O) devices are used to move information to and from the computer. The most common I/O devices include the keyboard, mouse, video display, and printer.

Other devices—such as terminals, printers, scanners, and so on—are sometimes attached to the computer. These are generally called *peripherals*.

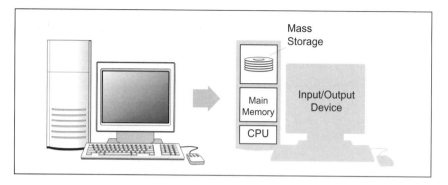

Figure 1-1
A typical computer system. The four parts of a single-user computer are shown.

1.2 One User or Many?

Workstations are more powerful than the typical personal computer.

The computer represented in Figure 1–1 is a *single-user* computer, either a *personal computer* or *workstation*. It has one keyboard and one video display, and is intended to serve just one person at a time. This is common with smaller computers.

Large computers, on the other hand, often have more power than one person can profitably use. These computers are commonly set up as *multiuser systems,* as shown in Figure 1–2. Note that the multiuser computer has the same basic parts as the single-user computer: CPU, main memory, mass storage, and I/O devices.

ASCII is a method for representing text; it is discussed in Chapter 18.

The I/O devices shown in Figure 1–2 are *character* or *ASCII terminals*, each consisting of a keyboard and a video monitor. Such terminals can display text but not graphics, and are affectionately called "dumb" terminals.

`telnet` is discussed in Chapters 3 and 22.

In some cases, a personal computer may be used instead of a dumb terminal to interact with a multiuser system. A *terminal-emulation program* running on the personal computer causes it to behave like an ASCII terminal. A utility called `telnet` allows the computers to communicate with each other.

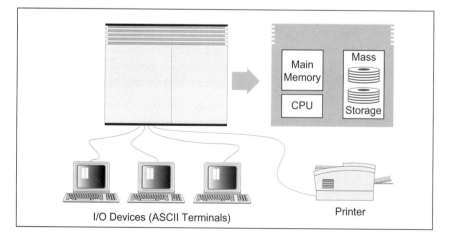

Figure 1-2
Multiuser computer system. This system is set up to handle as many as three users at a time. Some large systems can serve hundreds of users simultaneously.

I/O Devices (ASCII Terminals)   Printer

Bits, Bytes, Hertz, MIPS, and Flops

Computer memory is usually measured in bits and bytes. *Bit* is short for *binary digit*; a bit can store either a 0 or a 1. A *byte* is a grouping of eight bits; a byte can store a single character. The following prefixes are used for larger quantities:

kilo- (K) "thousand" (10^3)

mega- (M) "million" (10^6)

giga- (G) "billion" (10^9)

Sometimes these prefixes are meant as approximations—see Exercise 7.

Thus, 1 megabyte (Mbyte or MB) is approximately 1 million bytes of memory. A million bytes can hold a million characters, or about 500 typewritten pages.

A CPU may be rated by the number of bits it can process at a time. For example, a 32-bit CPU manipulates 32 bits at a time. Another way to say this is that the CPU has a 32-bit *word size*.

The rate at which words are processed by a CPU is determined by the *clock speed*. The *clock speed* is expressed in megahertz (MHz); 1 megahertz = 1 million pulses per second. Other things being equal, CPUs with larger word sizes and higher clock speeds are faster.

A computer's speed is sometimes expressed in terms of the number of arithmetic operations it can perform in a second. This is measured in *flops*, which is short for *floating-point operations per second*. Alternatively, a computer's speed may be expressed by the number of instructions it can execute in a second. This is measured in *MIPS*, which is short for *millions of instructions per second*.

1.3 Computer Networks

A server is computer hardware (or software) that provides a service to other hardware (or software).

Another way to accommodate multiple users is to link two or more computers together to form a *network*. Figure 1–3 shows a network consisting of three workstations (called *hosts*), a printer, and another computer called a *file server* that has no video display device but does have magnetic disks.

The hosts connected to the network may be full-fledged UNIX workstations, non-UNIX personal computers, or *diskless workstations*. A diskless workstation has only limited secondary memory, relying instead on the magnetic disks attached to the server. (The server serves the workstations by providing mass storage for them.)

Computer networking has become very popular. One reason for this is simple economics. By allowing users to share expensive resources such as printers, a network can be relatively economic to set up and operate.

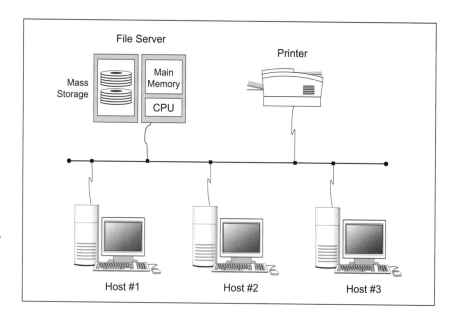

Figure 1-3
Computer network.
This network includes
four computers, one of
which is a server provid-
ing disk storage for the
other three.

1.4 The Operating System

As important as the computer hardware is, it can do nothing without software.
There are two general categories of software. Programs that allow users to solve
specific problems are called *applications*. Examples include word processors,
spreadsheets, and database management programs.

Software that provides support for creating and running applications is called
systems software. The most important systems software is the *operating system*
(OS), which performs three vital functions:

■ **Interaction with the user**. The OS handles the communication between the
user and the computer, passing commands from the user to the computer and
returning messages from the computer to the user.

■ **Management of other software**. The OS manages the way other software is
stored and run.

■ **Control of peripherals.** The OS controls all of the various peripheral devices
(printers, disk drives, terminals, and so on) that are attached to the computer.

1.5 Open and Closed Systems

Some operating systems are *proprietary* or *closed*, meaning they are developed
and owned by one company. Most proprietary operating systems are designed to
work only on certain types of computer hardware, making them *nonportable*. For
example, MS-DOS—the most popular operating system of the 1980s—was written

The Origins of UNIX

The UNIX story begins with a failed operating system, two computer scientists with time on their hands, and a computer game named *Space Travel*. The failed operating system was Multics, a joint venture involving General Electric, MIT, and the AT&T Bell Laboratories. Multics was envisioned as a great technological leap forward: an interactive, multiuser operating system that would be years ahead of anything then available. But the project was too ambitious, and by 1969 it was clear that Multics was in trouble. Reluctantly, Bell Labs withdrew from the project, leaving the Bell researchers with nothing to do.

A Bell researcher named Ken Thompson had written *Space Travel*, a computer game that allowed a Multics user to pilot an imaginary spacecraft to the major bodies of the solar system. While awaiting approval from Bell management for several new research projects, Thompson decided to rewrite *Space Travel* to run on a little-used PDP-7 minicomputer in the lab. He enlisted the aid of Dennis Ritchie, another Bell computer scientist who had worked on the Multics project.

It was no easy task. All programming had to be done on another machine, then transferred to the PDP-7 using punched paper tape. It did not take long for Thompson to wish that the PDP-7 had its own operating system, similar in some respects to Multics, but much simpler. So he wrote one. This was the first UNIX operating system, although it did not acquire that name until the following year. (The name was originally "Unics," a pun on Multics. Later this became UNIX.)

The PDP-7 had only about 9 Kbytes of main memory, less than some of today's household appliances. Thompson and Ritchie requested a larger computer. In exchange, they offered to produce a UNIX-based word-processing system for the Bell Labs patent department. They got their new computer—a PDP-11 with 24 Kbytes of main memory—and delivered the word-processing system in 1971. It was an immediate success, and UNIX was launched.

by Microsoft for machines having an Intel CPU. Likewise, the original Macintosh System was owned solely by Apple Computer and ran only on machines having a Motorola CPU.

In contrast, UNIX is a *nonproprietary* or *open* system. No single company is responsible for the development of UNIX and no single company owns it. Anyone may write an operating system that conforms to the published UNIX specifications. Moreover, UNIX has been adapted to run on a wide variety of computer hardware—in other words, UNIX is a *portable* operating system. Software is said to be portable if it can be moved from one type of computer to another with minimal changes. (This is not to be confused with a portable computer, which is computer hardware designed to be easily carried from place to place.)

UNIX and C

UNIX was originally written in assembly language, a primitive programming language. Since each type of computer has its own assembly language, early versions of UNIX could run only on the PDP-11 and closely related machines. But in 1973, UNIX was rewritten in C, a high-level programming language invented by Dennis Ritchie. It was much easier to write programs in C; just as important, C was designed to be a portable language, not tied to any particular type of computer hardware. As a result, UNIX became a portable operating system.

1.6 Multitasking and Time-Sharing

Background processes can run without interacting with the user.

UNIX is a *multitasking* operating system, meaning it enables the computer to work on more than one task at a time. With UNIX, you can run several programs "in the background" while you work on another task "in the foreground."

How does multitasking work? Although some computers actually can perform more than one task at a time, others cannot. However, by switching rapidly back and forth between tasks, performing a little here and a little there, a computer can create the illusion of doing many things simultaneously. This technique is called *time-sharing*, and it is feasible only because (a) the computer is very fast and (b) UNIX takes care of scheduling what is to be done and when.

UNIX is also capable of interacting with more than one user at a time—in other words, it is a *multiuser* operating system. This capability is especially important on large mainframe computers that must serve a large number of users; without it, everyone would have to wait his or her turn to use the computer.

1.7 Major Components of UNIX

The UNIX operating system consists of four main parts:

Many people consider "operating system" and "kernel" to be synonymous.

■ **Kernel.** The *kernel* is the master control program of the computer. It resides in the computer's main memory, and it manages the computer's resources. It is the kernel that handles the switching necessary to provide multitasking.

The file system is covered in Part II.

■ **File System.** UNIX organizes data into collections called *files*. Files may be grouped together into collections called *directory files* or *directories*.

Shells are covered in Part III.

■ **Shell.** The part of UNIX that interprets user commands and passes them on to the kernel is called the *shell*. A typical shell provides a *command-line interface*, where the user can type commands. This book covers the most common shells: the Bourne Shell, C Shell, TC Shell, Korn Shell, and Bourne-Again Shell (Bash).

■ **Utilities.** A *utility* is a useful software tool that is included as a standard part of the UNIX operating system. Utilities are often called *commands*.

Why So Many Versions of UNIX?

When UNIX was under development at AT&T's Bell Laboratories in the 1970s, AT&T was still prevented by law from competing in the computer industry. Since the company could not make a profit on UNIX, they gave it away, essentially free of charge.

UNIX became very popular at colleges and universities, where it was used for both teaching and research. (The low price tag undoubtedly had something to do with this popularity.) The early versions of UNIX were still quite crude, so academic computer scientists introduced their own improvements. Especially prominent in this effort was the Computer Systems Research Group at the University of California at Berkeley, which began producing its own versions of UNIX. By 1982, Berkeley Software Distribution (BSD) UNIX rivaled the AT&T versions in popularity.

Meanwhile, many computer companies produced their own versions of UNIX, often borrowing features from both AT&T and Berkeley UNIX. Of course, each version had its own name, usually ending in *x* (AIX, A/UX, HP-UX, Irix, Ultrix, and XENIX, to mention a few.) At one time there were as many as 200 variants of UNIX on the market.

1.8   Versions of UNIX

See "Why So Many Versions of UNIX?", this page.

When we say UNIX, we are really talking about a family of operating systems. In general, UNIX systems can trace their ancestry to AT&T System V UNIX, Berkeley Software Distribution (BSD) UNIX, or various UNIX-like systems:

■ **System V UNIX**. Most of the major commercial UNIX systems on the market today are based on AT&T UNIX, including AIX, Irix, Solaris, Tru64, Unicos, and UnixWare.

■ **BSD UNIX**. A number of operating systems have been derived from 4.4 BSD-Lite, the ultimate version of BSD UNIX, which was released in 1994. The most prominent of these are BSD/OS, FreeBSD, MacOS X, NetBSD, and OpenBSD.

■ **UNIX-like systems**. The UNIX-like operating systems (also called *work-alikes* or *clones*) behave very much like other UNIX systems, but do not use any software from AT&T. This category includes Hurd, Linux, Minix, and XINU.

Incidentally, the question is often asked, is it UNIX or Unix? Both forms are encountered. Since 1971, the name has been UNIX (all caps). However, this is now a trademark of the Open Group, and should properly be applied only to systems that are certified by that organization. For that reason, some people write Unix (mixed case) to refer to the entire family of operating systems, certified or not. In this book, we adhere to the earlier tradition and write UNIX throughout.

Linux and Other UNIX-Like Systems

In the early 1980s, AT&T still restricted the commercial use of the UNIX system. This led some companies to write their own operating systems that mimicked the behavior of UNIX without using any of AT&T's source code. These included systems such as Coherent, Idris, and Uniflex.

As UNIX spread in academia, it became popular for computer science courses on operating systems. Eventually, however, AT&T decided to restrict access to the internal code of UNIX. As a result, a number of computer science professors independently developed their own UNIX-like systems for teaching. The most prominent of these were Douglas Comer's XINU ("Xinu Is Not UNIX") and Andy Tanenbaum's Minix.

In 1991, a 21-year-old Finnish student named Linus Torvalds created his own operating system based on Minix. This became Linux, a UNIX-like system for personal computers. This system has proven to be an enormous success. Linux is available at no charge from the Free Software Foundation. Hundreds of volunteer programmers worldwide work to maintain and extend Linux.

1.9 UNIX Standards

See "A Brief History of UNIX Standardization" on page 11.

Traditionally, most UNIX systems have been similar enough that a person who learned to use one would have little trouble using any of the others. Even so, the differences could be irksome. A program might run well on one UNIX system but not on another, or it might give different results. This was an especially challenging problem for software vendors and organizations (such as the U. S. government) that had to maintain a variety of computer systems.

To address the problem of software portability, the Institute of Electrical and Electronics Engineers (IEEE) devised the Portable Operating System Interface (POSIX) standards to define how a standard operating system should behave. Systems and utilities which conform to the POSIX standards are said to be "POSIX-compliant." Most current UNIX systems are POSIX-compliant.

Another important organization promoting UNIX standardization is The Open Group, which actually owns the UNIX trademark. Before a company may apply the UNIX brand name to an operating system, that system must conform to the Single UNIX Specification defined by The Open Group.

1.10 Windows and Graphical User Interfaces

It is difficult to take full advantage of a multitasking operating system like UNIX if you can only see output from one process at a time on your monitor. Fortunately, most recent UNIX systems have the ability to divide the monitor screen into multiple areas called *windows* (Figure 1–4), each of which acts as if it

A Brief History of UNIX Standardization

Although similar in most respects, the many versions of UNIX were different enough to cause headaches for programmers, vendors, and users. For this reason, efforts began in the mid-1980s to define a UNIX standard.

In 1983, The Institute of Electrical and Electronics Engineers (IEEE) began work on a series of Portable Operating System Interface (POSIX) standards. The first POSIX standard was formally adopted by the American National Standards Institute (ANSI) in 1988. Most vendors of UNIX operating systems have modified their systems in accordance with the POSIX standards.

In 1984, the X/Open organization was created by several leading European computer companies. X/Open had as its mission the promotion of open (nonproprietary) operating systems, especially UNIX.

The Open Software Foundation (OSF), a consortium of major UNIX vendors (including IBM, Hewlett-Packard, and DEC) was formed in 1988. Its goal was to produce an alternative to AT&T UNIX that was not controlled by any one company.

AT&T was also aware of the need for standardization. In 1989, AT&T System V Release 4 (abbreviated "SVR4") was released. SVR4 combined the best features of the four most popular UNIX derivatives, which were SVR3, 4.3BSD, SunOS, and Microsoft XENIX.

In 1993, Novell acquired UNIX Systems Laboratories from AT&T. Later that year, Novell transferred ownership of the UNIX brand name to the X/Open organization. In 1995, Novell sold its UNIX business, including the UNIX source code (but not the UNIX trademark), to SCO.

In 1996, X/Open merged with the OSF to form The Open Group. As owner of the UNIX trademark, The Open Group defines the Single UNIX Specification, a set of standards that an operating system must meet to use the UNIX name.

In 1999, IEEE and The Open Group announced a joint effort to revise both the POSIX and the Single UNIX Specification. The revised standards were formally adopted by the International Organization for Standardization (ISO) in 2003.

were a separate monitor. Using a windowing system, you could read your electronic mail in one window, compose a reply in another window, and run a spreadsheet program from a third window, all at the same time.

The typical windowing system also offers what is called a *graphical user interface* (GUI or "gooey"), which allows you to work with pictures as well as character data. To run a particular program under a GUI, you might use a pointing device such

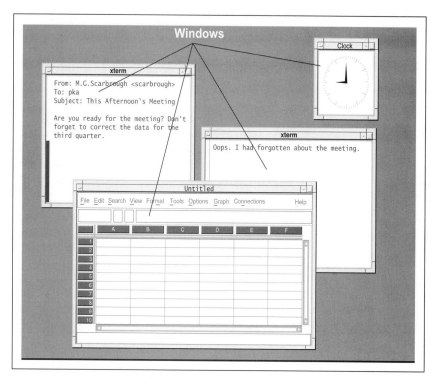

Figure 1-4
A windowing display.
Four windows are
shown; each window
acts as an independent
output device.

as a mouse to select an *icon* (a symbol) that represents that program, rather than having to remember and type a command. Because most people find it easier to work with pictures and pointing devices, GUIs have become very popular.

If you have used an Apple Macintosh or a PC running Microsoft Windows, you are already familiar with windows and GUIs. On UNIX systems, the GUI is usually based on the X Window System ("X" for short), which was originally developed at the Massachusetts Institute of Technology.

A server is software (or
hardware) that provides a
service to other software (or
hardware).

The X Window System works according to what is called a *client-server model*. In other words, X acts as a server for other programs (the clients) by providing a graphical user interface for them. This makes X especially well suited to networked computing because the clients and server can run on separate computers.

1.11 The Window Manager

Although the X Window System makes it possible to create a graphical user interface, X does not specify what the windows must look like or how they are manipulated by the user. That is the job of a program called the *window manager*. The window manager determines the "look and feel" of the GUI, controlling the appearance of the windows and determining how those windows are opened, closed, sized, resized, and moved.

Dozens of window managers have been created. The following are commonly used:

■ **Tab Window Manager** (twm). Originally developed at MIT and supplied as part of the X Window System, twm is a "plain vanilla" window manager that offers few frills. Even so, experienced UNIX programmers like twm because it can be configured to suit their personal tastes.

■ **Virtual Window Manager** (fvwm). Popular with Linux users, fvwm is free software derived from twm.

■ **Open Look Window Manager** (olwm). Sun Microsystems was the strongest promoter of Open Look, which has not been generally adopted by other manufacturers.

You will see how to begin using Motif in Chapter 4.

■ **Motif Window Manager** (mwm). Motif was developed by the Open Software Foundation (OSF), a consortium of several leading UNIX vendors. Motif was designed to have a "look and feel" similar to that of the IBM Presentation Manager and Microsoft Windows, two widely used GUIs for personal computers.

■ **Desktop Window Manager** (dtwm). Based on Motif, the Desktop Window Manager was developed for the Common Desktop Environment (discussed below).

1.12   Desktop Environment

The plethora of UNIX windowing systems has been a cause of confusion for system administrators and users. In 1993, six of the largest UNIX vendors started the Common Open Software Environment (COSE) initiative to address this problem. The result was the Common Desktop Environment (CDE).

You will see how to start using CDE in Chapter 5.

CDE is designed to provide a consistent look and feel, regardless of the variety of UNIX being used. The CDE user interface is organized around the idea of a "desktop," using *icons* or pictures to represent items—such as documents, files, and file folders—that might be found on a real desk. This approach is familiar to users of the Apple Macintosh and the Microsoft Windows operating systems. CDE also provides a new set of standard software tools, including a text editor, a calendar/datebook, and an electronic mail tool, in addition to the traditional UNIX utilities.

Other desktop environments are available, including the K Desktop Environment (KDE), the GNU Network Object Model Environment (Gnome), and XFce.

1.13   X Terminals

The X Window System was designed to be portable. As a result, X runs on virtually every kind of computer, from Macintoshes and PCs to supercomputers. This has contributed greatly to its success.

However, X will not run on a conventional character terminal—a terminal that can display text but not graphics—because considerable computing power is required to support a graphical user interface. This has led to the development of a hybrid input/output device called an *X terminal*, which has a CPU and enough internal memory to run X, but is not a complete computer in itself. (Most X terminals lack disk drives, for instance.) An X terminal is more expensive than a character-based terminal, but less expensive than a complete UNIX workstation.

Instead of purchasing an X terminal, many users run *X-terminal emulation programs* on their personal computers. Such programs allow a personal computer to act as if it were an X terminal.

1.14 Remote Access

Many users wish to connect to their UNIX system when working remotely (for example, while at home or traveling). Figure 1-5 shows four ways to do this.

Modem is short for "modulator-demodulator."

Figure 1-5(a) shows a personal computer and a UNIX system communicating using two modems. A *modem* converts outgoing digital data into signals for transmission over ordinary telephone lines (a process known as *modulation*). The receiving modem then converts the incoming telephone signals into digital form (*demodulation*).

The Internet is discussed in Part V.

Figure 1-5(b) shows another arrangement involving a personal computer and a standard modem. In this case, the modem communicates with an Internet Service Provider (ISP), which provides an Internet connection to the UNIX system.

Conventional modems are relatively slow. Figure 1-5(c) shows a system that provides faster data transmission. *Digital Subscriber Line* (DSL) technology uses sophisticated data-compression methods to transmit data at high rates over telephone lines.

Figure 1-5(d) shows another system for achieving faster data transmission rates. Some cable television companies provide data transmission over their coaxial cables using a special *cable modem*.

Other methods are used for gaining access to a remote computer system, including wireless and satellite technology. For more information about remote access, see the *Just Enough UNIX* website (`www.mhhe.com/andersen`).

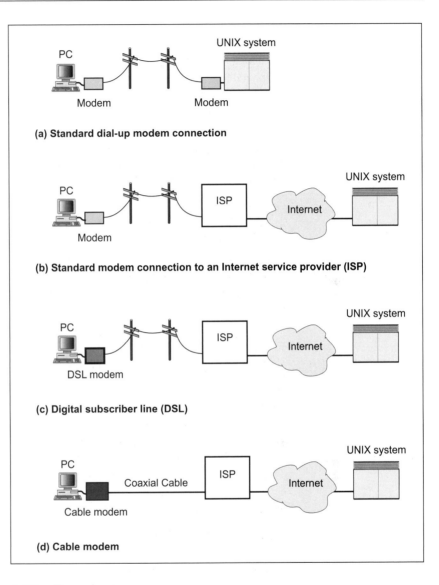

Figure 1-5
Remote access to a
UNIX system.

1.15   Exercises

1. Be sure you can define the following terms:

hardware	word size	shell
software	clock speed	file
CPU	flops	file system
main memory	MIPS	directory
secondary memory	server	utility
mass storage	client	command

external memory	host	window
I/O device	operating system	GUI
peripheral	proprietary	icon
network	portable OS	window manager
bit	open system	X terminal
byte	multitasking	terminal emulation
kilo-	time-sharing	modem
mega-	clone	ISP
giga-	kernel	DSL

2. What are the four main hardware components of most computer systems?

3. What are the main components of the UNIX operating system?

4. Name the most common UNIX shells.

5. Name the most commonly used X window managers.

6. Name three UNIX desktop environments.

7. When referring to the capacity of a computer's memory, computer scientists often use prefixes like kilo-, mega-, and giga- only approximately. For example, a kilobyte of memory is not exactly 1,000 bytes, but rather 2^{10} bytes. Likewise, a megabyte is really 2^{20} bytes, and a gigabyte is really 2^{30} bytes. What is the difference between a thousand and 2^{10}? A million (10^6) and 2^{20}? A billion (10^9) and 2^{30}?

YOUR UNIX ACCOUNT

Tutorials related to this
chapter are found in
Chapters 3, 4, and 5.

In one respect, UNIX is like your local bank. Just as you need a bank account to withdraw money (legally) from a bank, you also need an account to use a UNIX computer. In this chapter, you will learn what you need to know to obtain and begin using a UNIX account.

2.1 Your System Administrator

Every bank has a manager who sets bank policy, opens and closes customer accounts, balances the books, and generally sees that the bank operates smoothly. Of course, the manager does not necessarily do all of these things personally, but the manager is responsible to see that someone does.

Similarly, most UNIX installations have a *system administrator*, who sees that the system runs smoothly (most of the time, anyway). The system administrator's duties include

- Setting up the hardware;

- Installing software, including the UNIX operating system;

- Starting up the system (and shutting it down when necessary);

- Monitoring system usage;

- Backing up users' files;

- Creating new user accounts; and

- Troubleshooting.

The system administrator does not necessarily do all of these things personally—large computer installations typically divide these duties among several persons. Thus, when you read "system administrator," think "the system administrator or one of his or her assistants."

2.2 Your Account Name

A large UNIX installation may serve hundreds or thousands of users, each having his or her own account. To identify these accounts, each is given a unique name, which is typically based in some way on the user's real name or nickname. For example, the following would all be likely account names for a user named John P. Jones:

```
jpjones
```

```
jonesjp
```

```
jones
```

```
johnp
```

```
jpj
```

```
sparky
```

The policies for assigning account names vary. In some organizations, the system administrator chooses the name for you; in others, you may choose your own, subject to certain rules. The following rules are fairly typical:

■ Select a name that is at least three characters long, but no more than eight characters long.

■ Be sure that no other account has the same name.

■ Choose an account name that is related in some way to your real name or a nickname.

■ Use only numbers and lowercase letters; do not include uppercase letters or punctuation.

When you start a work session on the computer, you will be asked to *log in* by giving your account name:

```
login:
```

Because you use your account name when logging in, your account name is often referred to as your *login name* or *login*.

2.3 Your Password

Your login name is public knowledge. To prevent unauthorized use of your account, the computer also asks you for a secret *password*:

```
password:
```

By entering your password, you verify to the computer that you really are the person to whom the account belongs.

The system administrator will probably choose your first password for you. After that, you can (and should) choose your own passwords. A good password is one that is easy for you to remember, but difficult for someone else to guess. Here are some good general guidelines for selecting a password:

Your particular computer installation may have other rules as well—consult your system administrator.

- Choose a password that is at least six characters long. (Passwords can be as long as you like, but some systems only examine the first eight characters.)

- Combine numbers, upper- and lowercase letters, and punctuation.

- Make the password memorable, but avoid common names and any words that might be found in a dictionary.

- Do not use your social security number, your telephone number, your login, or any variation (forward or backward) of your login.

- Make sure a new password differs significantly from the old one.

A number of strategies exist for choosing a password. One is to misspell an easily remembered word or name. For example, neither `Chicago` nor `chicago` would be acceptable as passwords. But the following deliberate misspellings would be:

Do not use these examples—think up your own password.

`ch1Kagoh`

`Ch!.CAGO`

`Sh33?kago`

Another strategy is to form a password from the first letter of each word in an easily remembered phrase. Including punctuation is a good idea. For example:

`NiMyyd!` (**N**ot **i**n **M**y **y**ard **y**ou **d**on't!)

`Ihnybtf` (**I** **h**ave **n**ot **y**et **b**egun **t**o **f**ight)

`H,hotr` (**H**ome, **h**ome **o**n **t**he **r**ange)

`wtdatap` (**w**here **t**he **d**eer **a**nd **t**he **a**ntelope **p**lay)

Your password is the main line of protection for your account. Anyone who discovers your password can do nearly anything to your account—including deleting all of your files. Therefore, it is extremely important that you keep your password secure.

WARNING | MEMORIZE YOUR PASSWORD—DO NOT WRITE IT DOWN. AND NEVER DIVULGE YOUR PASSWORD TO ANYONE.

You will see how to change your password in the next chapter.

If you suspect that someone else has learned your password, you should change it immediately. In fact, it may be a good idea to change your password occasionally in any case, just to be safe.

2.4 Other Account Information

When your account is created, the system administrator sets up the following information in addition to the login name and password:

■ **Home Directory.** Your home directory is the place where all of your other files and directories reside. The home directory has a name, which is the same as your login name.

■ **Group ID.** You may be assigned to a group of users. In some organizations, groups are set up so that users in the same department or working on the same projects can easily share fles.

■ **Login Shell.** The system administrator will select a shell to start up automatically whenever you log in.

When you receive your UNIX account, be sure to ask what groups (if any) you have been assigned to and what your login shell is.

2.5 More Questions to Ask

There are a number of additional questions to ask your system administrator:

■ Which version of UNIX will I be using?

■ What kind of terminal will I be using? What is its `terminfo` code?

■ What are the erase, interrupt, stop, and continue keys?

■ Which printer(s) may I use?

■ How can I gain remote access to the system?

The rest of this chapter will explain what each of these questions means.

2.6 Versions of UNIX

You may recall that the name UNIX refers to a family of operating systems, most derived from either AT&T System V or Berkeley Software Distribution (BSD) UNIX. In addition, there are various UNIX-like systems in common use:

■ **System V UNIX**: AIX, Irix, Solaris, Tru64 Unix, Unicos, UnixWare

■ **BSD UNIX**: BSD/OS, Mac OS X, NetBSD, OpenBSD, ULTRIX

■ **UNIX-like systems**: Hurd, Linux, Minix, XINU

Ask your system administrator which kind of UNIX you will be using, and whether it is based on System V or BSD UNIX (or a UNIX-like system).

2.7 Termcap and Terminfo

As an open system, UNIX must be able to work with a wide variety of I/O devices. The UNIX system includes a database describing the operating characteristics of the many different terminals it can use. This is called either the `terminfo` ("terminal information") or `termcap` ("terminal capabilities") database.

When you log in, your system may request that you indicate the type of terminal device you are using by specifying its `terminfo` (or `termcap`) code. For example, suppose you were using a DEC VT 100 terminal. The code for this terminal is

`vt100`

Ask your system administrator which `terminfo` code(s) you should know, if any.

2.8 Special Keys

Figure 2-1 shows a typical computer keyboard. It has the same letter, number, and punctuation keys as a typewriter. It also has a number of special keys not found on the traditional typewriter. The following five keys are of particular interest:

■ (RETURN) Also called the (ENTER) or (NEWLINE) key, this is used to send commands to the shell.

■ (ESCAPE) This key, which may be labeled (ESC), is usually found near the upper left corner of the keyboard.

■ (ERASE) Various keys are used to erase characters. On many systems, this function is performed by a (BACKSPACE) or (DELETE) key, or by a combination of keys.

■ (BREAK) This key is (rarely) used during the login procedure.

■ (CONTROL) This may be labeled (Ctrl) on some terminals. It is used in combination with other keys to perform special functions.

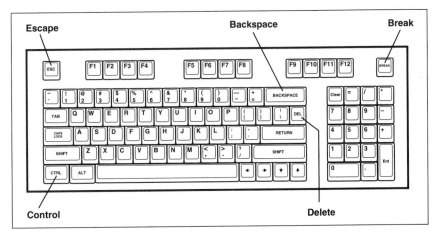

Figure 2-1
A computer keyboard, showing some of the special keys.

Of these, the (CONTROL) key deserves special mention. A large number of UNIX commands are executed by holding down the (CONTROL) key while simultaneously pressing another key. For example, on many terminals the erase function can be invoked by the key combination

(CONTROL)-(H)

When referring to this key combination in print, you will often see the notation ^H, where the caret (^) stands for the (CONTROL) key.

Later in the book, you will learn about many of the functions that involve the (CONTROL) key. For now, there are four special functions that you should ask about:

Function	Purpose	Key Combination		Alternative
erase	deletes a character	(CONTROL)-(H)	(^H)	(BACKSPACE)
interrupt	stops a program	(CONTROL)-(C)	(^C)	(DELETE)
stop	freezes the terminal	(CONTROL)-(S)	(^S)	?
continue	unfreezes the terminal	(CONTROL)-(Q)	(^Q)	?

Your system administrator can tell you which keys perform these functions.

Note that there may be more than one way to delete a character or interrupt a program. As shown in Appendix A, UNIX provides a way for you to change the keys that invoke these functions.

2.9 Printer Codes

Almost every UNIX system has a printer for producing paper output. (Paper output is called *hardcopy*.) A large computer installation may have many printers. Individual printers are identified by a code name, which typically reflects the type and location of the device. For example, suppose that one of the printers connected to your UNIX system were an HP LaserJet 4000, located in Room 12. The system administrator might give this printer one of the following code names:

hp4000-12

laserjet12

room12hp

You get the idea. There are no standard rules on naming printers, so it is a good idea to ask your system administrator for the names of the printers that are accessible from your system.

Teletypes and Terminals

When Thompson and Ritchie rewrote UNIX to run on the PDP-11 for the Bell Patent Department, the primary input/output devices were Teletype terminals. These were slow, noisy electromechanical devices that produced their output on rolls of paper.

The Teletype keyboard had the usual typewriter keys for upper- and lowercase letters, numbers, and punctuation. It also had a special "Control" key that was used in combination with other keys to perform special functions. (For example, holding down the Control key and typing the letter *B* caused a bell to ring.)

Although Teletypes are now obsolete, they are not entirely forgotten. The keyboards of newer I/O devices still have a Control key that is used in combination with other keys to perform special functions. In the vocabulary of UNIX, the abbreviation `tty` (short for Teletype) is still used to mean "terminal." And "print" is still used to mean "display output on a terminal," even for terminals that print to a video screen rather than paper.

2.10   Remote Access

The tutorials in Chapters 3, 4, and 5 presume that you will be working directly with your UNIX account using a terminal, a personal computer emulating a terminal, or a UNIX workstation.

However, you may need to work on your UNIX account remotely—while you are on the road, for instance. Remote access usually requires additional hardware and software that is beyond the scope of this book. Ask your UNIX system administrator or Internet Service Provider (ISP) about remote access:

■ What hardware and software do you recommend I use for remote access?

■ Is dial-up access available? If so, what telephone number(s) should I use?

■ What is the procedure for remote access?

■ Is there anything else I need to know?

Additional information on remote access can be found on the *Just Enough UNIX* web site (`www.mhhe.com/andersen`).

2.11 Exercises

1. Be sure you can define the following terms:

system administrator	home directory	`termcap` code
account name	group	control key
login name	login shell	interrupt
login	BSD	`tty`
logging in	System V	print
password	`terminfo` code	hardcopy

2. What version of UNIX will you be using? Is it based on AT&T or on BSD UNIX, or is it a UNIX-like system?

3. How are login names assigned for users on your system? Are you allowed to choose your own login, or is one chosen for you?

4. What are the rules for choosing a password on your system? Keeping those rules in mind, choose two or three passwords to use later. (Do not write down your passwords or divulge them to anyone.)

5. Which of the following would be good passwords for someone named Glynda Jones Davis, whose login name, phone number, and social security number are `gjdavis`, 555-2525, and 632-10-6854, respectively? Explain your reasoning.

`cat`	`Glynda7`	`tylerTwo`
`Smith`	`sivagjg`	`t555s632`
`5552525`	`Jones`	`532106854`
`KRoo2`	`jones`	`kangaroo`
`7cattz`	`NotSmith`	`trouble`
`Glynda`	`tiPPecanoe`	`trubble`

6. What kind of terminal will you be using? What is its `terminfo` (or `termcap`) code?

7. Which keys are used to erase input, interrupt a program, freeze the terminal, and unfreeze the terminal?

8. Which printer may you use? What is its code name?

9. What is the procedure for gaining remote access to your account?

# Chapter 3

GETTING STARTED

Skip this chapter if you are not using an ASCII terminal or terminal emulation software.

In this chapter, you will learn how to use an ASCII terminal (or a terminal-emulation program on a personal computer) to log into your UNIX account, change your password, and try out some UNIX commands. If you are working with an X terminal or workstation, you may wish to go on to Chapter 4, "Getting Started (X/Motif),"or Chapter 5, "Getting Started (CDE)".

If you haven't done so already, ask your instructor, system administrator, or consultant about setting up an account. You will need the following information:

■ Your login name;

■ Your password; and

■ The name of the computer you will be using.

This chapter describes local access to your UNIX account using a terminal or PC directly connected to the UNIX system. For information on remote access, ask your system administrator or Internet Service Provider (ISP). Or consult the *Just Enough UNIX* web site (`www.mhhe.com/andersen`).

3.1 Starting Up the Terminal

Skip this section if you are working remotely.

Some terminals are meant to be left on at all times, and should not be turned off. You cannot always tell by looking at the screen—your system may have a screen-saver program that blanks the display when it has been idle for a time. Therefore, the first step is to try to "wake up" the screen.

For a typical ASCII terminal, try these steps:

1. Press the spacebar or (RETURN) **key.** This is usually enough to cancel the screen-saver. If it does, go on to Section 3.3, "Obtaining a Login Prompt."

Double-check to be sure that the terminal is not already switched on before doing this.

2. Find the power switch and turn it on. The switch may be hidden under the front edge of the keyboard or on the back panel of the terminal. (See if you can find the power cord—the switch may be close to the point where the cord enters the terminal.) Turn on the terminal.

3. Allow the terminal to warm up. After a while, you should see a small, blinking line or rectangle on the terminal screen. This is the *cursor*. It shows where the next typed character will appear. Go on to Section 3.3, "Obtaining a Login Prompt."

If the "terminal" is actually a Windows or Macintosh computer emulating an ASCII terminal, try these steps:

1. Press the spacebar or (RETURN) **key, or move the mouse.** This is usually enough to cancel the screen-saver.

Double-check to be sure that the computer is not already switched on before doing this.

2. If necessary, find the power switch and turn it on. The switch may be hidden under the front edge of the keyboard or on the back panel of the terminal. (The switch may be close to the point where the cord enters the terminal.)

3. Allow the computer to boot up. Eventually, you should see the familiar Windows or Macintosh desktop.

4. Start the terminal-emulation/`telnet` **software.** How this is done depends on which software you are using. In most cases, you will double-click on an icon. Ask your system administrator for assistance.

3.2 Obtaining a Login Prompt

Now you must get the computer's attention. What you want is for the computer to show you a *login prompt*, indicating that it is ready for you to log in:

`login:`

If you see this on the screen, skip to the next section.

How you get a login prompt depends on whether your terminal is connected to one or many computer hosts.

If your terminal is connected to one host, try the following procedure for obtaining a login prompt:

1. Press (RETURN) **several times.** This may be enough to cause the computer to display a login prompt:

`login:`

If you get a login prompt, skip to the next section.

2. If the login prompt does not appear, try pressing (BREAK) **or** (RESET). Some systems may require that you press (BREAK) then (RETURN).

3. If Steps 1 and 2 do not work, see your system administrator.

If your terminal is connected to a terminal server, you must select a host computer. How this is done depends on the system. The following procedure is fairly typical:

1. Press (RETURN) **several times.** Often this will cause the terminal server to display a prompt. Prompts vary from system to system; here are some examples:

`Which computer?`

`Dial:`

`UNIVERSITY-NET>`

2. Enter the name of the host computer at the prompt. If you wanted to work with a machine named `merlin`, you would enter this name at the prompt:

`Which computer?merlin` (RETURN)

The chosen host computer should respond with a login prompt:

`login:`

If you get a login prompt, skip to the next section.

3. If Steps 1 and 2 do not work, consult your system administrator.

3.3   Logging In

If you have reached this point, you should see a login prompt on the screen:

`login:`

1. Enter your login name and press (RETURN). If your login name were `jsmith`, you would enter this after the prompt:

Do not enter `jsmith` (unless that is your login). Enter your login here.

`login:jsmith` (RETURN)

The computer will respond by prompting you for your password:

`password:`

2. Enter your password and press (RETURN).

Enter your password; it will not appear on the screen.

`password:`

Note that YOUR PASSWORD DOES NOT APPEAR ON THE SCREEN. The idea is to prevent others from looking over your shoulder and learning your password. (You will see how to change the password later.)

3. If you made an error, repeat Steps 1 and 2. If you made an error typing either your login or your password, the computer will inform you that your login is incorrect, and it will give you the chance to log in again:

Although this says "login incorrect," the same message is given if your password is incorrect.

`Login incorrect`
`login:`

If you see this, you must re-enter both your login and your password.

3.4   Messages

Once you gain access to the computer, it may print a variety of messages, including

■ Type of UNIX;

■ Message of the day from the system administrator;

■ Mail alert, telling you there is electronic mail waiting for you.

If you have mail, you will see how to read it later.

3.5 Setting the Terminal Type

Some UNIX systems are set up to ask you to specify your terminal type when you log in. If yours is such a system, it will show you a prompt like

```
Set terminal type (vt100):
```

Or perhaps

```
TERM (vt100):
```

The `terminfo` code in the parentheses represents the *default terminal type*; the computer assumes that this is the terminal you are using.

1. If your terminal matches the default type, simply press (RETURN). Then skip to the next section, "UNIX Shell Prompt."

2. Otherwise, enter the `terminfo` code for the type of terminal you are using. (This is something you should have obtained from your system administrator.) Be sure to press (RETURN) after the code.

3.6 UNIX Shell Prompt

At this point, you should see a *shell prompt*, which is simply the shell's way of telling you that it is ready to receive your instructions. If your login shell is the C Shell or TC Shell, the prompt is probably a percent sign:

```
%
```

If you are using the Bourne Shell, Korn Shell, or Bash as a login shell, the usual prompt is a dollar sign:

```
$
```

Other symbols are occasionally used for shell prompts, including the pound sign (#), the "greater than" sign (>), the asterisk (*), the "at" symbol (@), and the colon (:). Some systems are set up to include the host name as part of the prompt, like this:

```
merlin %
```

In this book, we will use the following as our "generic" prompt, to take the place of either the percent sign or the dollar sign:

In the examples that follow,   §
do not enter the prompt.

3.7   Terminal Troubles

Sometimes your terminal will not behave as you expect it to. Two problems are especially common:

■ **Everything you type appears in uppercase letters.** The UNIX system acts as if your terminal cannot handle lowercase letters.

■ **The usual erase key does not work.** The (BACKSPACE) or (DELETE) key does not erase characters as expected.

If either of these problems occurs, refer to Appendix A, "Taming Your Terminal."

3.8   Changing Your Password

Review Section 2.3 on selecting a password.

A good password is one that is easy for you to remember but difficult for someone else to figure out. Often the initial passwords assigned by system administrators fail these criteria. It is a good idea to change your password frequently to prevent unauthorized use of your account. If you have not already done so, you should take a minute to think about a password.

1. **Enter the** `passwd` **command at the shell prompt.** Note that this is `passwd`, not `password`:

`§ passwd` (RETURN)

The system will prompt for your old password:

`Old password:`

2. **Enter your old password, then press** (RETURN) **.** As usual, your password will not appear on the screen:

`Old password:` ▉▉▉▉▉▉

The computer will then ask you to enter your new password:

`New password:`

3. **Enter your new password, then press** (RETURN). As usual, your password will not appear on the screen:

`New password:` ▉▉▉▉▉▉

To ensure that you have made no mistakes, the computer will ask you to repeat your new password:

`Retype new password:`

4. **Repeat your new password.** If this is not done exactly as before, the system will not accept the new password, and you will have to start over:

`Retype new password:` ▉▉▉▉▉▉

You will know that the new password has been accepted when the shell prompt appears:

§

3.9 Trying Out Some UNIX Commands

Next, try a few UNIX commands to see how they work.

1. Start with the date **command.** Type date after the prompt, and press (RETURN) :

§ date (RETURN)

The computer will respond with the date and time. For example, if you were to give this command on Friday, August 13, 2004, at 8:35 pm (Eastern Daylight Time), the output would be something like

Fri Aug 13 20:35:41 EDT 2004

Note that this is the time for the host computer's locale, and that the time is given on the 24-hour clock.

2. Next, try the who **command.** Type who, followed by (RETURN) :

§ who (RETURN)

The computer will respond with a list of the users who are currently logged into the system. For example,

root	console	Aug 13	08:11
aadams	tty16	Aug 13	07:01
pgw	tty03	Aug 13	18:15
ben	tty18	Aug 13	11:32
jeff	tty12	Aug 13	09:45

The user's login name is listed first, followed by a code that identifies the line or *port* to which the user is connected. The date and time that the user logged in are also shown.

3. Try the who am i **command.** This command displays your login name:

§ who am i (RETURN)

3.10 Reading Your Mail

Skip this section if you have not received e-mail.

If you received a message telling you that you had received electronic mail, now is the time to read your mail.

1. Start the mail program. One of the following commands should work:

This usually works.

§ mailx (RETURN)

```
§ Mail (RETURN)

§ mail (RETURN)
```

The system will respond with a list of the messages. For example,

```
U   1 wards   Mon Aug 9 15:27   554/26358   "Class Roster"
N   2 aadams Fri Aug 13 8:59   40/1527   "Lunch"
N   3 gwc   Fri Aug 13   9:47   15/440   "Research Notes"
&
```

A *U* in the first column indicates an unread message left over from the last time you logged in; an *N* indicates a new message. The messages are numbered (from 1 to 3 in this case). The login name of the sender is shown, along with the date and time the message was received and the number of lines and characters the message contains (lines/characters). Finally, the subject of the message is given in quotes. The ampersand (&) on the last line is the *mail prompt*.

2. Read your message(s). Simply enter the message number after the mail prompt and press (RETURN) :

```
&2 (RETURN)
```

This will cause the second message to appear:

```
Message 2:
From aadams Fri Aug 13 8:59:01 2004
Date: Fri Aug 13 8:59:01
From: aadams (Abigail Adams)
To: (Your login name)
Subject: Lunch

Let's get together for lunch at 12:45 today. Okay?
&
```

Electronic mail—including the ways to send, save, and delete mail—is discussed in more detail in Part V.

3. Leave the mail utility. Typing *x* (for "exit") at the mail prompt will take you out of the mail utility, leaving the message(s) in the mailbox:

```
&x (RETURN)
```

3.11 Reading the UNIX Manual

Many UNIX systems come equipped with a detailed on-line manual that you can read using the man command. The manual describes the commands that are available on the system. To see how this is done, try the following command:

```
§ man cal (RETURN)
```

For more information on the UNIX manual, see Appendix B.

The cal command is one that we will use in later chapters; it displays a calendar on the screen. If your system has the on-line manual, you should see a description of cal. Otherwise, you may see the message

```
man: Command not found.
```

3.12 Logging Out

When you are finished working on the computer, you must "log out." This tells the system that you are finished using it.

1. If you are using the C Shell or TC Shell, try the `logout` **command:**

§ `logout` (RETURN)

2. For the Bourne Shell, Korn Shell, or Bash, try the `exit` **command:**

§ `exit` (RETURN)

3. If neither `logout` **nor** `exit` **works, try** ^D. Remember, the notation ^D means you should hold down the (CONTROL) key and type the letter *D*:

§ (CONTROL)–(D)

4. If necessary, log out from the terminal server. If you had to log onto a terminal server before selecting a computer host, you may also have to log out from the terminal server.

5. If nothing seems to work, ask for help. Do not leave without logging out first.

WARNING	NEVER LEAVE THE TERMINAL WITHOUT LOGGING OUT. ON SOME UNIX SYSTEMS, YOUR ACCOUNT MAY REMAIN OPEN EVEN IF THE TERMINAL IS TURNED OFF. THIS INVITES THE UNSCRUPULOUS TO GET INTO THE SYSTEM AND CAUSE TROUBLE.

3.13 Command Summary

Each of the commands listed here is entered at the shell prompt.

Changing Your Password

`passwd` (RETURN)	change password

Miscellaneous UNIX Commands

`date` (RETURN)	print current date and time
`who` (RETURN)	print a list of users currently logged in
`who am i` (RETURN)	print your login
`man cal` (RETURN)	show the manual page describing the `cal` command

Logging Out

`logout` (RETURN)	logout for C Shell or TC Shell
`exit` (RETURN)	logout for Bourne Shell, Korn Shell, or Bash
^D	optional logout command

3.14 Exercises

1. Be sure you can define the following terms:

cursor	login shell	shell
default	mail prompt	shell prompt

2. What kinds of terminals are connected to your UNIX system? Examine several different terminals and locate the (RETURN), (CONTROL), (BACKSPACE), (ESCAPE), and (BREAK) keys, and the ON/OFF switch.

3. See if your terminal has a key labeled "NO SCROLL." This key is supposed to "freeze" the terminal display. Press it and type your name. What happens on the screen? Now press the key again. What do you see?

4. On many terminals, the ^S key combination "freezes" the terminal. Try this key combination and type something on the keyboard. What happens? The key combination ^Q "unfreezes" the terminal, reversing the effects of ^S. Try this.

5. Does your keyboard have a key labeled "CAPS LOCK" or "CASE"? If so, press it and type something on the keyboard. What does this key do?

6. UNIX is *case-sensitive:* it distinguishes between upper- and lowercase letters. Try the commands listed below and note what each one does (if anything):

WHO (RETURN)

CAL 2004 (RETURN)

DATE (RETURN)

WHO AM I (RETURN)

Tutorial:
Getting Started (X/Motif)

Skip this chapter if your terminal does not run X, or if your system runs the Common Desktop Environment (CDE).

In this chapter, you will learn how to use an X terminal or workstation to log into your UNIX account, change your password, and try out some UNIX commands. If you haven't done so already, ask your instructor, system administrator, or consultant about setting up an account. You will need the following information:

■ Your login name;

■ Your password;

■ The name of the computer you will be using.

This chapter describes local access to your UNIX account. For information on remote access, ask your system administrator or Internet Service Provider (ISP). Or consult the *Just Enough UNIX* web site (www.mhhe.com/andersen).

If necessary, you can start X yourself—see Appendix C.

We assume that your system is set up to start the X server and window manager automatically. If this is not true for your system, you will have to start them yourself. In that case, log in according to the procedure presented in Sections 3.2 through 3.6; then refer to Appendix C, "Starting X and Motif."

4.1 Logging into the Display Manager

The X program that controls your login procedure is called the *display manager*.

1. Wake up the display. Most X terminals are equipped with a *screen saver*, a program that blanks out the screen when it has been idle for a time. Pressing a key or moving the mouse is usually enough to cancel the screen saver.

The display manager will show a login screen resembling Figure 4-1.

2. Enter your login name and press (RETURN) . If your login name were jsmith, you would enter this after the prompt:

Enter your login, not jsmith (unless that is your login).

```
login:jsmith (RETURN)
```

Figure 4-1
Login screen. The screen
presented by your dis-
play manager may look
somewhat different.

3. Enter your password and press (RETURN). Note that YOUR PASSWORD
DOES NOT APPEAR ON THE SCREEN. The idea is to prevent others from looking over your shoulder and learning your password. (You will see how to change
the password later.)

Enter your password here;
your password will not
appear on the screen.

`password:`

4. If you made an error, repeat Steps 2 and 3. If you made an error typing either
your login or your password, the computer will inform you that your login is incorrect, and it will give you the chance to log in again:

Although this says "login
incorrect," the same
message is given if your
password is incorrect.

```
Login incorrect
login:
```

If you see this, you must re-enter both your login and your password.

4.2 Root and xterm Windows

The root window is also
called the desktop.

Once you have successfully logged in, it may take the computer a minute or so to
start up the Motif window manager (mwm). Eventually, a window should appear,
as shown in Figure 4-2. The background is called the *root window*. The smaller
window is an xterm window. (You may also see a number of other windows,
depending on how your system administrator has configured the window
manager.)

 You will do most of your work in the xterm window. The name xterm is short
for "X Terminal," and as the name suggests, the xterm window emulates a
conventional terminal screen. Some of the parts of the xterm window are shown
in Figure 4-2. (Later in this chapter, you will learn what these do.)

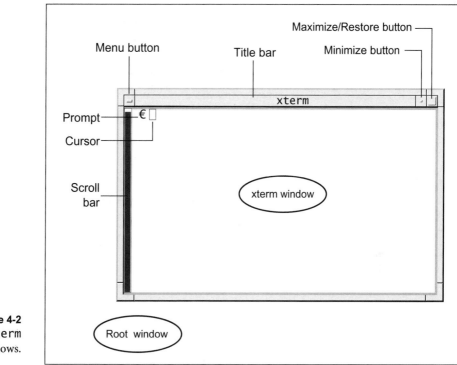

Figure 4-2
The root and `xterm`
windows.

4.3 Getting Acquainted with the Mouse

If you have previously worked with a personal computer, you are undoubtedly familiar with the use of a mouse with a GUI. As you move the mouse on its pad or the table top, an arrow-shaped pointer also moves on the screen.

Unlike many personal computers—which typically work with a mouse having just one or two buttons—the Motif Window Manager is designed to operate with a three-button mouse (Figure 4-3).

Unfortunately, there is no universally accepted standard that sets the functions of the mouse buttons—each system can be configured according to the administrator's (or user's) personal preferences. The following arrangement is fairly typical:

You may have to experiment to discover how the buttons work on your mouse.

■ **Left Button (#1).** The left button is generally used for command selection and activation. This includes pulling down menus, selecting menu items, moving windows, and pressing on-screen buttons.

■ **Middle Button (#2).** On some systems, this button is used to grab and manipulate window scroll bars.

■ **Right Button (#3).** This button has traditionally been used to obtain the "Root" menu.

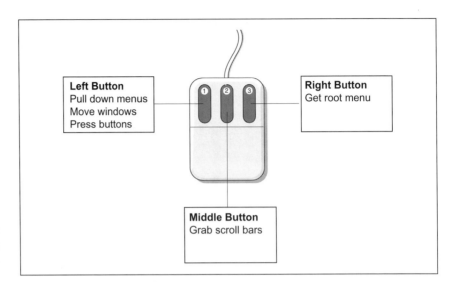

Figure 4-3
Three-button mouse.
The functions of the
buttons may be different
on your system.

There are three ways to activate a mouse button:

■ *Click.* Press and quickly release the button.

■ *Double-click.* Press and release the button twice in rapid succession.

■ *Drag.* Press and hold the button while moving the mouse.

4.4 Pulling Down the Window Menu

The window menu provides a number of useful commands for changing the size and position of the window. To see how this menu works—and to practice using the mouse—try resizing the xterm window:

1. Move the pointer to the window menu button. This button is found at the upper left corner of the xterm window:

Click here

2. Click once with the left mouse button.

A pull-down menu will appear (Figure 4-4). Take a moment to review the various options offered on the window menu. Note in particular the shortcuts and alternate key combinations. You need to understand what the various commands do:

■ **Restore.** Returns a window to its original size once it has been maximized.

■ **Move.** Allows you to move the window to a different position in the root window. (This option is not often used.)

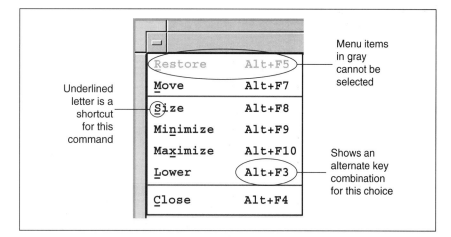

Underlined
letter is a
shortcut
for this
command

Menu items
in gray
cannot be
selected

Shows an
alternate key
combination
for this choice

Figure 4-4
Pull-down menu. This is
called a *pull-down menu*
because you pull it down
from the window frame.

■ **Size.** Allows you to change the size of the window. (This is not often used.)

Remember, an icon is a
small picture or symbol.

■ **Minimize.** Converts the window into an icon. (This is sometimes called the "iconify" command.) You can restore the window by double-clicking on the icon.

■ **Maximize.** Makes the `xterm` window grow to its full size.

■ **Lower.** Moves the current window behind other windows.

■ **Close.** Closes and eliminates the window, usually stopping any program that was running in it. Be careful not to confuse this with the Minimize command, which shrinks the window into an icon. (To confuse matters, on some windowing systems, "Close" does work just like "Minimize.")

3. Click once on Maximize with the left mouse button.

Restore	Alt+F5
Move	Alt+F7
Size	Alt+F8
Minimize	Alt+F9
Maximize	Alt+F10
Lower	Alt+F3
Close	Alt+F4

The Maximize command makes the `xterm` window grow to its full size. Note that you could have performed the same action by using either the one-letter command shortcut (`x`) or the alternate key combination (`Alt+F10`).

4. Click once on Restore with the left mouse button.

Restore	Alt+F5
Move	Alt+F7
Size	Alt+F8
Minimize	Alt+F9
Maximize	Alt+F10

The `xterm` window will return to its previous size. Note once again that you could have performed the same action by using either the one-letter command shortcut or the alternate key combination.

You will learn more about the other window menu options in the next section. For now, you should just close the menu.

4.5 Getting the Pop-Up Menus

Another kind of menu—a "pop-up" menu—appears when you click on the root window. The choices presented by these menus depend on how the system administrator has configured your system. Examine these menus:

1. Move the pointer to the root window.

2. Open a menu using the right button (#3). Depending on how your system is set up, you may have to hold down the mouse button.

A menu should appear. It might look something like this:

The root menu on your system might look very different from this.

Root Menu
New Window
Shuffle Up
Shuffle Down
Refresh
Restart...
Logout

Before going on, be sure that you understand the various options offered on the window menu:

■ **New Window.** This option starts another window, usually an `xterm` window.

■ **Shuffle up.** Just as you would shuffle a deck of cards, shuffling the windows puts some windows behind others. The shuffle up command takes the top window and places it behind the others in the root window. The second window then becomes the active one.

■ **Shuffle down.** This brings the rearmost window forward and places it in front of the others in the root window. This window then becomes the active window.

■ **Refresh.** Sometimes the images on the screen get jumbled. Refresh causes the computer to redraw the windows.

■ **Restart.** This stops the current mwm session and starts another one in its place.

■ **Logout.** You would use this command when you want to quit working on the machine. This closes all windows and stops any programs you have running.

3. Close the menu. On some systems, you do this by simply releasing the button. Other systems require that you click on the menu's title bar.

4. Open a menu using the left button. With the pointer on the root window, press (and if necessary, hold) the left button. Note what you see on the pop-up menu.

5. Close the menu and open another using the center button. Note again what you see. On many systems, this menu gives you options for logging into other machines on the network.

4.6   X Utilities

An application is a program that performs some useful function.

In your survey of the various pop-up menus, you may have discovered a menu that allows you to select various X utilities (also called X tools or clients). Some of the more common X utilities are listed below:

xbiff	Informs you when e-mail has arrived
xcalc	Brings up an on-screen calculator
xclock	Starts a clock in its own window
xedit	Starts a simple text editor
xterm	Starts another xterm window

4.7   Starting xterm from the Root Menu

Skip this section if there is no xterm or New Window menu option.

Now that you have seen how to get the root pop-up menus, you are ready to start another xterm window:

1. Move the pointer to the root window.

2. Press and hold the button that brings up the proper menu. This would be the menu showing an xterm or New Window option.

3. Without releasing the button, slide the pointer down to the New Window or xterm command.

The command will be highlighted.

4. Release the button.

Be patient—it may require a few seconds for the window to start up.

Starting one of the other X utilities listed on the menu—such as xcalc, xclock, and so on—is done similarly. (We leave it as an exercise for you to try these.)

4.8 Keyboard Focus

Although you may have multiple xterm windows open simultaneously, only one of these windows can receive input from the keyboard at a time. The window that gets the input is said to have the *keyboard focus*; this is sometimes called the *active window*. Most window managers change the color or shading of the frame and/or title bar of the active window to distinguish it from other windows.

There are two ways to select the window that will get the keyboard focus:

■ **Point-to-focus method.** On some systems, merely moving the pointer to an xterm window changes the focus to that window. (This is also referred to as the *point-to-type method.*)

■ **Click-to-focus method.** Some systems require that you point to a window and click the left mouse button. (This is also called the *click-to-type method.*)

Take a moment now to determine which method your system employs.

4.9 UNIX Shell Prompt

If you examine the contents of the xterm window, you will see a *shell prompt*, which is simply the shell's way of telling you that it is ready to receive your instructions. If your login shell is the C Shell or TC Shell, the prompt is probably a percent sign:

%

If you are using the Bourne Shell, Korn Shell, or Bourne-Again Shell (bash) as a login shell, the usual prompt is a dollar sign:

$

Other symbols are occasionally used for shell prompts, including the pound sign (#), the "greater than" sign (>), the asterisk (*), the "at" symbol (@), and the colon (:). Some systems are set up to show the host name as part of the prompt, like this:

merlin %

In this book, we will use the following as our "generic" prompt:

In the examples that follow,   §
do not enter the prompt.

4.10 Starting xterm Using a Command Line

You have already seen how to start a new `xterm` window using a pop-up menu. There is another way to open a new window:

1. Select one of the `xterm` windows to be the active window.

2. Enter the `xterm` command at the shell prompt. Note the ampersand (&) at the end of the command. This tells the shell to run the command "in the background" so that you can continue working in the current `xterm` window:

Be sure to include the
ampersand. ——————   § `xterm` & (RETURN)

3. Wait for the new window to start up.

4.11 Resizing a Window

You can easily change the size or shape of a window by dragging its corner:

1. Move the pointer to the bottom right corner of the window frame.

The shape of the pointer will change.

2. Drag the corner of the window.

You should see an outline of the new window position.

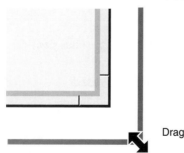

Drag

3. Release the mouse button.

The window will retain its new size and shape.

4.12 Moving a Window

Moving an xterm window is also very easy:

1. Move the pointer to the window's title bar.

2. Drag the window to the new position.

You should see an outline of the new window position.

3. Release the mouse button.

The window will remain in the new position.

4.13 Minimizing and Restoring a Window

In Motif, Minimize means iconify a window; Close means eliminate the window.

Under the Motif Window Manager, the Minimize command on the Window menu converts the window into an icon. This is sometimes called "iconifying" the window. This operation is not to be confused with the Close command, which eliminates the window entirely. (Not all window managers conform to this usage. If you use a different window manager, you may find that the Close command iconifies the window.)

1. Select one of the xterm windows to be the active window.

2. Open the window menu. Remember, this is done by clicking on the window menu button in the upper left-hand corner of the window frame.

3. Select the Minimize option.

The window will shrink to an icon.

4. Double-click on the icon.

This will restore the window to its previous size.

4.14 Changing Your Password

Review Section 2.3 on selecting a password.

A good password is one that is easy for you to remember but difficult for someone else to figure out. Often the initial passwords assigned by system administrators fail these criteria. It is a good idea to change your password frequently to prevent unauthorized use of your account. If you have not already done so, you should take a minute to think about a password.

1. Select an xterm window to be the active window.

2. Enter the passwd command at the shell prompt. Note that the command is passwd, not password:

§ passwd (RETURN)

The system will prompt for your old password:

Old password:

3. Enter your old password, then press (RETURN).

Your password will not
appear on the screen:

Old password: ▓▓▓▓▓▓▓

The computer will then ask you to enter your new password:

New password:

4. Enter your new password, then press (RETURN). Your password will not appear
as you type it:

Your password will not
appear on screen.

New password: ▓▓▓▓▓▓

To ensure that you have made no mistakes, the computer will ask you to repeat
your new password:

Retype new password:

5. Repeat your new password. If this is not done exactly as before, the system will
not accept the new password, and you will have to start over:

Retype new password: ▓▓▓▓▓▓

You will know that the new password has been accepted when the shell prompt
appears:

§

4.15   Trying Out Some UNIX Commands

Next, try a few UNIX commands to see how they work.

1. Select one of the xterm windows to be the active window.

2. Enter the date command. Type date after the prompt, and press (RETURN):

§ date (RETURN)

The computer will respond with the date and time. For example, if you were to
give this command on Friday, August 13, 2004, at 8:35 pm (Mountain Daylight
Time), the output would be something like

Fri Aug 13 20:35:41 MDT 2004

Note that this is the time for the host computer's locale, and that time is given on
the 24-hour clock.

3. Next, try the who command. Type who, followed by (RETURN):

§ who (RETURN)

The computer will respond with a list of the users who are currently logged into your host. For example,

root	console	Aug 13	08:11
aadams	tty16	Aug 13	07:01
pgw	tty03	Aug 13	18:15
ben	tty18	Aug 13	11:32
jeff	tty12	Aug 13	09:45

The user's login name is listed first, followed by a code that identifies the line or *port* to which the user is connected. The date and time that the user logged in are also shown.

4. Try the who am i **command.** This command prints your login name on the screen:

§ who am i (RETURN)

4.16 Reading Your Mail

Skip this section if you have not received e-mail.

If you have received electronic mail, now is the time to read it.

1. Select an xterm **window.**

2. Start the mail program. One of the following commands should work:

This usually works.

§ mailx (RETURN)

§ Mail (RETURN)

§ mail (RETURN)

The system will respond with a list of the messages. For example,

```
U  1 wards  Mon Aug 9 15:27  554/26358  "Class Roster"
N  2 aadams Fri Aug 13 8:59  40/1527    "Lunch"
N  3 gwc    Fri Aug 13 9:47  15/440     "Research Notes"
&
```

A *U* in the first column indicates an unread message left over from the last time you logged in; an *N* indicates a new message. The messages are numbered (from 1 to 3 in this case). The login name of the sender is shown, along with the date and time the message was received and the number of lines and characters the message contains (lines/characters). Finally, the subject of the message is given in quotes. The ampersand (&) on the last line is the *mail prompt*.

3. Read your message(s). Simply enter the message number after the mail prompt and press (RETURN):

&2 (RETURN)

This will cause the second message to appear:

```
Message 2:
From aadams Fri Aug 13 8:59:01 2004
Date: Fri Aug 13 8:59:01
From: aadams (Abigail Adams)
To: (Your login name)
Subject: Lunch

Let's get together for lunch at 12:45 today. Okay?
&
```

4. Leave the mail utility. Typing x (for "exit") at the mail prompt will take you out of the mail utility, leaving the message(s) in the mailbox:

&x (RETURN)

Electronic mail—including the ways to send, save, and delete mail—is discussed in more detail in Part V.

4.17   Reading the UNIX Manual

Many UNIX systems come equipped with a detailed on-line manual that you can read using the man command. The manual describes the commands that are available on the system. To see how this is done, try the following command:

§ man cal (RETURN)

The cal command is one that we will use in later chapters; it displays a calendar on the screen. If your system has the on-line manual, you should see a description of cal. (For more information on how to make sense of the manual, see Appendix B.) Otherwise, you may see the message

man: Command not found.

4.18   Logging Out

When you are finished working on the computer, you must "log out." This tells the system that you are finished using it.

| WARNING | NEVER LEAVE THE TERMINAL WITHOUT LOGGING OUT. ON SOME UNIX SYSTEMS, YOUR ACCOUNT MAY REMAIN OPEN EVEN IF THE TERMINAL IS TURNED OFF. THIS INVITES THE UNSCRUPULOUS TO GET INTO THE SYSTEM AND CAUSE TROUBLE. |

Unfortunately, the process for logging out varies from system to system. (When in doubt, check with your system administrator.)

■ **If Logout or Exit appears on the root menu, select this option.** You may have to wait a minute, but eventually the login screen should appear.

■ **If you see an icon labeled Logout, double-click on this icon.** This will either log you out or open up another window in which you can log out.

■ **If you see a window labeled Logout, double-click on this window.** Wait to see if the login screen appears.

When the login screen appears, the system is ready for the next user. If nothing seems to work, ask for help. Do not leave without logging out first.

4.19 Command Summary

Each of the commands listed here is entered in an xterm window at the shell prompt symbol.

Changing Your Password

passwd (RETURN)   change password

Opening an xterm Window

xterm & (RETURN)   start another xterm window

Miscellaneous UNIX Commands

date (RETURN)   print current date and time

who (RETURN)   print a list of users currently logged in

who am i (RETURN)   print your login

man cal (RETURN)   show the manual page describing the cal command

4.20 Exercises

1. Be sure you can define the following terms:

display manager	screen saver	desktop
root window	mouse	click
double-click	drag	menu
pull-down menu	maximize	minimize
pop-up menu	root menu	icon
keyboard focus	active window	mail prompt

2. See if your terminal has a key labeled "NO SCROLL." This key is supposed to "freeze" the terminal display. Press it and type your name. What happens on the screen? Now press the key again. What do you see?

3. On many terminals, the ^S key combination "freezes" the terminal. Try this key combination and type something on the keyboard. What happens? The key combination ^Q "unfreezes" the terminal, reversing the effects of ^S. Try this.

4. Does your keyboard have a key labeled "CAPS LOCK" or "CASE"? If so, press it and type something on the keyboard. What does this key do?

5. UNIX is *case-sensitive:* it distinguishes between upper- and lowercase letters. Try the commands listed below and note what each one does (if anything):

WHO (RETURN)

CAL 1999 (RETURN)

DATE (RETURN)

WHO AM I (RETURN)

6. The xbiff utility notifies you of the arrival of electronic mail by beeping and raising the flag on a mailbox icon. Try it. If xbiff is not available as a menu option, you can start it by entering the command

xbiff &

7. Experiment with the xcalc client program. If it is not available as a menu option, you can start xcalc with the command

xcalc &

8. Try the xclock client program. If it is not available as a menu option, you can start xclock with the command

xclock &

# Chapter 5

TUTORIAL:
GETTING STARTED (CDE)

Skip this chapter if your system does not run CDE.

In this chapter, you will learn to work with the Common Desktop Environment (CDE). If you haven't done so already, ask your instructor, system administrator, or consultant about setting up an account. You will need the following:

- Your login name;
- Your password;
- The name of the computer you will be using.

This chapter describes local access to your UNIX account. For information on remote access, ask your system administrator or Internet Service Provider (ISP). Or consult the *Just Enough UNIX* web site (`www.mhhe.com/andersen`).

5.1 Logging In

The CDE program that controls your login procedure is `dtlogin`. You do not have to start this program; it should already be running, waiting for you to log in.

1. If necessary, cancel the screen saver. A *screen saver* blanks out a screen that has been idle for a time. Press a key or move the mouse to cancel the screen saver.

You should then see a login screen that may look something like this:

The screen presented by your display manager will appear somewhat different.

2. Enter your login name in the box and press RETURN .

A password screen then appears:

3. Enter your password and press (RETURN). Note that YOUR PASSWORD DOES NOT APPEAR ON THE SCREEN. The idea is to prevent others from looking over your shoulder and learning your password. (You will see how to change the password later.)

4. If you made an error typing either your login name or password, repeat Steps 2 and 3. The computer will inform you that your login is incorrect, and it will give you the chance to log in again:

```
Login incorrect; please try again.
```

Although this says "login incorrect," the same message is given if your password is incorrect.

After you log in, your screen should resemble Figure 5-1. The background is called the *workspace*. Against this background is a `dtterm` or Terminal window and the CDE *Front Panel*. (You may see other windows or objects as well, depending on how your system administrator has set up your system.)

See Exercise 2 for information on changing and naming workspaces.

The Common Desktop Environment allows you to switch between four (or more) workspaces. This can be useful if you are working on multiple projects. By reserving a different workspace for each project, you can readily organize the tools and applications you need.

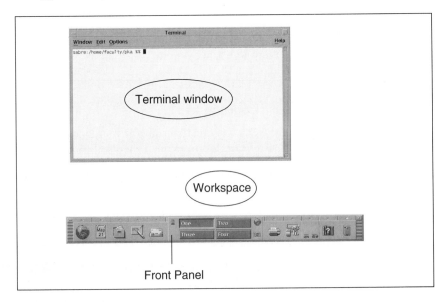

Figure 5-1
Common Desktop Environment (CDE), showing the Workspace, Terminal window, and Front Panel.

5.2 Getting Acquainted with the Mouse

If you have previously worked with a personal computer having a graphical user interface (GUI), you are undoubtedly familiar with the use of a mouse. As you move the mouse on its pad or the table top, an arrow-shaped pointer also moves on the screen.

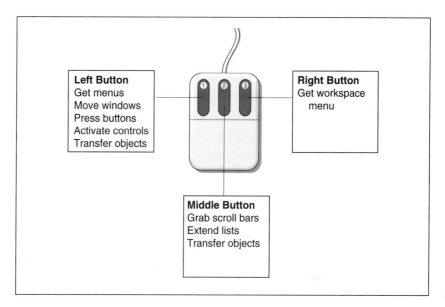

Figure 5-2
Three-button mouse.
The functions of the
buttons may be different
on your system.

Unlike many personal computers—which typically work with a mouse having just one or two buttons—the Desktop Window Manager is designed to operate with a three-button mouse (Figure 5-2).

See Exercise 6 for information on changing your mouse's behavior.

There is no universally accepted standard that sets the functions of the mouse buttons—each system can be configured according to the administrator's (or user's) personal preferences. The following arrangement is fairly typical:

You may have to experiment to discover how the buttons work on your mouse.

■ **Left Button (#1).** The left button is generally used for command selection and activation. This includes pulling down menus, selecting menu items, moving windows, and pressing on-screen buttons.

■ **Middle Button (#2).** This button is typically used to grab and move windows and scroll bars, to extend lists, and to transfer objects.

■ **Right Button (#3).** This button is often used to obtain pop-up menus.

There are several ways to activate a mouse button:

■ **Click.** Press and quickly release the button. This is done to select a window, icon, or menu option.

■ **Double-click.** Press and release the button twice in rapid succession. Double-clicking is done to start certain programs, to restore windows to their original size, and to close windows.

■ **Drag.** Press and hold the button while moving the mouse. This action is used to move objects—such as windows and icons—around the desktop.

■ **Drop.** Release the button after dragging an object to a new position.

5.3 Keyboard Focus

Although you may have multiple windows open simultaneously, only one of these windows can receive input from the keyboard at a time. The window that gets the input is said to have the *keyboard focus*; this is sometimes called the *active window*. Most window managers change the color or shading of the frame and/or title bar of the active window to distinguish it from other windows.

There are two ways to select the window that will get the keyboard focus:

The CDE Style Manager allows you to change the focussing method—see Exercise 5.

■ **Point-to-focus method.** On some systems, merely moving the pointer to a window changes the focus to that window. (This is also referred to as the *point-to-type method.*)

■ **Click-to-focus method.** Some systems require that you point to a window and click the left mouse button. (This is also called the *click-to-type method.*)

Take a moment now to determine which method your system employs.

5.4 The Terminal Emulator

You can open additional Terminal windows—see Exercises 7 and 8.

You will do much of your work in this book using the Terminal Emulator, also called `dtterm`. As its name suggests, the Terminal Emulator acts like a conventional terminal screen—in particular, a DEC VT220 terminal. The parts of the Terminal window are shown in Figure 5-3.

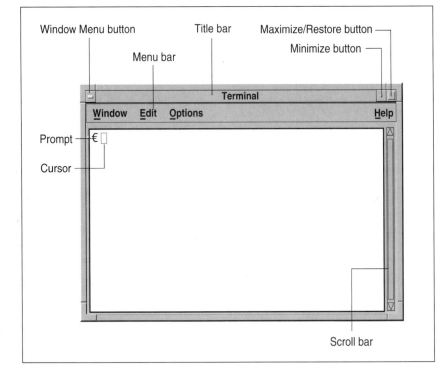

Figure 5-3
The Terminal Emulator or `dtterm` window.

■ **Window Menu button.** Pressing this button opens the Window Menu (see Section 5.5 below).

■ **Title bar.** The Title bar indicates the type of the window (i.e., Terminal), and is used to move the window.

■ **Menu bar.** Various pull-down menus are accessible from the menu bar.

■ **Maximize/Restore button.** This button enlarges the window to fill the screen or shrinks an enlarged window to normal size.

■ **Minimize button.** This button converts the window into an icon—that is, a small picture or symbol representing the window—and moves the icon to the edge of the workspace. (This is sometimes called "iconfying" the window.) The window can be restored by double-clicking on the icon.

■ **Scroll bar.** By dragging the scroll bar with the mouse, you can move up and down in the window.

5.5 Pulling Down the Window Menu

The Window Menu provides a number of useful commands for changing the size and position of the window. To see how this menu works—and to practice using the mouse—try resizing the Terminal window:

1. Move the pointer to the Window Menu button. This button is found at the upper left corner of the Terminal window:

Click here

2. Click once with the left mouse button.

A menu will appear (Figure 5-4). This is called a *pull-down* menu because you pull it down from the window frame. Take a moment to become familiar with the features of the menu. Note in particular the shortcuts and alternate key combinations. You need to understand what the various commands do:

■ **Restore:** Returns a window to its original size once it has been minimized or maximized.

■ **Move:** Allows you to move the window to a different position.

■ **Size:** Allows you to change the size of the window.

Remember, an icon is a small picture or symbol.

■ **Minimize:** Converts the window into an icon. (This is sometimes called the "iconify" command.) You can restore the window by double-clicking on the icon.

■ **Maximize:** Enlarges the window to fill the entire screen.

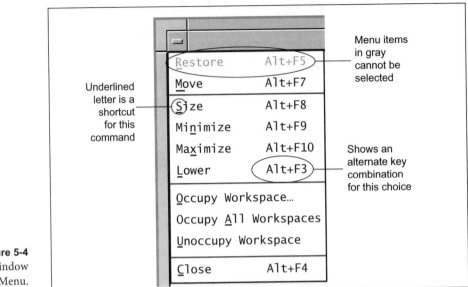

Menu items
in gray
cannot be
selected

Underlined
letter is a
shortcut
for this
command

Shows an
alternate key
combination
for this choice

Figure 5-4
Pull-down Window
Menu.

- **Lower:** Moves the current window behind other windows.

- **Occupy workspace:** Puts the window into another workspace.

- **Occupy all workspaces:** Puts the window into all workspaces.

You can also close a window
by double-clicking on the
Window Menu button.

- **Close:** Eliminates the window, usually stopping any program that was running in it. Do not confuse this with the Minimize command, which shrinks the window into an icon.

3. Click once on Maximize with the left mouse button.

The Maximize command makes the Terminal window grow to its full size. Note that you could have performed the same action by using either the one-letter command shortcut (x) or the alternate key combination (Alt+F10).

4. Click once on Restore with the left mouse button.

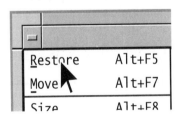

The Terminal window will return to its previous size. Note once again that you could have performed the same action by using either the one-letter command shortcut or the alternate key combination.

You will learn more about the other Window Menu options in the next section. For now, you should just close the menu.

5.6 Resizing a Window

You can easily change the size or shape of a window by dragging its corner:

1. Move the pointer to the bottom right corner of the window frame.

The shape of the pointer will change.

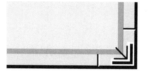

2. Drag the corner of the window.

You will see an outline of the new window position as you drag it:

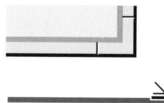

Drag

3. Release the mouse button.

The window will retain its new size and shape.

5.7 Moving a Window

Moving a Terminal window is also very easy:

1. Move the pointer to the window's title bar.

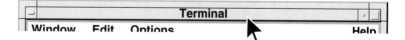

2. Drag the window to the new position.

You should see an outline of the new window position.

3. Release the mouse button.

The window should remain in the new position.

5.8   Minimizing and Restoring a Window

Minimize means iconify a window; Close means eliminate the window.

The Minimize command on the Window menu iconifies the window, converting it into an icon and moving it to the edge of the workspace. This operation is not to be confused with the Close command, which eliminates the window entirely.

1. **Make the Terminal window active.**

2. **Open the Window menu.** Remember, this is done by clicking on the Window Menu button in the upper left-hand corner of the window frame.

3. **Select the Minimize option.** The window will shrink to an icon placed off to the edge of the workspace.

4. **Double-click on the icon.** This will restore the window to its previous size.

5.9   UNIX Shell Prompt

If you examine the contents of the `dtterm` window, you will see a *shell prompt*, which is simply the shell's way of telling you that it is ready to receive your instructions. If your login shell is the C Shell or theTC Shell, the prompt is probably a percent sign:

```
%
```

If you are using the Bourne Shell, Korn Shell, or Bash as a login shell, the usual prompt is a dollar sign:

```
$
```

Other symbols are occasionally used for shell prompts, including the pound sign (#), the "greater than" sign (>), the asterisk (*), the "at" symbol (@), and the colon (:). Some systems are set up to include the host name as part of the prompt, like this:

```
merlin %
```

In this book, we will use the following as our "generic" prompt, to take the place of either the percent sign or the dollar sign:

In the examples that follow, do not enter the prompt.

```
§
```

5.10   Trying Out Some UNIX Commands

In this section, we will try some traditional UNIX commands to see how they work.

1. **Make the Terminal window active.**

2. **Enter the `date` command.** Type `date` after the prompt, and press (RETURN):

```
§ date (RETURN)
```

The computer will respond with the date and time. For example, if you were to give this command on Monday, August 13, 2007, at 8:35 pm (Eastern Standard Time), the output would be something like

```
Mon  Aug 13  20:35:41  EST  2007
```

Note that this is the time for the host computer's locale, and that time is given on the 24-hour clock.

3. Next, try the who **command.** Type who, followed by (RETURN):

§ who (RETURN)

The computer will respond with a list of the users who are currently logged into the system. For example,

```
root          console       Aug 13        08:11
aadams        tty16         Aug 13        07:01
pgw           tty03         Aug 13        18:15
ben           tty18         Aug 13        11:32
jeff          tty12         Aug 13        09:45
```

The user's login name is listed first, followed by a code that identifies the line or *port* to which the user is connected. The date and time that the user logged in are also shown.

4. Try the who am i **command.**

§ who am i (RETURN)

This prints your login name on the screen.

5.11 Changing Your Password

Review Section 2.3 on selecting a password.

A good password is one that is easy for you to remember but difficult for someone else to figure out. Often the initial passwords assigned by system administrators fail these criteria. It is a good idea to change your password frequently to prevent unauthorized use of your account. If you have not already done so, you should take a minute to think about a password.

1. Make the Terminal window active.

2. Enter the passwd **command at the shell prompt.** Note that this is passwd, not password:

§ passwd (RETURN)

The system will prompt for your old password:

Old password:

3. Enter your old password, then press (RETURN). Your password will not appear on the screen as you type:

```
Old password:
```

The computer will then ask you to enter your new password:

```
New password:
```

4. Enter your new password, then press (RETURN). As usual your password will not appear on the screen:

```
New password:
```

To ensure that you have made no mistakes, the computer will ask you to repeat your new password:

```
Retype new password:
```

5. Repeat your new password. If this is not done exactly as before, the system will not accept the new password, and you will have to start over:

```
Retype new password:
```

You will know that the new password has been accepted when the shell prompt appears:

§

5.12 Reading the UNIX Manual

Many UNIX systems come equipped with a detailed on-line manual that you can read using the man command. The manual describes the traditional UNIX commands that are available on the system. To see how this is done, try the following command in a Terminal window:

§ man cal (RETURN)

The cal command is one that we will use in later chapters; it displays a calendar on the screen. If your system has the on-line manual, you should see a description of cal. (For more information on how to make sense of the manual, see Appendix B.) Otherwise, you will see the message

```
man: Command not found.
```

5.13 The Front Panel

The Front Panel provides ready access to the powerful tools offered by the CDE. Figure 5-5 shows the parts of a typical Front Panel. (Because the Front Panel is readily customized, yours may appear somewhat different.)

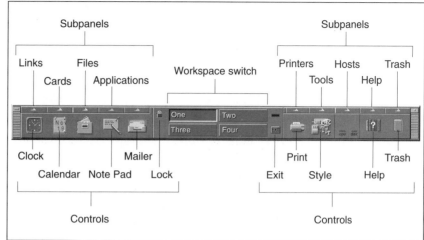

Figure 5-5
CDE Front Panel.

5.14 Using a Control

The icons on the Front Panel are called *controls*. The behavior of a control depends on how it is used:

■ **Click behavior.** Clicking on the icon may launch a software application or open a window. For example, clicking on the Calendar control starts the Calendar application; clicking on the Trash control opens a window showing the contents of the Trash Can.

■ **Drag-and-drop behavior.** In some cases, an object—such as a file—can be processed in some way by dropping it onto the icon. For example, an appointment file dropped on the Calendar control will be entered into the appointment calendar; a file dropped on the Trash control will be placed in the Trash Can.

■ **Indicator behavior.** Some controls provide information. Thus, the Calendar control displays the current date; the Trash control changes its appearance to show whether the Trash Can is empty or not.

Not all controls exhibit all three kinds of behavior. For instance, you can click on the Exit control to end your current computing session; but there is no drop or indicator behavior associated with the Exit control.

Let's see what happens when you click on the Calendar control:

1. **Click on the Calendar control.**

A calendar window will appear.

2. **Explore the Calendar.** Take some time to figure out how the calendar works. (See if you can change calendar views—daily, weekly, monthly, and yearly.)

3. **Close the Calendar window.** Double-click on the Window Menu button. (Or pull down the Window menu and select Close.)

5.15 Opening and Closing a Subpanel

A *subpanel* is a menu accessible from the Front Panel that lists additional controls. The following subpanels are typically available:

■ **Links.** This subpanel generally provides access to frequently used web applications, such as a browser. The clock application is often put here as well.

■ **Cards.** The controls for the Calendar, Address Manager, and other personal productivity applications may be listed here.

■ **Files.** Controls for various file- and disk-management tools are listed here.

■ **Applications.** Frequently used applications—including the Text Editor and Applications Manager—can be started from this subpanel.

■ **Mail.** The Mailer and other electronic mail tools are controlled from this subpanel.

■ **Printers.** Controls related to printing are grouped together on this subpanel.

■ **Tools.** Controls for frequently used software tools may be placed on this subpanel.

■ **Hosts.** The Terminal and Console controls are available on this subpanel.

■ **Help.** Various on-line Help viewers are listed here.

■ **Trash.** The Trash Can and Empty Trash controls are found on this subpanel.

It is easy to open and close a subpanel:

1. **Click the up-button to open.**

The subpanel opens, and the up-button becomes a down-button.

2. **Click the down-button to close.**

The subpanel closes, and the down-button becomes an up-button again.

There are two other ways to close a subpanel. You can double-click on the Window menu button. Or you can click on one of the controls listed on the subpanel, which will activate the control and, at the same time, close the subpanel.

5.16   Tearing Off a Subpanel

You can "tear off" a subpanel and drag it to another location. The subpanel will remain open even after you click on one of its controls.

1. **Open the subpanel.**

2. **Grab the top of the subpanel.**

3. **Drag the subpanel away from the Front Panel.**

5.17   Promoting a Control to the Front Panel

You have probably noticed that every control shown on the Front Panel also appears on the underlying subpanel. You can "promote" a frequently used control from the subpanel to the Front Panel:

1. **Open the subpanel.** Try the Applications subpanel.

2. **Move the pointer to the control you want to promote.** You will use the Text Editor frequently in later chapters; let's promote it to the Front Panel.

3. **Press and hold the #3 mouse button.**

Another menu will appear.

4. **Select Promote to Front Panel.**

5. **Release the mouse button.**

The subpanel will close and the promoted icon will appear on the Front Panel.

5.18   Adding a Control to a Subpanel

It is easy to add a control to a subpanel:

1. **Open and tear-off the Applications subpanel.** Remember, tearing-off a subpanel keeps it open.

2. **Click on the Applications control.**

The Applications Manager window will appear.

3. **Double-click on Desktop_Apps.** You may have to scroll up or down (or resize the window) to find the Desktop_Apps icon in the Applications Manager window. Double-clicking on this icon opens the Desktop Applications window.

4. **Find the Calculator icon.**

5. Drag and drop the Calculator on the "Install Icon" box on the Applications subpanel.

```
[   ]  Install Icon
```

The calculator control will appear on the subpanel.

5.19 Getting Help

The Common Desktop Environment provides an extensive Help System. Information is organized in *volumes*, like books in a library. Each of the standard CDE applications has its own Help volumes; other applications may also have volumes in the system. There are several ways to obtain help:

■ **Help key.** On most systems, this is the *F1* key. Pressing it provides help that is appropriate for the particular application or window you are using. (This is called *context-sensitive* help.)

■ **Help menu.** Most application windows include a pull-down Help menu on the Menu bar. This is usually linked to the help volumes for that application.

■ **Help Manager.** Help Manager allows you to examine any volume in the Help System.

Let's use Help Manager to search for a particular topic:

1. Double-click on the Help Manager control. If you do not see the control on the Front Panel, look for it on the Help subpanel.

We leave it as an exercise for you to explore the Top Level Help volume.

The Help Viewer will appear. The viewer is open to the *Top Level Volume*, which provides an overview and introduction to the Common Desktop Environment.

2. Click on the Index... button.

The Index Search dialog box will appear.

3. Select the All Volumes button. Note that you can search the current volume, selected volumes, or the entire Help library.

4. Select the Entries With: button.

5. Enter a topic or keyword in the box. To find information on the Calendar Manager, for example, enter *calendar* in the box.

6. Press Start Search.

Help Manager will list index entries that contain the word *calendar*. A typical item in the list will look like this:

```
+87   Calendar Help
```

This means that the requested topic appears 87 times under the index entry for the Calendar. The plus sign (+) indicates that the topics themselves are not shown.

7. **Click on the index entry to expand the list.**

The plus sign changes to a minus sign (–), and the topics appear under that index entry.

8. **Click on a topic to read about it in the Help Viewer.**

5.20 Logging Out

When you are finished working on the computer, you must "log out." This tells the system that you are finished using it.

1. **On the front Panel, press the Exit control.**

2. **Wait for the login screen to appear.**

When you see the login screen, the system is then ready for the next user.

5.21 Command Summary

Each of the commands listed here is entered in a Terminal window at the shell prompt.

Changing Your Password

passwd (RETURN)   change password

Miscellaneous UNIX Commands

date (RETURN)   print current date and time

who (RETURN)   print a list of users currently logged in

who am i (RETURN)   print your login

man cal (RETURN)   show the manual page describing the cal command

5.22 Exercises

1. Be sure you can define the following terms:

Front Panel	screen saver	desktop
Workspace	mouse	click
double-click	drag	menu
pull-down menu	maximize	minimize
pop-up menu	subpanel	icon
keyboard focus	active window	shell prompt

2. You can change workspaces using the appropriate button in the Workspace switch. (Try it.) By default, the buttons are designated One, Two, Three, and Four. You can give a button a more descriptive name using the Rename option on the button's pop-up menu. (Try it.)

3. The Top Level Help Volume provides a good introduction to the Common Desktop Environment. Use Help Manager to open and read through the Top Level Volume.

4. The CDE Style Manager allows you to change the appearance and behavior of the desktop. For example, you can choose a patterned backdrop for the current workspace, and you can select a color palette for the backdrop, window frames, and other components. Open the Style Manager, click on Backdrop, and try out the various patterns. Then click on Colors and try the available color palettes.

5. Using the CDE Style Manager, you can choose between the point-to-focus method and the click-to-focus method. Try it. Open the Style Manager, click on Keyboard, and select the option you want.

6. The Style Manager allows you to change the behavior of the mouse, including the functions of the buttons. Open the Style Manager, click on Mouse, and select the option(s) you want.

7. The CDE normally opens one Terminal Emulator window when you log in. You can have several Terminal windows running simultaneously. To start a Terminal window, open the Hosts subpanel and click on This Host or Terminal.

8. Another way to start a new Terminal is to enter the dtterm command in an existing terminal window. Try it:

Be sure to include the ampersand.   § dtterm & (RETURN)

PART II
UNIX FILE SYSTEM

# Chapter 6

THE UNIX FILE SYSTEM

Tutorials related to this chapter are found in Chapters 7, 8, and 9.

The *file system* is the part of UNIX that organizes and keeps track of data. In this chapter, you will learn how to use the UNIX file system to manage your data.

6.1 Files and Directories

If you have previously used a computer, you are undoubtedly familiar with files. Most computer users know that a *file* is a collection of related information— anything from a chocolate cake recipe to a computer program—which is stored in secondary memory.

To UNIX, everything is a file.

UNIX expands the usual definition of *file* to include anything from which data can be taken or to which data can be sent. Hence, a file may be something stored in secondary memory; but it can also refer to the various input/output devices (keyboard, video display, printer, and so on) that can provide or accept data. Since that describes virtually everything the operating system deals with, it is often said that everything is a file to UNIX.

There are three general kinds of UNIX files:

■ **Ordinary files.** These are the common computer files, what people usually have in mind when they say "files." Most of your work on UNIX will involve ordinary files, which are also called *regular files*.

■ **Special files.** Also called *device files*, special files represent physical devices such as terminals, printers, and other peripherals. Although you will frequently use special files, you will rarely (if ever) create or modify one.

■ **Directory files.** Ordinary and special files are organized into collections called *directory files* or *directories*. Whereas ordinary files hold information, directories can hold other files and directories.

You will most often work with ordinary files and directory files, so those will be the focus of this chapter.

6.2 Binary and Text Files

Ordinary UNIX files can be divided into two categories:

■ **Text files.** As the name suggests, a *text file* contains information in the form of text that you can read. Such files can be created and modified using a program called a *text editor*. Because text is generally represented by ASCII code, text files are often called *ASCII files*.

■ **Binary files.** A *binary file* is an ordinary file containing non-textual data. In most cases, binary files are intended to be read and processed by computer programs rather than human users. (If you were to attempt to read or modify binary code using a conventional text editor, its contents would appear undecipherable.)

6.3 Home and Working Directories

When you first log into your UNIX account, you enter what is known as your *home directory*. This is where you will keep any files or directories that you create. The name of your home directory is usually the same as your login name.

After you have logged into your home directory, you are free to move to other directories in the system. Whichever directory you happen to be working in at the time is called your *current directory* or *working directory*. When you first log in, your working directory is your home directory.

Each user on the system is given a home directory. On a typical large UNIX system, there may be hundreds of these home directories, each containing scores of other files and directories.

6.4 The UNIX File Tree

Figure 6-1 is a simplified diagram of a typical UNIX system. It looks something like an upside-down tree, with its root at the top. In fact, the directory at the very top, the one that contains all of the other directories, is called the *root*. Various other directories reside inside the root directory:

bin   This directory contains the software for the shell and the most commonly used UNIX commands. Although bin is short for "binary," you may want to think of it as a "bin" for holding useful software tools.

dev   The name is short for "devices"; this directory holds the special files needed to operate peripheral devices such as terminals and printers.

etc   Various administrative files are kept in this directory, including the list of users that are authorized to use the system, as well as their passwords.

home   Users' home directories are kept here. On some large systems there may be several directories holding user files.

tmp   Temporary files are often kept in this directory.

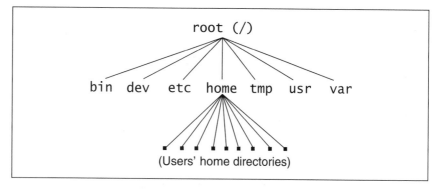

Figure 6-1
Directory structure of a
typical UNIX system.
Users' home directories
are kept in the directory
home in this system.

usr   Some versions of UNIX keep users' home directories in usr; others keep
        such useful things as the on-line manual pages here.

var   Files containing information that varies frequently are kept in the var di-
        rectory. An example would be user mailboxes, which are typically found
        in the /var/mail directory.

Although your particular UNIX system may be set up a bit differently, all UNIX
systems have a root directory at the top.

A directory will sometimes be referred to as the "parent" or the "child" of another
directory. For example, root is the parent of bin, dev, etc, home, tmp, usr, and
var; these directories, in turn, are the children of root. (Child directories are
often called *subdirectories*.) Note that every directory except root has exactly one
parent, but may have many children.

6.5 File and Directory Names

Every file and directory has a name. The name of your home directory is usually
the same as your login, and you normally cannot rename it. However, you must
choose names for any other files and directories you make. On most UNIX
systems, file names may comprise from one to 255 of the following characters, in
any combination:

Some older systems limit
file names to 14 characters.

- Uppercase letters (A to Z);

- Lowercase letters (a to z);

- Numerals (0 to 9);

- Period (.), underscore (_), and comma (,).

A space or a special
character in a file name is
likely to confuse the shell.

In most cases, you should avoid file names that contain spaces or any of the
following special characters:

& * \ | [ ] { } $ < > ( ) # ? ' " / ; ^ ! ~ %

Also, avoid using UNIX command names as file names.

It is a good idea to choose descriptive names that give an idea about the contents of the file. Some users also prefer short file names (to save typing).

Consider using *filename extensions*. A filename extension is a suffix attached to the file name to identify the data kept in the file. An extension typically consists of a few characters separated from the rest of the file name by a period. For example, if you were writing a book, you might put each chapter in its own file:

> *Some non-UNIX operating systems do not allow long filename extensions or multiple extensions.*

```
mybook.ch1
mybook.ch1.v2
mybook.ch2
mybook.ch3.revised
mybook.appendix1.old
```

This book follows the convention that ordinary file names are given in lowercase letters, while directory names inside users' home directories are capitalized. This will help you distinguish at a glance directories from ordinary files. You do not have to observe this convention with your own files and directories.

6.6 Absolute Pathnames

To use a file in your current directory, all you need is the file's name. However, if the file is located in another directory, you will need to know the file's *pathname*. A pathname is an address that shows the file's position in the file system.

> *An absolute pathname shows how to find a file, beginning at the root.*

Absolute or *full* pathnames give the location of a file in relation to the top of the file system. The simplest full pathname is for the root directory, which is represented by a slash:

```
/
```

The absolute pathnames for the root's child directories, shown in Figure 6–1, are

```
/bin            /dev            /etc
/home           /tmp            /usr
/var
```

> *All absolute pathnames begin with a slash.*

Note that each of these begins with a slash (/), which tells you that the path starts at the root. Note too that this is a *forward* slash, not a backslash (\).

Figure 6–2 shows home and two of the users' home directories it contains (jack and jill). You have already seen that the pathname for home is

```
/home
```

The absolute pathname for the user directory jill is

```
/home/jill
```

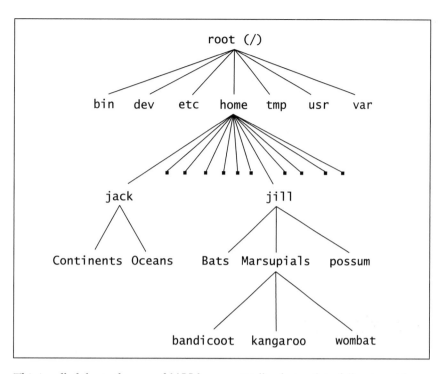

Figure 6-2
The home directories
jack and jill. A large
UNIX system may con-
tain hundreds of home
directories.

This is called the *pathname* of jill because it tells what path to follow to get from the root directory to jill. In this case, the path goes from the root, to the directory home, and finally to jill. Continuing further, the subdirectory Marsupials has the absolute pathname

/home/jill/Marsupials

Ordinary files also have absolute pathnames. For example, the pathname of the file wombat is

/home/jill/Marsupials/wombat

This means that wombat may be found by starting at the root, moving down to the directory home, then to the user directory jill, to the directory Marsupials, and finally to the file wombat itself.

You may have noticed that the slash (/) serves two purposes in pathnames. The first slash represents the root; other slashes stand as separators between file names.

As you can imagine, a full pathname can be unwieldy. Fortunately, you can abbreviate some pathnames. A tilde (~) by itself stands for your home directory's pathname; a tilde preceding a user name stands for that user's home directory. Thus,

~ represents the absolute pathname of your home directory

~jack represents the absolute pathname of the home directory jack

6.7 Relative Pathnames

A relative pathname shows how to find a file, beginning at your working directory.

More often than not, you are interested in the position of a file or directory relative to your current working directory. Relative pathnames start from the working directory rather than the root.

When writing out a relative pathname, a single period or dot (.) is the shorthand notation for your current working directory. Similarly, two dots (..) are used to signify the parent of your working directory—the one above it in the directory structure. These are usually called "dot" and "dotdot." Hence

Both "dot" and "dotdot" are links—see Section 6.14.

. ("dot") represents the current working directory

.. ("dotdot") is the parent of the current working directory

For files in the current directory, the relative pathname is easy: it is simply the name of the file. Suppose you were working in the directory jack shown in Figure 6–2. The relative pathnames of the two directories in jack would be

```
Continents   Oceans
```

The parent of jack is home. Therefore, the relative pathname of home would be

```
..
```

Suppose now that you wanted the relative pathname of the directory that contains home, which is the root directory. From the directory jack this would be

```
../..
```

To find the Marsupials directory from the directory jack, you would first move up to home (represented by "dotdot"), then down to jill, and finally down to Marsupials itself. Putting this altogether, the relative pathname becomes

```
../jill/Marsupials
```

While absolute pathnames always begin with a slash (/), representing the root directory, relative pathnames begin either with "dot" (.), "dotdot" (..), or the name of a file or directory in your current working directory.

6.8 Listing Files

You now know how to write absolute pathnames and relative pathnames, but you may reasonably wonder what good this is. To answer that, consider how pathnames may be used with a few UNIX commands. Start with the ls ("list") command.

Suppose jack is working in his home directory, and he wants to remind himself which files he has in his home directory. He would type the command

§ ls (RETURN)

The response would be

```
Continents  Oceans
```

Now suppose jack wants to know what jill has in her Marsupials directory. From his home directory, he would use the ls command with the pathname of Marsupials:

§ ls ../jill/Marsupials ⌐RETURN⌐

The computer's answer would be

```
bandicoot  kangaroo  wombat
```

Thus, without leaving home, jack can list files in a distant directory—even a directory belonging to another user—if he knows the directory's pathname.

6.9   Hidden Files and Directories

A *hidden* (or *invisible*) file is one that is not listed when you use the simple ls command. A file or directory will be hidden if its name begins with a period. For example,

```
.hidden    .jim   .lost    .profile    .login    .  ..
```

would all be hidden—they would not be listed by the simple ls command. To list all of the files in a directory, including the hidden ones, requires the ls –a ("list all") command. Suppose, for example, that jack is working in his home directory, and he types

§ ls -a ⌐RETURN⌐

He would see

```
.  ..   Continents  Oceans
```

Similarly, if jack were to use this command with the pathname of jill's Marsupials directory, he would see something like this:

§ ls -a ../jill/Marsupials ⌐RETURN⌐

```
.  ..   bandicoot  kangaroo  wombat
```

Note that "dot" (.) and "dotdot" (..) are both names of hidden directories, and that both appear when jack uses the ls -a command. Remember, "dot" is just another name for the current directory; "dotdot" refers to the parent of the current directory.

6.10   Renaming and Moving Files

The ls command takes one pathname; now consider a command that uses two. The mv ("move") command has the general form

mv *pathname1 pathname2*

This means "move the file found at *pathname1* to the position specified by *pathname2*." To see how this works, consider how jill might tidy up her home directory using mv.

The file name possum is wrong because the proper name for the animal is "opossum." If jill is still working in her home directory, the pathname of the file possum is just the file name. To change the name of the file without changing its location, she simply uses mv with the new name:

§ mv possum opossum (RETURN)

This means "move the contents of possum (in the current directory) into the file opossum (also in the current directory)." Since there is no existing opossum file, one is created, and the old file name disappears.

Next, jill remembers that the opossum is a marsupial, and therefore should be moved to the Marsupials directory. The mv command will do the trick:

§ mv opossum Marsupials (RETURN)

This means "move opossum from the current directory into the Marsupials directory." Thus jill can use the mv command twice, once to rename a file and again to move it to another directory. The end result is shown in Figure 6–3.

jill could have moved the file and renamed it at the same time using the command

§ mv possum Marsupials/opossum (RETURN)

This means "move the contents of possum to the Marsupials directory and into a file named opossum."

WARNING   BE CAREFUL WHEN MOVING OR RENAMING A FILE. IF A FILE HAVING THE SAME PATHNAME ALREADY EXISTS, THE EXISTING FILE WILL BE OVERWRITTEN.

6.11 Creating a File

There are four common ways to create a UNIX file:

1. Copy an existing file.

2. Redirect the "standard output" from a UNIX utility.

3. Use a text editor.

4. Write a computer program that opens new files.

Of these, (1) and (2) are considered in this chapter; (3) is covered later in the book. (Consult a book on your favorite programming language to see how to write a program that creates files.)

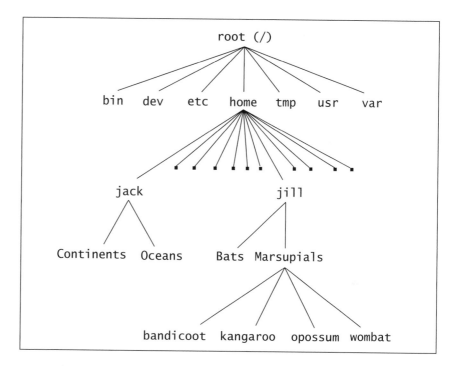

Figure 6-3
The home directory after the file possum was renamed opossum, then moved to the Marsupials directory.

6.12   Copying Files

The cp ("copy") command has the form

cp *pathname1   pathname2*

This means "copy the file found at *pathname1* and place the copy in the position specified by *pathname2*." Suppose that jack has developed a sudden interest in wombats and asks jill for a copy of her file on the subject. From her home directory, jill uses the command

§ cp Marsupials/wombat ../jack/Continents (RETURN)

to make a copy of the wombat file and put it in the Continents directory. The result is shown in Figure 6–4.

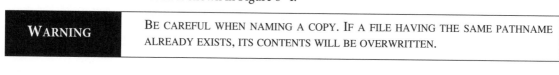

| WARNING | BE CAREFUL WHEN NAMING A COPY. IF A FILE HAVING THE SAME PATHNAME ALREADY EXISTS, ITS CONTENTS WILL BE OVERWRITTEN. |

6.13   Creating a File by Redirection

Redirection puts the output into a file rather than the terminal screen.

The second method of creating a new file is to redirect the output of a command. In other words, instead of displaying the results of the command on the screen, UNIX puts the results into a file. As an example, consider what happens if jill moves to her Marsupials directory and issues the ls command:

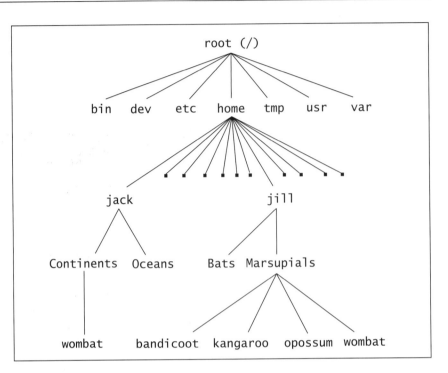

Figure 6-4
The home directory
after `jill` places a copy
of wombat in Conti-
nents.

§ ls ⟨RETURN⟩
bandicoot kangaroo opossum wombat

Think of the redirection
symbol (>) as an arrow
pointing to the file where
the output should go.

Suppose now that she wants to redirect this list into a file named `filelist`. She does this using the *output redirection symbol* (>):

§ ls > filelist ⟨RETURN⟩
§

Usually, the standard
output is the terminal
screen, and the standard
input is the keyboard.

This time, nothing appears on the screen because the output was rerouted into the file. In UNIX terminology, the information was redirected from the *standard output* (the terminal screen) to the file. If `jill` lists her files now, she will see that there is a new one named `filelist` in the directory:

§ ls ⟨RETURN⟩
bandicoot filelist kangaroo opossum wombat

Redirection is powerful and convenient, but it can be dangerous. If you redirect the output into a file that already exists, the original contents of the file will be lost.

WARNING	REDIRECTION INTO AN EXISTING FILE WILL OVERWRITE WHATEVER IS ALREADY IN THE FILE.

If you want to add something to the end of an existing file while keeping the original contents, you can use the *append* operation. This requires two redirection symbols (>>):

Appending adds the output
to the end of the file.

```
§ ls >> filelist (RETURN)
§
```

6.14 Links

Although we have been saying that directory files contain other files and directories, that is not precisely true. If you could look inside a directory, you would find no files. Instead, you would see a list of the files that are supposed to be "contained" in that directory. The names on the list refer to the storage locations that actually hold the files. We say that the files are "linked" to the directory.

Generally, a *link* is a name that refers to a file. UNIX allows more than one link to the same file, so a file can have more than one name.

Directory files always contain at least two links: "dot" (.), which is a link to the directory itself; and "dotdot" (..), a link to the parent directory. Most ordinary files are created with just one link.

You can create more links to a file using the ln ("link") command:

§ ln *filename newfilename* (RETURN)

where *filename* is the name of an existing file, and *newfilename* is the new name you want to link to the file.

6.15 The Long Listing

The UNIX operating system is designed to make it easy for users to share files. However, there are times when you do not want others to copy, move, or even examine the contents of your files and directories. You can easily control access to the files in your home directory.

The ls -l ("list –long") command shows the current access permissions on a file or directory:

§ ls -l (RETURN)

This produces listings that look something like this:

```
drwxrwx---   2 you engr     12 Apr  1 15:53 Cal
-rw-rw----   1 you engr    997 Mar 31 10:53 fun
-rw-rw----   1 you engr    401 Mar 31 10:30 summer.2007
```

Let's decipher the first listing:

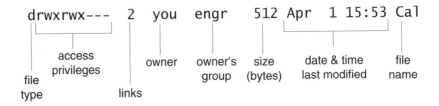

- **File type.** A *d* in the leftmost position indicates a directory. An ordinary file will have a hyphen (–) in this position.

Access privileges are
discussed in Section 6.16
- **Access privileges.** These nine positions show who has permission to do what with the file or directory. (More will be said about these later.)

- **Links.** Remember, a *link* is a pseudonym for a file or directory. Directory files always have at least two links, because each directory contains the hidden entry "dot" (.) as a pseudonym for itself and "dotdot" (..) as a pseudonym for the parent directory. Most ordinary files have just one link, but you can create more using the ln command.

- **Owner.** This is the login of the person who owns the file.

- **Owner's group.** A *group* is a collection of users to which the owner of the file belongs. (On Berkeley systems, ls –l does not list the group name; to see it, you have to use the ls –lg command.)

- **Size.** The size of the file is given in bytes.

- **Date and time.** The date and time the file was last modified is shown here.

- **File name.** The name of the file or directory is listed last.

6.16 Access Privileges

In the previous section, we saw how the ls –l ("list –long") command can be used to get information on a file, including the access privileges. The nine entries showing the access permissions deserve a closer look:

rwxrwx---

Basically, there are three things that can be done to an ordinary file:

r   **Read.** Examine (but not change) the contents of the file.

w   **Write.** Change the contents of a file.

x   **Execute.** If the file contains a program, run that program.

Likewise, there are three things that can be done to a directory:

r   **Read.** List the contents of the directory using the ls command.

w   *Write.* Change the contents of the directory by creating new files or removing existing files. (To edit an existing file requires write permission on that file.)

x   *Execute.* "Search" the directory using `ls -l`. Also, move to the directory from another directory, and copy files from the directory.

When deciding who can have access to a file, UNIX recognizes three categories of users:

- *Owner.* The owner of the file or directory.

- *Group.* Other users belonging to the user's group.

- *Public.* All other users on the system.

The first three permissions show what the owner may do; the next three show what the group may do; the last three show what the public may do. For example,

rwxrwx---   owner has read, write, and execute privileges

            group has read, write, and execute privileges

            public has no privileges

rw-rw----   owner has read and write privileges

            group has read and write privileges

            public has no privileges

r--r--r--   owner has read privileges only

            group has read privileges only

            public has read privileges only

6.17   Changing File Modes

The access privileges are sometimes called the *mode* of the file or directory. To change the mode, you use the `chmod` ("change mode") command. `chmod` uses the following notation:

u   user (owner) of the file

g   group

o   others (public)

a   all (owner, group, and public)

=   assign a permission

+   add a permission

-   remove a permission

A few examples will help you see how chmod is used. To give the owner execute permission without changing any other permissions, you would use

§ chmod u+x *filename* (RETURN)

Note that there are no spaces between u and +, or between + and x.

To remove read and write permissions from group members, you would use

§ chmod g-rw *filename* (RETURN)

The following command will give everyone read permissions while removing any other permissions:

§ chmod a=r *filename* (RETURN)

To give the user read and write permissions and everyone else read privileges, use

Do not put space(s) after the comma.   § chmod u=rw,go=r *filename* (RETURN)

6.18 Exercises

1. What are the rules for naming UNIX files and directories?

2. Which of the following would be valid names for ordinary UNIX files? Explain.

foo	guess?	book.chap1	BOOK.chap2
2good2Btrue	{2bad}	>right>	<left<
name	rank*	serial#	^up^
el_paso	w.lafayette	New York	/slash\
.hideNseek	.357	747	passwd

3. Which of the following would be valid directory names? Explain.

doo_wa	dir1	Dir2	Directory.3
*Hook	|Line|	"Sinker"	money.$
Game	Set	Match	sticks
[Groucho]	'Chico'	Harpo.#	Karl?
.hideNseek	.357	747	passwd

Exercises 4 through 11 refer to the hypothetical UNIX file system previously shown in Figure 6–4. (Hint: It may be helpful to sketch the directory structure as you go along.) These exercises should be done in order.

4. What are the absolute pathnames for root, bin, jill, and kangaroo?

5. Suppose that Marsupials is now your working directory. What are the relative pathnames of root, bin, jill, and kangaroo?

6. jack has two subdirectories, Continents and Oceans.

a. What are the absolute pathnames of Continents and Oceans?

b. From Oceans, what are the relative pathnames of root, etc, and bandi-coot?

7. Imagine that jack sets up additional subdirectories to hold geographical information. Continents contains Africa, Antarctica, Asia, Australia, Europe, NAmerica, and SAmerica. Each of these directories contains subdirectories for individual countries or regions. For example, NAmerica contains the subdirectories Canada, CentralAm, Mexico, and USA. Assuming every file and directory to be in its proper place, give the absolute pathnames of the following directories:

a. Norway;

b. India;

c. Egypt;

d. Argentina.

8. Suppose jack's working directory is USA. Show how he could accomplish the following tasks, *using a single command line and relative pathnames in each case*:

a. List the contents of the Marsupials directory belonging to jill.

b. List the contents of Australia.

c. Make a copy of jill's file kangaroo, and place it under the name kangaroo in his Australia directory.

9. Repeat the previous problem using absolute pathnames.

10. The directory Canada has twelve subdirectories, one for each of the ten provinces and two territories. Suppose jack's working directory is SAmerica. Show how he could accomplish the following tasks, *using a single command line and relative pathnames in each case*:

a. List the contents of BC, the directory for British Columbia, Canada.

b. Place a copy of the file for Vancouver, British Columbia, in the directory jill.

11. Repeat the previous problem using absolute pathnames.

12. Suppose you have a file named stuff in your working directory. Specify the command(s) you would use to do the following:

a. Give everyone permission to read stuff; do not change any other privileges.

b. Permit the owner and group members to read and write the file; remove all privileges from everyone else.

c. Remove writing privileges from everyone but the owner.

d. Give the owner and group members permission to execute stuff while giving the owner sole permission to read or write it.

13. Suppose you have a directory named MyStuff in your working directory. Specify the command(s) you would use to do the following:

a. Give everyone permission to list files in MyStuff; do not change any other privileges.

b. Permit the owner and group members to list, remove, or add files; remove all privileges from everyone else.

c. Remove writing privileges from everyone but the owner.

d. Give the owner and group members permission to execute MyStuff while giving the owner sole permission to read or write it.

Chapter

7

TUTORIAL: WORKING WITH FILES

In this chapter, you will learn how to create, view, copy, rename, and print files. All of your work will take place in your home directory—you'll see how to make subdirectories in the next chapter.

7.1 Printing a Calendar

Many of the examples in this chapter make use of the UNIX utility cal, which displays a calendar for any month or any year from AD 1 to AD 9999. To see how this works, try some examples:

1. Print a calendar for a given month. For example, to show the calendar for the twelfth month of the year 2007, type the command

§ cal 12 2007 ⟨RETURN⟩

The computer will respond with the calendar:

```
   December 2007
 S  M Tu  W Th  F  S
                   1
 2  3  4  5  6  7  8
 9 10 11 12 13 14 15
16 17 18 19 20 21 22
23 24 25 26 27 28 29
30 31
```

2. Print a calendar for an entire year. To do this, specify the year but not the month:

§ cal 2007 ⟨RETURN⟩

A calendar for the year 2007 should have appeared on your screen, although it probably scrolled by too fast for you to read it all. Don't worry; in a moment you will see how to save this calendar in a file that you can examine at your leisure.

7.2 Creating a File by Redirection

Many UNIX commands print their output on the standard output, usually the computer screen. However, the UNIX shell allows you to redirect the output into a file. Let's do this using the `cal` command.

The rules for naming UNIX files are given in Section 6.5.

1. Select a name for the file. Remember to use descriptive file names. An appropriate name for a file holding the calendar for the year 2007 would be 2007.

2. Enter the `cal` command, followed by the redirection operator (>) and the file name. To put the calendar for the year 2007 into the file 2007, type

Think of > as an arrow pointing where the output will go.

§ `cal 2007 > 2007` (RETURN)

This time, the calendar does not appear on the screen; instead, the standard output from `cal` has been redirected into the file 2007.

The UNIX shell does not tell you when it has successfully created a file by redirection.

3. List the file names in your current working directory. How do you know if the new file was created? You can check this by listing the files in your working directory using the `ls` command:

§ `ls` (RETURN)

The name of the new file should appear:

2007

Redirection created a file named 2007 in your home directory. Had there already been a file named 2007, its contents would have been replaced.

WARNING	REDIRECTION INTO AN EXISTING FILE WILL OVERWRITE WHATEVER IS ALREADY IN THE FILE.

7.3 Viewing a File with cat

Catenate means "join together," which is one of the functions of `cat`.

Suppose you want to see the **contents** of a file, not just its name. One way to do this is by the use of the `cat` ("catenate") command.

■ **Type `cat`, followed by the file name.** Thus, to look at the 2007 file, type

§ `cat 2007` (RETURN)

This displays the file, but it scrolls by so fast that the first few lines cannot be read. Fortunately, UNIX provides a more convenient means of viewing files.

7.4 Viewing with more

The `more` command allows you to display a file, one screen at a time.

1. Enter the `more` command and the file name. To view the file 2007, type the command line

§ `more 2007` (RETURN)

This will display as much of the file as will fit on the screen at one time. If the entire file does not fit, a message will appear in the lower corner of the screen, telling you that more remains to be seen:

```
--More--
```

2. To see more of the file, press the space bar. This will show you the next screenful.

3. To exit without viewing the entire file, type q or Q (for quit). It is not necessary to press (RETURN):

```
q
```

You will know that you are out of the more program when you see the UNIX shell prompt:

```
§
```

7.5   Viewing with pg

Some UNIX systems offer the pg ("page") command as an alternative to more.

1. Enter the pg command and the file name. To view the file 2007, type the command line

```
§ pg 2007 (RETURN)
```

This will display as much of the file as will fit on the screen at one time. If the entire file does not fit, a colon (:) appears at the bottom of the screen to indicate that more of the file remains to be seen.

```
:
```

2. To see more, press (RETURN). This will show you the next screenful of the file.

3. To exit without viewing the whole file, type q or Q (for quit). It is not necessary to press (RETURN):

```
q
```

You will know that you are out of the pg program when you see the UNIX shell prompt:

```
§
```

7.6   Chaining Files Together with cat

You previously used the cat command to view the contents of a file. When given a single file name, cat simply displays the contents of that file; when two or more file names are used together, cat displays all of the files, one after another. This can be used to join together the contents of multiple files.

Your next task is to use cat to make a calendar for the summer months of 2007. First, use the cal utility to make three files:

§ cal 6 2007 > jun.2007 (RETURN)
§ cal 7 2007 > jul.2007 (RETURN)
§ cal 8 2007 > aug.2007 (RETURN)

1. View the files with cat. Enter the cat command followed by the file names:

§ cat jun.2007 jul.2007 aug.2007 (RETURN)

The contents of the files will be displayed, one right after another:

```
      June 2007
 S  M Tu  W Th  F  S
                1  2
 3  4  5  6  7  8  9
10 11 12 13 14 15 16
17 18 19 20 21 22 23
24 25 26 27 28 29 30
      July 2007
 S  M Tu  W Th  F  S
 1  2  3  4  5  6  7
 8  9 10 11 12 13 14
15 16 17 18 19 20 21
22 23 24 25 26 27 28
29 30 31
     August 2007
 S  M Tu  W Th  F  S
          1  2  3  4
 5  6  7  8  9 10 11
12 13 14 15 16 17 18
19 20 21 22 23 24 25
26 27 28 29 30 31
```

2. Use cat again, but redirect the output into another file. For example, to create a file named summer.2007, enter the command

§ cat jun.2007 jul.2007 aug.2007 > summer.2007 (RETURN)

This creates a new file containing a three-month calendar. Note that the redirection operator is required here.

3. List the files.

§ ls (RETURN)

The new file should appear:

2007   aug.2007   jul.2007   jun.2007   summer.2007

7.7 Appending to a File

The UNIX shell allows you to add information to the end of an existing file, an operation called *appending*.

■ **Type the command, the append operator, and the name of the file.** To append the calendar for September 2007 to the file `summer.2007`, type the following line, making sure to use the append symbol (>>):

§ `cal 9 2007 >> summer.2007` (RETURN)

Had you used the regular redirection symbol (>), the calendar for September would have replaced the calendars for June, July, and August that were already in the file. Instead, the September calendar was added to the end of the `summer.2007` file.

7.8 Copying a File with cp

The `cp` ("copy") command is used to copy files. We will use it to make a copy of the file `summer.2007`.

1. **Think of a name for the copy.** The usual rules for naming UNIX files apply. An appropriate name for a file containing a calendar for the summer of 2007 might be `SUMM.2007`.

WARNING	BE CAREFUL WHEN NAMING A COPY. IF A FILE HAVING THE SAME PATHNAME ALREADY EXISTS, ITS CONTENTS WILL BE OVERWRITTEN.

2. **Enter the `cp` command, followed by the names of the original file and the copy.** To make a copy of `summer.2007` named `SUMM.2007`, type

This means "copy `summer.2007` into `SUMM.2007`."

§ `cp summer.2007 SUMM.2007` (RETURN)

In this case, there is no existing file with the name `SUMM.2007`, so one is created.

3. **Verify that the new file appears.** UNIX does not alert you that a file has been copied, so you will have to check this yourself using the `ls` command:

§ `ls` (RETURN)

The computer will list all of the files in the current directory, including the new file:

`2007   SUMM.2007   aug.2007   jul.2007   jun.2007   summer.2007`

There is just one small problem with this example: the convention in this book is to use lowercase letters for file names, and to capitalize directory names. (You don't have to do this, but it helps distinguish files from directories.) `SUMM.2007` is an ordinary file, not a directory, so in the next section you will give it a different name.

7.9   Renaming a File with mv

The `mv` ("move") command is used for renaming files. (It is also used for moving files to other directories, as you will see in the next chapter.)

1. Choose a new name for the file. As usual, you should choose names that are short and descriptive. An appropriate name for a file containing a calendar for the summer of 2007 might be `vacation.2007`.

WARNING	BE CAREFUL WHEN RENAMING A FILE. IF A FILE HAVING THE SAME PATHNAME ALREADY EXISTS, THE EXISTING FILE WILL BE OVERWRITTEN.

2. Enter the `mv` command, followed by the old name and the new name. To rename SUMM.2007 as `vacation.2007`, type the command line

§ `mv SUMM.2007 vacation.2007` (RETURN)

3. Verify that the new file name appears in the directory. Because UNIX does not tell you that the file has been renamed, you will have to check this yourself using the `ls` command:

§ `ls` (RETURN)

The computer will list all of the files in the current directory:

`2007 aug.2007 jul.2007 jun.2007 summer.2007 vacation.2007`

The difference between `cp` (copy) and `mv` (move) is that `cp` creates a new file, leaving the old file intact, while `mv` simply renames the old file.

7.10   Printing on the Default Printer

Frequently, you are likely to require hardcopy output from your files. How you produce this depends on the number and type of printers available to you, as well as the type of UNIX you are using.

■ **Enter the simple line printer command, followed by the file name.** If you are using Berkeley UNIX, enter the `lpr` ("line printer") command:

§ `lpr 2007` (RETURN)

On AT&T UNIX, enter the `lp` command:

§ `lp 2007` (RETURN)

7.11 Printing on Other Printers

If your computer system has more than one printer attached to it, the simple line printer command used in the previous section will send your files to the default printer. You can specify another printer with the -P or -d option. To do this, you first have to know the code for the printer you are to use; ask your instructor, consultant, or system administrator.

■ **Enter the line printer command and specify the printer and the file to be printed.** On Berkeley UNIX you would type the following command, making sure to insert the proper printer code in place of *code*:

§ lpr -P*code* 2007 (RETURN)

Note that there is a space before the -P and before the file name, but not between the -P and the printer code.

On AT&T UNIX, you would type the following command, inserting the printer code in place of *code*:

§ lp -d*code* 2007 (RETURN)

Here again, there is a space before -d and before the file name, but not between the -d and the printer code.

7.12 Removing Unneeded Files

When a file is no longer useful, you should remove it so that it won't take up valuable storage space. This is done with the rm ("remove") command, which takes the pathname of the file to be removed. Since you probably don't need two copies of the summer 2007 calendar, remove one of them.

1. **Use the ls command to check the file name.** Since on many systems you cannot retrieve a file once it has been removed, it is a good idea to be sure of the file name:

§ ls (RETURN)

2007 aug.2007 jul.2007 jun.2007 summer.2007 vacation.2007

2. **Type rm, followed by the file's pathname.** To remove vacation.2007, type the command line

§ rm vacation.2007 (RETURN)

3. **Verify that the file is gone.** UNIX does not tell you that the file has been removed, so you will have to check this yourself using the ls command:

§ ls (RETURN)

2007   aug.2007   jul.2007   jun.2007   summer.2007

7.13 Command Summary

Each command is typed in after the UNIX shell prompt, and each is terminated by a (RETURN). Note that *file*, *file1*, and *file2* may be simple file names or pathnames.

Making Calendars

cal *m year*	show a calendar for month *m* (1-12) of *year* (1–9999)
cal *year*	show a calendar for *year*
cal *year* > *file*	redirect calendar for *year* into *file*
cal *year* >> *file*	append calendar for *year* to *file*

Listing and Viewing Files

ls	list files in working directory
cat *file*	show contents of *file* all at once
more *file*	show contents of *file* one screen at a time; press spacebar to continue or q to quit
pg *file*	Like more. Press (RETURN) to see next screen, q to quit

Printing Files

lpr *file*	send *file* to default line printer (BSD UNIX)
lp *file*	send *file* to default line printer (AT&T UNIX)
lpr -P*code file*	send *file* to printer designated by *code* (BSD)
lp -d*code file*	send *file* to printer designated by *code* (AT&T)

Copying, Renaming, and Removing Files

cp *file1 file2*	copy *file1* into *file2*; retain both copies of the file
mv *file1 file2*	move (i.e., rename) *file1* to *file2*; retain only *file2*
rm *file*	remove (i.e., delete) *file*

7.14 Exercises

1. What are the rules for selecting UNIX file names?

2. Because of the need to make certain adjustments to the calendar, the month of September 1752 was a very unusual one. What was different about it?

3. The echo command takes a line that you type in and repeats it back on the screen. Thus if you type

echo This is fun! (RETURN)

The computer will respond with

This is fun!

Redirect this phrase into a file named fun.

4. Using the commands who, who am i, and date, append to the fun file (see Exercise 3 above) a list of the users currently logged onto the computer, your login, and the current date.

5. A hidden file has a name that begins with a period (.). Use the cal utility and the redirection operator (>) to create a file named .hidden, then use ls to list your files. Do you see the .hidden file? Now try the ls -a command. Does .hidden appear? What other hidden file entries do you see?

6. Many UNIX systems offer a utility named file, which classifies files according to their contents. The utility examines the file and tries to determine what kind of information it may contain. Some of the classifications used by file are

ascii text	c program text	commands
data	directory	empty
English text	executable	

Try out the file command on the files and directories in your system. Does file always classify files correctly?

# Chapter 8

TUTORIAL: WORKING WITH DIRECTORIES

A directory is a file that contains other files and directories. In this chapter, you will see how to create directories, move files between directories, rename files, and delete directories you no longer need.

8.1 Your Directory Structure Thus Far

If you have carefully followed the examples in the text and worked through all of the end-of-chapter exercises, your file system should resemble the structure shown in Figure 8–1. At this point, your home directory contains no subdirectories. You are now ready to create new subdirectories inside your home directory.

Figure 8-1
Your file system after completing the previous chapter.

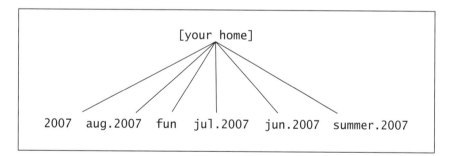

8.2 Creating a Subdirectory

It's time to make a directory to hold the calendars you made in the previous chapter. For this we use the mkdir ("make directory") command.

1. Select an appropriate name for the new directory. The rules for naming directories are the same as for files. (However, in this book we will capitalize the names of any new directories we create to distinguish them from ordinary files.) A descriptive name for a directory to hold calendars would be Cal.

Note that the directory name Cal differs from the cal command—remember, UNIX is case-sensitive.

2. Enter mkdir followed by the new directory name. Remember to capitalize the directory name:

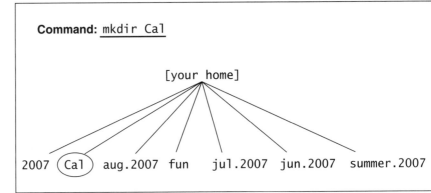

Figure 8-2
Your file system after creating the subdirectory Cal. At this point, Cal contains no files.

§ mkdir Cal (RETURN)

3. Use the ls command to see that the new directory exists:

§ ls (RETURN)

The new directory name should appear, along with the names of the files you made before:

2007   Cal   aug.2007   fun   jul.2007   jun.2007   summer.2007

(If you have been following the examples in the text, your file system should resemble Figure 8–2.)

8.3 Moving Files between Directories

Recall that you previously used mv to rename a file.

When a new subdirectory is first created, it contains no files. In this section, you will see how to move a file to a new subdirectory using the mv ("move") command, which you previously used to rename files.

1. Type the mv command, the file's name, and the destination directory's name. To put 2007 into the directory Cal, enter the command line

§ mv 2007 Cal (RETURN)

This puts 2007 inside Cal (see Figure 8–3).

2. List the files in your home directory. Check to see that 2007 has indeed been moved:

§ ls (RETURN)

The 2007 file will not appear because it is now inside the Cal subdirectory:

Cal aug.2007 fun jul.2007 jun.2007 summer.2007

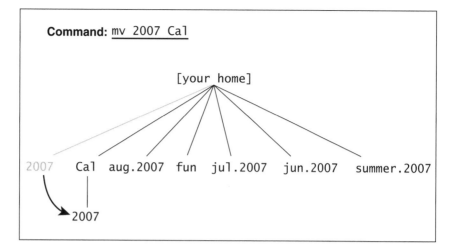

Command: <u>mv 2007 Cal</u>

[your home]

2007   Cal   aug.2007   fun   jul.2007   jun.2007   summer.2007

2007

Figure 8-3
Moving the file 2007
into Cal.

8.4   Creating Directories Using Pathnames

Your next task is to create a subdirectory inside Cal to hold monthly calendars. A good, descriptive name for this directory is Months. Since this is to go inside Cal, the pathname of the new directory relative to your home directory will be Cal/Months.

■ **Enter the mkdir command, followed by the pathname of the new directory.** Thus, to create a directory Months inside the directory Cal, type

Remember to capitalize
Months to emphasize that
it is a directory name.

§ mkdir Cal/Months (RETURN)

With the creation of Months, your directory structure should resemble the one shown in Figure 8–4.

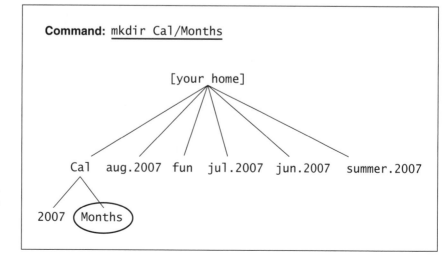

Command: <u>mkdir Cal/Months</u>

[your home]

Cal   aug.2007   fun   jul.2007   jun.2007   summer.2007

2007   (Months)

Figure 8-4
Directory structure after
creation of the subdirec-
tory Months.

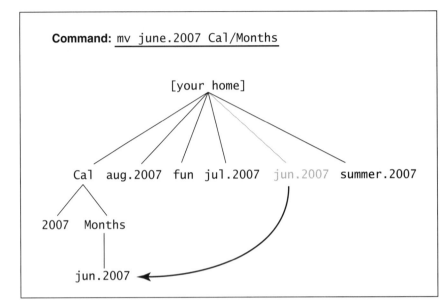

Figure 8-5
Directory structure after
moving jun.2007 into
the subdirectory
Months.

8.5 Using Pathnames to Move Files

In this section, you will move a file into the Months directory, using a pathname to specify the file's new location.

1. Enter the mv command, the file name, and the new pathname. Thus, to move the file jun.2007 into Months, type

§ mv jun.2007 Cal/Months (RETURN)

At this point, your directory structure should look something like Figure 8–5.

2. List the files in the current directory. The ls command should show that jun.2007 is no longer in the current directory:

§ ls (RETURN)
Cal aug.2007 fun jul.2007 summer.2007

8.6 Using Pathnames to Move and Rename Files

In this section, you will move a file and rename it with one command, using a pathname to specify both the file's new location and its new name.

■ **Enter the mv command, the file name, and the new pathname.** To move the file aug.2007 into Months, and rename it 08.2007, type

§ mv aug.2007 Cal/Months/08.2007 (RETURN)

The result of this operation is shown in Figure 8–6.

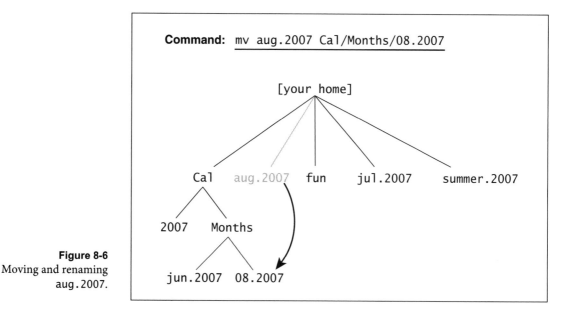

Figure 8-6
Moving and renaming
aug.2007.

8.7 Working in a Distant Directory

As you have seen, the simple `ls` command only lists files and directories in the current working directory. To list files in another directory, you must give `ls` that directory's pathname. As you will see in this section, you can work with the files in the directory `Months` without leaving your home directory.

1. Enter the list command, followed by the pathname of the directory you wish to examine. Thus, to see the contents of `Months`, type:

§ `ls Cal/Months` (RETURN)

You should see

`08.2007   jun.2007`

2. Enter the `cat` command, followed by the pathname of the file you want to view. You can view the contents of the file `08.2007` from your home directory using the `cat` command with the appropriate pathname:

§ `cat Cal/Months/08.2007` (RETURN)

The contents of `08.2007` will appear on the screen:

```
    August 2007
 S  M Tu  W Th  F  S
          1  2  3  4
 5  6  7  8  9 10 11
12 13 14 15 16 17 18
19 20 21 22 23 24 25
26 27 28 29 30 31
```

8.8 Changing Your Working Directory

You can change your current working directory using the cd ("change directory") command with the pathname of the target directory.

■ **Enter the cd command followed by the pathname of the target directory.** Thus, to move to the subdirectory Months, type

§ cd Cal/Months (RETURN)

This makes Months your working directory.

8.9 Returning to Your Home Directory

To return to your home directory, you **could** use cd with either the absolute or the relative pathname of your home directory. However, there is a much easier way.

■ **Enter the cd command without a pathname.** This will always get you back to your home directory, regardless of where you are in the file structure:

§ cd (RETURN)

8.10 Printing Your Working Directory

As you might imagine, it is easy to get lost among the hundreds of directories in a large UNIX system. The pwd ("print working directory") command always displays the absolute pathname of your current working directory.

■ **Type pwd.** This will print your location relative to the root:

§ pwd (RETURN)

8.11 Removing Directories

A directory that is no longer needed may be removed using the rmdir ("remove directory") command. You cannot remove a directory unless it is first emptied of files and other directories. This is a safety feature, intended to prevent you from accidentally throwing away files that you meant to keep.

1. **Enter the rmdir command, followed by the pathname of the directory.** To remove the subdirectory Cal, type

§ rmdir Cal (RETURN)

If the directory contains files, the shell will respond with a message such as

rmdir: Cal: Directory not empty

2. **If necessary, use rm to remove any files in the directory.** Then repeat step 1. Because you will need the Cal directory to complete the exercises, do not remove it yet.

8.12 Command Summary

Each of these commands is typed in after the UNIX prompt, and each is terminated by a (RETURN). *Dir* and *file* represent the pathnames of a directory and a file, respectively.

mkdir *Dir*	make a directory having the pathname *Dir*
mv *file Dir*	move *file* into the directory *Dir*
cd *Dir*	change to directory having the pathname *Dir*
cd	change to home directory
rmdir *Dir*	remove (i.e., delete) the directory *Dir*
pwd	print working directory's pathname

8.13 Exercises

1. What are the rules for naming UNIX directories?

2. What is the absolute pathname of your home directory?

3. Create a new directory Misc and move the file fun inside this new directory.

4. Without leaving your home directory, create a directory named Vacations inside Cal. Then move summer.2007 into this new directory.

5. Prepare a sketch of your directory structure after completing Exercises 2 through 4 above.

# Chapter 9

TUTORIAL: USING FILE MANAGER

Skip this chapter if your system does not have CDE.

In previous chapters, you have seen how to use traditional UNIX utilities for working with files and directories. File Manager provides alternative file-processing tools that take full advantage of the CDE graphical user interface.

9.1 Your File Structure Thus Far

If you have followed the examples and worked through all of the end-of-chapter exercises in the previous two chapters, your file system should resemble the one shown in Figure 9–1.

In this chapter, you will use File Manager to do the following:

In CDE, directories are called folders.

■ Create a new folder (directory) named `Years`.

■ Move the file `2007` into the folder `Years`.

■ Move the file `jul.2007` to the `Months` folder.

■ Print the file `jun.2007` on your default printer.

■ Change the name of the file `08.2007` to `aug.2007`.

■ Delete the file `fun` and the folder `Misc`.

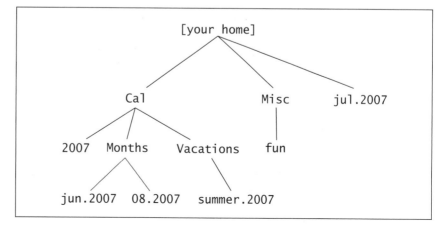

Figure 9-1
Your file system after completing the previous two chapters.

9.2   Starting File Manager

Start the File Manager:

■ **Click on the File Manager control.** This is usually located on the Front Panel:

If the control is not visible on the Front Panel, look for it on the File subpanel.

The File Manager window (Figure 9–2) will open your home folder.

Note the various parts of the window:

■ **Window Menu button, Minimize button, and Maximize/Restore button.**
These perform the usual functions on the window.

■ **Menu bar.** Note in particular the menu labeled Selected—it lists actions that can be performed on a selected file or folder.

■ **Iconic path.** The pathname of the current folder (in this example, the home folder for jsmith) is depicted graphically as a row of folder icons:

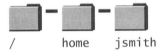

■ **Status line.** Here, the current folder's path is shown using traditional UNIX notation:

/home/jsmith

■ **View area.** Also called the Object Viewing area, this is where the contents of the folder are shown. (More about this later.)

■ **Message line.** This gives the total number of objects (files and folders) and the number of hidden objects contained in the current folder.

In general, three types of objects may appear in the File Manager's View area:

■ **Action icons.** An action icon, also known as an *application icon*, represents a software tool, application, or command. Double-clicking or dropping a file on an action icon will launch the tool, application, or command.

■ **File icons.** These icons represent ordinary files. A distinctive icon is used to indicate the type or format of the data in the file. Thus, a different icon will be used for a text file than for a spreadsheet file.

■ **Folder icons.** A folder is simply a directory—that is, a file that can contain other files, directories, and action icons.

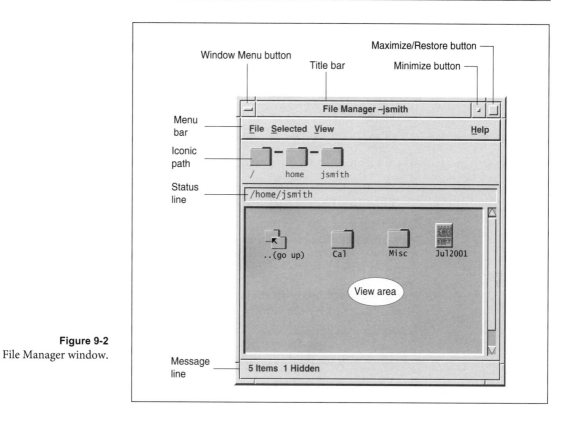

Figure 9-2
File Manager window.

9.3 Changing Your Working Folder

There are several ways to move through the folder tree:

■ **To move to a subfolder, double-click on its icon.** For example, double-clicking on Cal will put you into that folder:

Cal

■ **To move to the parent folder, double-click on the .. (go up) icon.** The icon looks like this:

.. (go up)

- **Go to any folder in the current path by double-clicking on its icon.** Remember, the current path is shown iconically below the Menu bar:

/   home   jsmith

- **To go home, open the File menu and choose the Go Home option.**

Take a moment to try out each of these options.

9.4 Displaying a Pop-up Menu

A pop-up menu is associated with each object (file icon, folder icon, or action icon) in File Manager. This menu provides information on the object's properties, and it allows you to perform various operations on the object. Let's get the pop-up menu for the file jun.2007:

1. If necessary, move to the folder containing the object. We want the file jun.2007, which is contained in the Months folder inside the Cal folder.

2. Point to the object's icon. Move the pointer to the jun.2007 icon.

3. Click with the right (#3) mouse button.

The pop-up menu will appear:

jun.2007
Properties...
Put in Workspace
Put in Trash
Help
Open
Print

Note that the file name is listed at the top of the menu. Below the file name appears a list of options:

- **Properties.** This option allows you to find out useful information about a file or folder: who owns it; how large it is; when it was created; when it was last modified; and who has permission to read, write, and execute it.

You can also drag the file to the Workspace.

- **Put in Workspace.** If you select this option, a copy of the object's icon will be placed on the Workspace backdrop. In effect, this gives the object two icons, one in the original folder, the other on the backdrop.

- **Put in Trash.** As you might expect, this option moves the file to the Trash Can. (More about this later.)

■ **Help.** This tells you the data type of the file.

The next section of the menu is a list of the actions you can perform on the object. The first item in the list is always the *default action*, which is what occurs when you double-click on the object's icon:

■ **Open.** If the object is a folder, this action causes the contents of the folder to appear in the File Manager window. If the object is a file, this typically starts up the application program that created the file, then loads the contents of the file.

■ **Print.** This action prints a hard copy of the file on the default printer.

Always keep in mind that any option on the pop-up menu is also available on the Selected menu.

9.5 Printing Using the Printer Control

There are several ways to print a file on the default printer. The simplest is to use the Printer control on the Front Panel:

1. Drag and drop the file on the Printer control. The control should be visible on the Front Panel.

The Print dialog box will appear.

2. Specify the print options. You can change printers (the default printer is listed), request more than one copy, have page numbers printed, and so on.

3. Select Print.

The file should print on the default printer.

9.6 Printing from the Pop-Up Menu

You can also print from the file's pop-up menu:

1. Open the pop-up menu. Point to the file icon and press the right (#3) mouse button.

2. Select Print.

The Print dialog box will appear, as before.

3. Specify the print options and select Print.

The file should print on the default printer.

9.7 Printing from the Selected Menu

You can print a file from File Manager's Selected menu:

1. Select the file to be printed. Click on the file icon.

2. Open the Selected menu. This menu is located on the File Manager menu bar.

3. Select Print.

The Print dialog box will appear, as before.

4. Specify the print options and select Print.

The file should print on the default printer.

9.8 Creating a New Folder

Let's create a new folder in the `Cal` folder:

1. Move to the parent folder. The parent folder in this case is `Cal`.

2. Pull down the File menu and choose New Folder.

A dialog box will appear.

The rules for naming files and directories are summarized in Section 6.5.

3. Type a new name into the New Folder field. Since the new folder will hold yearly calendars, an appropriate name would be `Years`.

4. Click OK or press (RETURN).

The new folder will appear in the View area.

9.9 Moving or Copying to a Nearby Folder

You can also use the Move to... option on the Selected menu.

You can move a file from one folder to another simply by dragging and dropping. For this to work, however, you must be able to see both icons—the icon for the file and the icon for the destination folder—in the same File Manager window. For example, let's move the file 2007 into the folder `Years`, both of which are contained in `Cal`:

1. Obtain a File Manager view showing the file and the folder. In this case, you need to be in the `Cal` folder.

2. Drag and drop the file onto the destination folder. Drag the file 2007 and drop it on the folder `Years`.

You can also copy using the Copy To... option on Selected menu.

If you hold down the (CONTROL) key while dragging and dropping, the file will be *copied* to the new location instead of merely being moved.

9.10 Moving or Copying to a Distant Folder

The method used in the previous section for moving a file works only if the file and the destination folder are visible in the File Manager at the same time. This is true if both have the same parent folder. Otherwise, you must open a second File Manager window:

1. Go to the folder containing the file. We are going to move the file `jul.2007` (which should be located in your home folder) to the folder `Months`.

2. Open a second File Manager window. We want to put the file in the folder Months, which cannot be seen from your home folder; for this, another File Manager window is needed. Double-click on the File Manager control.

A new File Manager window will appear, showing your home folder.

3. Make the destination folder visible in the second File Manager window. By moving down to the Cal folder, you should be able to see the Months folder.

4. Drag and drop the file onto the destination folder.

As before, holding down the (CONTROL) key while dragging and dropping causes the file to be *copied* to the new location.

As we shall see in the next section, a folder (including any files or folders it contains) can be moved or copied the same way as a file.

9.11   Deleting an Object

Our next task is to delete the Misc folder and its contents. You can delete an object by putting it in the Trash Can. The easiest way to do this is by dragging and dropping:

You can also use the Put in Trash option on the pop-up or Selected menu.

■ **Drag and drop the object on the Trash Can.** To remove the folder Misc, drag and drop it on the Trash Can control.

Note that the Trash Can changes shape to indicate that it is no longer empty.

An object placed in the Trash Can is not deleted immediately, but remains there until it is either retrieved or shredded. You can retrieve an object by dragging it out of the Trash Can; on some systems, shredding occurs automatically when you log out. If you do not want to wait until then, you can shred the trash yourself:

1. Double-click on the Trash Can icon. This opens a view of the trash.

2. Select the object(s) to be shredded. To select several objects, drag the pointer across them, or hold down the (CONTROL) key while you click on the icons individually. To select all of the objects in the Trash Can, pull down the File menu and choose Select All.

To shred all objects in the Trash can, you can open the Trash subpanel and double-click on the Empty Trash control.

3. Select Shred. This option is available on the File menu and the object's pop-up menu; either may be used.

A dialog box will appear, asking you to confirm whether you really want to shred the trash. Keep in mind that on many systems, a shredded object cannot be recovered.

4. Click OK. The selected objects will be shredded and removed from the Trash Can.

5. Close the Trash Can window.

9.12 Renaming an Object

You can also use the Rename option on the Selected menu.

If you have been carefully following the examples and exercises thus far, you should have a folder named Months that contains three files: 08.2007, jul.2007, and jun.2007. A better name for the first file would be aug.2007. Let's rename the file:

1. If necessary, select a File Manager window to be active.

2. Go to the folder containing the file. Move to the folder Months, which is inside the folder Cal.

3. Click on the file name. Do not click on the icon itself, but on the name below the icon. In this case, click on 08.2007.

4. Type the new file name. Type the new name aug.2007. You can backspace to delete erroneous characters.

5. Press the (RETURN) **key.** If you decide not to change the name, either press (ESC) or click outside the name.

Keep in mind that you cannot have two objects sharing the same name in the same folder.

9.13 Selecting a Tree View

File Manager gives you the choice of several ways to view your files and folders. We have been using the Single Folder view, which is the default view.

You can also choose a *tree view*, which resembles in concept the kind of upside-down tree structures we have been drawing (such as in Figure 9–1). The main difference is that File Manager draws "squared-off" trees in which the branches grow down and to the right (Figure 9–3).

There are three different tree view options:

■ **Folders only.** This is the default tree view. It shows just the folders in the tree. To see any files in a particular folder, you must double-click on that folder.

■ **Folders, then Files.** This option shows the folders in the tree. To see any sub-folders, you simply click on the [+] button next to the folder. Click again to show files inside the subfolders.

■ **Folders and Files.** This option shows all folders and files, as in Figure 9–3.

Try a tree view:

1. Move to the folder that will appear at the top of the tree. For now, go to your home folder.

2. Pull down the View menu and choose Set View Options.

A dialog box will appear.

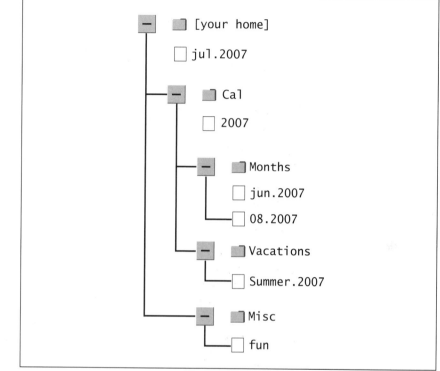

Figure 9-3
File Manager's tree view. This is an alternative way to represent the file structure shown in Figure 9-1. A [–] button shows that a folder is open to view; closed folders would have a [+] button.

3. **Select the By Tree option.**

4. **Select one of the tree view options.**

5. **Click OK.**

9.14 Exercises

1. Prepare a sketch of your file structure after completing this chapter.

2. File Manager offers several ways to represent files and folders:

Names shows the names of all objects, but not their icons. Folders are marked by a slash (/) appended to their names; executable files have an asterisk (*) appended.

Large icons shows names and large icons. (This is the default representation.)

Small icons shows names and small icons.

Name, date, size ... shows additional information about the file or folder.

To try out these representations, pull down the View menu and select Set View Options. Then select the appropriate button in the dialog box.

3. By default, File Manager lists files and folders alphabetically by name. However, you can choose a different sorting order:

File type sorts by the object type.

Date sorts by the date the files were last modified, either in ascending order (oldest files first) or descending order (newest first).

Size sorts according to size, either in ascending order (smallest files first) or descending order (largest first).

To try out these options, pull down the View menu and select Set View Options. Then select the appropriate buttons in the dialog box.

4. When you accumulate a large number of files and folders, you may occasionally have trouble finding the particular one you want. File Manager can search for a file or folder according to its name or contents. To search by name, pull down the File menu and select Find. A dialog box will appear. Enter the file or folder name, specify a search folder, and press Start. Try it. (For searching by a file's contents, see the next exercise.)

5. Refer to the CDE Help volumes to learn how to search for a file by its contents. Then try this procedure on one of your files.

6. Using the Properties option on the Selected or pop-up menu, you can control who is permitted to read, write, or execute a file. Try it on one of your files.

PART III
UNIX SHELLS

# Chapter 10

UNIX SHELLS

Tutorials related to this
chapter are found in
Chapters 11 and 12.

The *shell* is the UNIX command processor. When you type a command and press
(RETURN), it is the shell that interprets the command and takes the appropriate
action. In this chapter, you will see how the shell works.

10.1 Common Shells

Although dozens of shells have been written for the UNIX operating system, only
a handful are in widespread use. The UNIX shells discussed in this chapter can be
grouped into two "families." The first is the Bourne Shell family:

■ **Bourne Shell** (sh). Written by Steven Bourne at AT&T's Bell Labs, sh was the
first major UNIX shell. It has been a part of nearly every UNIX system since Version 7 was released in 1979.

■ **Korn Shell** (ksh). The Korn Shell was created by David Korn at AT&T as an
improved Bourne Shell. The first version of ksh was released in 1986, with major
upgrades in 1988 and 1993.

■ **Bourne Again Shell** (bash). Originally written by Brian Fox for the GNU
project of the Free Software Foundation, bash was released publicly in 1988.
Further development of bash has been carried on by Chet Ramey, who released
Version 2.0 in 1996.

The second family of shells is the C Shell family:

■ **C Shell** (csh). The C Shell was written by Bill Joy (who also wrote the vi editor) at the University of California at Berkeley. This shell was included with BSD
UNIX in 1979, and has been found on most subsequent UNIX systems.

■ **TC Shell** (tcsh). An improved version of the C Shell, the TC Shell was developed in the late 1970s and early 1980s by a number of programmers (most notably Ken Greer at Carnegie-Mellon University and Paul Placeway at Ohio State).

10.2 Your Login Shell

When your UNIX account was created, the system administrator selected a shell for you. This is called your *login shell*, because it is the shell you use each time you log in.

Once you have worked with the various shells available on your system, you may decide to change your login shell. On some systems, you can do this yourself using the chsh ("change shell") command; on others, the system administrator must make the change for you.

10.3 How the Shell Processes Commands

The entire process can be summarized this way:

1. The shell displays a prompt symbol on the screen. The prompt tells you the shell is ready to receive your commands.

2. You type in a command. As you type, the shell stores the characters and also echoes them back to the terminal screen.

3. You type (RETURN). This is the signal for the shell to interpret the command and start working on it.

4. The shell interprets your command. In most cases, the shell looks for the appropriate software to run your command. If the shell can't find the right software, it gives you an error message; otherwise, the shell asks the kernel to run it.

5. The kernel runs the requested software. While the command is running, the shell "goes to sleep." When the kernel finishes, it "wakes up" the shell.

6. The shell displays a prompt symbol. This indicates that the shell is once again ready to receive your commands.

We will say more about the search path in Part VI.

How does the shell know where to find software to run (Step 4)? The answer is that the shell looks through a predetermined list of directories called the *search path*.

This is a good place to point out the difference between a program and a process in UNIX jargon. A *program* is a set of coded instructions contained in a file. An example of a program is the ls command: it is just a sequence of computer instructions contained in the file /bin/ls. Similarly, your login shell is also just another program residing in the directory /bin.

A process is a running program.

A *process* is what you get whenever the computer runs a program. Thus, when you issue the ls command, the computer creates an ls process by running the program in the file /bin/ls. Likewise, when you log in, the computer looks in the file containing the shell program and creates a shell process for you.

The important thing to remember is that there is only one copy of the ls program, but there may be many active ls processes. In the same way, there is only one copy of each shell program, but there may be many active shell processes.

10.4 Options and Arguments

The typical UNIX command can take one or more options which modify what the command does. Table 10-1 shows some options for the `ls` ("list") command.

Most commands allow you to specify multiple options. Thus, to prepare a reversed long listing of all files in the directory *Dir*, flagging directories and executable files, you could type

Note that each option is preceded by a hyphen.

§ `ls -a -l -r -F` *Dir* (RETURN)

Or you could combine the options:

§ `ls -alrF` *Dir* (RETURN)

Incidentally, anything that follows the command name—including the options and file names—is generally referred to as an *argument*.

Table 10-1
Some options for the `ls` ("list") command.

Command	Effect
`ls`	List files in the current directory (except hidden files)
`ls -a`	List all files in the current directory, including hidden files
`ls -F`	Flag the files: show a slash (/) after each directory and an asterisk (*) after each executable file
`ls -l`	Print "long" list of files (except hidden files)
`ls -r`	List files in reverse order
`ls -s`	List files by size
`ls -t`	List files by time of last modification
`ls -u`	List files by time of last access

10.5 Standard Input, Output, and Error

Whenever you run a UNIX command or other program, the operating system opens up three standard channels for input and output:

■ **Standard input.** The standard input (or `stdin`) is the file where the program normally looks for input.

■ **Standard output.** The standard output (`stdout`) is the file where the program sends output.

■ **Standard error.** The standard error (`stderr`) is the file where the program sends error messages.

Remember: to UNIX, everything is a file.

Although we have defined `stdin`, `stdout`, and `stderr` as files, keep in mind that a UNIX file is nearly *anything* that can send or receive data. Most of the time we use "standard input" to mean the keyboard, and both "standard output" and "standard error" to mean the terminal screen.

Much of the power of UNIX derives from the shell's ability to reroute the standard input/output channels. A UNIX program is typically designed so that its standard input can be the keyboard, an ordinary file, or another program. Likewise, its standard output and standard error can be the terminal screen, an ordinary file, or another program.

10.6 Redirection

As we have said, the "standard output" is usually the terminal screen. However, the shell allows you to redirect the standard output so that the output goes into an ordinary file instead. For example, you have already seen how to use the output redirection operator (>) to create a file containing a calendar:

§ cal 2007 > calendar.file (RETURN)

You can add output to a file using the append operator (>>):

§ cal 2008 >> calendar.file (RETURN)

It is also possible to redirect the standard input so that a process takes its input from an ordinary file rather than the keyboard. For example, the mail command allows you to send and read electronic mail. To send the contents of the file my.message to the user jones, you could enter the command line

§ mail jones < my.message (RETURN)

You can combine input and output redirection in the same command line. For example, the following command line invokes the wc utility to count the lines, words, and characters in the file input, then redirects the results into the file output:

§ wc < input > output (RETURN)

10.7 Grouping Commands

Normally you type one command at a time, following each command by a (RETURN), which is the signal for the shell to begin its work. However, it is possible to put multiple commands on the same line, if you separate the commands with semicolons. Thus the command line

§ who; ls; cal (RETURN)

has the same effect as the three separate command lines

§ who (RETURN)
§ ls (RETURN)
§ cal (RETURN)

Grouping commands can be especially useful when you want to redirect the output into a file. You could make a calendar for the summer of 2007 in three steps:

```
§ cal 6 2007 > summer.2007 (RETURN)
§ cal 7 2007 >> summer.2007 (RETURN)
§ cal 8 2007 >> summer.2007 (RETURN)
```

You could accomplish the same thing with just one line:

```
§ (cal 6 2007; cal 7 2007; cal 8 2007) > summer.2007 (RETURN)
```

Note the parentheses; these are necessary to make sure the calendars for June, July, and August are all redirected into the same file. Suppose you were to omit the parentheses, like this:

```
§ cal 6 2007; cal 7 2007; cal 8 2007 > summer.2007 (RETURN)
```

In this case, the calendars for June and July would appear on the screen, and only the August calendar would be redirected into the file.

10.8   Pipes

Suppose you wanted to display the calendars for the years 2007, 2008, and 2009, one right after the other. You could type the command line

```
§ cal 2007; cal 2008; cal 2009 (RETURN)
```

This will print the calendars on the standard output, but they will scroll by so fast that you cannot read them. One way around this problem is to redirect the output into a file:

```
§ (cal 2007; cal 2008; cal 2009) > temp (RETURN)
```

Now you can view the contents of temp using the more or pg utility:

```
§ more temp (RETURN)
```

or

```
§ pg temp (RETURN)
```

This will work, but it requires that you create a temporary file just to look at the output from the commands. You can avoid creating a file by using what is called a *pipe*, which connects the output from one utility to the input of another. A vertical bar (|) is the pipe symbol. You would pipe the output from command1 to command2 like this:

```
command1 | command2
```

Thus, to view the calendars for 2007, 2008, and 2009, we can pipe the output of the cal utility to either more or pg:

§ (cal 2007; cal 2008; cal 2009) | more (RETURN)

or

§ (cal 2007; cal 2008; cal 2009) | pg (RETURN)

Note how this differs from redirection with > or >>. Redirection places the output from a utility into an ordinary file; the piping operation directs the output to another utility.

10.9 Tees

A *tee* allows you to do two things at once: (1) save the output from a command in a file, and (2) pipe the output to another command. We could take the output from *command1* and send it to the file *outfile* and to *command2* like this:

command1 | tee *outfile* | *command2*

Thus the command line

§ (cal 2008; cal 2009) | tee calfile | more (RETURN)

places copies of the calendars for 2008 and 2009 into the file calfile as they are also displayed on the terminal screen by more.

10.10 Filters

A *filter* takes a stream of data from its standard input, transforms the data in some way, and sends the results to the standard output. Table 10-2 shows some of the filters commonly found on UNIX systems.

Filters are often used with pipes and tees. Consider the sort utility, which, as you might expect, sorts its input. Suppose you wanted to list, alphabetically by their login names, the users currently logged onto your machine. You could do this by piping the output from who into sort:

§ who | sort (RETURN)

You can also give sort the name of a file to sort:

sort is discussed in
Chapter 11.

§ sort poems (RETURN)

This would sort the lines of the file poems alphabetically. By default, the sort utility puts blanks first, then uppercase letters, then lowercase letters. This order can be reversed using the -r option:

§ sort -r poems (RETURN)

The sort utility takes many other options, some of which are discussed in Chapter 11.

Table 10-2
Some UNIX filters.

Filter	Function
cat	Catenate and display text
comm	Compare sorted files, selecting or rejecting lines common to both
crypt	Encode or decode text
cut	Cut out selected fields from input lines
diff	Display line-by-line differences between two files
egrep	Search text for a pattern using full regular expressions
fgrep	Search text for a character string
fmt	Format text
grep	Search a file for a pattern
head	Display the beginning (head) of a file
less	Show text, one screenful at a time
more	Show text, one screenful at a time
nl	Number lines
paste	Merge lines of text
pg	Show text, one screenful at a time
pr	Format and print text
sort	Sort and/or merge text
spell	Check for spelling errors
tail	Display last part of a file
tr	Translate characters
uniq	Display lines in a file that are unique
wc	Count number of lines, words, and characters in text

10.11 Wildcards

Wildcards are also called metacharacters.

Typing and retyping file names can be a nuisance, especially if the names are long or there are very many of them. You can abbreviate file names using *wildcards*, which are characters that can stand for other characters (just as a joker in a pack of cards can stand for other cards in the pack).

The wildcard symbols are the asterisk (*), the question mark (?), and the square brackets [ ]. To see how these symbols are used, suppose that you had a directory named Fun containing the following files:

backgammon	backpacking	baseball	basketball
biking	blackjack	boxing	bridge
camping	canoeing	checkers	chess
crossword	dancing	eating	fencing
fishing	football	golf	hearts
hiking	karate	poker	rugby
sailing	skiing	softball	swimming
team1	team2	team3	team4
teamA	teamB	teamC	teamD
teamM	teamW	teamX	teamY
teamZ	track	wrestling	

The asterisk matches one or more characters.

The asterisk (*) is by far the most commonly used wildcard. It matches any character or string of characters, including blanks. As you can see, the directory Fun contains a large number of files. Using wildcards you can avoid having to list all of them when you are interested in just a few. For example, the command

§ ls f* (RETURN)

will list only those files beginning in *f*:

fencing fishing football

The command

§ ls *ball (RETURN)

will cause the shell to list the files that end in *ball*:

baseball basketball football softball

You are not limited to using a single asterisk. For instance, the command

§ ls *ack* (RETURN)

will list file names that contain the sequence of letters *ack:*

backgammon backpacking blackjack track

WARNING	THE ASTERISK WILDCARD MUST BE USED WITH CARE. THE rm * COMMAND, FOR EXAMPLE, CAN ERASE ALL OF THE FILES IN THE CURRENT DIRECTORY.

The question mark matches a single character.

The question mark (?) wildcard matches just one character at a time. For example,

§ ls ?iking (RETURN)
biking hiking

The brackets specify the character(s) to match.

The square brackets [ ] instruct the shell to match any characters that appear inside the brackets. For example

```
§ ls team[ABXYZ] (RETURN)
teamA teamB teamX teamY teamZ
```

You can also indicate a range of characters, rather than list each character:

```
§ ls team[1-4] (RETURN)
team1 team2 team3 team4
```

You can combine the wildcards *, ?, and [ ]. Suppose you wanted to list all of the files in the directory Fun that begin with the letters *a*, *b*, or *c*. This command will do the trick:

```
§ ls [abc]* (RETURN)
```

The bracketed letters tell the shell to look for any file names that have *a*, *b*, or *c* at the beginning. The asterisk matches any other sequence of letters. The result is the list

```
backgammon backpacking baseball basketball biking blackjack
boxing bridge camping canoeing checkers chess crossword
```

Likewise, to list all of the files having names that end with any letter from *m* through *z*, you could use the command

```
§ ls *[m-z] (RETURN)
```

The asterisk matches any sequence of characters; the brackets match only letters from *m* through *z* that appear at the end of the file name.

```
backgammon checkers chess hearts
```

10.12 Quoting Special Characters

You will recall that UNIX file names should not contain any of the following special characters:

```
& * \ | [ ] { } $ < > ( ) # ? ' " / ; ^ ! ~ %
```

By now it should be clear why: each of these characters has a special meaning to the shell. But sometimes this can be a problem. You may want to use a special character in its usual, everyday meaning. Consider, for example, the command line

```
§ echo What time is it? (RETURN)
```

The shell will interpret the question mark as a wildcard, and it will try to find a file name to match it. Unless you happen to have a file with a three-character name beginning with *it*, the shell will not be able to find a match, and it will complain:

```
§ echo: No match.
```

If you want the shell to treat a question mark as a question mark, not as a special character, you must quote it. One way to do this is to write a backslash (\) immediately before the question mark:

Without the backslash, ? is treated as a wildcard.

§ echo What time is it\? (RETURN)

This produces the output

What time is it?

Note that the backslash does not appear in the output; its only purpose is to cancel the special meaning of the question mark.

The backslash only works on a single character. Thus, to produce the output

**** STARS ****

you would have to place a backslash in front of each of the special characters:

§ echo **** STARS **** (RETURN)

Quoting each special character individually can be tedious. Alternatively, you can quote the entire string of characters all at once using single quotes:

Without the single quotes, the asterisks would be treated as wildcards.

§ echo '**** STARS ****' (RETURN)

The single quotes ('...') used here should not be confused with the backquotes (`...`). Backquotes, which are also called *grave* accent marks, are used to enclose commands that you want the shell to run. Thus, the command line

The backquotes run the date command.

§ echo It is now `date`. (RETURN)

will produce output that looks something like this

It is now Mon Aug 13 16:04:41 EST 2007.

where the shell has run the date utility and included the result in the output from echo. In contrast, this is what would happen if you left off the backquotes:

§ echo It is now date. (RETURN)
It is now date.

Double quotes are less powerful than single quotes.

Double quotes ("...") are like single quotes but less powerful. Putting double quotes around a string of characters cancels the special meaning of any of the characters except the dollar sign ($), backquotes (`...`), or backslash (\).

The different ways of quoting special characters are summarized in Table 10-3.

Table 10-3
Quoting special characters. Here, string represents any string of characters.

Quote	Effect
\	Cancel the special meaning of the next character
'string'	Cancel the special meaning of any characters in string
"string"	Cancel the special meaning of any characters except $, ``, and \
`string`	Run any commands in string; output replaces `string`

10.13 Background Processing

As we said before, UNIX is a multitasking operating system, which means that it can run more than one program for you at the same time. You can start a command and put it in the "background," to continue running while you work on another task in the foreground.

Processes that can run unattended are often put in the background.

Running a background process is simple: Type an ampersand (&) at the end of the command line before pressing (RETURN). Consider a hypothetical long-running program called longrun. You could run this program in background with the command

§ longrun & (RETURN)

If you were running the Bourne Shell, you would then see something like this:

3216 is the process identification number (PID).

```
3216
§
```

Running the C Shell, TC Shell, Korn Shell, or Bash, you would see something like this:

[1] is the job number; 3216 is the PID.

```
[1]      3216
§
```

Whichever shell you are using, it assigns a *process identification number* or PID to every process running in the background. The C Shell, TC Shell, Korn Shell, and Bash also assign a *job number,* which is the number in brackets. A prompt then lets you know that the shell is ready to process another command line, even if longrun is not yet finished:

§

The PID is important if you want to terminate a background job before it finishes. This is done with the kill command. To kill background process number 3216, for example, you would use the command

§ kill 3216 (RETURN)

Incidentally, some hard-to-kill processes require stronger medicine. Using kill with the -9 option will usually deal with them:

§ kill -9 3216 (RETURN)

Table 10-4
Job control commands. Here, *n* represents a job number.

Command	Effect
bg %*n*	Send process *n* to the background
fg %*n*	Bring process *n* to the foreground
jobs	List jobs
kill %*n*	Kill (terminate) process *n*
stop %*n*	Stop (suspend) process *n*

10.14 More Shell Features

The C Shell, TC Shell, Korn Shell, and Bash offer the same functionality as the original Bourne Shell. In addition, these shells include some features not present in the Bourne Shell:

■ **Job control.** All of the common shells allow you to run processes in the background with the ampersand (&) and eliminate them with the `kill` command. The C Shell, TC Shell, Korn Shell, and Bash also have *job control,* which makes it easier to manage background processes. Job control commands (Table 10-4) allow you to stop processes temporarily, move foreground processes to the background and back again, and kill processes.

■ **Command history.** The C Shell, TC Shell, Korn Shell, and Bash `history` mechanism maintains a list of the most recent commands you have entered, and gives you a convenient way to repeat a command from the list.

■ **Filename completion.** Using the *filename completion* feature (found in the C Shell, TC Shell, and Bash), you can type a command and part of a filename, then have the shell complete the filename for you.

These additional shell features are discussed in greater detail in Chapter 12.

10.15 Exercises

1. Be sure you can define each of the following terms:

shell	program	process
option	argument	standard input
standard output	grave accent	redirection
pipe	tee	filter
metacharacter	wildcard	quote
background process	foreground process	process id number
PID	job number	job control

2. What would each of the following commands do?

```
echo *
echo /*
echo \*
echo "*"
echo
echo */*
rm *        [Careful—do not try this!]
```

For Exercises 3–6, suppose your working directory contained the following files:

backgammon	backpacking	baseball	basketball
biking	blackjack	boxing	bridge
camping	canoeing	checkers	chess
crossword	dancing	eating	fencing
fishing	football	golf	hearts
hiking	karate	poker	rugby
sailing	skiing	softball	swimming
team1	team2	team3	team4
teamA	teamB	teamC	teamD
teamM	teamW	teamX	teamY
teamZ	track	wrestling	

3. How would you use cat to show the contents of the files ending in *ing*?

4. How would you list any files containing *x* or *X* (in this case, boxing and teamX)?

5. How would you show the contents of files with names containing *o*?

6. How would you show the contents of the files backgammon, backpacking, and blackjack using just one command?

TUTORIAL:
WORKING WITH THE SHELL

In this chapter, you will gain experience using the shell as a command interpreter. You will practice grouping commands; working with wildcards, filters, pipes, and tees; and running commands in the background.

11.1 Grouping Commands

First try grouping several commands on the same command line, using semicolons as command separators. Then redirect the output into a file:

1. Enter the commands on one line, separated by semicolons. You can print your working directory, the calendar for September 2007, and the current date and time with this command line:

§ pwd; cal 9 2007; date (RETURN)

2. Run the same commands again, but redirect the output into a file. Be sure to put parentheses around the commands:

Without the parentheses, only the output from date would go into the file.

§ (pwd; cal 9 2007; date) > out1.tmp (RETURN)
§

Nothing appears on the screen except the prompt because the output was redirected into out1.tmp instead of going to the standard output.

3. Use the cat command to check on the contents of the file.

§ cat out1.tmp (RETURN)

You should see something like this:

```
/home/yourlogin
    September 2007
 S  M Tu  W Th  F  S
                    1
 2  3  4  5  6  7  8
 9 10 11 12 13 14 15
16 17 18 19 20 21 22
23 24 25 26 27 28 29
```

```
30
Sat  Dec 29   13:21:46  MST   2007
```

11.2 Creating a File with cat

cat prints on the standard output the contents of any file(s) specified as arguments.

The cat command is one of the simplest—and most useful—of the UNIX utilities. You have already used cat to view and to combine ("catenate") files. As you will see in this section, cat can also serve as a "quick and dirty" alternative to a text editor.

1. Invoke cat without an input file, redirecting the output into the file you want to create. If cat is not given an input file to read, it reads from the standard input. Thus, to create a file named out2.tmp, type

```
§ cat  > out2.tmp (RETURN)
```

At this point, you should see nothing happening on the screen, because cat is waiting for you to enter text.

2. Type the text you want to put into the file. For example,

```
My Bonnie looked into the gas tank, (RETURN)
The contents she wanted to see. (RETURN)
I lit a match to assist her: (RETURN)
Oh, bring back my Bonnie to me! (RETURN)
```

3. Generate an end-of-file (EOF) signal. This is done by typing

```
(CONTROL) - (D)
§
```

The prompt tells you that cat has finished and you are back in the shell.

4. Check the file. The cat command will show that the text has been stored in the file:

```
§ cat out2.tmp  (RETURN)
```

You should see something like this:

```
My Bonnie looked into the gas tank,
The contents she wanted to see.
I lit a match to assist her:
Oh, bring back my Bonnie to me!
```

You can also indicate explicitly that you want cat to read the standard input by typing a hyphen (-) instead of a file name. Try it:

1. Invoke cat with a hyphen instead of an input file, redirecting the output into the file you want to create. Thus, to create a file named out3.tmp, type

The hyphen tells cat to read from the standard input.

```
§ cat - > out3.tmp (RETURN)
```

At this point, you should see nothing happening on the screen, because cat is waiting for you to enter text.

2. Type the text you want to put into the file. For example,

```
There once was a fellow named Frank, RETURN
who drove around town in a tank. RETURN
It was noisy and dark, RETURN
and quite hard to park, RETURN
But it got him good rates at the bank. RETURN
```

3. Generate an end-of-file (EOF) signal. This is done by typing

```
CONTROL - D
§
```

4. Check the file. The cat command will show that the text has been stored in the file:

```
§ cat out3.tmp RETURN
```

You should see something like this:

Keep out1.tmp, out2.tmp, and out3.tmp—you will use them later in the chapter.

```
There once was a fellow named Frank,
who drove around town in a tank.
It was noisy and dark,
and quite hard to park,
But it got him good rates at the bank.
```

The cat utility is not a replacement for a text editor—cat does not allow you to change or delete text from a file—but it can be useful in creating short text files.

11.3 Using Wildcards

If you worked through the previous sections carefully, you should now have three new files in your directory named out1.tmp, out2.tmp, and out3.tmp.

■ **Examine the files using the cat command and the asterisk wildcard (*).** Thus, to view the files that begin in *out*, type

```
§ cat out*  RETURN
```

To view all of the files ending in *.tmp,* type the command line

```
§ cat *.tmp RETURN
```

■ **Examine the files using the cat command and the question mark (?).** Recall that the question mark matches any single character. Thus, to view the files out1.tmp, out2.tmp, and out3.tmp, type

```
§ cat out?.tmp  RETURN
```

The file names `out1.tmp`, `out2.tmp`, and `out3.tmp` differ only by one character—a number in the fourth position—and the question mark can stand for any of the numbers.

■ **Examine the files using the `cat` command and the brackets.** The brackets can be used to indicate a range of letters or numerals. To view the files `out1.tmp`, `out2.tmp`, and `out3.tmp`, type

§ `cat out[1-3].tmp` ⓇETURN

11.4 Using wc

The `wc` ("word count") filter counts the lines, words, and characters in a file or collection of files. It has the following general form:

Items in square brackets are optional.

`wc [-lcw] filelist`

where `filelist` is a list of one or more file pathnames. You can apply various options so that `wc` prints only the number of lines (`-l`), or the number of words (`-w`), or the number of characters (`-c`). The `wc` command is very simple to use:

■ **Enter the `wc` command and the file name.** Try it on the `out2.tmp` file:

§ `wc *2.tmp` ⓇETURN

This produces the output

```
4        27        133   out2.tmp
```

showing that there are 4 lines, 27 words, and 133 characters in the `out2.tmp` file. (To `wc`, a "word" is simply any group of characters followed by blanks, tabs, or newlines.)

■ **Run the `wc` command on multiple files.** Try this command line:

§ `wc *[2-3].tmp` ⓇETURN

This runs `wc` on `out2.tmp` and `out3.tmp`, producing the output

```
4        27        133   out2.tmp
5        33        160   out3.tmp
9        60        293   total
```

Note that `wc` shows the line, word, and character counts for the files individually, as well as the totals for both files.

11.5 Using grep

The `grep` filter searches line by line through specified input files for a pattern of characters. Any line containing the desired pattern is printed on the standard output. The format of `grep` is

Items in square brackets are optional.

`grep [-cilnv]` *pattern* [*filelist*]

See Appendix D to learn
about regular expressions.

The *pattern* may be a simple word or string of characters, or it may be a *regular expression*. A regular expression is a compact notation that specifies a general string of characters, in much the same way that a wildcard represents a set of file names. Regular expressions are discussed in Appendix D.

■ **Search for a particular word in a set of files.** Thus, to search the files out1.tmp, out2.tmp, and out3.tmp for lines containing the word *tank*, you would use the command

§ grep tank *tmp (RETURN)

Any lines containing the pattern *tank* are listed on the screen:

out2.tmp:My Bonnie looked into the gas tank,
out3.tmp:who drove around town in a tank.

■ **Search using the line-number option.** The -n option causes grep to print the number of any line containing the pattern:

§ grep -n tank *tmp (RETURN)

The word *tank* occurs on the first line of out2.tmp and on the second line of out3.tmp. Hence, grep prints

out2.tmp:1:My Bonnie looked into the gas tank,
out3.tmp:2:who drove around town in a tank.

■ **Search using the list-only option.** The -l option causes grep to list only the names of the files containing the pattern. For example,

§ grep -l Bonnie *tmp (RETURN)
out2.tmp

■ **Reverse the sense of the test.** The -v option causes grep to list the lines that do **not** contain the pattern. For example,

§ grep -v dark out3.tmp (RETURN)

There once was a fellow named Frank,
who drove around town in a tank.
and quite hard to park.
But it got him good rates at the bank.

11.6   Using sort

As you might expect, sort sorts the lines in a file or collection of files. It can also merge two or more files without sorting them. The sort command has the general format

Items in square brackets are
optional.

sort [-bcdfimMnortuyz] [-*field*] [*filelist*]

As you can see, sort takes quite a large number of options, only a few of which will be discussed in this section. A *field* is a sequence of characters bounded by white space. (The individual words in a line of text might be considered as fields, for example.) Sorting is normally done according to the first field in each line, but you can specify that other fields be examined instead.

■ **Perform a simple sort on the first field of the files.** The following command line will list the sorted contents of out1.tmp, out2.tmp, and out3.tmp:

```
§ sort *.tmp RETURN
                       1
     September 2007
  2  3  4  5  6  7  8
  9 10 11 12 13 14 15
  S  M Tu  W Th  F  S
/home/yourlogin
16 17 18 19 20 21 22
23 24 25 26 27 28 29
30
But it got him good rates at the bank.
I lit a match to assist her:
It was noisy and dark,
My Bonnie looked into the gas tank,
Oh, bring back my Bonnie to me!
Sat  Dec 29   13:21:46  MST   2007
The contents she wanted to see.
There once was a fellow named Frank,
and quite hard to park,
who drove around town in a tank.
```

The sorting order is also called the collating sequence.

This may appear strange until you understand the sorting order that the sort utility employs. This varies from system to system, but the following is typical:

1. Control characters

2. White space (i.e., blanks and tabs)

3. Numerals

4. Uppercase letters

5. Lowercase letters

You can apply various options to modify the sorting order. Here are just a few possibilities:

sort -b   Ignore leading blanks

sort -f   Fold upper- and lowercase letters together (ignore case)

sort -n   Numeric sort (e.g., 1 precedes 10)

sort -r   Reverse usual order (e.g., Z precedes a)

■ **Sort on the first field, ignoring leading blanks and case.** Specifying a field off-set of +0 will cause sort to examine the first field of each line:

§ sort -bf +0 *.tmp (RETURN)

```
/home/yourlogin
                            1
16 17 18 19 20 21 22
 2  3  4  5  6  7  8
23 24 25 26 27 28 29
30
 9 10 11 12 13 14 15
and quite hard to park.
But it got him good rates at the bank.
I lit a match to assist her:
It was noisy and dark,
My Bonnie looked into the gas tank,
   Oh, bring back my Bonnie to me!
 S  M Tu  W Th  F  S
Sat Dec 29   13:21:46  MST   2007
    September 2007
The contents she wanted to see.
There once was a fellow named Frank,
who drove around town in a tank.
```

■ **Sort on the second field of the files.** Specifying a field offset of +1 will cause sort to skip the first field of each line and examine the second field. Try this on the file out3.tmp:

§ sort -bf +1 out3.tmp (RETURN)

```
who drove around town in a tank.
But it got him good rates at the bank.
There once was a fellow named Frank,
and quite hard to park.
It was noisy and dark,
```

There is much more to the sort utility than we can detail here. If you want to know more, refer to the UNIX manual.

11.7 Pipes and Tees

A pipe connects the standard output from one utility to the standard input of another utility. A tee allows you to take the output from a command and direct it into a file and to another command. In this section, you will practice using pipes and tees.

■ **View the calendars for 2007 and 2008, one page at a time.** One of the following command lines will do:

§ (cal 2007; cal 2008) | more (RETURN)

Or

§ (cal 2007; cal 2008) | pg ⟨RETURN⟩

■ **View the calendars for 2007 and 2008, and create a file containing these calendars.** This requires a tee and two pipes:

§ (cal 2007; cal 2008) | tee calfile | more ⟨RETURN⟩

■ **List the files in the root's subdirectories, one page at a time.** Either of the following commands will work to pipe the output from ls to the more or pg utility:

§ ls -a /* | more ⟨RETURN⟩

or

§ ls -a /* | pg ⟨RETURN⟩

■ **List the files in the root's subdirectories and create a file containing this listing.** This can be done using two pipes and a tee:

§ ls -a /* | tee root.list | more ⟨RETURN⟩

This places a list of the root and its subdirectories into the file root.list as this list is also displayed on the terminal screen.

■ **Count the files in the root's subdirectories.** This can be done with the command line

§ ls -a /* | wc -l ⟨RETURN⟩

■ **Print a long listing of the root's subdirectories, sorted by size (largest first).** The fifth field in a long listing gives the file size. To perform a reverse numerical sort (-rn) on the fifth field, skip the first four fields (+4):

§ ls -al /* | sort -rn +4 | more ⟨RETURN⟩

■ **Make a long listing of the root's subdirectories; sort it by size; send it to the standard output and to a file.** The fifth field in a long file listing normally shows the size of the file. To sort on the fifth field, skip the first four fields (+4):

§ ls -al /* | sort -n +4 | tee list.by.size | more ⟨RETURN⟩

■ **Find a file among the root's subdirectories.** Thus, to find the file passwd, enter the command line

§ ls -a /* | grep passwd ⟨RETURN⟩

11.8 Sleeping

The sleep command creates a process that "sleeps" for a specified period of time. In other words, sleep waits a specified number of seconds before returning to the shell. It has the general format

```
sleep n
```

Exercise 1 deals with the accuracy of the sleep command.

where n is a nonnegative integer that indicates the number of seconds the process is to sleep. On most systems, the sleep utility does not count seconds very accurately, so n is only an approximation.

1. Run the sleep command. To sleep for about 15 seconds, enter

§ sleep 15 (RETURN)

2. Use sleep to delay execution of another command. This is a common application of the sleep utility. For example,

§ (sleep 60; echo I am awake now) (RETURN)

3. Wait for the process to finish. When sleep finishes, echo will print

I am awake now

11.9   Interrupting a Foreground Process

If you start a long-running process such as sleep the usual way (that is, in the foreground), you cannot work on any other commands until it finishes. If for some reason you do not wish to wait that long, you must interrupt the process. This is done with the (CONTROL) - (C) key combination.

1. Start the process. For example,

§ (sleep 120; echo I am awake now) (RETURN)

2. Interrupt the process. Type

(CONTROL) – (C)

This will interrupt sleep and invoke the echo command:

^CI am awake now
§

11.10   Running a Background Process

As we said before, UNIX allows you to run a process in the "background" while you work on another task in the foreground. This is useful for long-running processes, especially those that do not require your attention. As an example of such a long-running process, we will once again use the sleep command.

1. Start a long-running process in the background. For example,

§ (sleep 60; echo I am awake now)& (RETURN)

If you are running the Bourne shell, you should see something like this:

The number you see will likely be different.

3271

In this example, the shell assigned a process identification (PID) number of 3271. (The actual PID on your system may be different.)

If you are running C Shell, TC Shell, Korn Shell, or Bash, you should see

The numbers you see will likely be different.

```
[1]      3271
```

Here, [1] is the job number and 3271 is the PID.

The shell will display a prompt to let you know it is ready for more commands:

§

2. Check status of the process. Enter the ps ("process status") command to check on what is happening:

§ ps (RETURN)

You might see something like this (the PIDs will be different):

```
PID  TTY  TIME   COMMAND
3140 p0   0:01   sh
3271 p0   0:00   sleep 60
3290 p0   0:00   ps
§
```

Note that there are three processes: the shell (sh in this example); sleep; and the ps command itself.

3. Wait for the process to finish. After approximately 60 seconds, you should get the message:

```
I am awake now
§
```

11.11 Killing a Background Process

Sometimes it is necessary to terminate a background process. This is done with the kill command. To see how this works, try the same background process you used in the previous section.

1. Start the background process. Be sure to note the PID:

```
§ (sleep 60; echo Stop this command) &  (RETURN)
3310
§
```

2. Kill the process. Type kill, a space, and the PID number:

§ kill 3310 (RETURN)

Some systems will tell you when a background job has been killed:

```
Terminated  (sleep 60; echo Stop this command)
§
```

11.12   Command Summary

Counting Lines, Words, and Characters

wc *file(s)*	count lines, words, and characters in *file(s)*
wc -1 *file(s)*	count the lines in *file(s)*

Searching

grep *pattern file(s)*	print line(s) in *file(s)* containing *pattern*
grep -n *pattern file(s)*	as before, but print line numbers as well
grep -1 *pattern file(s)*	print the name of any file containing *pattern*
grep -v *pattern file(s)*	print line(s) *not* containing *pattern*

Sorting

sort *file(s)*	sort *file(s)* observing the usual collating sequence
sort -b *file(s)*	sort, ignoring leading blanks
sort -f *file(s)*	sort, folding lowercase and uppercase together (ignore case)
sort -n *file(s)*	sort numerically (1 before 10, etc.)
sort -r *file(s)*	reverse sort (9 before 0, Z before A, *etc.*)
sort +*n* *file(s)*	sort on field $n + 1$ (skip n fields)

Sleeping

sleep *n*	sleep *n* seconds

Foreground and Background Processing

^C	interrupt (kill) a foreground process
^D	generate end-of-file signal
^Z	stop (suspend) a foreground process
command &	run command in background
ps	obtain process status
kill *n*	terminate background process *n*

11.13 Exercises

1. How accurately does the `sleep` command count seconds? Try the following command to find out:

```
(date; sleep 60; date)
```

2. Refer to the `man` entry for `cat` to determine what each of the following commands is supposed to do:

cat -e *file*
cat -s *file*
cat -t *file*
cat -u *file*
cat -v *file*
cat -vet *file*

3. Refer to the `man` entry for `grep` to determine what each of the following commands is supposed to do:

grep -c *pattern* *file*
grep -i *pattern* *file*
grep -l *pattern* *file*
grep -n *pattern* *file*
grep -v *pattern* *file*

4. Refer to the `man` entry for `sort` to determine what each of the following commands is supposed to do:

sort -d
sort -m
sort -M
sort -n
sort -o
sort -r
sort -t
sort -u
sort -y
sort -z
sort -nr

5. The -R ("recursive") option causes `ls` to list not only the files in the specified directory, but also the files inside any subdirectories. How could you use this with an appropriate pipe-and-filter arrangement to determine whether a file exists in your account?

# Chapter 12

TUTORIAL: USING ADDITIONAL SHELL FEATURES

In this chapter, you will learn about three features offered by the C Shell (`csh`), TC Shell (`tcsh`), Korn Shell (`ksh`), and Bourne Again Shell (`bash`) that are not found in the original Bourne Shell (`sh`):

- Command history
- Job control
- Filename completion

12.1 Checking Your Shell

There are two ways to determine which shell you are using:

- **Check the login shell.** The command line

Do not omit the $ before SHELL.

§ echo $SHELL (RETURN)

will list the pathname of your login shell.

For example, if you are using `csh`, you might see something like

`/bin/csh`

The exact pathname may be different, depending on how your system is set up.

or perhaps

`/usr/bin/csh`

For `tcsh`, the pathname will be something like `/bin/tcsh` or `/usr/bin/tcsh`; for `ksh`, you might see `/bin/ksh` or `/usr/bin/ksh`; for `bash`, you will see something like `/bin/bash` or `/usr/bin/bash`.

- **Check the process status.** The `ps` ("process status") utility shows which processes are running:

§ ps (RETURN)

You should see the name of your shell. For example, if your login shell is `csh`, you would see something like this (although the PIDs will likely be different):

Some versions of ps will also list the ps process itself.

```
PID TTY       TIME   CMD
2046 pts/5    0:01   csh
§
```

12.2 Trying a Different Shell

Skip this section if you do not want to try a different shell.

You may wish to try a shell other than the one that was selected as your login shell. The shell is contained in a file like any other utility; and like any other utility, you can run a shell by entering the name of the file at the prompt.

1. Check to see whether the shell is available. The `which` utility will look through a predetermined list of directories—the *search path*—to find a file you specify. For example, to check for `tcsh`, enter the command

§ which tcsh (RETURN)

If `tcsh` is found, its pathname will be listed:

§ /usr/bin/tcsh

Otherwise, you will see a message telling you that `tcsh` was not located in the search path:

This lists the directories in the search path.

```
no tcsh in /usr/bin /usr/local/bin /usr/ucb...
```

2. Run the shell if it is available. You can run a shell simply by entering its filename. For example, to run the TC Shell, enter the command

§ tcsh (RETURN)

3. Check to see that the shell is running. Use the `ps` utility for this:

§ ps (RETURN)

Two shell processes should be listed: your original login shell and the shell you just started. Hence, if your login shell were `csh` and you started up `tcsh`, you would see something like this:

```
PID TTY       TIME   CMD
2144 pts/5    0:00   tcsh
2046 pts/5    0:00   csh
§
```

In this example, `tcsh` is running as a *subshell* under the control of the login shell, which is `csh`.

12.3 Setting up the History Mechanism

The history mechanism "remembers" the most recent commands you have issued, and allows you to repeat those commands quickly.

To use history with csh or tcsh, you must first specify how many commands are to be remembered; otherwise, only the single most recent command will be retained (which is not very useful). By default, the ksh history mechanism remembers the most recent 128 commands; bash retains 500 commands.

Most users set the history mechanism to record about 100 commands. However, for the purposes of this chapter, we will set the number much lower.

■ **Set the number of commands to be recorded.** Set history to remember your most recent 10 commands. If you are using csh or tcsh, type

(csh or tcsh) § set history = 10 (RETURN)

If you are using ksh or bash, type

(ksh or bash). § HISTSIZE=10 (RETURN)

Note that there should be no spaces on either side of the equals sign (=) when setting HISTSIZE.

Startup files are discussed in Part VII. Normally, the commands to set history or HISTSIZE are put in a startup file, so you do not have to remember to set them yourself each time you log in.

■ **Enter some commands.** We will need some commands to practice on. Enter the following ten command lines:

§ cal 1 2007 (RETURN)
§ cal 2 2007 (RETURN)
§ cal 3 2007 (RETURN)
§ cal 4 2007 (RETURN)
§ cal 5 2007 (RETURN)
§ ls (RETURN)
§ sleep 5 (RETURN)
§ echo Echo (RETURN)
§ (sleep 5; echo That was a short nap) (RETURN)
§ pwd (RETURN)

12.4 Using the History Mechanism

Now we are ready to try out the history mechanism.

1. Run the history command. Type

§ history (Return)

You should see a numbered list of the most recently executed commands, with the history command itself appearing as the last item on the list:

Numbering may vary on
your system.

```
1   cal 2 2007
2   cal 3 2007
3   cal 4 2007
4   cal 5 2007
5   ls
6   sleep 5
7   echo Echo
8   (sleep 5; echo That was a short nap)
9   pwd
10  history
```

Note that the first `cal` command (`cal 1 2007`) is no longer listed because we configured `history` to remember just ten commands. If you enter more than ten commands, the oldest commands are discarded from the list.

2. Repeat the most recent command on the list. If you are using `csh`, `tcsh`, or `bash`, this is done by typing two exclamation marks at the prompt. Try it:

(csh, tcsh, or bash)   § `!!` (Return)

If you are using `ksh`, enter an *r* (for "repeat'):

(ksh)   § `r` (Return)

Because the most recent command was `history`, you should see another listing of commands, as before:

Numbering may vary.

```
1   cal 3 2007
2   cal 4 2007
3   cal 5 2007
4   ls
5   sleep 5
6   echo echo
7   (sleep 5; echo That was a short nap)
8   pwd
9   history
10  history
```

Once again, the oldest command was discarded from the list.

3. Repeat a command by number. To repeat the seventh command on the list using `csh`, `tcsh`, or `bash`, type

(csh, tcsh, or bash)   § `!7` (Return)

To repeat the seventh command on the list using `ksh`, type an *r*, a space, and a *7*:

(ksh)   § `r 7` (Return)

The seventh command should run:

```
(sleep 5; echo That was a short nap)
That was a short nap
§
```

4. Repeat a command by entering the first letter(s) of the command line. The shell will repeat the most recent command line that begins with the letter(s) you specify. Thus, to repeat a command line that starts with the letter *p*, type

(csh, tcsh, or bash)   § !p (**Return**)

or

(ksh)   § r p (**Return**)

The most recent command beginning with *p* will run:

pwd

Take some time now to practice using the history mechanism.

12.5 Using Job Control

In the previous chapter, we saw how to run a process in the background. The capability of running background processes is available in the original Bourne Shell and subsequent shells.

In addition, csh, tcsh, ksh, and bash have a feature called *job control*, which provides greater flexibility in dealing with background processes. In this section you will see how to use job control to suspend a job, move it to the background, and kill it. Table 12-1 lists the process-control commands we will use.

In the examples that follow, the output shown is what you would get if you were using tcsh on a Sun Solaris system. Your results should be similar.

1. Start the process in the foreground. To practice, use the sleep utility to create a long-running process:

§ (sleep 1800; echo I am awake now) (RETURN)

This process will require about 1800 seconds (30 minutes) to complete. A process such as this should be run in the background, so you can continue working in the foreground.

2. Stop (suspend) the job. This is done with the key combination

(CONTROL) – (Z)

The shell will tell you that the job has been suspended

Some shells will say "stopped," not "suspended."   ^Z
Suspended (user)

Command	Effect
(CONTROL)-(C)	Interrupt (terminate) a foreground process
(CONTROL)-(Z)	Stop (suspend) a foreground process
bg %n	Send process n to the background
fg %n	Bring process n to the foreground
jobs	List jobs
kill %n	Kill (terminate) process n
stop %n	Stop (suspend) background process n

3. Check the status of the job. Enter the jobs command:

§ jobs (RETURN)

This will list, by job number, each job and its status. In this case, there is just one job:

[1] + Suspended (user)   (sleep 1800; echo I am awake now)

At this point, you have four choices:

■ **Background processing.** Move the job to the background using the bg ("background") command.

■ **Foreground processing.** Resume running the job in the foreground using the fg ("foreground") command.

■ **Suspension.** Do nothing and leave the job suspended. (You will not be allowed to exit the shell if you leave a job suspended—you will have to kill the job or start it running again.)

■ **Termination.** Terminate the job using the kill command.

Let's run the command in background.

4. Move the stopped job to the background. Use the bg command and the job number. Note the percent sign (%) preceding the job number:

§ bg %1 (RETURN)

The shell will indicate that the process is now running in the background. You might see a message similar to the following (note the & at the end of the line):

[1]   (sleep 1800; echo I am awake now) &

Once again, you have four choices:

■ **Background processing.** Do nothing and leave the job running in the background. After about 30 minutes, you will see the message "I am awake now". While the job is running in the background, you will be able to continue working in the foreground.

- **Foreground processing.** Bring the job to the foreground using the `fg` command. In about 30 minutes, you will see the message "`I am awake now`". While the job is running in the foreground, you will not be able to enter other commands.

- **Suspension.** Suspend (stop) the job again using the `stop` command. (You will have to kill the job or restart it before leaving the shell.)

- **Termination.** Terminate the job using the `kill` command.

There seems to be little reason to keep this particular process going, so let's kill it.

5. **Kill the job.** To kill job number 1, enter

§ `kill %1` (RETURN)

The shell will respond with a prompt:

§

6. **Check the status of the job.** Use the `jobs` command as before:

§ `jobs` (RETURN)

The `jobs` command will show immediately whether you successfully killed the job. You may see no jobs listed at all; or you may see something like this:

`[1]   Terminated    ( sleep 1800; echo I am awake now )`

Sometimes, however, the `kill` command fails, and `jobs` will indicate that the process is still running:

`[1] Running       ( sleep 1800; echo I am awake now )`

In this case, you should try the steps discussed in the next section.

12.6 Killing a Stubborn Job

Use the commands in this section if the usual `kill` command does not work.

If the simple `kill` command fails, stronger measures are necessary:

1. **Bring the job to the foreground.** Use the `fg` command with the job number:

§ `fg %1` (RETURN)

2. **Interrupt the job.** Use the ^C key combination:

(CONTROL)–(C)

If that does not work, there is one more thing you can do.

3. **If necessary, kill the job using the –9 option.** To kill job number 1, enter

§ `kill -9 %1` (RETURN)

Although some processes ignore the simple `kill` command, none can ignore `kill -9`.

12.7 Filename Completion (csh, tcsh, or bash)

Filename completion in ksh is very different from the other shells, and won't be covered here.

We have already seen how wildcards (such as *) can be used to match file names in commands. *Filename completion* performs a similar function: type a command and the beginning of a filename, then press a special key ((Tab) in tcsh or bash, (Esc) in csh), and the shell completes the filename for you.

Filename completion is always available in tcsh and bash; in csh, you must first set the filec variable:

Normally, filec is set in a startup file—see Part VII.

§ set filec (RETURN)

If you followed the examples in the previous chapter, you should have files named out1.tmp, out2.tmp, and out3.tmp in your home directory. Work on these:

1. Type the command name and the first few characters of the file name. Let's use cat to view the contents of out1.tmp. In csh, type

(csh)

§ cat out (Esc)

In tcsh or bash, type

(tcsh or bash)

§ cat out (Tab)

In this case, there are several files that begin in *out*; therefore, the shell will beep because it is not able to determine which one you mean.

2. List the matching filenames. Type ^D to do this:

In some other contexts, ^D sends an end-of-file signal.

§ (Control)-(D)

The shell will list the files in the current directory that begin in *out*, and it will display the command line again as you left it:

```
out1.tmp   out2.tmp   out3.tmp
§ cat out
```

3. Add enough characters to identify the file you want. To view out1.tmp, type a *1*, then press either (Esc) or (Tab) as before:

(csh)

§ cat out1 (Esc)

or

(tcsh or bash)

§ cat out1 (Tab)

The shell will complete the filename for you:

§ cat out1.tmp

4. Press (RETURN) to execute the command.

The contents of the file out1.tmp should appear.

12.8 Exiting the Shell

If you started a shell other than your login shell, you will need to exit the subshell before you can log out.

1. Exit the subshell when you are finished with it. Use the `exit` command to leave the new shell:

§ `exit` (RETURN)

This should terminate the subshell process and return you to your login shell. You should see the original shell prompt:

§

However, if you still have suspended jobs, you will receive a warning:

`There are stopped jobs.`

2. If necessary, deal with any stopped jobs. Either restart the stopped jobs using bg, or terminate the stopped jobs using `kill`. Then repeat Step 1.

3. Log out.

12.9 Command Summary

Shells and Subshells

`echo $SHELL`	check login shell
`which` *file*	look in search path for *file*
shellfile	run shell contained in *shellfile*
`exit`	exit a subshell

Command History

`set history = ` *n*	record *n* commands (`csh` or `tcsh`)
`HISTSIZE=`*n*	record *n* commands (`ksh` or `bash`)
`!!`	repeat last command (`csh`, `tcsh`, `bash`)
`r`	repeat last command (`ksh`)
`!`*n*	repeat *n*th command (`csh`, `tcsh`, `bash`)
`r` *n*	repeat *n*th command (`ksh`)
`!`*str*	repeat last command starting with *str* (`csh`, `tcsh`, `bash`)
`r` *str*	repeat last command starting with *str* (`ksh`)

Filename Completion

`set filec`	set up filename completion (`csh`)
fil (Esc)	complete filename starting with *fil* (`csh`)
fil (Tab)	complete filename starting with *fil* (`tcsh` or `bash`)
^D	list matching files

Job Control

^C	kill a foreground process
^Z	stop (suspend) a foreground process
`bg` *%n*	move job *n* to background
`fg` *%n*	move job *n* to foreground
`jobs`	list status of all jobs
`kill` *%n*	kill job *n*
`kill -9` *%n*	definitely kill job *n*
`stop` *%n*	stop (suspend) background process *n*

12.10 Exercises

1. Each of the shells discussed in this chapter provides a method for alternating between two directories. If you are using `tcsh`, `bash`, or `ksh`, the command

§ `cd -` (RETURN)

will return you to your previous working directory. The same effect can be achieved in `csh` using the `pushd` ("push directory") command:

§ `pushd` (RETURN)

Try the command (`cd -` or `pushd`) that works with your shell.

2. You have seen how the `which` utility can be used to look through your search path for the file containing a specified command. On some systems, however, there may be more than one file holding a particular command. The `whereis` utility will list all of the files that may contain that command, not just the one that is executed when you type its name. For example, to list all of the files containing the TC Shell, use the command

§ `whereis tcsh` (RETURN)

Try it.

3. Normally, the `history` list is discarded when you log out. However, both `csh` and `tcsh` allow you to save your history list between login sessions. To do this, you must set `savehist`. Hence,

§ `set savehist` ⃝RETURN

Try this on your system.

4. After you have had a chance to try out a new shell, you may want to use it as your login shell. On some systems, the system administrator must change login shells for you. On other systems, you may select your own login shell using either `chsh` ("change shell") or `passwd -s`. See which method your system uses.

PART IV
TEXT EDITORS

# Chapter 13

Text Editors

Chapters 14 through 17
contain tutorials on the use
of text editors.

A *text editor* is a program that you can use to create and modify files. UNIX systems typically offer a choice of text editors. In this chapter, you will learn about UNIX text editors in general.

13.1 Text Editors versus Word Processors

Before learning what a text editor is, you should understand what it is not. *A text editor is not a word processor.* True, both text editors and word processors are used to create and edit text files, but that is where the similarity ends.

A word processor typically does more than a text editor. Besides adding text to a file, most word processing programs allow you to control the appearance of the text—the page layout, paragraph styles, typefaces, and so on—when it is printed. With some word processor programs, you can create tables, enter mathematical equations, and insert graphics.

In contrast, a text editor does just that: edit text. Most text editors have limited text formatting capabilities. Generally speaking, a text editor is not intended to format text for printing; it is intended for creating and modifying ordinary text or ASCII files. Although this might seem limiting at first, remember that UNIX systems typically store information in the form of ASCII files. For example, a computer program or shell script would be stored as an ASCII file.

13.2 UNIX Text Editors

A number of different text editors are available on most UNIX systems. The following are perhaps the most widely used:

The name of this editor is
pronounced "vee-eye".

■ vi. This editor was written by Bill Joy, a graduate student at the University of California at Berkeley (who also wrote the C Shell and later became one of the founders of Sun Microsystems). Although originally found only on Berkeley UNIX, vi is now the standard editor on POSIX-compliant systems.

■ emacs. Originally written by Richard Stallman at MIT, emacs is a powerful, feature-rich editor known for its flexibility: emacs can be personalized to fit the tastes of the user. Some versions of emacs supported windowing before windowing systems became common on UNIX.

- pico. This editor was developed at the University of Washington for composing messages in the pine mail program. The menu structure of pico makes it especially easy for beginners to learn.

- xedit. This X client is a simple window-based text editor. It is available on most systems that run X. (We will not cover xedit in this book.)

- CDE Text Editor. The Common Desktop Environment (CDE) includes a simple, yet powerful, text editor.

We will examine vi, emacs, pico, and Text Editor in this and subsequent chapters.

13.3 How a Text Editor Works

Regardless of the text editor you choose, the process of editing a text file can be summarized as follows:

1. You start the editor and give it the name of a file to edit.

2. If you specified an existing file, the editor makes a copy of it and places the copy in a temporary workspace called the *work buffer*. If you are creating a new file, the editor simply opens up an empty work buffer.

3. You use editor commands to add, delete, and/or change the text in the work buffer. When you are satisfied with the changes you have made, you tell the editor to save or write them into the file.

4. The editor saves in a file the contents of the work buffer. If you are editing an existing file, the editor replaces the original file with the updated version in the buffer.

Note that you do not work directly on the file, but only on the copy that is in the buffer. This means that if you leave the editor without writing your changes into the file, the changes are lost, and the original file is not altered.

13.4 Line, Screen, and GUI Editors

All editors do much the same things, but some are decidedly easier to use than others. The original UNIX editor ed is called a *line editor* because it makes changes in the buffer line by line. To make a change using a line editor, you must first specify the line where you want the change to be made, and then you must specify the change itself. This can be a lot of work for even minor changes. Furthermore, it can be difficult to keep in mind the way the changes fit into the text as a whole because you are working with just one line at a time.

Screen editors are sometimes called *visual editors*; vi is short for "visual."

A *full-screen editor*, on the other hand, allows you to view and to work with as much of the work buffer as will fit on your screen. You can easily move the cursor around the screen, making changes to characters, words, and paragraphs as well as lines. Any changes you make are always apparent because the screen is updated immediately. And you can see clearly how the changes affect the rest of the text because you can view many lines at the same time. vi, emacs, and pico are full-screen editors.

The proliferation of graphical user interfaces (GUIs) has led to the development of a new class of full-screen text editors that are designed to take full advantage of the pointer and mouse. The CDE Text Editor is an example of this class of editor.

13.5   Spell and Look

The vi editor lacks a built-in spell-checker.

For the benefit of people who occasionally misspell words, UNIX offers the spell utility. spell goes through a file and checks every word against the UNIX word list (sometimes called a "dictionary"). When spell encounters words or groups of characters that are not on the word list, it displays them on the screen.

Although spell is very useful, it has its limitations. It cannot detect grammatical errors or words used incorrectly. (Few spelling checkers can.) Thus if you wrote "up" when you meant "down," or "wait" instead of "weight," spell cannot help you. Nor can it correct misspelled words, as some spell-checkers do.

A related utility named look allows you to look up words on the word list that is used by spell. You will learn how to use both look and spell in the chapters on vi and emacs.

13.6   Command-Line Editing

Command-line editing is discussed in Chapter 14 (vi) and Chapter 15 (emacs).

Usually, we think of using an editor to edit ordinary text files. However, some shells—including tcsh, ksh, and bash—allow you to use vi or emacs commands to edit command lines. If you make a mistake entering a command, you need not cancel the entire command and start over; you can use the editor to correct the command.

13.7   Which Editor Is Right for Me?

The choice of an editor depends on availability and personal preference. Here are some considerations:

■ vi. Because the POSIX standard specifies vi as the standard editor, it is likely to be found on every UNIX system. It works well on dumb terminals and terminal emulators. However, it does not have the flexibility of emacs.

■ emacs. Although not officially a standard editor, emacs is widely available. It can be used on a dumb terminal or terminal emulator. It can be customized to suit your tastes. Some users prefer it to vi.

■ pico. In general, pico is easier to learn than either vi or emacs, and would therefore be a good choice for a beginner. The user interface for pico is very similar to that of the pine mail program; if you use pine, you will find it easy to use pico as well. Moreover, pico can run on a dumb terminal or terminal emulator. Its major drawback is that it might not be available on your system.

■ CDE Text Editor. Arguably the most powerful editor—and the easiest to learn—Text Editor will naturally be the first choice of anyone working in the Common Desktop Environment. However, you cannot run Text Editor on a dumb terminal or terminal emulator.

Thus, if your concern is to learn one editor that will be universally available on all standard UNIX systems, you should consider vi (although emacs would be a very close second). For ease of use, choose pico or Text Editor.

A final point: All text editors work on text files, and a text file created by one editor can be read and modified by another editor. As a result, you are not restricted to any one editor. You might choose to learn two editors—say, Text Editor for when you are able to work with the Common Desktop Environment, and vi or emacs for other situations.

13.8 Exercises

1. Be sure you can define the following terms:

text editor	word processor	work buffer
cursor	line editor	screen editor
GUI editor	word list	dictionary

2. Which text editors are available on your system?

# Chapter 14

TUTORIAL:
EDITING WITH VI

Skip this chapter if you do not intend to use vi.

The visual editor vi is the standard text editor on POSIX-compliant systems. In this chapter, you will see how to use the vi editor to create and edit text files and to edit command lines.

14.1 vi Modes

To use vi, you have to know something about its operating modes (Figure 14-1). When you first enter the vi editor, it is set to the *command mode*. This means that vi will treat all keystrokes as editing commands, and not as text to be entered into the file. Pressing (Return), (Backspace), or the space bar while in the command mode moves the cursor without introducing new lines or spaces into the text.

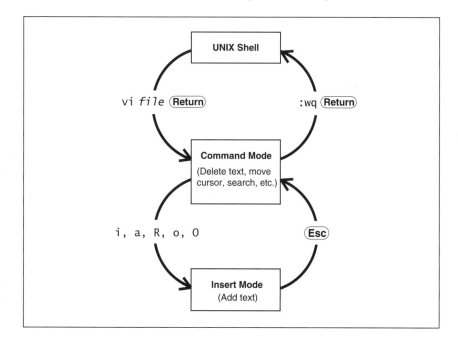

Figure 14-1
Operating modes of the visual editor vi.

To add text to the file, you must switch to the *insert mode*, which you can do using any of the following commands:

i   insert text to the left of the current cursor location

I   Insert text to the left of the current line

a   append text to the right of the cursor

A   Append text to the end of the current line

R   Replace (type over) existing text

o   open a new line below the current line and move the cursor there

O   Open a new line above the current line and move the cursor there

None of these insert-mode commands appears on the screen, but everything typed afterward does. Pressing the (Esc) key returns vi to the command mode.

In general, you use the insert mode when adding text to the file, and the command mode for everything else (moving around the file, deleting text, etc.).

Perhaps the most common difficulty that beginning vi users have is remembering which mode they are working in. When in doubt, hit the (Esc) key a couple of times to get back to the command mode. (If the terminal beeps or the screen flashes when you press (Esc), that is a signal that you are already in the command mode.)

14.2 Opening a New File

If you haven't already done so, log in and set your terminal. Then follow the examples.

1. Select a name for the new file. The name should be descriptive. Thus, a good name for a file that will contain poetry might be poems.

2. Enter the vi command, followed by the name of the new file. To create a file named poems, type the command line

§ vi poems (Return)

If your terminal is set properly, you should see something like this:

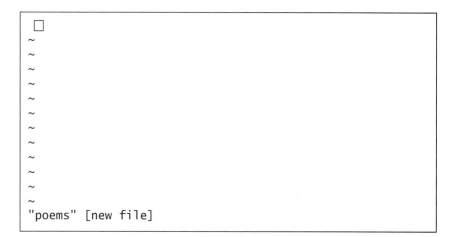

The tildes (~) mark empty lines in the work buffer.

The box on the first line represents the *cursor*, which shows the point at which any new text would be entered. (The actual appearance of the cursor depends on the particular type of terminal you are using.)

14.3 Inserting Text

1. Switch to insert mode. This is done using the i ("insert") command. Type

The *i* does not appear on screen.

i

This command does not appear on the screen, but everything you type subsequently will.

2. Enter text into the work buffer. Try typing in the following lines of verse (ignore any mistakes for now—you'll see how to correct them later):

Mary had a little lamb, (Return)
A little cheese, (Return)
A little ham. (Return)
Burp!☐

Although these lines appear on the terminal screen, they are not yet saved in the file. Remember, you must "write" these lines from the buffer into the file to save them.

14.4 Writing Text to the File

1. Press (Esc) **to get back into the command mode:**

(Esc)

2. Enter the Write command. Type a colon (:), a *w*, and a (Return). Note that the cursor jumps to the bottom of the screen when you type the colon:

This command appears at
the bottom of the screen as
you type.
:w (Return)

The computer will respond with a message that shows the number of lines and characters that were saved in the file:

"poems" [New file] 4 lines, 61 characters

3. **Leave the** vi **editor.** This is done using the Quit command.

:q (Return)

The computer will answer with the shell prompt to let you know you are out of vi and back in the UNIX shell:

§

14.5   Moving the Cursor

When editing a file, you will often need to move the cursor around the file. Moving the vi cursor is always done in the command mode.

1. **Reopen the file using** vi. To open the file named poems, type the command

§ vi poems (Return)

This will cause vi to copy the contents of the file into the work buffer, then display this on the screen:

```
Mary had a little lamb,
A little cheese,
A little ham.
Burp!
~
~
~
~
~
"poems" 4 lines, 61 characters
```

Note that the cursor is positioned over the first character in the work buffer.

2. **If necessary, put** vi **into the command mode.** If you are unsure which mode you're working in, simply press the (Esc) key to get into the command mode.

3. **Move the cursor.** Many computer keyboards have arrow keys—also called *cursor-control keys*—that move the cursor one space at a time in the direction indicated:

These may not work on
your machine.
← ↓ ↑ →

In the command mode, the h, j, k, l, (Space), (Backspace), ⊖ (hyphen), and (Return) keys may be used in place of the arrow keys:

On many terminals, holding a key down causes its function to be repeated rapidly. This can be useful when you want to move quickly through the file.

h   move one space left

j   move one space down

k   move one space up

l   move one space right

The (Space), (Backspace), ⊖ (hyphen), and (Return) keys may also be used to move the cursor in the command mode:

(Space)   move one space right

(Backspace)   move one space left

⊖   move to beginning of previous line

(Return)   move to beginning of next line down

Practice using the various cursor-control keys until you get a feel for how they work.

14.6 Replacing Text

You have seen how to create a new text file using the vi editor. Now you will see how to edit existing text by typing over it with new text.

1. If the file is closed, open it using the vi editor. To edit the file poems, type

§ vi poems (Return)

This will put a copy of the file poems into the work buffer and display it for you on the screen.

2. If necessary, put vi into the command mode. When you invoke the vi editor, it should start up in the command mode. You can always make sure vi is in the command mode by pressing (Esc):

(Esc)

3. Move the cursor to the text you intend to replace. Use the arrow and/or alternative cursor-control keys discussed in the previous section. In the file poems you might want to replace *Burp!* with something more suitable. (Mary is very polite and would never burp at the dinner table.) Move the cursor down to the fourth line and position it over the *B* in *Burp*.

4. Type the Replace command. In the command mode, type an uppercase *R* (for "Replace"). The *R* does not appear on the screen, but it does take vi from the command mode into the insert mode.

This command does not appear on the screen.

R

5. Enter the new text. Whatever you type now will be written over the old text. To replace *Burp!* with *Delicious!*, type

`Delicious!`

Note how *Delicious!* is written right over the offending *Burp!*.

6. Return to the command mode. Pressing the (**Esc**) key puts vi back into the command mode:

(**Esc**)

At this point, you have made changes to the text in the work buffer, but these changes have not yet been saved in the file.

14.7 Writing the File and Quitting the Editor

If you want to save the changes you have made to the work buffer, you must "write" these changes into the file. (Remember, the editor always works on a copy of the file.)

1. Put vi into the command mode. Press the (**Esc**) key.

2. To save your work, write the changes into the file. From the command mode, press the colon (:) key, then the *w* key. Note that when you press the colon, the cursor jumps to the bottom of the screen:

This appears at the bottom of the screen.

`:w` (**Return**)

The editor will show you how many lines and characters were written to the file:

`"poems" 4 lines, 66 characters`

Note that the cursor returned to the last character you typed. This will allow you to continue editing the file, if you wish.

3. If you are finished with the file, quit the editor. This is done using the Quit command.

`:q` (**Return**)

The computer will answer with the shell prompt to let you know you are out of vi and back in the UNIX shell:

§

If you try to quit the file without saving your changes, the computer will respond with the message

`No write since last change (:q! overrides)`

At times, you may decide not to save the changes you have made. In that case, do not write the changes into the file, but enter the command

This quits the editor without saving the changes you made.

`:q!` (**Return**)

14.8 Appending Text

In this section, you will see how to add text to the file using the a ("append") command.

1. If the file is not already open, reopen it. To edit the file poems, type

§ vi poems (Return)

This will put a copy of the file poems into the work buffer and display it for you on the screen.

2. If necessary, put vi **into the command mode.** Remember, you can always make sure vi is in the command mode by pressing (Esc):

(Esc)

3. Position the cursor. Keep in mind that the Append command adds the text to the right of the cursor position. Move the cursor to the bottom of the file.

4. Enter the Append command. Just type the letter *a*:

This command does not   a
appear on the screen.

Now type the following lines (hit (Return) at the end of each line to start a new line):

(Return)
Mary had a polar bear (Return)
Whose fur was white as snow, (Return)
And everywhere that big bear went (Return)
The people (Return)
let it go. (Return)

5. Return to the command mode. Hit (Esc):

(Esc)

6. If you are finished editing, write to the file and quit the editor. You can do this in one step by typing:

This appears at the bottom   :wq (Return)
of the screen.

The computer will respond with a message telling you how many lines and characters were written into the file:

"poems" 9 lines, 175 characters

The prompt (§) indicates that you are back in the UNIX shell:

§

14.9 Joining Two Lines

In vi , the J ("join") command allows you to join two lines together.

1. **If the file is not already open, open it.** To edit the file `poems`, type

§ vi poems (Return)

This will put a copy of the file `poems` into the work buffer and display it for you on the screen. Note that in this example, the last two lines of the poem are the ones that should be joined together:

```
The people
let it go.
```

2. **If necessary, press (Esc) to put vi into the command mode.**

3. **Move the cursor to the first of the two lines you want to join.** The cursor can be put anywhere on that line:

Put the cursor on the first of the two lines.

```
The people
let it go.
```

4. **Enter the Join command.** Just type the capital letter *J*:

This command does not appear on the screen.

J

The editor will join the lines:

```
The people let it go.
```

5. **If you are finished, write the changes to the file and quit the editor.**

This appears at the bottom of the screen.

:wq (Return)

The computer will indicate how many lines and characters were saved in the file:

```
poems  8 lines, 174 characters
```

The prompt (§) indicates that you are back in the UNIX shell:

§

14.10 More Ways to Insert Text

Four more insert-mode commands are frequently useful:

A   Append text to the end of the current line

I   Insert text at the beginning of the current line

o   open a new line below the current line and move the cursor there

O   Open a new line above the current line and move the cursor there

The exercises at the end of this chapter will give you the opportunity to try out these commands.

14.11 Correcting Mistakes

Everyone makes an occasional error, so vi thoughtfully provides several means of correcting mistakes. These commands work only in the command mode. (When in doubt, hit (Esc) to get into the command mode.)

x   delete one character

dd   delete entire line

u   undo most recent change

U   Undo any changes made to current line

:q!   quit without saving changes

To delete a single character, move the cursor over that character and press the *x* key. To delete an entire line, type *dd*. To delete *n* lines (where *n* is any positive integer), move the cursor to the first of the lines to be deleted and type *ndd*.

If you make a change and then think better of it, you can undo the most recent change by the u ("undo") command

(Esc)u (Return)

If you want to undo several changes to the line you are currently working on, you can restore the current line to its previous condition with the U ("Undo") command:

(Esc)U (Return)

Note, however, that U works only so long as you remain on the line; if you go to another line, you cannot go back and use the U command to undo the changes.

If you make too many changes to undo with the u or U commands, you can always use the command

(Esc):q! (Return)

which quits the text editor without saving any changes.

14.12 Writing to a Different File

Sometimes, it is convenient to make changes to a file and save those changes under a different file name. Because we plan to try out the spell utility later in this chapter, let's create a file to contain misspelled words:

1. If the file is not already open, open it. To edit the file poems, type

§ vi poems (Return)

2. Make changes. Use the R ("Replace") command to introduce a few misspelled words into the file poems:

<u>Marye</u> had a <u>wittle</u> <u>wamb</u>,
A <u>wittle</u> cheese,
A <u>wittle</u> ham.
<u>Delisious</u>!

Mary had a polar <u>beer</u>
Whose <u>fir</u> was white as snow,
And everywhere that big <u>bare</u> went
The people let it go.

3. Write the changes to a different file. Use the :w ("write") command, as before, but this time specify a new file name. Since the new file is to contain misspelled words, call it misspelled. Type the command

(Esc):w misspelled (Return)

You will be notified that the text has been saved in a new file:

"misspelled" [New file] 9 lines, 176 characters

4. Quit without saving changes. You have written the misspellings into the file misspelled; you do not need to save them in poems as well. Use the command

:q! (Return)

14.13 Using spell

If spell is not available on your system, try ispell instead.

spell is a UNIX utility that checks your spelling. Unlike many spell-checkers that are supplied as part of a word processor or text editor, spell is an entirely separate program. Consequently, you will not use spell at the same time you are editing a file with vi.

1. If you are still working in vi, quit the editor. To save your changes and quit, type

(Esc):wq (Return)

2. At the shell prompt, enter the spell command and the file name.

§ spell misspelled (Return)

The spell utility searches through the file and prints any words that are not found on the UNIX word list:

Delisious
Marye
wamb
wittle

Note that although wittle appears three times in the file, it is listed only once by spell. Note too that spell caught the unusual spelling of Mary; the word list includes many proper names. But spell missed some words: beer, fir, and bare. The reason is simple: these are legitimate words in spell's word list. Remember, spell does not really check for spelling errors; rather, it looks for groups of characters that do not match those in its word list. Consequently, it will not detect words that are used out of context.

14.14 Finding Text

The vi editor can locate particular words or groupings of characters anywhere in the file. This is useful when correcting spelling errors. For example, spell identified the misspelled word Delisious in the file misspelled.

1. Open the file if it is not already open. Suppose you want to correct the misspelled words in the file misspelled. Type

§ vi misspelled (Return)

2. If necessary, put vi into the command mode.

3. Type a slash (/) followed by the word or characters you want to find. Note that when you type the slash, the cursor jumps to the bottom of the screen:

This appears at the bottom of the screen.

/Delisious (Return)

When you press (Return), the cursor will move to the place where the word is located. You may then use vi's editing commands to edit the text.

4. Enter a slash (/) to search for further occurrences of the same word or characters. There is no need to type the word again:

(Esc)/ (Return)

When vi can find no other instances of this word, it will tell you so:

Pattern not found

5. Search backward through the file from the current cursor location. Use a question mark (?) to do this:

(Esc)?wittle (Return)

This will find one of the occurrences of the word wittle. To check for the next occurrence, type

(Esc)? (Return)

14.15 Global Substitution

"Global" means "comprehensive."

The forward search (/) and backward search (?) commands provide a quick way to find an error in a file. Once you have found the error, you can use the vi editor commands to make the necessary change. Although this approach works well if there are only one or two such changes to make, it is even faster to make the changes using the Global Substitution command.

1. **If necessary, put** vi **into the command mode.**

2. **Enter the Global Substitution command.** This is a "colon"command having the form

:%s/*old*/*new*/g (Return)

where % specifies that all lines of the file be examined, s is short for "substitute", *old* represents the old text that you want to replace, *new* represents the new text, and g stands for "global." Thus, to replace all occurrences of *wittle* with *little*, type

This line appears at the bottom of the screen.

:%s/wittle/little/g (Return)

3. **Write the changes into the file.**

See Exercise 15 for a variation on the Global Substitution command.

If you have not already done so, you may wish to take a moment now to correct the remaining errors in your misspelled file.

14.16 Jumping around the File

The vi editor provides a convenient way to move the cursor rapidly to a specific line in the file.

1. **If necessary, open the file with** vi.

2. **In the command mode, type the line number and the Go command.** Thus, to go to the seventh line of the file, type

This command does not appear on screen.

7G

in which the G stands for "Go."

3. **To go to the bottom of the file, type** G. No line number is necessary:

This command does not appear on screen.

G

You can also jump a certain number of lines above or below your current position:

■ **Jump backward.** Enter the number of lines you wish to jump, followed by a minus sign (–). Thus, to jump back 9 lines from your current position, type

This command does not appear on screen.

9–

■ **Jump forward.** Enter the number of lines you wish to jump, followed by a plus sign (+). Thus, to jump forward 5 lines from your current position, type

This command does not appear on screen.

5+

14.17   Setting Line Numbers

Of course, if you are to be jumping forward or backward to specific lines, it would be helpful to be able to number the lines.

1. **Put** vi **into the command mode.**

2. **Enter the Set Numbers command.** Type the line

This command appears at the bottom of the screen.

```
:set nu (Return)
```

This causes line numbers to be placed down the left-hand margin:

The line numbers appear on the screen but are not written into the work buffer or the file.

```
1 Mary had a little lamb,
2 A little cheese,
3 A little ham.
4 Delicious!
5
6 Mary had a polar bear
7 Whose fur was white as snow,
8 And everywhere that big bear went
9 The people let it go.
```

3. **To remove the line numbers, enter the Set No Numbers command.** In the command mode, type

```
:set nonu (Return)
```

14.18   Buffers and More Buffers

Recall that vi actually works on a copy of the file in the work buffer. While using vi, you have access to other buffers as well. There are 36 of these:

- unnamed buffer

- named buffers "a, "b, "c, ... ,"z

- numbered buffers "1, "2, "3, ...,"9

The unnamed buffer is sometimes called the *general-purpose buffer*. When you change or delete text, the old text is not thrown away immediately. Instead, vi moves the old material into the unnamed buffer, and holds it there until you change or delete more material. The advantage of this is that it allows you to change your mind and restore the deleted text using the "undo" command:

```
u
```

This puts the old text back where it came from. Since vi has only one unnamed buffer, the undo command can only restore the most recent change you made; previous changes are lost.

The named buffers and numbered buffers are useful for moving blocks of text around a file or between different files. In the next section, for example, you will move four lines of text from one place in a file to another. You will do this by positioning the cursor at the beginning of the block of text and issuing the command

```
"a4yy
```

This is best understood when read backwards: yy stands for "yank," which means in this case "copy"; the 4 refers to four lines of text; and "a (double quote-a) specifies a particular named buffer. Therefore, this command tells vi to copy four lines of text and place them in the named buffer "a.

To retrieve the text from the named buffer, place the cursor where you want the text to go and type the command

```
"ap
```

which tells vi to "put" a copy of the contents of the named buffer "a into the work buffer.

Remember that buffers are only temporary storage locations; their contents are lost once you leave vi.

14.19 Yanking Text

Let's use a named buffer to move blocks of text around in the file:

1. Use vi to open the file. If you have been following the examples thus far, open the file poems.

2. In the command mode, move the cursor to the first of the lines you wish to copy. To copy the second poem, move the cursor to the first line of the poem:

```
Mary had a polar bear
```

3. Yank the lines into a named buffer. Thus, to copy four lines into named buffer "a, type the following line (no (Return) is required):

This command does not appear on screen.

```
"a4yy
```

Although the command itself does not appear on the screen, the computer usually puts a message at the bottom of the screen:

On some systems, this message does not appear.

```
4 lines yanked
```

14.20 Putting Text

Once you have yanked text into a buffer, the text will remain in that buffer until you either put more text in its place or you leave the editor. You can put (copy) the text from the buffer to the file:

1. **Move the cursor to the place you want to put the text.** In the current example, move the cursor down to the last line in the file.

2. **Put the lines of the named buffer into the work buffer.** The following command will put a copy of the contents of the named buffer `"a` below the current cursor location.

This command does not appear on screen.

```
"ap
```

The four lines of the second poem should appear. The computer will also tell you how many lines were placed:

```
4 lines
```

If you try the Put command on a buffer that has nothing in it, the computer will respond with an error message such as

Buffers are also called registers.

```
Nothing in register a
```

The contents of the named buffer are not changed by the Put operation; you could put the same four lines into the text again if you wanted to.

3. **Write the changes into the file.**

WARNING	Remember that buffers are only temporary storage locations; their contents are lost once you quit `vi`.

14.21 Moving Text between Files

The named and numbered buffers are also used to transfer text from one file to another.

1. **If necessary, put `vi` into the command mode.**

2. **Move the cursor to the first of the lines you want to transfer.** Suppose you want to copy the first four lines of `poems` into a new file. Make sure the cursor is on the first line of the lines that you wish to transfer.

3. **Yank the lines into a named buffer.** To yank four lines into the buffer `"m`, type

This command does not appear on screen.

```
"m4yy
```

The computer will print the number of lines that were yanked:

```
4 lines yanked
```

4. **Enter the Edit File command.** Type `:e` followed by the name of the file that is to receive the yanked text. Thus, to put the text into the file `stuff`, type

```
:e stuff (Return)
```

This tells the editor that you want to work on the file `stuff`. The editor will close the file `poems` and attempt to open a file named `stuff`. If there is no file named `stuff` in your current directory, the editor opens an empty work buffer:

☐
~
~
~
~
~
~
```
"stuff" No such file or directory
```

5. Put the lines. To put lines from "m into the newly opened work buffer, type

This command does not appear on screen.

```
"mp
```

You should see something like this appear on the screen:

```
Mary had a little lamb,
A little cheese,
A little ham.
Delicious!
4 lines
```

6. Write the lines into the file. This is done the usual way:

(Esc):w(Return)

The editor will tell you the size of the new file that you just created:

```
"stuff" [New file] 5 lines, 109 characters
```

Note that the new lines were entered below the original cursor position, leaving a blank line at the top of the file. As a result, the new file contains five lines, not four.

7. Edit the file as necessary, then save the changes and quit the editor.

14.22 Command-Line Editing (tcsh, ksh, bash)

Skip this section if you are using sh or csh.

Suppose you are using sh or csh, and that you make a mistake typing a command at the prompt. Your options are limited: either backspace to the error and retype the rest of the command, or cancel the command entirely with (Control)-(U) and start over.

In contrast, tcsh, ksh, and bash give you the ability to edit commands using either the emacs or vi editor. This way, you can correct errors without having to retype all or part of the command line.

The first step is to select an editor. In this chapter, we want to use vi editing commands:

Normally, a startup file is used for this—see Part VII.

■ **Select an editor.** If you are using tcsh and wish to select vi as your editor, enter

(tcsh)   § bindkey -v (RETURN)

If you are using `ksh`, enter

(ksh)   § VISUAL=vi (RETURN)

If you are using `bash`, enter

(bash)   § set -o vi (RETURN)

Once you have done this, you will be able to edit command lines using `vi`.

1. Type an erroneous command line. Type the following command line, leaving the cursor at the end of the line (do not press (RETURN)):

§ echoe I never make misstayyks ever

Note that there are two misspelled words in this command line: *echoe* should be *echo*, and *misstayyks* should be *mistakes*.

2. Press (Esc) put `vi` into command mode.

3. Move the cursor to the first error. In the `vi` command mode, the following keys will move the cursor along the command line:

These are the same commands used to move the cursor left and right along a line in a file.

h or (Backspace) move one space back (left)

l or (Space)   move one space forward (right)

On some keyboards, the arrow keys (← and →) may be used to move the cursor left or right along the command line.

4. Correct the command name. You will need to change *echoe* to *echo* by deleting the extra *e*. You can use many of the same commands you used to edit files: x to delete a character, R to type over text, i to insert text, and so on.

5. Correct the remaining spelling errors. Move the cursor to *misstayyks* and change it to *mistakes*.

6. Continue editing the line as needed. Delete *ever* and insert it (with a comma) after *never*. When you finish, the command line should look something like this:

§ echo I never, ever make mistakes

7. Execute the command. Press (RETURN).

The computer should echo the message:

I never, ever make mistakes

14.23 Command Summary

You must press (Return) after a UNIX shell command (such as vi or spell) or a
vi command that begins with a slash (/), question mark (?), or colon (:). Press
(Esc) to obtain the vi command mode. Note that vi commands beginning with
a colon (:) or slash (/) appear at the bottom of the screen, but none of the other
vi commands appear on-screen.

Opening, Writing, and Closing Files (use (Return))

vi *file*	open file named *file* (UNIX shell command)
:w	write changes into default file
:w *file*	write changes into file named *file*
:q	quit vi
:wq	write changes into file and quit vi
:q!	quit without writing changes into file

Inserting Text (vi command mode)

a	add text to the right of the current cursor location
i	insert text to the left of the cursor
0	Open up a new line above the current line
o	open up a new line below the current line
R	Replace (type over) text
(Esc)	return to command mode

Moving the Cursor (vi command mode)

←↓↑→	move one space in direction indicated
h	move one space left
j	move one space down
k	move one space up
l	move one space right
(Spacebar)	move one space right
(Backspace)	move one space left
(Return)	move to beginning of next line down
⊖ (hyphen)	move to beginning of previous line

Correcting Mistakes (vi command mode)

x	delete one character
dd	delete entire line
$n$dd	delete n lines
u	"undo" most recent change
U	"undo" all changes on current line

Checking Spelling (UNIX shell command)

spell *file*	list misspelled words found in *file*
ispell *file*	list misspelled words found in *file*

Searching (vi command mode)

/*word*	search forward for the first occurrence of *word*
/	continue search for the next occurrence of *word*
?*word*	search backward for the first occurrence of *word*
?	continue search backward for the next occurrence of *word*

Jumping to a Line (vi command mode)

n+	jump forward (down) n lines
n-	jump backward (up) n lines
nG	Go to line number n
G	Go to the bottom of the file

Setting Line Numbers (vi command mode)

:set nu	set line numbers on the screen
:set nonu	remove line numbers

Yanking and Putting (vi command mode)

"k$n$yy	yank (copy) n lines into buffer "k
"kp	put the contents of buffer "k below the current line

Substituting Text Globally (vi command mode)

:%s/*old*/*new*/g	replace *old* by *new* everywhere in the file

Editing Another File (vi command mode)

:e *file*	edit *file*

Selecting an Editor for Command-Line Editing (UNIX shell commands)

`bindkey -v`   select `vi` (for `tcsh`)

`VISUAL=vi`   select `vi` (for `ksh`)

`set -o vi`   select `vi` (for `bash`)

14.24 Exercises

1. If there are any typos in your file `poems`, use the `vi` editor to correct them.

2. Specify which `vi` mode you would use to **(a)** delete a line; **(b)** yank a line; **(c)** write over old text; **(d)** move the cursor; **(e)** add text to a new line above the current cursor position.

3. How do you get from the `vi` command mode to the insert mode? How do you get back again?

4. Describe what happens when the following `vi` commands are given:

```
"z10yy
"kp
u
```

5. You have already seen how the `vi` command a allows you to insert text to the right of the current cursor position. The command A is also used to insert text, but at the end of the current line. Using the `vi` editor, open the file `poems`, type an A, and enter the following line:

`This demonstrates the A command.`

6. The `vi` command I ("Insert") allows you to insert text. How does it differ from the i ("insert") command?

7. The `vi` command o ("open") opens an empty line below the current cursor position. Try out this command.

8. The `vi` command O ("Open") opens an empty line above the current cursor position. Try out this command.

9. Use the `vi` editor to create a file named `747art`. Enter the following text, being sure to press (Return) each time the cursor nears the right edge of the screen:

> It is hard to deny, yet rarely said, that the creative impulse was redirected at some point early in this century, or perhaps in the 19th, away from some of its normal artistic channels and into new ones associated with engineering and technology. Quite apart from being useful, a Boeing 747 is a far more impressive aesthetic object than what passes for "art" in our contemporary museums.
>
> --Tom Bethell

Make sure to write this into the file before you quit the vi editor.

10. Most computer terminals have a useful feature called *wraparound*. Try an experiment to find out whether your terminal does:

a. Open a new file named wrap and begin typing in the quote by Tom Bethell (see the previous problem), only this time do not press (Return) when the cursor reaches the end of the screen. Instead, keep typing and observe what happens. If the cursor automatically moves down to the next line as you type, your terminal has wraparound—it wraps a long line around to the next line to fit it on the screen. If, on the other hand, the cursor remains at the end of the line as you type, your terminal lacks wraparound.

b. Continue typing in the entire Bethell quote without pressing the (Return) key. (This may be a bit difficult if your terminal does not have the wraparound feature, but do the best you can.) Write the quote into the file and quit the vi editor.

c. Reopen the file wrap. How many lines and characters do you see on the screen? How many lines and characters does the editor say are in the file? (Moral #1: What you see on the screen is not necessarily what you get in the file. Moral #2: If you want to start a new line, press (Return)—don't rely on the wraparound.)

11. If you are unsure of the spelling of a word, you can use the look utility to check its spelling in the UNIX word list. Suppose you wanted to know how to spell *relief*. Is it "*i* before *e*" or "*e* before *i*"? At the UNIX shell prompt, type look, followed by the word in question:

§ look relief (Return)

If the word appears on the UNIX word list, look will print it on the screen:

relief
§

Try a misspelled word (e.g., "releif").

If the word is not on the list, look will print nothing. Instead, you will see the UNIX shell prompt:

§

You can also use look to examine all of the words on the UNIX word list that begin with a particular sequence of letters. To see the words that begin with *rel*, type

§ look rel (Return)

Use look to determine whether the following are found in the UNIX word list: **(a)** your first name; **(b)** your last name; **(c)** the last name of the current vice president; **(d)** Kabul, the capital of Afghanistan; **(e)** herpetologist; **(f)** ornithology.

12. One of the requirements for a good UNIX password is that it not be a common word or name. Some UNIX installations will not accept as a password any word in the internal word list. Use look to see whether these passwords are listed: **(a)** Hi54Luck; **(b)** 4Tune8; **(c)** 1DayMayB; **(d)** Much2Gr8; **(e)** 14DRoad; **(f)** FOR@ward; **(g)** gin/GER; **(h)** hydro.GEN.

13. Use `spell` on the files that you created in the previous chapters. If `spell` reports an error in a file, open that file and use the Search (/) command to find the misspelled words. Make the necessary corrections.

14. In a previous exercise, you created a file named `747art`. Open this file and use the search commands to locate the sentence beginning with the word `Quite`. Yank the lines that contain this entire sentence. (You may have to take a few words from the preceding sentence as well.) Use the `edit` command to transfer these lines to a new file `art`.

15. There is a modification of the previous Global Substitution command that you might find useful:

`:%s/wittle/little/gc` (Return)

The `c` at the end of the command line stands for "confirm." Under this option, the editor will show you each change and ask you for confirmation before actually making the change:

```
Marye had a wittle wamb
            ^^^^^^
```

If you want to make the change, type `y` (for *yes*); otherwise, type `n` (for *no*).

# Chapter 15

TUTORIAL:
EDITING WITH EMACS

Skip this chapter if you do not intend to use emacs.

The emacs editor is found on most UNIX systems. In this chapter, you will see how to use emacs to create and edit a text file.

15.1 Starting emacs

■ **Start** emacs. Enter the emacs command at the UNIX shell prompt

§ emacs (Return)

In a moment, you should see the emacs screen, as shown in Figure 15-1.

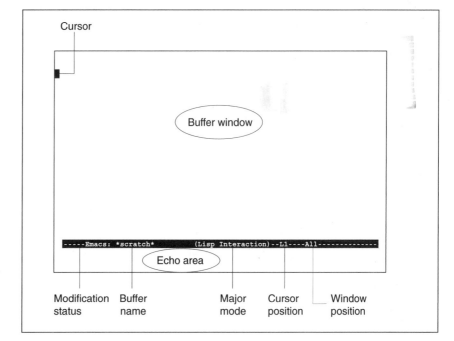

Figure 15-1
The emacs screen. The dark band near the bottom of the screen is the Mode Line.

15.2 The emacs Screen

Take a moment to identify the various parts of the emacs screen:

■ **Buffer window.** This is the place where you enter text or modify text. It shows the contents of the work buffer.

■ **Cursor.** The cursor is a small box that marks your current location in the buffer. Any character you type is inserted to the left of the cursor.

■ **Echo Area.** Also called the *minibuffer*, this is an area at the bottom of the screen in which messages and one-line commands appear.

■ **Mode Line.** Located above the Echo Area, the Mode Line is a contrasting (reverse-video) band that provides useful information about the status of the buffer and the editor.

Let's examine the Mode Line in greater detail. The Mode Line in Figure 15-1 includes the following information:

■ **Modification status.** Dashes (--) in this position show that no changes have been made to the text. When you make changes, asterisks (**) appear instead.

■ **Buffer name.** Every buffer has a name. If the contents of the buffer were obtained from a file, the file name will appear in the Mode Line. "Scratch" is used for a new buffer that has not yet been saved to a file.

■ **Major mode.** An emacs *mode* is a set of features that can speed specialized tasks, such as editing C, Lisp, or Fortran programs. Some commands behave slightly differently in different modes. (We will not discuss emacs modes in this book.)

■ **Cursor position.** "L1" shows that the cursor is currently positioned on Line 1.

■ **Window position.** "All" means that the current buffer fits entirely in the emacs window. For longer buffers, "Top" indicates that the window is positioned to show the top of the buffer, and "Bot" means the window is positioned at the bottom of the buffer. A percentage (e.g., "15%") indicates that 15% of the buffer is above the top of the window.

15.3 Command Notation

Many emacs commands require that you use the (Control) key in combination with other keys. In traditional emacs notation, (Control) is indicated by C-. For example, the command sequence to save changes in a file is

(Control)-(X)   (Control)-(S)

In emacs notation, this command sequence is written as C-x C-s.

Other emacs commands require that you use the (Meta) key, denoted M-. Thus, the command to move to the top of the buffer is the combination

(Meta)-(V)

In emacs notation, this command sequence is written as M-v. If your keyboard does not have a (Meta) key, you can use the (Alt) key instead:

(Alt)-(V)

Alternatively, you can press *and release* the (Escape) or (Esc) key, then press the (V) key:

(Esc) (V)

This would be written in emacs notation as <ESC>v.

Other common abbreviations used in the emacs manual are <Return> or <RET> for the (Return) key; <Delete> or <Del> for the (Delete) key; and <SPC> for the (Spacebar).

15.4   Entering Text

Let's put some text into the buffer:

■ **Enter the text.** Type the following lines of verse:

```
    Poem #1 (Return)
Mary had a little lamb, (Return)
A little cheese, (Return)
A little ham. (Return)
Burp!□
```

Although these lines appear in the emacs buffer window, they are not yet saved in the file. That is the next step.

15.5   Saving Text to a File

1. Use the Save command. This is the key combination C-x C-s. First hold down the (Control) key while pressing the (X) key; then hold down the (Control) key while pressing the (S) key:

(Control)-(X)   (Control)-(S)

A prompt will appear in the Echo Area:

```
File to save: ~/
```

The rules for naming files and directories are summarized in Section 6.5.

2. Enter a valid file name. It is a good idea to select a descriptive name for the file. Try the name poems:

```
File to save: ~/poems
```

3. Press (Return). Note that a message appears in the Echo Area, telling you what just happened:

```
Wrote /home/yourlogin/poems
```

15.6 Ending the Editing Session

We have created a new file; now let's exit the emacs editor.

1. Use the Exit command. This is the combination C-x C-c:

(Control)-(X) (Control)-(C)

This puts you back into the UNIX shell. You should see the UNIX prompt:

§

2. Check that the new file exists. The ls command should list the file:

§ ls (Return)

3. Check the contents of the file. The cat command will show the contents:

§ cat poems (Return)

15.7 Finding a File

Let's reopen the file you just created:

1. Restart emacs.

§ emacs (Return)

2. Select the Find File command. The command is C-x C-f:

(Control)-(X) (Control)-(F)

A prompt will appear in the echo area:

Find file: ~/

3. Enter a valid file name. Thus, to open the file poems, enter the file name after the prompt:

Find file: ~/poems

4. Press (Return). Note that the file name appears in the Mode Line.

15.8 Moving the Cursor

When editing a file, you will often need to move the cursor around the file. There are a number of commands for doing this:

■ **Use the arrow keys to move the cursor.** Many computer keyboards have arrow keys—also called *cursor-control keys*—that move the cursor one space at a time in the direction indicated:

These may not work on your machine.   ← ↓ ↑ →

■ **Use the alternative cursor-control keys to move the cursor.** A number of commands may be used in place of the arrow keys:

On many terminals, holding a key down causes its function to be repeated rapidly. This can be useful when you want to move quickly through the file.

C-f   move one space forward (right)

C-b   move one space back (left)

C-p   move to previous line (one line up)

C-n   move to next line (one line down)

C-a   move to the beginning of the current line

C-e   move to the end of the current line

15.9   Correcting Text

Of course, you need to be able to correct errors and make changes to text. There are a number of commands that can be used to delete characters from the buffer:

\<Del\>   ((Delete) key) delete the character to the left of the cursor

C-d   delete the character under the cursor

Let's make changes to the current buffer.

1. Move the cursor to the right of the text to be deleted. In the buffer poems you might want to replace *Burp!* with something more suitable. (Mary is very polite and would never burp at the dinner table.) Position the cursor to the right of *Burp!*.

2. Delete the unwanted text. Use the (Delete) key (\<Del\>) to remove the characters. Note that the cursor moves back one space each time you press (Delete).

3. Enter the new text. Whatever you type now will be entered into the work buffer. Try Delicious!:

Delicious! (Return)

4. Continue entering text. Let's add another poem to the buffer:

(Return)
    Poem #2 (Return)
Mary had a polar bear (Return)
Whose fur was white as snow, (Return)
And everywhere that big bear went (Return)
The people let it go. (Return)

5. Quit emacs. As before, use the Quit (C-x C-c) command:

(Control)-(X)   (Control)-(C)

Because you have not saved the most recent changes, emacs will prompt you to save the file:

```
Save file ~/poems? (y, n, !, q, C-r, or C-h)
```

6. Answer Yes. Press the *y* key:

```
y
```

This will save the changes in the file poems. Something else happens as well: The previous contents of the file poems are placed in a new file named poems~. That way, you do not lose the original file.

15.10 Opening a File from the Command Line

You can start emacs and open a file at the same time:

■ **Restart emacs and reopen the file.** To open the file named poems, type the command line

§ emacs poems⟨Return⟩

This causes emacs to copy the contents of the file into the buffer and position the cursor in the upper left corner of the screen.

15.11 Searching for Text

You can move through a file to find a specified word, character, or string of characters using an *incremental search* (I-search). In an incremental search, emacs does not wait until you have completely specified the string of characters you want; instead, it begins searching while you are typing the string.

1. Enter the Search command. The command is C-s:

⟨Control⟩-⟨S⟩

In response, a prompt appears in the Echo Area:

```
I-search:
```

2. Enter the character or string of characters you want to find. Suppose you want to find the word *ham* in the buffer. Type the letter *h* at the prompt:

```
I-search: h
```

Note that when you typed the *h*, emacs positioned the cursor to the right of the *h* in *had*. Now add the letter *a*:

```
I-search: ha
```

This time, emacs moved the cursor to the right of the *a* in *had*. Finally, type *m*:

```
I-search: ham
```

Obviously, *had* contains the letters *ha* but not *m*, so emacs searches forward through the file until it finds a string of characters that matches the pattern. In this case, *ham* is the next string that works. The editor repositions the cursor at the end of this word.

3. If necessary, modify the search string. Suppose you were really interested in finding all the strings containing the characters *ha*. You can modify the search string by pressing the (Delete) key to remove the last letter of the previous search string:

```
I-search: ha
```

Note that the cursor jumped back to the word *had*.

4. Find the next occurrence of the search string. In this example, *had*, *ham*, and *that* will match the search string; emacs has found the first word. To find *ham*, type the search command C-s:

(Control)-(S)

Note that the cursor jumped to the right of the word *ham*.

5. Repeat search for string. Type the Search command C-s again:

(Control)-(S)

The cursor jumps down to the word *had* in the second poem. Use the search command C-s again:

(Control)-(S)

The cursor jumps to the word *that*. Repeat the Search command C-s one more time:

(Control)-(S)

Since there are no more occurrences of the pattern *ha*, emacs gives you a message:

```
Failing I-Search
```

6. Terminate the search. Once you are finished searching the file, you can end the search and leave the cursor at its new position by pressing (Return).

The C-s command searches forward through the buffer, starting at the current location of the cursor. Any text above the cursor is not searched.

In contrast, the C-r command searches *backwards* from the current cursor location. Any text below the current cursor location is not searched.

15.12   Killing and Yanking

Killing and yanking are often called cutting and pasting.

You may sometimes need to move a block of text—also called a *region* of text— from one place to another within a buffer. To do this, you must first put the text into a temporary storage location called a *Kill Ring*. In emacs terminology, this is called *killing* the text. Then you can move the cursor to another point in the buffer and retrieve the text from the Kill Ring. This is called *yanking* the text.

1. Move the cursor to the beginning of the text to be moved. In the poems file, move the cursor to the start of the first poem.

2. Mark the beginning of the text region. Use the C-@ ("Set Mark") command:

The C-<SPC> command
may be used on some
keyboards.

(Control)-(@)

You should see a message that the mark has been set:

Mark Set

3. Move the cursor to the end of the text region. Move the cursor to the end of the first poem.

4. Kill the text. The C-w ("Kill Region") command causes the text region to be removed from the work buffer into the Kill Ring:

(Control)-(W)

5. Move the cursor to the new location. Move to the end of the poems file.

6. Yank the text. The C-y ("Yank") command copies text from the temporary buffer into the work buffer:

(Control)-(Y)

You can paste the text again, if you wish. Try it:

(Control)-(Y)

15.13 Undoing Changes

You probably would not want to save the most recent changes made in the poems buffer. (There is no need for two copies of Poem #1, nor should Poem #1 come after Poem #2.) The emacs editor allows you to "undo" recent changes:

1. Give the Undo command. Type C-x u:

(Control)-(X) (U)

This will undo the effect of the most recent command.

2. Repeat the Undo command. Try the alternate Undo command C-_ (which may or may not work on your keyboard):

Here, _ is the underscore.   (Control)-(⌒)

This should undo the next most recent command. (If this does not work, try the C-x u command instead.)

3. Repeat as needed. When you finish, the first poem should be back in its original position.

15.14 Saving to a Different File

1. Make changes in the buffer. Because we will want to try out the spell-checker, first use emacs to introduce some misspelled words (underlined below) into the file poems:

```
      Poem #1
Marye had a wittle wamb,
A wittle cheese,
A wittle ham.
Delisious!
```

```
      Poem #2
Mary had a polar beer
Whose fir was white as snow,
And everywhere that big bare went
The people let it go.
```

2. Save the changes. Use the Write (C-x C-w) command:

⟨Control⟩-Ⓧ   ⟨Control⟩-Ⓦ

emacs will tell you the current file name in the Echo Area:

File to save: ~/poems

3. Replace the file name. Delete the current file name, and replace it with another. In this case, try misspelled:

File to save: ~/misspelled

4. Press ⟨Return⟩. The changes will be saved in the file misspelled. The original file poems will remained unchanged.

15.15 Using spell

If spell is not available on your system, try ispell instead.

spell is a UNIX utility that checks your spelling. Unlike many spell-checkers that are supplied as part of a word processor or text editor, spell is an entirely separate program. Consequently, you will not use spell while you are editing a file with emacs.

1. If you are working in emacs, **write the file and quit the editor.** Recall that the command sequence to do this is C-x C-s followed by C-x C-c.

2. At the shell prompt, enter the spell **command and the file name.**

§ spell misspelled ⟨Return⟩

The spell utility searches through the file and prints any words that are not found on the UNIX word list:

```
Delisious
Marye
wamb
wittle
```

Note that although *wittle* appears three times in the file, it is listed only once by spell. Note too that spell caught the unusual spelling of *Mary*; the word list includes many proper names. But spell missed some words: *beer*, *fir*, and *bare*.

The reason is simple: these are legitimate words in `spell`'s word list. Remember, `spell` does not really check for spelling errors; rather, it looks for groups of characters that do not match those in its word list. It will not detect words used out of context.

15.16 Reading the emacs Tutorial

We have barely scratched the surface of emacs; an entire book could be written on the subject. To learn more, you can refer to the `emacs` on-line tutorial:

1. If necessary, start `emacs`. Enter the `emacs` command at the UNIX shell prompt

§ emacs (Return)

2. Start the `emacs` tutorial. The command is C-m t:

(Control)–(M) (T)

This will open a new window containing the tutorial.

3. Work through the tutorial.

4. Cancel the tutorial. The `emacs` Cancel command is C-g:

(Control)–(G)

15.17 Command-Line Editing (tcsh, ksh, bash)

Skip this section if you are using `sh` or `csh`.

If you make a mistake typing a command while using either `sh` or `csh`, your options are limited: either backspace to the error and retype the rest of the command, or cancel the command entirely with (Control)–(C) and start over.

In contrast, `tcsh`, `ksh`, and `bash` give you the ability to edit commands using either the `vi` or `emacs` editor. This way, you can correct errors without having to retype all or part of the command line.

The first step is to specify that you want to use `emacs` editing commands.

Normally, a startup file is used for this—see Part VII.

■ **Select an editor.** If you are using `tcsh` and wish to select `emacs`, enter the command

(tcsh) § bindkey -e (RETURN)

If you are using `ksh`, enter

(ksh) § VISUAL=emacs (RETURN)

When using `bash`, enter

(bash) § set -o emacs (RETURN)

Once you have done this, you will be able to edit shell command lines using `emacs`.

1. Type an erroneous command line. Type the following command line, leaving the cursor at the end of the line (do not press (RETURN)):

§ echoe I never make misstayyks ever

Note that there are two misspelled words in this command line: *echoe* should be *echo*, and *misstayyks* should be *mistakes*. Also, we will move the word *ever* from the end of the line to a position right of the word *never*.

2. Move the cursor to the first error. The following emacs key combinations will move the keys along the command line:

These are the same
commands used to move
the cursor left and right
along a line in a file.

C-f   move one space forward (right)

C-b   move one space back (left)

On some keyboards, the arrow keys (← and →) may be used to move the cursor left or right along the command line.

3. Correct the command name. You will need to change *echoe* to *echo* by deleting the extra *e*. Use the same commands you used previously to delete characters:

<Del>   ((Delete) key) delete the character to the left of the cursor

C-d   delete the character under the cursor

4. Correct the remaining spelling errors. Move the cursor to *misstayyks* and change it to *mistakes*.

5. Continue editing the line as needed. Delete *ever* and insert it (with a comma) after *never*. When you finish, the command line should look something like this:

§ echo I never, ever make mistakes

6. Execute the command. Press (Return).

The computer should echo the message:

I never, ever make mistakes

15.18 Command Summary

Opening, Writing, and Closing Files

emacs *file*	open *file* (UNIX shell command)
C-x C-s	save buffer in current file
C-x C-w	write buffer to a file specified by user in echo area
C-x C-f	find a file and copy it into the buffer
C-x C-c	Exit emacs session

Moving the Cursor

←↓↑→	move one space in direction indicated
C-f	move one space forward (right)
C-b	move one space back (left)
C-p	move to previous line (one line up)
C-n	move to next line (one line down)
C-a	move to the beginning of the current line
C-e	move to the end of the current line

Deleting Text

<Del>	(Delete key) delete the character to the left of the cursor
C-d	delete the character under the cursor

Searching for Text

C-s	search forward through the buffer for string of characters
C-r	search backward through the buffer for string of characters

Killing and Yanking Text

C-@	mark start of text block
C-w	kill (cut) text from buffer into Kill Ring
C-y	yank (paste) the text from Kill Ring into buffer

Undoing Changes

C-x u	undo most recent command
C-_	alternate undo command

Miscellaneous Commands

spell *file*	check *file* for spelling errors (UNIX command)
ispell *file*	check *file* for spelling errors (UNIX command)
C-m t	run tutorial
C-g	cancel or stop a command

Selecting an Editor for Command-Line Editing (UNIX shell commands)

bindkey -e	select emacs (for tcsh)
VISUAL=emacs	select emacs (for ksh)
set -o emacs	select emacs (for bash)

15.19 Exercises

1. If there are any typos in your file poems, use the emacs editor to correct them.

2. Using the emacs editor, create a new file named 747art and type in the following quote:

> It is hard to deny, yet rarely said, that the creative impulse was redirected at some point early in this century, or perhaps in the 19th, away from some of its normal artistic channels and into new ones associated with engineering and technology. Quite apart from being useful, a Boeing 747 is a far more impressive aesthetic object than what passes for "art" in our contemporary museums.
>
> --Tom Bethell

Make sure to write this into the file before you quit the editor.

3. Use spell on the files that you created in the previous chapters. If spell reports an error in a file, open that file and use the Search command to find the misspelled words. Make the necessary corrections.

4. If you are unsure of the spelling of a word, you can use the look utility to check its spelling in the UNIX word list. Suppose you wanted to know how to spell *relief*. Is it "*i* before *e*" or "*e* before *i*"? **At the UNIX shell prompt, type** look, **followed by the word in question:**

§ look relief (Return)

If the word appears on the UNIX word list, look will print it on the screen:

relief

Try a misspelled word (e.g., "releif").

If the word is not on the list, `look` will print nothing. Instead, you will see the UNIX shell prompt:

§

You can also use `look` to examine all of the words on the UNIX word list that begin with a particular sequence of letters. To see the words that begin with *rel*, type

§ `look rel` (Return)

Use `look` to determine whether the following are found in the UNIX word list: **(a)** your first name; **(b)** your last name; **(c)** the last name of the current vice president; **(d)** Kabul, the capital of Afghanistan; **(e)** herpetologist; **(f)** ornithology.

5. One of the requirements for a good UNIX password is that it not be a common word or name. Some UNIX installations will not accept any word in the internal word list. Use `look` to see whether any of these passwords is listed: **(a)** Hi54Luck; **(b)** 4Tune8; **(c)** 1DayMayB; **(d)** Much2Gr8; **(e)** 14DRoad; **(f)** FOR@ward; **(g)** gin/GER; **(h)** hydro.GEN.

# Chapter 16

TUTORIAL:
EDITING WITH PICO

Skip this chapter if you do
not intend to use pico.

The pico text editor is an easy-to-use text editor available on many UNIX systems. In this chapter, you will see how to use pico to create and edit a text file.

16.1 Starting pico

■ **Start pico.** Enter the pico command at the UNIX shell prompt

§ pico (Return)

If all goes well, you should see the pico window, as shown in Figure 16-1. Take a moment to identify the various parts of the window.

■ **Status line.** The dark bar at the top of the window shows the current version of pico, the name of the file being edited, and other information concerning the status of the file.

■ **Content area.** This is the place where you enter text or modify text. It shows the contents of the work buffer.

■ **Cursor.** This is a small black box that marks your current location in the content area.

■ **Message line.** Located below the content area and above the menu bar, the message line is the place where pico displays messages and prompts.

■ **Menu bar.** The menu bar or command list occupies the last two rows of the window. It lists frequently used pico commands. You can enter one of these commands by holding down the (Control) key—represented by a caret (∧)—while pressing another key.

Twelve commands are listed on the Menu bar:

∧G   Get Help. Provides more information regarding the various functions.

∧X   Exit. Ends the pico session. You will be prompted for the name of a file into which your work may be saved.

∧O   Write Out. Saves your work in a file without ending the editing session.

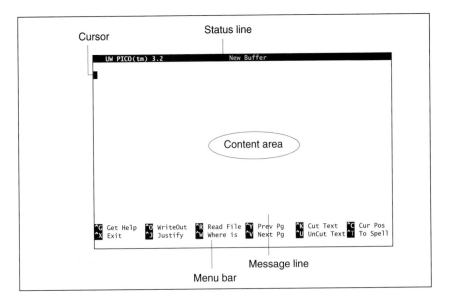

Figure 16-1
The pico window.

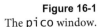

∧J   Justify. Adjusts the appearance of the paragraph where the cursor is sitting.

∧R   Read File. Allows you to copy a file into the buffer. You will be prompted for the name of the file.

∧W   Where Is. Searches the buffer for characters or words that you specify.

∧Y   Previous Page (Prev Pg). Scrolls back (up) one page.

∧V   Next Page (Next Pg). Scrolls forward (down) one page.

∧K   Cut Text. Cuts text from the buffer and saves it temporarily. The text can be pasted back into the buffer.

∧U   UnCut Text. Pastes cut text into the buffer.

∧C   Current Position (Cur Pos). Shows the line number of the current cursor location, and lists the total number of lines and characters in the file.

∧T   To Spell. Starts the spell-checker.

16.2 Entering Text

The cursor shows where text is to be entered into the Content Area.

■ **Enter the text.** Try typing in the following lines of verse:

```
Mary had a little lamb, (Return)
A little cheese, (Return)
A little ham. (Return)
Burp!█
```

The spell-checker will find the next occurrence of *wittle* and ask whether you want to replace it with *little*:

```
Replace "wittle" with "little"?
```

4. Enter y for yes. The correction will be made and the next error will be found:

```
Replace "wittle" with "little"?
```

5. Continue correcting the misspellings.

Note that the spell-checker misses some words: beer, fir, and bare. The reason is simple: these are legitimate words in the UNIX word list. Remember, the spell-checker does not really check for spelling errors; rather, it looks for groups of characters that do not match those in its word list. Consequently, it will not detect words that are used out of context.

16.10 Cutting and Pasting

You may occasionally need to move large blocks of text around within a file. This is done by storing the text in a temporary buffer.

1. Move the cursor to the beginning of the text block. In the poems file, move the cursor to the start of the first poem.

2. Mark the beginning of the text block. Use the ^^ command:

(Control)-(^)

You should see a message that the mark has been set:

```
[Mark Set]
```

3. Move the cursor to the end of the text block. Move the cursor to the end of the first poem. Note that the text is highlighted:

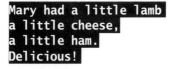

4. Cut the text. The ^K ("Cut") command causes the text to be removed from the work buffer into a temporary storage buffer:

(Control)-(K)

5. Move the cursor to the new location. Move to the end of the poems file.

6. Paste the text. The ^U ("Uncut") command copies text from the temporary buffer into the work buffer:

(Control)-(U)

You can paste the text multiple times, if you wish:

(Control)-(U)

16.11 Exiting without Saving Changes

There is no reason to save the most recent changes in the file poems. You can discard the changes by exiting pico without writing out the changes.

1. Select the Exit command. Type ^X.

You will be asked whether you want to save the modified buffer:

Save modified buffer (ANSWERING "No" WILL DESTROY CHANGES) ?

2. Answer n for no at the prompt.

The buffer will not be written out to the file.

16.12 Command Summary

Opening, Writing, and Closing Files

pico *file*	open *file* (UNIX shell command)
^O	write out to a file without ending the editing session
^R	read file into the buffer
^X	exit pico session

Searching for Text

^W	search the buffer for characters or words

Moving the Cursor

←↓↑→	move one space in direction indicated
^F	move one space forward (right)
^B	move one space back (left)
^P	move to previous line (one line up)
^N	move to next line (one line down)
^A	move to beginning of the current line
^E	move to end of the current line
^Y	scroll back (up) one page
^V	scroll forward (down) one page

Cutting, Pasting, and Deleting Text

^^	mark start of text block
^K	cut text from work buffer and save temporarily
^U	uncut (paste) text previously cut from the work buffer
^D	delete text at the current cursor position
(Backspace)	delete text to the left of the cursor
(Delete)	delete text to the left of the cursor

Miscellaneous Commands

^C	show line number of the current cursor location
^G	get help
^J	justify paragraph where the cursor is sitting
^T	start spell-checker

16.13 Exercises

1. If there are any typos in your file poems, use the pico editor to correct them.

2. Using the pico editor, create a new file named 747art and type in the following quote:

> It is hard to deny, yet rarely said, that the creative impulse was redirected at some point early in this century, or perhaps in the 19th, away from some of its normal artistic channels and into new ones associated with engineering and technology. Quite apart from being useful, a Boeing 747 is a far more impressive aesthetic object than what passes for "art" in our contemporary museums.
>
> --Tom Bethell

Make sure to write this into the file before you quit the editor.

3. The Get Help (^G) command provides useful information on the various pico commands. Use it to determine how the Current Position (^C) command works, then try out this command in one of your files.

4. Use the Get Help command to determine how the Justify (^J) command works. Then try out the Justify (^J) command on one of your files.

# Chapter 17

TUTORIAL:
EDITING WITH TEXT EDITOR

Skip this chapter if you are
not using CDE or Text
Editor.

Text Editor is a tool provided by the Common Desktop Environment for creating
and editing text files. If you have previously used a word processor, you should
have no trouble learning to use Text Editor.

17.1 Starting Text Editor

1. Open the Applications subpanel.

2. Click on the Text Editor icon.

An Editor window will appear (Figure 17-1), with the cursor positioned at the top
of the window.

17.2 Entering Text

Putting text into the window is easy:

1. If necessary, select the Editor window.

2. Type the text. Errors can be deleted by backspacing. Enter the following lines:

```
Poem #1 (Return)
Mary had a little lamb, (Return)
A little cheese, (Return)
A little ham. (Return)
Burp! (Return)
(Return)
Poem #2 (Return)
Mary had a polar bear, (Return)
whose fur was white as snow. (Return)
And everywhere that big bear went, (Return)
The people let it go. (Return)
```

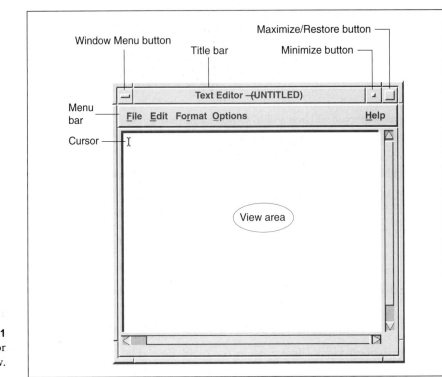

Window Menu button

Title bar

Maximize/Restore button

Minimize button

Menu bar

Cursor

View area

Figure 17-1
The CDE Text Editor window.

17.3 Saving to a File

The next step is to save in a file the lines you just entered:

The menu remains open if you use the right (#3) mouse button.

1. **Pull down the File menu.** You can use either the mouse or the alternate key combination (Alt)-(F).

2. **Choose Save (needed).** Either click on the Save option or press the *S* key.

A "Save As" dialog will appear.

3. If necessary, type a path or folder name in the box. By default, your current directory path will appear in the window. If that is acceptable, there is no need to change this.

4. Enter a valid file name. By default, UNTITLED appears in the box. It is a good idea to select a descriptive name for the file. Try the name poems.

5. Press OK. This will cause the lines to be copied from the screen to the file.

If you entered the name of an existing file, you will be asked whether you want to replace the existing file with the contents of the Editor window.

17.4   Ending the Editing Session

1. Pull down the File menu.

2. Click on Close. Alternatively, you can press the *C* key or Alt+F4.

The Editor window will disappear.

17.5   Re-opening a File

Let's re-open the file you just created. First, restart the Editor:

1. Open the Applications subpanel.

2. Click on the Text Editor icon. Wait for the Editor window to reappear.

At this point, the editor is open to an empty buffer.

Next open the file:

1. Pull down the File menu.

2. Choose Open....

A dialog box will appear.

3. Enter a file name. To open the file poems, type this name into the box labeled "Enter a file name."

4. Press OK.

The contents of the file poems will appear in the Editor window.

Keep in mind that it is a copy of poems that you see in the window; the file itself is not changed until you save the changes.

17.6 Overstriking Text

In most cases, you will operate the Editor in the *insert* mode. That is, characters you type are inserted to the left of the cursor, and any existing text moves over to make room. However, at times you may want to replace the existing text by typing over it. For this, put the editor into *overstrike* mode:

You can move the cursor using the keyboard arrow keys, or by pointing and clicking at the new location.

1. Position the cursor. In the file poems you might want to replace *Burp!* with something more suitable. (Mary is very polite and would never burp at the dinner table.) Position the cursor to the left of the *B* in Burp.

2. Pull down the Options menu. Use the mouse or the alternate key combination (Alt)–(O).

3. Select Overstrike. Click on Overstrike or press the *O* key.

Note that a check mark appears next to the option to show it has been selected.

4. Type the new text over the old text. Enter *Delicious!* over the offensive *Burp!*.

5. Return to insert mode. Pull down the Options menu and de-select Overstrike.

The check mark will disappear, showing that the overstrike option is no longer in effect.

17.7 Copying, Cutting and Pasting

You can move blocks of text around within a file or between two different files using a temporary buffer called a *clipboard*. Open the file poems and follow these steps:

1. Select the text. Position the cursor at the beginning of Poem #1, then hold down the left (#1) mouse button while dragging the cursor over the first poem. The selected text will be highlighted.

2. Pull down the Edit menu and choose Copy. The selected text will be copied from the window into the clipboard. (Alternatively, you can use the Cut command, which copies the text into the clipboard and removes it from the window.)

3. Move the cursor to the new location. Position it below Poem #2.

4. Pull down the Edit menu and choose Paste.

The text will be copied from the clipboard into the window.

The Paste operation *copies* text from the clipboard to the window.

5. Repeat pasting as needed. Since the Paste operation leaves the text in the clipboard unchanged, it is available for pasting as many times as you wish. Try it—paste another copy of the text at the bottom of the file. When you are finished, the window should look something like this:

```
Poem #1
Mary had a little lamb,
A little cheese,
A little ham.
Delicious!

Poem #2
Mary had a polar bear,
whose fur was white as snow.
And everywhere that big bear went,
The people let it go.
Poem #1
Mary had a little lamb,
A little cheese,
A little ham.
Delicious!
Poem #1
Mary had a little lamb,
A little cheese,
A little ham.
Delicious!
```

17.8 Undoing a Change

There is no reason to have three copies of Poem #1 in the poems file—one is quite enough. The Undo command will reverse the effect of the most recent Cut, Paste, Clear, Replace, Include, Format, or Undo command. Try it:

■ **Pull down the Edit menu and choose Undo.** If the last operation was a Paste, the pasted text should disappear from the Editor window.

If you select Undo again, the text is pasted back into the file—remember, Undo can "undo" itself.

17.9 Deleting Text

We still have a redundant copy of Poem #1 in the file poems. You can either clear it or delete it. Clearing replaces the text with spaces; deleting removes it entirely. Let's delete it:

1. **Select the text to be deleted.** Drag the cursor over the second copy of Poem #1.

2. **Pull down the Edit menu and choose Delete.**

The selected text disappears.

3. Pull down the File menu and choose Save.

The changed text will be saved in the current file, which is poems.

17.10 Saving to a Different File

Later in this chapter we will try out the Editor's spell-checker. For this, we will need a copy of the file poems.

1. Pull down the File menu and select the Save As... option.

The Save As window will appear.

2. Enter the new file name. Since the new file will contained misspelled words, name it misspelled.

3. Press OK.

Note that the title of the Editor window changes to show the new file name.

Any changes you save now will go into the new file misspelled; the original file poems will remain unchanged.

17.11 Finding and Changing Text

You can quickly search through a file to find—and replace—a specified string of characters using the Find/Change command. Because we plan to test the spell-checker later in this chapter, let's use this command to introduce some misspellings into the file misspelled:

1. Pull down the Edit menu and select Find/Change....

The Find/Change window will appear.

2. **Enter the search string in the Find box.** Enter the word *little*.

3. **Enter the replacement string in the Change box.** Enter the misspelling *wittle*. (To find a word rather than change it, leave the Change box blank.)

4. **Press Find button.** The first occurrence of *little* is highlighted.

If for some reason you do not want to make the change, skip this step.

5. **To change the string, press the Change button.** The highlighted search string *little* will be replaced by *wittle*. (The Change All command replaces every occurrence of *little*.)

6. **Continue finding and changing.** When you have changed all instances of the search string *little* in the file, you will see a message:

`Unable to find the string little in the current document.`

Use the Find/Change command to misspell more words (underlined below):

```
Poem #1
Marye had a wittle wamb,
A wittle cheese,
A wittle ham.
Delisious!

Poem #2
Mary had a polar beer
Whose fir was white as snow,
And everywhere that big bare went
The people let it go.
```

17.12 Spell-Checking

Text Editor includes a spell-checker which we can use to find and correct some of the errors in the file `misspelled`:

1. **Pull down the Edit menu and select Check Spelling....**

The spell-checker will search through the file and highlight the first word that appears to be misspelled. The Spelling Checker dialog box will appear, showing the misspelling and a list of possible corrections.

2. Skip or correct the word. Press Skip if you do not want to change the word. (Skip All will cause the spell checker to ignore the word everywhere it occurs in the file.) Or select the desired spelling from the list of alternatives and press Change. (Change All will make the same change throughout the file.)

3. Continue checking and correcting.

4. Close the Spelling Checker window to end the session.

Note that the spell-checker misses some words: beer, fir, and bare. The reason is simple: these are legitimate words in the editor's word list. Remember, the spell-checker does not really check for spelling errors; rather, it looks for groups of characters that do not match those in its word list. Consequently, it will not detect words that are used out of context.

17.13 Closing without Saving

Any changes not saved in a file are lost when you close the Editor. Sometimes, this can be an advantage—you may decide not to keep the changes. Suppose, for example, that you wanted to retain the misspelled words in the file misspelled. If you have not yet saved the corrections made by the spell-checker, simply close the Editor without saving the file:

1. Pull down the File menu and choose Close.

You will be asked whether to save the changes to the file.

2. Select No.

The Editor window will disappear; no changes will be saved in the file.

17.14 Command Summary

File menu

New	open new window for editing
Open...	copy existing file into window for editing
Include	include copy of an existing file in window
Save	copy text from window into current file
Save As...	write text from window into file specified by user
Print	print contents of window
Close	close window and end editing session

Edit menu

Undo	reverse effect of most recent change
Cut	remove selected text from window and place in clipboard
Copy	copy selected text from window into clipboard
Paste	write text from clipboard into window
Clear	replace selected text with spaces
Delete	delete selected text
Select All	select all text in window
Find/Change...	search and replace text in window
Check Spelling...	find and correct spelling errors in window

Format menu

Settings...	set paragraph alignment and margin widths
Paragraph	apply settings to current paragraph
All	apply settings to all text in window

Options menu

Overstrike	allow typing new text over existing text
Wrap to fit	adjust line lengths to fit in window
Status Line	open status line at bottom of window
Backup on Save	make backup copy when file is saved

17.15 Exercises

1. If there are any typos remaining in the file poems, use the editor to correct them.

2. Using the editor, create a new file named 747art and type in the following:

> It is hard to deny, yet rarely said, that the creative impulse was redirected at some point early in this century, or perhaps in the 19th, away from some of its normal artistic channels and into new ones associated with engineering and technology. Quite apart from being useful, a Boeing 747 is a far more impressive aesthetic object than what passes for "art" in our contemporary museums.

> --Tom Bethell

Make sure to copy this into the file before you close the editor.

3. Use the Text Editor Help menu to find information on the Settings available on the Format menu.

4. The Status Line (available on the Options menu) shows (1) the number of text lines in the file; (2) the line where the cursor is located; and (3) whether the Overstrike mode has been selected. Try it.

5. Use the Text Editor Help menu to find out how to format and print a file.

6. What does the Wrap to Fit option do?

7. What do the New and Include options do?

PART V
NETWORKS

# Chapter 18

NETWORKS

Related tutorials are found
in Chapters 19 through 25.

A *network* is a group of computers that are interconnected to share information
and resources. In this chapter, you will learn about networking of computers. You
will also learn about various programs that allow you to communicate with other
computer users.

18.1 Local Area Networks (LANs)

Computer networks are often classified according to size and geographical
coverage. A *Local Area Network* or LAN consists of computers that are close to
one another—often in the same building.

As shown in Figure 18-1, local area networks can be laid out in a variety of
configurations, which are often called *topologies*. Each of these arrangements has
it advantages and drawbacks; however, from the standpoint of the average
computer user, they all appear to be very similar.

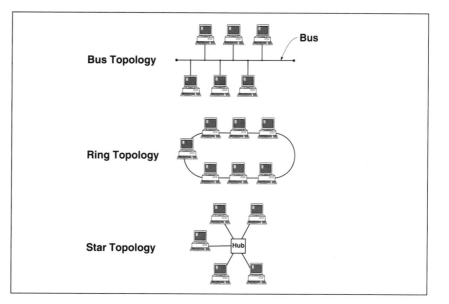

Figure 18-1
Typical topologies for
local area networks
(LANs).

There is no generally accepted definition of how "local" a network must be to qualify as a local area network. Some LANs may be large enough to span a university campus or an entire city—although you may occasionally hear the terms *Campus Area Network* (CAN) or *Metropolitan Area Network* (MAN) used to describe these networks. Any network larger than this is generally called a *Wide Area Network* or WAN.

The most common way to create a WAN is by linking together two or more LANs, as shown in Figure 18-2. The LANs may be located at widely separated sites, perhaps in different cities or even on different continents. Each LAN is equipped with a special-purpose computer called a *gateway* to handle communications with the other LANs making up the network. In many cases, the gateways communicate over a high-speed data channel called a *backbone*.

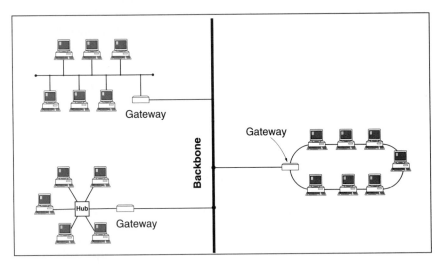

Figure 18-2
A wide area network (WAN) consisting of several LANs connected to a high-speed back- bone.

18.2 The Internet

An internet is a network of networks.

The linking together of networks to form larger networks is called *internetworking*. Networks created this way can themselves be linked together to form still larger networks. The end result of this process, repeated many times, has been the creation of a super-internetwork called the *Internet*. It is now connected to thousands of other networks around the world. The Internet permits users to exchange electronic mail, to transfer files, and to log in and work on remote machines almost anywhere on earth.

The Internet grew out of a government research project. (See "A Brief History of the Internet" on page 219.) But the government does not own the Internet. In fact, no one "owns" any more of the Internet than their particular LAN or WAN. Nor is there a president, CEO, or board of directors for the entire Internet. (However, many of the networks making up the Internet are governed by presidents, CEOs, and/or boards of directors.) The closest thing to a central governing authority for the Internet is a voluntary international organization called the Internet Society

A Brief History of the Internet

What is now known as the Internet originated in work sponsored by the Advanced Research Projects Agency (ARPA), an agency of the U.S. Department of Defense. In the late 1960s, ARPA became interested in creating a long-distance network that could function even when some of its nodes were disabled (such as might happen in a war or other national emergency). The proposed network would use a communication method called *packet-switching*, in which messages are broken into units called *packets* and sent over the network, to be reassembled at their destinations. If part of the network fails, the packets are automatically rerouted to a working part of the system.

ARPA awarded a contract to Bolt Baranek and Newman, a Massachusetts consulting firm, to develop software for a packet-switching network. ARPANET, as it was called, began operations in 1969. It initially linked four computers located at UCLA, Stanford, UC Santa Barbara, and the University of Utah. Other hosts were soon added, at a rate of about twenty per year throughout the 1970s.

A vital step in the development of the Internet occurred in 1974. Vinton Cerf and Robert Kahn described how computers could communicate using TCP/IP (Transmission Control Protocol/Internet Protocol). These protocols were tested on ARPANET, and would in time become the basis for the worldwide Internet.

Although funded by the Defense Department, ARPANET remained essentially a civilian research project. As such, it was not really suited for the day-to-day requirements of the armed forces. A separate military network named MILNET was formed in 1983. Three years later, in 1986, the National Science Foundation (NSF) created the NSFNET to provide access to five national supercomputing centers. NSFNET featured a high-speed, transcontinental backbone.

ARPANET, MILNET, and NSFNET were funded and administered by different agencies; however, they were also interconnected, and it became common to think of them as a single entity. In 1991, Congress made it official by passing the High-Performance Computing Act, which combined all of the government-sponsored networks into one National Research and Education Network, or NREN.

The National Information Infrastructure Act was passed in 1993 to promote private-sector development of the Internet. Government funding was reduced, and the cost of maintaining the Internet backbone was shifted to commercial operators such as MCI, Sprint, and America Online.

The recent growth of the Internet has been phenomenal. It took twenty years to reach 100,000 hosts, but less than three more years to exceed a million hosts. Since then, the number of hosts has been doubling every year or so, with no end in sight.

Other Notable Networks

ARPANET was not open to the general public; most of its host computers belonged to defense contractors or universities doing government-funded research. But the researchers at ARPANET were not the only ones interested in networks. The 1970s and 1980s saw the development of a number of other WANs, some of which are still in existence:

■ **Telenet.** Not to be confused with the `telnet` program, Telenet was a commercial version of ARPANET created in 1974.

■ **UUCP.** The abbreviation UUCP is short for "UNIX to UNIX copy." This is not really a network, but rather a set of programs designed for distributing UNIX software updates and electronic mail over ordinary long-distance telephone lines. However, some people do talk of the "uucp network."

■ **Usenet**. Begun in 1979, the UNIX Users' Network or Usenet was initially intended for sharing information between the University of North Carolina and Duke University using UUCP. Usenet has grown into a decentralized network known for its electronic news groups.

■ **BITNET**. The name is short for "Because It's Time Network." BITNET was started at the City University of New York (CUNY) in 1981. It has since expanded to include more than 2,000 computers around the world. BITNET handles electronic mail, terminal-to-terminal messages, and file transfers.

(ISOC). Various advisory boards and task forces operating under the aegis of ISOC periodically issue whatever rules and standards that are needed to keep the Internet humming along.

18.3 Internet Protocols

A protocol is a set of rules that computers must follow to communicate.

Nearly every type of computer system can communicate over the Internet. This is possible only because everyone using the Internet has agreed to observe certain communications rules, or *protocols*, which govern how messages are sent, received, and interpreted. The most important of these are the *Transmission Control Protocol* (TCP) and the *Internet Protocol* (IP), which are usually lumped together and referred to by their acronyms: TCP/IP.

TCP and IP are designed for communication over dedicated, high-speed transmission lines. Other protocols, intended for use over conventional telephone lines, are the *Point-to-Point Protocol* (PPP) and the older *Serial Line Internet Protocol* (SLIP). Many commercial Internet providers offer PPP (or SLIP) connections to users who do not need (or cannot afford) a full TCP/IP connection.

18.4 IP Addresses and Domain Names

Every host on the Internet has a unique address. An Internet or IP address consists of four numbers separated by periods (usually called "dots"):

`128.46.126.96`

This particular address belongs to a workstation named `fairway`, which is part of the Engineering Computing Network (ECN) at Purdue University. That same host also has a unique name, called a *domain name*:

`fairway.ecn.purdue.edu`

This particular name has four parts:

Not all domain names have four parts. For instance, some hosts are not part of a subnet.

The *top-level domain* or TLD (`edu` in this case) denotes the kind of organization that owns the host. Seven top-level domains have traditionally been used in the United States:

`com`	commercial organization	`mil`	military agency
`edu`	educational institution	`net`	network support organization
`gov`	government agency	`org`	nonprofit organization
`int`	international organization		

Domain names for hosts outside the United States usually indicate the country or region where the hosts are located. Some geographical domains are listed below:

AR	Argentina	DE	Germany	PK	Pakistan
AU	Australia	IN	India	PH	Philippines
AT	Austria	ID	Indonesia	RU	Russia
BR	Brazil	IL	Israel	SA	Saudi Arabia
CA	Canada	IT	Italy	ES	Spain
CL	Chile	JP	Japan	SE	Sweden
CN	China	MX	Mexico	CH	Switzerland
DK	Denmark	NL	Netherlands	TW	Taiwan
FI	Finland	NZ	New Zealand	GB	United Kingdom
FR	France	NO	Norway	US	United States

Other top-level domains have been defined:

aero	air-transport industry	museum	museums
biz	businesses	name	individuals
coop	cooperatives	pro	professionals
info	all users		

18.5 Electronic Mail

One of the most popular features of the UNIX operating system is electronic mail (e-mail or E-mail), which allows you to exchange text messages with other users. There are three standard UNIX mail programs:

■ **Original UNIX mailer** mail. Although superseded by newer mail programs, mail is still available on most UNIX systems.

■ **Berkeley mail program** Mail. This program has more features and is easier to use than the original mail program.

You will see how to use Mail and mailx in the next chapter.

■ **System V mailer** mailx. The x stands for "extended." The mailx program is based on Berkeley Mail.

Of these, the original mail program is not often used. (In fact, some systems are set up so that the mail command calls up one of the other mailers.) In addition to these standard mail programs, your system may offer a choice of other mailers:

■ elm. Written by Dave Taylor in 1986, the elm mailer is a powerful, menu-driven alternative to the standard UNIX mail programs.

You can learn about pine in Chapter 20.

■ pine. From the same people who wrote the pico text editor, pine is intended to be an easy-to-use alternative to elm. (pine stands for "pine is not elm.")

■ RMAIL. The RMAIL program is built into some versions of the emacs editor.

■ mh. Unlike the other mailers listed here, mh is actually a collection of programs rather than a single program. It originated at the Rand Corporation, and is especially useful for handling high volumes of mail. A related program called xmh provides a graphical interface to mh that runs under the X Window System.

Mailer is discussed in Chapter 21.

■ Mailer. The Common Desktop Environment (CDE) includes a powerful mail-handling program called Mailer.

In this book, we will concentrate on the standard mailers Mail and mailx, the pine mail program, and Mailer.

18.6 Internet Mail Addresses

Whichever mail program you prefer, you need to know how to address e-mail. An Internet mail address consists of the recipient's login name, followed by the "at" symbol (@) and the domain name of the recipient's host computer:

adam@fairway.ecn.purdue.edu

1. Start the mail program and enter the recipient's address. To practice, you might specify yourself as recipient:

§ mailx yourlogin (Return)

or

§ Mail yourlogin (Return)

You will be asked for a subject:

Subject:

2. Specify a subject.

Subject: Test Message #3 (Return)

3. Enter your message. For example,

There once was a fellow named Lester,
Whose knowledge grew lesser and lesser.
It at last grew so small,
He knew nothing at all;
So they hired him as a professor.

4. Start the editor. Begin a new line, then type a tilde (~), followed by a *v* (for visual editor), then (Return):

(Return)
~v (Return)
(Return)

This will bring up the vi editor and place your message in the buffer:

There once was a fellow named Lester,
Whose knowledge grew lesser and lesser.
It at last grew so small,
He knew nothing at all;
So they hired him as a professor.
~
~
~
/tmp/Re24223 6 lines, 163 characters

On some systems, the Subject line will also appear in the buffer.

5. Use the vi commands to edit the message. If you are following along with the example, you might try changing "Lester" to "Chester.")

6. When you finish editing, save the changes into the file and quit the editor. Do this with the usual commands:

(Esc) :wq (Return)

This will put you back in the mail program. You may see a prompt of some sort:

(continue)

7. **Send the message.** This is done the usual way:

(Return)

(Control)-(D)

You may be asked to specify carbon copies.

Cc:

8. **Send the carbon copies, if any.** Press (Return) if you do not wish to send any copies:

Cc: (Return)

This will get you out of the mail program and back into the UNIX shell:

§

19.4 Your Mailboxes

The mail program uses two kinds of mailboxes. Your *system mailbox* is a file that holds mail you have received but have not read, deleted, or saved to another file. On many systems, this file is located in the /var/spool/mail directory, and has the same name as your user ID. For example, if your user ID is jdoe, then your system mailbox is the file /var/spool/mail/jdoe.

In addition to the system mailbox, you may have a *personal mailbox*. This is a file named mbox in your home directory. Any mail messages you have read but not deleted or saved in another file are automatically put into your mbox file when you quit the mail program.

Many shells (including sh, ksh, and bash) will check your system mailbox periodically and notify you of any new messages:

New mail has arrived.

You can also use the biff or xbiff program to alert you when new mail arrives. These programs are discussed in the exercises.

19.5 Reading Your Mail

You can read the messages in your system mailbox with the same electronic mail program that you used to send messages:

1. **Start the mail program without specifying a recipient.** How you do this depends on whether your system uses mailx or Mail:

§ mailx (Return)

or

§ Mail (Return)

The mail program will list the messages in your system mailbox:

```
>U 1 yourlogin Thu Nov 22 15:27 15/433 "Test Message #1"
 N 2 yourlogin Thu Nov 22 15:35 27/573
 N 3 yourlogin Thu Nov 22 15:42 19/559 "Test Message #3"
 &
```

The > in the first column points to the current message. A U indicates a previously unread message; N indicates a new message. The messages are numbered (1 through 3 in this case). The login name and address of the sender is shown, along with the date and time the message was received and the number of lines and characters the message contains (lines/characters). The subject of the message is given in quotes.

The ampersand (&) on the last line is the *mail prompt*. It tells you that the mail program is awaiting your instructions. Some systems use a question mark (?) as a prompt.

2. If necessary, list the next screenful of messages. If there are too many messages in your mailbox to list on one screen (perhaps because you have many admirers or have not been keeping up with your mail), you can list the next screenful by typing a z at the mail prompt:

&z (Return)

You can list the previous screenful of messages again by typing z- (z hyphen):

&z- (Return)

To list the current screenful of messages, enter h at the mail prompt:

&h (Return)

3. Select a message to read. To do this, simply type in the message number at the prompt and press (Return). To see the first message, for example, type

&1 (Return)

This will cause the first message to appear:

```
Message 1:
From yourlogin Day Month Time Year
Date: Day Month Time Year
From: yourlogin (Your name)
To: (Your login name)

Subject: Test Message #1

Don't be alarmed.
This is only a test.
&
```

The mail program places some additional lines at the top of a message before sending it on. These lines make up the *mail header*, which contains such information as the name, the login, and the address of the person who sent the message. Note that the mail header makes it difficult to send an anonymous mail message!

Once you have read the message, there are a number of things you can do with it. Without leaving the mail program, you can reply to the message, save it in a file, or delete it.

19.6 Replying to a Message

Next we will see how to respond to e-mail. While you are still in the mail program, use the R ("Reply") command:

1. Enter the Reply command and specify a message number. Thus, to reply to the second message, type

&R1 (Return)

This tells the mail program that you want to reply to the user who sent the first message. The mail program will take care of addressing your reply; it even fills in the Subject field for you.

Subject: Re: Test Message #1

2. Enter your message. This is done as you did before:

What a relief.

3. Send the message. Press (Return), then (Control)-(D):

(Return)
(Control)-(D)

19.7 Saving Messages

You may decide to keep some messages for future reference. You can save a message in a file with the s ("save") command.

■ **Enter the Save command, followed by the message number.** Thus, to save the message 1 in a file named message1.file1, type

&s1 message1.file1 (Return)

This creates a new file in your home directory named message1.file1, and places in it the text of the message, including the mail header. (If you already have a file named message1.file1 in your home directory, the message is appended to the file.) The original message is deleted from your system mailbox. The mail program will tell you that the message has been saved.

19.8   Deleting Messages

Some messages are not worth saving. You should delete these with the d ("delete") command.

1. Enter the Delete command, followed by the message number. For example, to delete the third message, type

&d3 (Return)

Normally, the mail program does not tell you that it has deleted a message. Instead, it will simply show you a mail prompt:

&

2. Check that the message has been deleted. The h ("headers") command will list the messages remaining in the mailbox:

&h (Return)

A deleted message will no longer appear in the list of mail headers.

19.9   Restoring Deleted Messages

What if you delete a message by accident and want to get it back? If you have not exited the mail program, you can retrieve deleted messages using the Undelete command.

■ **Enter the Undelete command, followed by the message number.** For example, to restore the third message, type

&u3 (Return)

19.10   Quitting the Mail Program

The x command is useful when you accidentally deleted a message you want to keep.

There are two common ways you can quit the e-mail program after reading your mail, which differ in what is done to the messages in your mailbox. The q ("quit") command puts any messages that you read, but did not delete, into a file named mbox in your home directory. Unread messages are left in the system mailbox. The x ("exit") command quits the mail program without changing the mailbox, restoring any deleted messages.

Of these, the q command is more commonly used:

■ **Type q, then (Return):**

&q (Return)

Some versions of the mail program will tell how many messages were saved in the mailbox and how many were placed in your mbox file:

```
Saved 1 message....
```

19.11 Reading Your mbox File

Your mbox file receives messages that you have read but have not deleted or saved in another file. The -f ("file") option allows you to read and process the messages in your mbox file, just as you did with the messages in your system mailbox.

1. **Start the mail program with the -f option.**

§ `mailx -f` (Return)

or

§ `Mail -f` (Return)

The mail program will list the messages in your mbox.

2. **Process the messages.** Use the usual mail commands.

3. **Quit the mail program.** Either the q or the x command will do this.

19.12 Using finger

The `finger` utility tells you the real name of the person who has a particular login name. It can be useful when you are trying to guess a person's e-mail address.

■ **Enter the `finger` command, giving the person's login as an argument.** The first time, try it on your own login:

§ `finger yourlogin`(Return)

When entered without an argument, `finger` lists everyone who is currently logged in.

You should see information about the user—in this case, yourself. However, if the `finger` command is not available, the system will say so:

`finger: Command not found`

Some versions of `finger` can tell you the login name, given the user's last name.

■ **Enter the `finger` command, giving the person's last name as an argument.** Try it on your own name:

§ `finger yourname`(Return)

This will produce either a list of users having your last name or an error message.

19.13 Getting Help

Any time you forget what commands are used by `mailx` or `Mail`, type the `?` ("help") command after the mail prompt. This will display a list of commands.

```
h                          print out active message headers
m [user list]              mail to specific users
n                          goto and type next message
p [message list]           print messages
pre [message list]         send messages back to system mailbox
q                          quit (unresolved messages in mbox)
R [message list]           reply to sender (only) of messages
r [message list]           reply to sender and recipients
s [message list] file      append messages to file
t [message list]           type messages (same as print)
top [message list]         show top lines of messages
u [message list]           undelete messages
v [message list]           edit messages with display editor
w [message list] file      append to file, without from line
x                          quit, do not change system mailbox
z                          display next page of headers
z-                         display previous page of headers
!                          shell escape
```

A [message list] consists of integers, ranges of same, or user names separated by spaces. If omitted, Mail uses the current message.

19.14 Command Summary

Some of the commands discussed in this chapter are UNIX shell commands; others work only within `mailx` or `Mail`. All of these commands must be terminated by a (Return).

Reading Mail in Your Mailbox (UNIX shell commands)

`mailx`	list e-mail messages received
`Mail`	list e-mail messages received

Reading Mail in Your mbox File (UNIX shell commands)

`mailx -f`	list messages stored in mbox file
`Mail -f`	list messages stored in mbox file

Listing, Deleting, Saving, and Replying (mailx or Mail command)

z	list next screenful of messages
z-	list previous screenful of messages
d*n*	delete message number *n*
s*n* *file*	save message number *n* in *file*
R*n*	Reply to the sender of message number *n*
r*n*	same as R*n*, but also sends reply to everyone who received the original message

Note that R and r may have the reverse effects on some systems.

^D	send a message

Sending Mail (UNIX shell commands)

`mailx` *user@host*	mail a message to *user@host*
`Mail` *user@host*	mail a message to *user@host*

Mailing a File (UNIX shell commands)

`mailx` *user@host < file*	mail *file* to *user@host*
`Mail` *user@host < file*	mail *file* to *user@host*

Editing a Message Using vi (mailx or Mail tilde escapes)

~v	call up visual editor to edit current message

Identifying a User

`finger` *user*	get the real name of the user with login *user*

19.15 Exercises

1. Find someone with an account on your computer (or on the same network) and practice using mailx or Mail to exchange messages.

2. As you have seen, the s ("save") command is used inside the mail program to append a message to a file. The w ("write") command also appends messages to files. Mail yourself a message, then use the w command to put it into a file. Exit the mail program and examine the contents of the new file. What is the difference between w and s?

3. The mail S ("save") command will save a mail message in a file that has the same name as the sender's login. (If such a file already exists, the message will be appended to the file.) Try out the S command.

4. The mail programs mailx and Mail make use of so-called *tilde escapes*. These are mail commands that begin with a tilde (~). You have seen how to use the tilde escape sequence ~v to edit a message using the vi editor. Find out about other tilde escapes. Start up the mail program as if you were going to send a message. However, instead of typing a message, enter the tilde escape sequence

~? (Return)

to display a list of the tilde escapes. What do the following tilde escapes do?

~p

~h

~q

~r

~s

~x

5. You have seen how to mail a file using the redirection operator on the command line. Thus, to send the file *myfile* to *user@host*, the command is

§ mailx *user@host* < *myfile* (Return)

or

§ Mail *user@host* < *myfile* (Return)

When the message is received, it will not have a subject. You can remedy this using the -s ("subject") option, like this:

§ mailx -s "This is the subject" *user@host* < *myfile* (Return)

or

§ Mail -s "This is the subject" *user@host* < *myfile* (Return)

Try out the -s option by mailing a file to yourself.

6. An electronic mail message may pass through a number of intermediate stops before reaching its destination. The -v ("verbose") option allows you to track the progress of your message as it is delivered:

§ mailx -v *user@host* (Return)

or

§ Mail -v *user@host* (Return)

Try the -v option, preferably on a message that is to travel a long distance.

7. The from command lists the mail headers in your system mailbox without actually starting the mail program. Try it:

§ from (Return)

8. The biff utility alerts you when you receive mail. (Believe it or not, this utility was named for a dog that belonged to a graduate student in the Computer Science Department at the University of California at Berkeley.) You can activate biff with the command line

§ biff y (Return)

To deactivate biff, enter

§ biff n (Return)

When new mail arrives, biff will print a notice, including the login of the sender, the subject line, and the first few lines of the message. Try it.

9. The X client xbiff creates a picture of a mailbox on the screen. When you receive new mail, xbiff emits a sound and raises the flag on the mailbox. You can start xbiff with the command

§ xbiff & (Return)

If you are running X, try out xbiff.

10. Study Appendix H to learn how write and talk work. Then find someone with an account on your computer (or on the same network) and practice using write or talk to exchange messages.

TUTORIAL:
PROCESSING MAIL WITH PINE

In this chapter, you will see how to use the University of Washington's news and mail program pine to send and receive electronic mail. Although pine is not a standard UNIX utility, it is widely available on UNIX systems.

20.1 Starting pine

■ **Start pine.** Enter the pine command at the UNIX shell prompt

§ pine (Return)

You should see the pine Main Menu window, as shown in Figure 20-1.

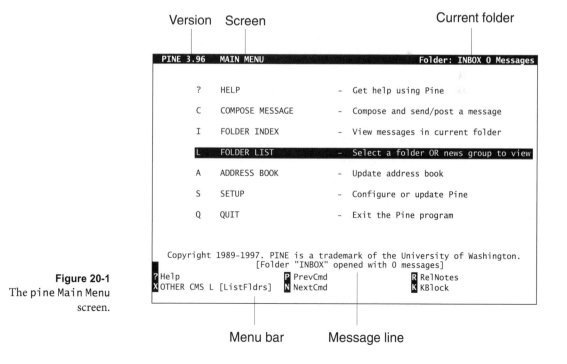

Figure 20-1
The pine Main Menu
screen.

20.2 Composing and Sending a Message

Begin by creating and sending a message to yourself:

1. Choose the Compose Message option. Press the *C* key. The COMPOSE MES-
SAGE screen will appear, as shown in Figure 20-2. Note that the cursor is initially
located in the To: field.

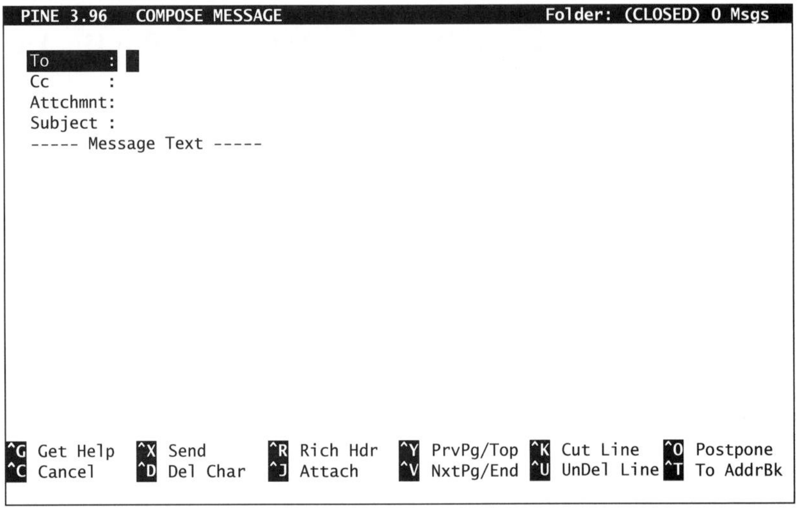

```
  PINE 3.96    COMPOSE MESSAGE                          Folder: (CLOSED) 0 Msgs

    To       : █
    Cc       :
    Attchmnt:
    Subject :
    ----- Message Text -----










  ^G Get Help  ^X  Send      ^R Rich Hdr  ^Y PrvPg/Top  ^K Cut Line   ^O Postpone
  ^C Cancel    ^D  Del Char  ^J Attach    ^V NxtPg/End  ^U UnDel Line ^T To AddrBk
```

Figure 20-2
COMPOSE MESSAGE
screen. The cursor is initially positioned in the
To: field.

Use the arrow keys to move
the cursor.

2. Enter the mail address of the recipient. When you are trying out pine for the
first time, type in your own address and press (**Return**):

To   : *yourlogin@yourhost*(**Return**)

The cursor should now be positioned in the Cc: (Carbon copy) field.

3. Enter addresses of persons who are to receive a copy of the message. If you
do not want to send copies, leave the Cc: field blank. Press (**Return**):

Cc   : (**Return**)

The cursor should now be positioned in the Attchmnt: (Attachment) field.

4. Attach a file. You can attach nearly any UNIX file to your message, even if the
format of the file is one that pine cannot read. Assuming you still have a file
named poems in your home directory, enter this file name in the Attchmnt:
field:

Attchmnt:poems (**Return**)

You should see a message informing you that the file has been attached, and the
cursor should now be located in the Subject: field.

5. Enter a subject. Choose a short title that summarizes the purpose or content of the message:

`Subject :Test Message #1` (Return)

You might wish to review the chapter on `pico`.

6. Compose the message. If you have previously used the `pico` text editor, the `pine` editing tools will be familiar. Enter a simple message:

`Do not be alarmed -- this is only a test.`

7. Send the message. The command is ^X:

(Control)-(X)

You will be asked to confirm that you want to send the message:

`Send message?`

8. Confirm. Enter *Y* for "Yes" (or *N* for "No").

You will be returned to the Main Menu. In the Message Line, you will see a message confirming that the mail was sent:

`[Message sent and copied to sent-mail]`

20.3   Listing Your Folders

In `pine`, a *folder* is a file for holding messages. A new user typically has three mail folders:

- `INBOX` holds messages you have received.

- `sent-mail` holds copies of messages you have sent.

- `saved-messages` holds mail you have saved.

The current folder is listed in the upper right corner of the screen. If the INBOX is listed, you can view its contents using the Folder Index command:

Do this if the current folder is the INBOX.

- **Enter the Folder Index command.** From the `Main Menu`, press the *I* key.

You should see a numbered list of messages received:

These are called mail headers.

```
+ A 1 Aug  9  Jane Doe            (515K)    Re: Good Book
  D 2 Aug 18  jim@MegaMicro.com   (2,011)   Sale!
+ N 3 Aug 20  Your Name           (1,361)   Test Message #1
```

If you see such a list, skip to the next section.

If INBOX is not your current folder, you can use the Folder List command to select it:

1. Enter the Folder List command. From the `Main Menu` screen, press the *L* key:

`L`

What you see now depends on how your account has been set up. In the simplest scheme, the INBOX, sent-mail, and saved-messages will be listed:

INBOX   sent-mail   saved-messages

A collection is a group of related folders.

However, it may be that your system administrator has created separate collections for, say, mail folders and news folders. In that case, you will see a screen that looks something like this:

```
  PINE 3.96    FOLDER LIST                      <mail/[]> sent-mail 0 Msgs


--------------------------------------------------------------------------
Folder-collection <mail/[]>  **Default for Saves**                  (Local)
--------------------------------------------------------------------------
                   [ Select Here to See Expanded List ]


--------------------------------------------------------------------------
News-collection <News on news.server.edu>                          (Remote)
--------------------------------------------------------------------------
                   [ Select Here to See Expanded List ]

```

2. If necessary, view the expanded list in the mail collection. Under the mail collection, highlight the line

[Select Here to See Expanded List]

and press the *V* key:

V

3. View the folder. Use the *P*, *N*, or arrow keys to highlight the INBOX folder, and press *V*:

V

This brings up the FOLDER INDEX screen. You should see a numbered list of mail headers:

These are called mail headers.

```
+ A 1 Aug  9  Jane Doe              (515K)   Re: Good Book
  S 2 Aug 18  jim@MegaMicro.com    (2,011)   Sale!
+ N 3 Aug 20  Your Name            (1,361)   Test Message #1
```

20.4 Mail Headers

Let's examine the structure of the mail header:

```
+ N 3 Aug 20  Your Name            (1,361)   Test Message #1
```

The + at the beginning of the line indicates that the message was sent directly to you—no one else received a carbon copy. This is followed by a letter indicating the status of the message:

N   New message. You have not yet viewed this particular message.

A   Answered message. You have replied to the sender of the message.

S   Saved message. You have saved a copy of the message.

Next comes the message number (3), followed by the date (Aug 20), the name of the sender (Your Name), the size of the message (1,361), and the Subject (Test Message #1).

20.5 Reading Your Mail

Let's retrieve the message you just sent yourself. Assuming that the current folder is the INBOX, follow these steps:

Use the *P, N,* or ↓↑ keys to scroll through the list.

1. **Highlight the message of interest.** Scroll up or down the list of mail headers. (This will not be necessary if you have just one message in your INBOX.)

2. **View the message.** Press the *V* key:

V

This will open a MESSAGE TEXT viewer, in which you will see the body of the message (but not the attachment).

20.6 Viewing and Saving an Attachment

1. **View the attachment index.** From the MESSAGE TEXT viewer, press the *V* key again:

V

This brings up the ATTACHMENT INDEX viewer, which shows a list of items. The first item in the list is the body of the message, while the second is the attachment we are looking for.

2. **View the attachment.** Scroll to the second entry and press the *V* key:

V

This brings up the ATTACHED TEXT viewer, in which the text of the attachment appears.

3. **Save the attachment.** You can copy the attachment into a file in your home directory by pressing the *S* key:

S

You will be prompted for a file name:

Copy attachment to file in home directory:

4. **Specify a file.** Enter a valid file name at the prompt:

Copy attachment to file in home directory: poems.mail (Return)

The mail program will confirm that the message was saved in a file.

5. Return to the message text. You must exit the ATTACHED TEXT viewer and the ATTACHMENT INDEX viewer. Press the *E* key twice:

E
E

You should now see the MESSAGE TEXT viewer.

20.7 Replying to a Message

Let's reply to the message you just read:

1. Use the Reply command. In the MESSAGE TEXT screen, Press the *R* key:

R

You will be asked whether the original message is to be included:

`Include original message in Reply?`

2. Answer Yes. Press the *Y* key:

Y

A COMPOSE MESSAGE screen will appear, with the original message (each line marked by a >) already in place:

`On Aug 20 Your Name wrote:`

`>Do not be alarmed -- this is only a test.`
`>`

3. Compose your reply. This is done using the same editing tools you used before:

`On Aug 20 Your Name wrote:`

`Do not be alarmed -- this is only a test.`
`>`
`Do not worry -- I am not alarmed by your silly test.`

4. Send the message. Remember, the command is ^X:

(Control)–(X)

As before, you will have to confirm that you really want to send the message.

Note that attachments are not normally sent as part of the reply, even when you include the body of the original message in your reply.

20.8   Saving the Message in a Folder

The Save command allows you to save the current message in a pine folder, usually the saved-messages folder. You can do this from the MESSAGE TEXT screen:

1. Use the Save command. Press the *S* key:

S

You will be prompted for the folder name:

SAVE to folder in <mail/[]> [saved-messages]:

The default folder (in this case, saved-messages) is listed in square brackets. Unless you specify another folder, the message will go to the default folder.

Skip this step if the default is saved-messages.

2. If necessary, select the correct folder. Use the To Folders (To Fldrs) command ^T to bring up a list of folders available:

(Control)–(T)

Highlight the saved-messages folder and press *S* (for Select):

[saved-messages]
S

This will return you to the MESSAGE TEXT screen.

The message is copied to saved-messages and deleted from INBOX.

3. Press (Return). You will be told that the message has been copied and deleted:

[Message 3 copied to "saved-messages" and deleted]

4. Check the index. Press the *I* key:

I

The message will be marked for deletion:

+ D 3 Aug 20 Your Name   (1,361) Test Message #1

Expunge means "erase."

The message is not actually deleted at this time; in fact, you can decide to "undelete" the message. When you leave pine, you will be asked if you want to *expunge* the deleted messages from the INBOX.

20.9   Getting Help

You probably noticed that the menu bar in every pine screen includes a Help option. The Help screens in pine are *context-sensitive*, meaning that the content of the screen is selected to be appropriate for the screen you are currently viewing.

1. Select the Help command. From most screens, simply press the *?* key. (In the COMPOSE MESSAGE screen, the command is ^G.)

2. Read the Help screen. You can move to the next page by pressing (Spacebar) (Spc); you can move to the previous page by pressing the *-* key.

3. Exit the Help screen. Press the *E* key:

E

20.10 Quitting pine

1. **Select the Quit command. Press the *Q* key:**

Q

You will be asked to confirm your command:

Really quit pine?

2. **Answer Yes at the prompt.** Press the *Y* key:

Y

20.11 Using finger

The finger utility tells you the real name of the person who has a particular login name. It can be useful when you are trying to guess a person's e-mail address.

■ **Enter the finger command, giving the person's login as an argument.** The first time, try it on your own login:

§ finger *your-login* (Return)

When entered without an argument, finger lists everyone who is currently logged in.

You should see information about the user—in this case, yourself. However, if the finger command is not available, the system will say so:

finger: Command not found

Some versions of finger can tell you the login name, given the user's last name.

■ **Enter the finger command, giving the person's last name as an argument.** Try it on your own name:

§ finger *your-name* (Return)

This will produce either a list of users having your last name or an error message.

20.12   Command Summary

Starting pine (UNIX shell command)

pine   start pine

Main Menu Screen

?   open Help screen

C   open COMPOSE MESSAGE screen

I   view messages in current folder

L   select a folder to view

Q   exit the pine program

COMPOSE MESSAGE Screen

^G   get Help

^C   cancel message

^X   send message

^D   delete character

^Y   go to previous page

^V   go to next page

^K   cut line

^U   undelete line

MESSAGE TEXT VIEWER

?   get Help

V   view ATTACHMENT or ATTACHMENT INDEX

R   reply to message

E   export message to a UNIX file

S   save message in pine folder

ATTACHMENT INDEX VIEWER

V   view attachment

S   save attachment

E   exit viewer

20.13   Exercises

1. Find someone with an account on your computer (or on the same network) and practice using pine to exchange messages.

2. The `pine` mail program allows you to create an address book, containing the names and e-mail addresses of people with whom you correspond frequently. Use the `pine` Help command to see how this is done.

3. One alternative to saving a message in the **saved-messages** folder is to export it to a UNIX file. Use the `pine` Help command to see how this is done.

4. The `from` command lists the mail headers in your system mailbox without actually starting the mail program. Try it:

§ `from` (Return)

5. The `biff` utility alerts you when you receive mail. (Believe it or not, this utility was named for a dog that belonged to a graduate student in the Computer Science Department at the University of California at Berkeley.) You can activate `biff` with the command line

§ `biff y` (Return)

To deactivate `biff`, enter

§ `biff n` (Return)

When new mail arrives, `biff` will print a notice, including the login of the sender, the subject line, and the first few lines of the message. Try it.

6. The X client `xbiff` creates a picture of a mailbox on the screen. When you receive new mail, `xbiff` emits a sound and raises the flag on the mailbox. You can start `xbiff` with the command

§ `xbiff &` (Return)

If you are running X, try out `xbiff`.

7. Study Appendix H to learn how `write` and `talk` work. Then find someone with an account on your computer (or on the same network) and practice using `write` or `talk` to exchange messages.

TUTORIAL:
PROCESSING MAIL WITH MAILER

Skip this chapter if your
system does not run CDE.

The Common Desktop Environment includes Mailer, a powerful program for handling electronic mail. In this chapter, you will see how to use Mailer to compose, send, read, and store messages and attachments.

21.1 Starting Mailer

■ **Start Mailer.** Double-click on the Mailer control on the Front Panel. Note that the Mailer icon appears in one of two forms, depending on whether you have received new mail:

(New mail)

The Mailer main window will appear, as shown in Figure 21-1.

Take a moment to identify the parts of the Mailer window:

■ **Window Menu button, Minimize button, and Maximize/Restore button.** These perform the usual functions on the window.

■ **Title bar.** The title bar lists the pathname of the *mailbox*, which is a file that holds messages you have received.

■ **Header List.** Each message has a *mail header* which lists the message's sender, its subject, the date and time it was sent, and its size. The header for the current message is highlighted. You can select the message to view by clicking on its header.

■ **Message buttons.** Frequently used commands are available by pressing buttons. These commands are also available from the various menus of the Menu bar.

■ **Sash.** By dragging the sash up or down, you can resize the Header List area and the Message View.

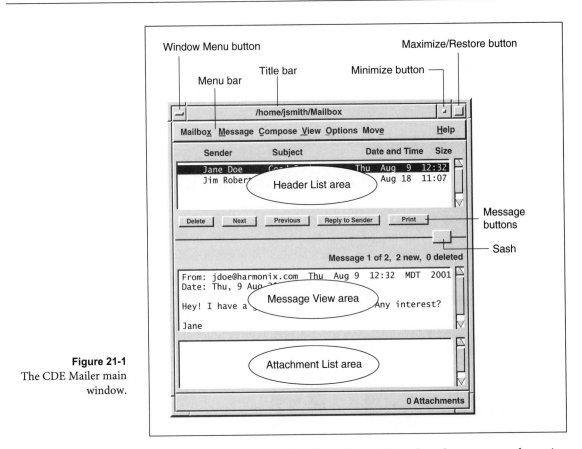

Figure 21-1
The CDE Mailer main
window.

■ **Message View area.** The header and text of the selected message are shown in this area.

■ **Attachment List area.** If there are any attachments to the selected message, their icons will be shown here.

21.2 Composing a Message

If you have a new account, you may not have received any mail yet. However, you can begin by sending a message to yourself:

1. Pull down the Compose menu and choose the New Message option.

The New Message window will appear, as shown in Figure 21-2.

2. Enter the mail address of the recipient in the To: Field. When you are trying out Mailer for the first time, type in your own address and press (**Return**):

yourlogin@yourhost (**Return**)

The Subject: field should now be active.

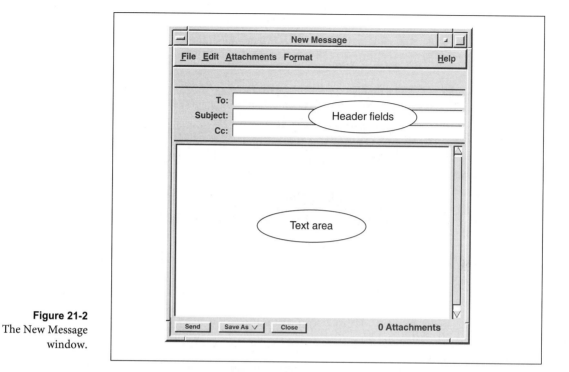

Figure 21-2
The New Message
window.

3. Enter a subject in the Subject: field. Choose a short title that summarizes the purpose or content of the message:

```
Test Message #1  (Return)
```

The Cc: (Carbon copy) field should now be active.

4. Enter addresses of persons who are to receive a copy of the message. If you do not want to send copies, leave the Cc: field blank. Press (Return):

```
(Return)
```

The cursor should now be positioned in the Text area.

5. Compose the message. Composing in the Mailer is very similar to editing with the Text Editor. Enter a simple message:

```
Do not be alarmed -- this is only a test.
```

21.3 Adding an Attachment

An *attachment* is a file that is sent along with an e-mail message. Attachments may be used to transmit plain or formatted text, images, sounds, or executable code. Attaching a file is straightforward:

1. Pull down the Attachments menu and choose Add File. The Attachment menu is found on the Menu bar of the New Message window.

The Mailer Add dialog box will appear.

2. **Select the file to attach.** Try attaching the file poems from your previous work.

3. **Click Add.**

The dialog box will disappear, an Attachment List area will open up below the Text area, and the attachment's icon will be placed on the list.

If you change your mind, you can remove an attachment by selecting the Delete option on the Attachments menu. And if you change your mind again, you can restore the attachment using the Undelete option.

21.4   Sending the Message

Once you have addressed and composed your message and have added any attachments, you are ready to send it:

■ **Send the Message.** Click the Send button on the New Message window.

The New Message window will disappear.

21.5   Reading Your Mail

Let's read the message you just sent yourself:

1. **Pull down the Mailbox menu and select Check for New Mail.**

If the header does not appear, wait and try again.

The new message's header should appear on the Header list.

2. **Highlight the message of interest**. Click on the message's header.

The text of the message will appear in the Message View area.

21.6   Viewing an Attachment

1. **If necessary, open the Attachment list.** Pull down the Attachments menu and select Show List.

The attachment icon should be visible in the Attachment List area.

2. **Open the attachment.** Double-clicking on the attachment icon causes the attachment to open.

21.7   Replying to a Message

Mailer allows you to choose one of four ways to reply to a message:

■ **Reply to the sender only.** Your reply goes only to the person who sent the original message.

■ **Reply to the sender and include the original message.** Your reply will include a copy of the original message, set off by a symbol such as the right angle bracket (>).

■ **Reply to the sender and all recipients.** Your reply goes to the sender of the original message and to anyone on the Cc: list of the original message.

■ **Reply to the sender and all recipients, and include the original message.** The sender and every recipient of the original message will receive your reply, including a copy of the original message. The original message will be set off by a symbol such as the right angle bracket (>).

Let's reply to the message you just received, including the text of the original message in the reply:

1. **Select the message to which you want to reply.** Simply click on the appropriate header in the Header List.

2. **Pull down the Compose menu and choose Reply to Sender, Include.**

A Compose window will appear, having the To: and Subject: fields already filled in for you.

3. **Compose your reply.** This is done using the same editing tools you used before:

```
On Aug 20 Your Name wrote:

>Do not be alarmed -- this is only a test.
>
Do not worry -- I am not alarmed by your silly test.
```

4. **Add an attachment, if desired.**

5. **Send the message.** Press the Send button.

21.8 Saving a Message in a File

The Save as Text command allows you to save the current message in a file:

1. **Select the message to be saved. Click on the message header.**

2. **Pull down the Message menu and select Save as Text.**

A dialog box will appear.

3. **Enter the path or folder name, file name, etc.**

4. **Press Save.**

If there are attachments, you will be given a warning that they will not be saved in the file automatically—you must do this yourself.

21.9 Saving an Attachment in a File

You can also save an attachment in a file:

You can also use the Save As option on the Attachments menu.

1. **Point to the attachment icon and press the right (#3) button.**

A pop-up menu will appear.

2. Select Save As.

A dialog box will open.

3. Enter the path or folder name, file name, etc.

4. Press Save.

21.10 Printing a Message

It is easy to print a hard copy of a message:

1. Select a message. Click on the message header.

The Print One option prints one copy on the default printer.

2. Pull down the Message menu and select the Print... option.

A dialog box will open.

3. Enter the printer name, number of copies, etc.

4. Press Print.

21.11 Deleting a Message

Once you have saved and printed a message, there is no reason to keep it in the inbox:

1. Select the message to be deleted. Click on the message header.

2. Pull down the Message menu and select Delete.

You can also use the Destroy Deleted Messages option on the Mailbox menu.

Deleted messages are not removed from the mailbox immediately—in most cases, they are actually removed (or "destroyed") when you log out. This gives you the chance to retrieve a deleted message using one of the Undelete commands on the Message menu.

21.12 Quitting Mailer

■ **Pull down the Mailbox menu and select Close.**

21.13 Exercises

1. Find someone with an account on your computer (or on the same network) and practice using Mailer to exchange messages.

2. The Signature option on the Options menu allows you to enter text that will be included at the end of every message you send. Create your own signature file.

3. Sometimes you receive a message that you want to pass on to someone else. You can do this by pulling down the Mailbox menu and selecting either Forward or Forward, No Attachments. Try it.

4. You can set up Mailer so that it will send an automatic reply to anyone who sends you a message. This is usually called *vacation mail* because it is convenient when you have to be away from your office for a time. A typical vacation mail message might look something like this:

```
I am on vacation, and will read your message regarding
 $SUBJECT  when I return.
```

The subject line from the original message is inserted in your reply in place of the string $SUBJECT. You can set up a vacation mail message using Vacation Message on the Options menu.

5. Using the View menu, you can choose to list messages by Date/Time, Sender, Subject, Size, or Status. Take some time to try out each of these options. What does the Abbreviated Headers option do?

6. Mailer allows you to create additional mailboxes for organizing mail. Refer to the relevant Help volume to find out how to create, open, and close a mailbox.

7. The Search option on the Message menu allows you to search a mailbox for a particular message. Refer to the relevant Help volume to find out how to use Search.

8. A mail *alias* is an alternate name for one or more users. If you regularly send the same message to a group of users, you can save yourself time by creating an alias for the entire group. For example, you might refer to your friends by the alias *friends*. If you then send a message to *friends*, it will be sent to everyone listed under that alias. Refer to the relevant Help volume to find out how to use the Aliases option

TUTORIAL:
LOGGING IN REMOTELY

Running either `rlogin` or `telnet` on your local UNIX host, you can work on a remote computer system on which you have an account. The difference is that `rlogin` allows you to connect only to another UNIX system; `telnet` can connect to UNIX and non-UNIX hosts.

`rlogin` and `telnet` are security risks. Secure alternatives are discussed in Part VI.

Both `rlogin` and `telnet` transmit data (including passwords) in readable form. To prevent someone from intercepting and reading your data, some system administrators replace `rlogin` and `telnet` with a secure alternative such as Secure Shell (SSH).

22.1 Running rlogin

In this section you will see how to use `rlogin` to log into your account on a remote UNIX host. (If you do not have an account on another machine, you can practice with your local account.)

1. Start the `rlogin` program, specifying the remote host and your remote login name. Thus, if you had an account named `jsmith` on the remote UNIX host `merlin.podunku.edu`, you would type

§ `rlogin merlin.podunku.edu -l jsmith` (Return)

On some systems, that will be enough to get you into the remote system; no password is needed. Other systems will require that you enter a password:

`password:`

2. If necessary, enter the password that you use for the remote host. This may not be the same as the password used on your local host.

3. When you finish working on your remote account, log out from that account. One of the following commands should work (see Chapter 3):

§ `logout` (Return)

§ `exit` (Return)

§ (CONTROL)-(D)

22.2 Running telnet

In this section you will see how to use `telnet` to log into a remote host—either a UNIX or non-UNIX computer—on which you have an account. (If you do not have an account on another machine, you can practice with your local account.)

1. Start the `telnet` program.

§ `telnet` (Return)

You will receive the `telnet` prompt:

`telnet>`

2. Enter the Open command, followed by the Internet address of the remote machine. Thus, if you had an account on `merlin.podunku.edu`, you would type

`telnet> open merlin.podunku.edu` (Return)

The `telnet` program will try to connect to the remote host. If the connection is successfully made, the remote host will display a login prompt:

```
Trying . . .
Connected to merlin.podunku.edu.
Escape character is '^]'

SunOS UNIX (merlin.podunku.edu)
login:
```

3. Log into your remote account. Follow the procedure set out in Chapter 3, "Getting Started." Once you have logged in, you can run the usual UNIX commands (but not the X Window System) on the remote host.

22.3 telnet Commands

When you logged in using `telnet`, you probably noticed a message about an "escape character" that may have looked something like this:

`Escape character is '^]'`

This means that the `telnet` program uses the (Control)-(]) key combination as an escape sequence. (This is not to be confused with the (Esc) key that is used with the `vi` editor.) The `telnet` escape character allows you to suspend your work on the remote host and give commands to the `telnet` program itself.

1. Enter the `telnet` escape character. On most systems, this is the ^] combination:

§ (Control)-(])

The computer will respond with the `telnet` prompt:

`telnet>`

2. Display the list of `telnet` **commands.** Enter a question mark (?) at the prompt:

`telnet> ?` (Return)

The program will respond with a list of commands:

```
close    close current connection
display  display operating parameters
mode     line-by-line or character-at-a-time mode
open     connect to a site
quit     exit telnet
send     transmit special characters
set      set operating parameters
toggle   toggle operating parameters
z        suspend telnet
?        print help information
```

3. Display a detailed command description. To get more information on any of these commands, type the command name followed by a question mark:

`telnet> close ?` (Return)

The `telnet` program will show you a description of the `close` command:

`close   closes current connection`

That does not tell you anything more than you already knew. However, some of the other commands give you considerably more information; take a moment and try them out.

4. Exit the `telnet` **command mode.** This is done by pressing the (Return) key at the `telnet` prompt:

`telnet>` (Return)

This will put you back into your remote UNIX account.

22.4   Ending the telnet Session

Once you have finished working on the remote host, you should log out from that machine and end the `telnet` session.

1. Log out from your remote account. This is done the usual way (see Chapter 3). One of the following commands should work:

§ `logout` (Return)

§ `exit` (Return)

§ (CONTROL)-(D)

When you have logged out, you will see a `telnet` prompt:

```
telnet>
```

At this point you could, if you wish, open another remote session using the **open** command.

2. **Quit the telnet program.** Enter quit at the prompt:

```
telnet> quit (Return)
```

You will see a UNIX shell prompt:

§

22.5   A Shortcut Method

There is a quicker way to run a telnet session:

1. Enter the telnet command, followed by the Internet address of the remote machine. Thus, if you had an account on the host computer merlin.po-dunku.edu, you would type

```
§ telnet merlin.podunku.edu (Return)
```

Eventually, you will see the login prompt:

```
login:
```

2. **Log into your remote account as usual.**

3. **When finished, close the connection.**

```
telnet> close (Return)
```

This will usually log you out of the remote account and quit telnet. You should see a UNIX shell prompt:

§

22.6   Connecting to Guest Accounts

Normally, you must have an account on any remote host to which you want to connect using telnet. However, a number of special telnet accounts exist on the Internet to provide services to the public. There are two ways to log into such an account.

The first—and perhaps most common—method requires that you connect to the host computer using telnet, then log into the account using a special login name and password. (Many systems do not require a password.) For example, you can reach the online catalog of the Washington State University library this way:

```
§ telnet griffin.wsu.edu (Return)
```

When you reach the server, it will prompt you for a login:

```
login:
```

The login to be used is library; no password is required for this particular service.

The second method is to use telnet to log into the server through a special "port," designated by number. It is usually unnecessary to provide either a login or password. For example, Melvyl, the University of California's on-line catalog can be reached using the command line

§ telnet melvyl.ucop.edu 23 (Return)

Note the number 23; this is the port number.

22.7 Command Summary

Each of these commands is typed in after the UNIX prompt, and each is terminated by a (Return). The address of the remote host is represented by *host*.

Remote Login Commands (UNIX shell prompt)

rlogin *host*	log into a remote UNIX computer named *host*
telnet *host*	log into a remote computer named *host*
telnet	start up the telnet program

Telnet Commands (Telnet Prompt)

open *host*	open connection to computer *host*
?	print telnet help
close	close connection to remote host
quit	quit telnet session

22.8 Exercises

1. If you have an account on a remote UNIX machine, log into that account using rlogin.

2. If you have an account on a non-UNIX machine that is connected to the network, log into that account using telnet.

3. Use telnet to connect to the Washington State University library.

4. Use telnet to connect to Melvyl at the University of California.

# Chapter 23

TUTORIAL:
TRANSFERRING FILES

Both `rcp` ("remote copy") and `ftp` ("file transfer protocol") allow you to transfer files between two computer systems on which you have accounts. The `rcp` utility is designed to work with two UNIX systems; `ftp` can also get files from non-UNIX hosts. Moreover, `ftp` can be used to obtain files from public file servers.

Many system administrators replace `rcp` and `telnet` utilities with secure alternatives.

Secure alternatives to `rcp` and `telnet` are discussed in Part VI.

23.1 Running rcp

In this section you will see how to use `rcp` to obtain a file from a remote UNIX host. For `rcp` to work, three conditions must be met:

■ You must have an account on the remote UNIX host.

■ Both hosts must "trust" each other. (That is, certain files exist on each host listing the other as being trustworthy.)

■ You must have permission to copy the file.

Assuming that these conditions are met, the procedure for copying the file is very simple:

■ **Enter the `rcp` command, specifying the remote host and remote file, then the local host and the new file name.** For example, if you wanted to copy the file *myfile* from the remote UNIX host *farhost*, you would type

§ `rcp` *farhost*:*myfile* *mycopy* (Return)

The name of the remote host is separated by a semicolon from the pathname of the file on the remote host. Note that no password is needed. The `rcp` utility will simply refuse to work if you do not have an account on the remote host or the hosts do not trust each other.

23.2 Running ftp

In this section you will see how to use ftp to copy files from a remote host—either a UNIX or non-UNIX computer—on which you have an account.

1. Start the ftp program.

§ ftp (Return)

You will receive the ftp prompt:

ftp>

2. Enter the open command, followed by the Internet address of the remote machine. Thus, if you had an account on farhost.xyz.edu, type

ftp> open farhost.xyz.edu (Return)

The ftp program will try to connect to the remote host. If the connection is successfully made, the remote host will prompt for your login name:

Connected to farhost.xyz.edu.
220 farhost.xyz.edu FTP server (Version 4.179) ready.
Name (farhost.xyz.edu):

3. Enter your login name. Be sure to use the login name for the remote account, not that on your local account, if they are different. For example, if you had an account named smithj on the remote host, you would type

Do not enter smithj
(unless that is your login).
Enter *your* login here.

Name (farhost.xyz.edu): smithj (Return)

The remote host will prompt for your password:

331 Password required for smithj
Password:

4. Enter your password. Of course, the password does not show on screen as you type it.

Enter your password here; it
will not appear on the
screen.

Password:▨▨▨▨▨

You will be notified when you have successfully logged in:

230 User smithj logged in.
ftp>

23.3 ftp Help

The ftp program takes dozens of commands. Fortunately, one of those commands is help, which lists and describes the set of ftp commands.

1. Enter the help command at the ftp prompt. There are two ways to do this. Either type the word help, or a single question mark (?):

ftp> ? (Return)

The computer will respond with a list of commands:

!	dir	nput	rmdir
$	disconnect	nmap	runique
account	form	ntrans	send
append	get	open	status
ascii	glob	prompt	struct
bell	hash	proxy	sunique
binary	help	sendport	tenex
bye	lcd	put	trace
case	ls	pwd	type
cd	macdef	quit	user
cdup	mdelete	quote	verbose
close	mdir	recv	?
cr	mkdir	remotehelp	
delete	mls	rename	
debug	mode	reset	

Some of these are similar to UNIX commands that are already familiar to you (such as cd, ls, mkdir, and pwd). Others are peculiar to the ftp program.

2. Obtain a description of a command. Enter the help or ? command, followed by the command you are interested in. For example, to get a description of the delete command, enter the command line

ftp> ? delete (Return)

The program will respond with a short description of the command that will give you an idea of how it is used:

delete   delete remote file

23.4 Getting a File

One of the reasons to use ftp is to get a copy of a file from a remote host. This is done with the get command.

1. Move to the remote directory containing the file you want. Like the UNIX shell, `ftp` uses the `cd` command to change the working directory. Thus, if you wanted to get a file from the subdirectory `Marsupials`, you would type

Enter the pathname of the directory containing the file you want.

```
ftp> cd Marsupials (Return)
```

Depending on how `ftp` has been set up on your system, you may see a message that looks something like this:

```
250 CWD command successful.
```

2. List the files to find the one you want. With `ftp`, as with the UNIX shell, you can do this with the `ls` command:

```
ftp> ls (Return)
```

This command will list the files in the current directory on the remote host. It usually tells you how many bytes of information were transferred across the network:

```
200 PORT command successful.
150 Opening ASCII mode data connection for file list.
bandicoot
kangaroo
opossum
wombat
226 Transfer complete
38 bytes received in 0.0042 seconds (8.9 Kbytes/sec)
```

3. Select the file transfer mode. As far as `ftp` is concerned, there are two types of files. An *ASCII file* contains text; a *binary file* contains other kinds of information (such as graphics, audio recordings, or compressed text). Depending on the type of information that is in the file, enter either `ascii` or `binary` at the `ftp` prompt:

```
ftp> ascii (Return)
```

The `ftp` program will confirm your selection:

```
200 Type set to A.
>
```

4. Get the file. Enter the `get` command, followed by the name of the original file, then the name you want to give the local copy. For example, suppose you want to get a copy of the file `wombat` from the remote host, and that you want to name it `wombat.copy` on your local host. You would enter this line:

```
ftp> get wombat wombat.copy (Return)
```

In most cases, `ftp` will inform you that the transfer was successful:

```
200 PORT command successful.
150 Opening ASCII mode data connection for wombat (7014
```

```
bytes)
226 Transfer complete
7224 bytes received in 0.8 seconds (8.8 Kbytes/sec)
ftp>
```

23.5 Sending a File

Using ftp, you can also send a file from your local host to the remote host—the reverse of the operation described in the previous section. This is done with the put command.

1. Specify the file type. Remember, ftp distinguishes between ASCII files containing text and binary files containing other kinds of information (graphical, audio, etc.). Select the proper file transfer mode by entering either ascii or binary at the ftp prompt:

```
ftp> ascii (Return)
```

The ftp program will confirm your selection:

```
200 Type set to A.
>
```

2. Send the file. Enter the put command, followed by the name of the original file, then the name you want to give the remote copy. For example, suppose you wanted to send a copy of the file meeting.events from the local host, and that you want to name it meeting.events.copy on your remote host. You would enter this line:

```
ftp> put meeting.events meeting.events.copy (Return)
```

ftp will inform you that the transfer was successful:

```
200 PORT command successful.
150 Opening ASCII mode data connection for meeting.events
226 Transfer complete
local: meeting.events  remote: meeting.events.copy
2878 bytes received in 0.033 seconds (86 Kbytes/sec)
ftp>
```

23.6 Ending the ftp Session

Once you have finished working on the remote host, you should end the ftp session.

■ **Quit the ftp program.** Enter quit at the ftp prompt:

```
ftp> quit (Return)
```

You will see a UNIX shell prompt:

§

23.7 A Shortcut Method

There is a quicker way to run an `ftp` session:

1. Enter the `ftp` command, followed by the Internet address of the remote machine. Thus, if you had an account on the host `farhost.xyz.edu`, you would type

§ `ftp farhost.xyz.edu` (Return)

2. Log into your remote account as usual. This will require that you enter your login and password at the appropriate prompts.

3. When finished, close the connection using the `quit` command.

`ftp> quit` (Return)

This will log you out and quit `ftp`. You should see a UNIX shell prompt:

§

23.8 Getting Files with Anonymous ftp

Originally, `ftp` was intended to allow you to transfer files between two computers on which you have accounts. However, *anonymous* `ftp` allows you to get files from hosts on which you do not have an account. These hosts are called *public ftp servers*.

For example, the United States Census Bureau maintains a server that you can reach by anonymous `ftp`.

1. Start the `ftp` program and specify the server you want. For example, to connect to the Census Bureau's public `ftp` server, you would enter the command

§ `ftp ftp.census.gov` (Return)

When you reach the server, it will identify itself and prompt for your login name:

```
Connected to ftp.census.gov.
220-          U.S. Department of Commerce, Bureau of Census
220-************************************************************
```

Various warning and disclaimers appear here. ─────────────────────────

```
220 blue.census.gov FTP server ready.
Name (ftp.census.gov:yourlogin):
```

2. Enter the guest login name at the prompt. Some servers expect you to enter "`guest`" as your login; others require "`anonymous`." For the Census Bureau server, use "`anonymous`":

The server will notify you that it has accepted the login name; it may also prompt you for a password:

Some servers require you to enter "guest" as your login name.

```
Name (ftp.census.gov:yourlogin): anonymous (Return)
```

```
331 Guest login ok, send e-mail address as password.
Password:
```

3. If necessary, enter the guest password. Some systems require no password; others use "guest" or "anonymous." The Census Bureau server asks for your e-mail address. Thus, if your address were jsmith@merlin.podunku.edu, you would enter this at the prompt:

Enter the required guest password here; it will not appear on the screen.

```
Password:▮▮▮▮▮▮▮▮
```

4. Use ftp commands to find and transfer files.

5. When you are finished, quit ftp as before.

23.9 File-Compression Programs

Large files are often compressed to save storage space and decrease the time needed to transfer them over the network. Depending on the file and the compression technique, a compressed text file may occupy as little as 40% of the memory required by the original.

A compressed file is typically distinguished from a normal file by a file name suffix, which indicates the program that was used to compress the file. Some of the more common compression/decompression programs, and their file name suffixes, are listed in Table 23-1.

Table 23-1
File compression/decompression programs.

Compression	Decompression	Suffix	Sample File Name
compress	uncompress, zcat	.Z	textfile.Z
cpio	cpio	.cpio	textfile.cpio
gzip	gunzip	.gz	textfile.gz
pack	unpack	.z	textfile.z
pax	pax	.pax	testfile.pax
Stuffit	unsit	.Sit	textfile.Sit
Packit	unpit	.pit	textfile.pit
PKZIP	PKUNZIP	.ZIP	textfile.ZIP
tar	tar	.tar	textfile.tar

Strictly speaking, `cpio`, `tar`, and `pax` are not compression programs; they are *file archive programs*. Such programs can combine a number of files and directories into a single file—called an *archive file*—for storage on tape or transferring across the Internet. An archive file is often compressed before it is transferred.

Of the programs listed above, `compress` and `tar` are the ones most commonly found on UNIX systems. The procedure for preparing a file or set of files for compression using `tar` and `compress` is fairly straightforward, as you will see in the next few sections.

23.10 Creating an Archive File

The `tar` program is normally used to prepare multiple files and directories for storage or transfer. If you are working with just one file, you will probably not bother with `tar`; in that case, skip this section.

1. Create an archive file using `tar`. To archive all of the files in a directory, run the `tar` program with the `-cf` option, giving a name for the archive file and specifying the directory that is to be processed. Thus, to create an archive file named `marsupials.tar` containing the files from the `Marsupials` directory, you would enter

Here, `-c` means "create"; f peceeds the `tar` file. ────────/

§ `tar -cf marsupials.tar Marsupials` (Return)

2. Check that the `tar` file has been created. Enter the `ls` command to list the files:

§ `ls` (Return)

You should see the names of both the original directory and the `tar` file:

Note that `tar` does not alter the original directory.

`Marsupials marsupials.tar`

3. Verify the contents of the `tar` file. This is done with the `-t` ("table of contents") option:

§ `tar -tf marsupials.tar` (Return)

The `tar` program will list the files that were bundled together to make the archive file. Next, the `tar` file will need to be compressed.

23.11 Compressing Files

The most common compression program found on UNIX systems is `compress`, which is very simple to operate:

1. Compress the file. This is done by typing the `compress` command, followed by the name of the file to be compressed:

§ `compress marsupials.tar` (Return)

2. Check that the compressed file has been created. Once again, enter the `ls` command to list the files:

§ `ls` (Return)

You should see the names of both the original directory and the newly compressed file:

The `compress` *program attaches the .Z suffix automatically.*

`Marsupials marsupials.tar.Z`

Once you have compressed the file, it is ready to be transferred by `ftp`. When using `ftp` to send a compressed file, be sure to specify `binary` (not `ascii`) file transfer type.

23.12 Uncompressing Files

Once the compressed file has been transferred to its destination, it must be uncompressed. The `uncompress` command is used to restore files that have been processed with `compress`. If you are working with a compressed `tar` file, you should uncompress it before untarring it.

1. Enter the `uncompress` command, followed by the name of the file to be restored. The file should have the `.Z` suffix:

§ `uncompress marsupials.tar.Z` (Return)

2. List the files. The compressed file will be gone, replaced by its uncompressed version:

§ `ls` (Return)
`marsupials.tar`

In this example, the uncompressed file is an archive (`tar`) file; you must "untar" it to convert it back into a directory.

23.13 Restoring tar Files

The `tar` command is used with the `-x` ("extract") option to restore an archive file:

1. If necessary, create a directory to hold the untarred files. In this case, create a directory named `Marsupials2`:

§ `mkdir Marsupials2` (Return)

Some versions of `tar` *do not allow the* `-C` *option, but put the untarred file in the current directory.*

2. Enter the Extract command. Type `tar -xf`, followed by the name of the `tar` file, the `-C` ("change directory") option, and finally the name of the directory where you want the untarred directory to go:

§ `tar -xf marsupials.tar -C Marsupials2` (Return)

3. Check the directory. The newly untarred `Marsupials` directory should appear inside the `Marsupials2` directory:

§ ls Marsupials2 (Return)
Marsupials

If you list the contents of the Marsupials directory, you should see the files contained.

23.14 Command Summary

Each of the UNIX commands listed here is typed at the shell prompt and terminated by (Return). Each of the ftp commands is typed at the ftp prompt and terminated by (Return).

Remote Copy Command (UNIX shell prompt)

rcp *farhost:file mycopy*	copy *file* from *farhost* as *mycopy*

File Transfer Commands (UNIX shell prompt)

ftp *farhost*	log into a remote computer named *farhost*
ftp	start up the ftp program

ftp Commands (ftp Prompt)

open *farhost*	open connection to computer *farhost*
?	print ftp help
get *file mycopy*	get remote *file*; save locally as *mycopy*
put *file mycopy*	send local *file* to remote host as *mycopy*
quit	close connection to remote host

tar Commands (UNIX Shell Prompt)

tar -cf *file.tar Dir*	make tar file *file.tar* from directory *Dir*
tar -tf *file.tar*	print table of contents for *file.tar*.
tar -xf *file.tar Dir*	extract file(s) from *file.tar* to directory *Dir*

compress Commands (UNIX Shell Prompt)

compress *file*	compress *file* (creates file named *file.Z*).
uncompress *file.Z*	restore *file.Z*

# Chapter 24

COMPUTER SECURITY

Good computer security can prevent the unauthorized use—or misuse—of computer resources. Inadequate computer security can be costly:

■ In January 2000, the names, addresses, and credit card information belonging to 200,000 customers were stolen from an online business. The thief attempted to extort money from the business; when no payment was made, information belonging to some 25,000 customers was posted on a Web site.

■ In May 2002, a Queensland (Australia) court sentenced a computer technician to two years in jail. He had deliberately caused an automated sewage system to dump a million liters of raw sewage into public parks and streams.

■ In December 2002, federal prosecutors charged a former Wall Street systems administrator with securities fraud. They alleged that the systems administrator planted a "logic bomb" designed to delete files on more than a thousand of his employer's computers. He had purchased stock options hoping to profit when the company's stock price fell.

In an annual survey of computer security professionals conducted by the Computer Security Institute (CSI) and the Federal Bureau of Investigation (FBI), 70% of respondents reported attacks on their computer systems. The CSI/FBI estimated that 251 organizations lost a total of $202 million in 2002 because of computer security problems.

24.1 Attacks

We can identify three general categories of attacks on computer systems:

■ **Information theft.** Information theft occurs when private data is read or copied by an unauthorized person.

■ **Intrusion.** In an intrusion attack, an unauthorized user gains access to the computer system and its resources. An intruder might delete or alter files, bring the computer system down, or use the computer to launch attacks on other systems.

Hackers, Crackers, Phreakers, and Script Kiddies

Journalists frequently use the term "hacker" to refer to anyone who compromises computer security. Originally, however, a *hacker* was someone who was especially skillful or clever at programming.

A *cracker* is someone who intentionally circumvents security measures so as to break into ("crack") a computer system. Crackers may do this simply for the challenge, or they may have malicious intent. (A system administrator may hire a *tiger team* of crackers—called *sneakers* or *samurai*—to test system security.)

Phreakers are crackers who specialize in exploiting security holes in the telephone network, with the goal of making long-distance telephone calls without paying for them.

Script kiddies are fairly unsophisticated crackers who use programs ("scripts") written by others to detect and exploit holes in computer security.

Despite the attention given to crackers in the press, insiders—disgruntled employees and careless users—pose the greatest danger to computer security.

■ **Denial of service.** A denial-of-service attack prevents the legitimate use of computer resources by authorized users. The most direct way to do this is to cut the wire connecting the computer to the outside world (a *physical or infrastructure denial-of-service* attack). More common are various methods of flooding the computer system with more data than it can handle.

All three kinds of attacks may be carried out in concert. Thus, a "sniffer" program may be used to intercept usernames and passwords sent over the Internet (information theft), enabling unauthorized users to log into computer accounts that do not belong to them (intrusion), from which they can attempt to overload other computers (denial of service).

Attacks may be pressed directly by individuals or groups (see "Hackers, Crackers, Phreakers, and Script Kiddies," this page) or by malicious programs (see "Trap Doors, Viruses, Trojan Horses, and Worms," next page).

24.2 Traditional UNIX Security

In the old days of mainframes, security meant keeping the computer safe behind glass and locked doors. Only a few trained computer operators were allowed to have direct access to the machine. The machines themselves were not generally connected to other machines, and programs ran in batch mode.

Trap Doors, Viruses, Trojan Horses, and Worms

Occasionally, computer programmers will deliberately create a *back door* or *trap door*, which is a secret hole in a system's security. For example, a system designer may provide a special back door that will allow a service technician to gain access without an account or password. This convenience comes at the price of reduced security. A cracker who discovers the backdoor will be able to enter the system also.

A *logic bomb* is destructive code lurking in a program—such as an operating system or application—that performs some undesirable action when certain conditions occur. For example, a logic bomb might cause the system to crash at noon on a certain date. Logic bombs may be unintentional (the result of bad programming) or deliberate.

A *trojan horse* is a malicious program disguised as a benign one. When run by an unsuspecting user, a trojan horse appears to do something useful while also doing something destructive in the background. A *mockingbird* is a type of trojan horse that mimics a login program for the purpose of collecting login names and passwords.

A *virus* is a computer program that attaches itself to another program or data file. A virus program may install a back door, trojan horse, or logic bomb. Most viruses infect personal computers running some version of Microsoft Windows; few viruses have been created to infect Unix systems.

A *worm* is a program that makes copies of itself and sends them over a network to infect other systems.

UNIX was designed from the start as a multiuser, time-sharing OS. One of the challenges was to allow authorized users access to the computer while keeping each user's data secure from the others. From the user's standpoint, UNIX security involves three processes:

■ **Authentication.** To use their UNIX accounts, users are required to prove their identities by providing a password. The process of proving one's identity is called *authentication*.

■ **Access control.** Authorized users are given personal accounts on the computer, and are able to prevent anyone else from using their files without permission.

■ **Encryption.** Sensitive data can be kept from prying eyes by encryption—that is, by transforming the data to be unreadable by someone who does not possess the proper "key." The Unix password file is encrypted to prevent anyone from reading passwords.

These three themes—authentication, access control, and encryption—recur throughout our discussion of computer security. We will have more to say about each one later.

24.3 UNIX Security Holes

The designers of UNIX wanted to promote information sharing; their primary concern was not security. UNIX systems have traditionally offered a number of utilities for working between multiple computer accounts and multiple hosts:

■ `ftp` (file transfer program) allows a user to transfer files to and from a remote host.

■ `rcp` (remote file copy) copies files between UNIX machines.

■ `rlogin` (remote login) opens a terminal for running commands on a remote host.

■ `rsh` (remote shell) executes shell commands on a remote host.

■ `telnet` is used to communicate between hosts using the TELNET protocol.

Unfortunately, because these utilities transmit unencrypted passwords, a cracker can use a "sniffer" program to intercept the passwords as they travel over the network.

Even worse, the traditional *r-utilities* `rcp`, `rlogin`, and `rsh` allow users to bypass the password requirement entirely. Users may place a file named `.rhosts` ("remote hosts") in their remote accounts containing a list of hosts and user accounts that are to be "trusted." When the `.rhosts` file is used, the *r*-utilities allow remote access from a trusted account on a trusted host without a password.

Unfortunately, the `.rhosts` file creates a serious security hole for any computer connected to the Internet. A cracker can masquerade as a trusted user—a technique called *spoofing*—to gain access to an account without a password. The cracker then has easy access to the accounts listed in the `.rhosts` file.

The X Window System opens up other potential security holes. Data traveling over the network between the X client and server can be intercepted and read.

Various secure alternatives to the traditional remote-computing utilities have been developed. One of the most popular is Secure Shell (SSH), which is discussed in Section 24.10 and in Chapters 25 and 26.

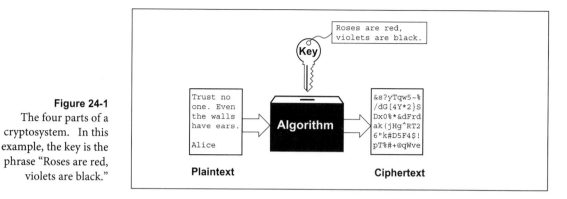

Figure 24-1
The four parts of a cryptosystem. In this example, the key is the phrase "Roses are red, violets are black."

24.4 Cryptography

Cryptography (literally "hidden writing") may be defined as the art and science of concealing the meaning of communications. As shown in Figure 24-1, cryptography generally involves four components:

■ **Plaintext.** The original, unencrypted message is called *plaintext* or *cleartext*. The purpose of an encryption scheme is to conceal the meaning of the plaintext to make it unreadable by unauthorized persons.

■ **Ciphertext.** A message that has been encrypted is called *ciphertext* or *cryptogram*.

■ **Algorithm.** In general, an *algorithm* is a finite sequence of steps that will accomplish a given task. The task for an *encryption algorithm* is to transform plaintext into ciphertext (or vice versa).

■ **Key.** An *encryption key* is information—such as a word, number, or phrase—that is required by a cryptographic algorithm to encrypt or decrypt a message. All other things being equal, the longer and more random the key, the more secure the encryption.

Altogether, the algorithm, keys, plaintext, and ciphertext constitute what is called a *cryptosystem*.

In the following sections, we will consider three types of cryptosystems: secret-key encryption, public-key encryption, and one-way encryption.

24.5 Secret-Key Encryption

Figure 24-2 shows the process of *secret-key encryption*. Also called *conventional* or *symmetric* encryption, this approach uses the same key to encrypt and decrypt a message.

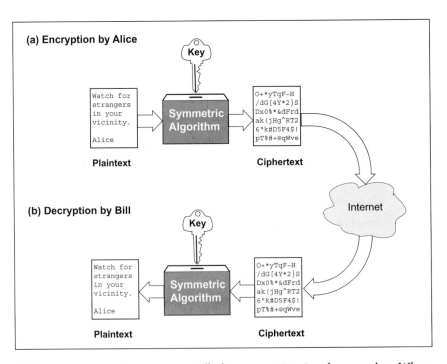

Figure 24-2
Secret-key encryption.
(a) Alice uses the secret
key for encryption.
(b) Bill uses the same
key for decryption.

If Alice wants to send a message to Bill, she encrypts it using the secret key. When he receives the encrypted message, Bill uses the same key and algorithm to decrypt it. If Stan intercepts the message, he cannot easily decrypt it because he lacks the key.

Secret-key cryptosystems have the advantage of being fast and relatively secure. However, such systems have one huge weakness: How do you distribute the key to authorized users while ensuring that other parties do not get the key as well?

Popular secret-key encryption methods include 3DES (Triple Data Encryption Standard), Blowfish, IDEA (International Data Encryption Algorithm), and AES (Advanced Encryption Standard).

24.6 Public-Key Encryption

Figure 24-3 depicts *public-key encryption*, which is also called *asymmetric* encryption. This approach uses two keys, one to encrypt, the other to decrypt. The public key (as the name implies) may be known by everyone. In contrast, the private key is kept secret by its owner.

If Alice wants to send a secret message to Bill, she uses Bill's public key to encrypt it. When he receives the message, Bill uses his private key to decrypt it. If Stan happens to intercept the message, he cannot read it because he lacks Bill's private key.

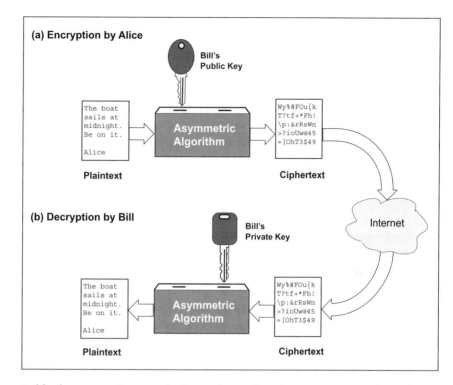

Figure 24-3
Public-key encryption.
(a) Alice uses Bill's public key for encryption.
(b) Bill uses his private
key for decryption.

Public-key encryption can also be used to authenticate messages, as shown in Figure 24-4. A message encrypted with a person's private key can be decrypted by anyone using the sender's public key. Thus, Bill can encrypt a message using his private key and send it to Alice, Mary, and Jane. They can decrypt the message using Bill's public key and be assured that it is an authentic message from Bill (or someone using Bill's private key). If Stan tries to impersonate Bill by sending a message that was encrypted using a different private key, the message will not decrypt properly using Bill's public key.

The advantage of public-key encryption is that it reduces (but does not entirely eliminate) the key-management problem: there is no need to figure out how to arrange a secure channel for distributing a secret key to the proper users.

The disadvantage of public-key encryption is that it requires much more computation—and is therefore much slower—than conventional secret-key encryption. (One way to overcome this speed disadvantage is to use a secret-key algorithm to encrypt a long message, then use a public-key algorithm to encrypt the message key.)

The best known public-key algorithm is RSA (for Rivest, Shamir, and Adleman, its developers). Other public-key systems are associated with the names Diffie-Hellman and ElGamal.

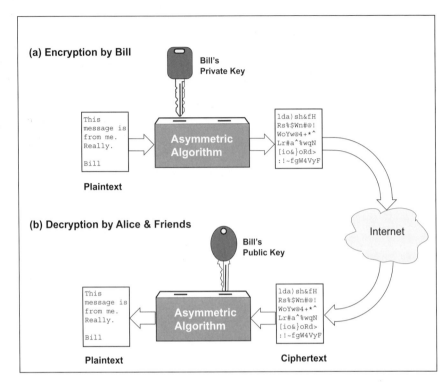

24.7 One-Way Encryption

Figure 24-5 shows the process of *one-way encryption*, which uses an algorithm called a *hash function*. In general, a hash function takes input text and converts it into a single string called the *message digest, hash value, or fingerprint*. Hash functions have a variety of applications in computer science.

In general, a hash function accepts input text of any length and produces a single string of fixed length. In other words, regardless of the size of the input, the hash value is always the same length.

For cryptographic use, a hash function should not be invertible—that is, given the hash value, it should be impossible to compute or guess the original text from the hash value, even if the hash algorithm is known. Consequently, the hash function can be used to encrypt a message but not decrypt it.

At first glance, a encryption scheme that cannot be reversed might seem useless, even silly—much like a lock that can be closed but not re-opened. However, one-way encryption is used in a surprising variety of ways:

No one but you ever needs to know your password.

■ **Password security.** Using a one-way hash function, the password is encrypted and stored in the passwd file. When the user logs in and provides a password, it can be encrypted with the same hash function and compared with the encrypted password on file. If the two match, the proper password was given. Decryption is

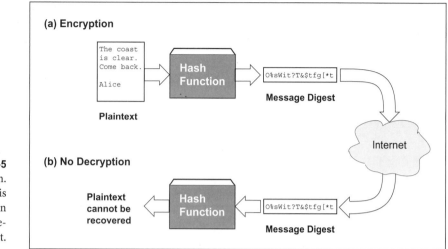

Figure 24-5
One-way encryption.
The hash function is
used for encryption
only; it is not used to re-
cover the plaintext.

never needed because the user already knows his or her own password, and there is no reason for anyone else to know it.

■ **Key generation.** The best key for a conventional encryption method would be a long string of random characters. However, a long, random key is difficult to remember. Some encryption systems employ a hash function to create a random key from an easily remembered password or passphrase supplied by the user.

■ **Data integrity.** A hash function can be used to ensure that a message has not been garbled in transmission. To see how this is done, suppose that Alice wishes to send a file to Bill as an e-mail attachment. She uses the hash function to compute a hash value for the attachment and includes the hash value in her e-mail message. When Bill receives the message, he makes a copy of the attached file and runs the same hash function on it. He then compares the resulting hash value to the one Alice provided. If the two hash values match, the file has not been garbled. (For added security, Alice can encrypt the hash value using her private key to make sure that no one intercepts the message and substitutes their own hash value and file attachment.)

24.8 Enhanced Authentication

To protect sensitive computer systems—especially those connected to the Internet—a number of measures are used to supplement the traditional UNIX password security system:

■ **One-time passwords.** To foil crackers who try to steal or guess passwords, users are admonished to change their passwords frequently. Taken to the extreme, the password could be changed at the end of each login session, although this would be inconvenient if done using the `passwd` command. Instead, a one-time password system automatically generates a new password for each remote login. The most widely used one-time password systems are S/Key and OPIE ("One-time Passwords in Everything").

■ **Physical tokens.** In addition to a password, some systems require that the user display some kind of token such as a smart card or a special badge.

■ **Biometrics.** Physical tokens can be lost, stolen, or forged. Some systems rely instead on distinctive physical characteristics such as fingerprints, retinal scans, or voiceprints.

■ **Authentication servers.** An authentication server performs authentication for other systems on a local network. The best known example is the Kerberos system from MIT. A user who requests a service (such as printing a file on a network printer) must first be approved by the authentication server, which issues a temporary "ticket" authorizing the requested service.

24.9 Internet Access Control

File permissions are discussed in Chapter 6.

We have already seen how to restrict access to files using the chmod utility. Access control becomes much more difficult with networked computers. Various hardware and software measures are used to provide better access control:

■ **Firewalls.** A firewall is a system designed to restrict access to a computer or network. A firewall may be implemented as hardware or software (or both). Most firewalls perform *packet filtering*, a process in which incoming and outgoing IP packets are examined according to a set of rules. Only those packets which satisfy certain criteria are allowed to pass. A firewall may also prevent outsiders from discovering the structure of the protected network.

■ **Proxy servers.** A proxy server is similar to a firewall in that both control access to resources on a private network. A proxy server, however, sits between a client and a server and examines requests for services made by the client. The proxy server determines whether the request should be forwarded to the server.

■ **Content filters.** A content filter examines an e-mail message or web page to determine whether it is suitable for transmission. Those that are deemed objectionable are prevented from passing. For example, parents may install a content server to prevent their children from viewing web pages containing pornographic or violent images.

24.10 Secure Shell

SSH is pronounced letter-by-letter: "S-S-H."

Secure Shell (SSH) uses strong encryption to make secure network connections between computers. Despite its name, SSH is not really a shell—a command interpreter—but rather a secure alternative to the UNIX "r-commands":

■ scp (secure file copy) copies files between UNIX machines. It is a secure replacement for the original rcp (remote file copy) utility.

Security Acronyms

Here is a selection of important acronyms related to secure computing on the Internet:

IPSec. The Internet Engineering Task Force has developed the *IP Security Protocol* (IPSec) as a standard for secure communications on the Internet.

SSL. Netscape Communications Corporation developed the *Secure Sockets Layer* (SSL) to provide secure and private transmission over the Internet. SSL is optimized for HTTP, but also handles FTP and TELNET.

SHTML. The *Secure Hypertext Markup Language* or SHTML was designed for providing security for financial transactions over the Web.

S/MIME. The *Secure Multi-Purpose Internet Mail Extensions* (S/MIME) add digital signatures and encryption to the original MIME standard for electronic mail.

TLS. Based on SSL, *Transport Layer Security* (TLS) is another protocol for secure and private transmission over the Internet.

VPN. Organizations can avoid the expense of setting up their own computer networks by creating a *Virtual Private Network* (VPN) instead. A typical VPN connects computers via the Internet, encrypting all communications to prevent unauthorized access.

- `slogin` (secure login) opens a terminal for running commands on a remote host. It replaces `rlogin` (remote login).

- `ssh` (secure remote shell) is a secure alternative to `rsh` (remote shell), which executes shell commands on a remote host.

SSH can also serve as a secure replacement for `ftp` (file transfer program) for transferring files to and from a remote host, and for `telnet` for remote access using the TELNET protocol.

Used generically, the name Secure Shell refers to a protocol. Recall that a protocol is a set of communications rules that govern how messages are to be sent, received, and interpreted. The SSH protocol deals with authentication, encryption and data integrity.

Two different SSH protocols exist. The original Secure Shell protocol was written in 1995 by Tatu Ylönen at the Helsinki University of Technology in response to an attack on the university's computer network. This was Secure Shell Version 1, denoted SSH-1.

Later in 1995, Ylönen founded SSH Communications Security Ltd. to develop and commercialize Secure Shell. This was followed by a number of revisions of the original SSH-1 protocol (most notably SSH-1.3 and SSH-1.5).

In 1996, SSH Communications Security Ltd. introduced a new protocol, called SSH-2. The new protocol addresses a number of weaknesses in SSH-1 and provides additional functionality.

SSH-1 is discussed in the next chapter; SSH-2 is discussed in Chapter 26.

SSH-1 and SSH-2 are related, but incompatible, protocols. That is to say, a program that uses only SSH-1 will not be able to communicate with one that uses only SSH-2. Fortunately, many SSH-2 products are also backwardly-compatible with SSH-1.

Anyone is free to write a software product that implements the SSH protocols. Dozens of such products are available for UNIX and non-UNIX operating systems, including the Amiga, BeOs, Java, Mac OS X, OS/2, Palm Pilot, VMS, and Windows. Some of the better known SSH products are listed below:

- SSH1 and SSH2 from SSH Communications Security Ltd. (`www.ssh.com`)

- OpenSSH from the OpenBSD project (`www.openssh.com`)

- F-Secure SSH from F-Secure Corporation (`www.f-secure.com`)

- SecureCRT from VanDyke Software (`www.vandyke.com`)

A list of SSH implementations may be found on the following web site:

`http://www.freessh.org`

The authors of *SSH, The Secure Shell: The Definitive Guide* compare a number of commercial SSH products on their web site:

`http://www.snailbook.com/software.html`

24.11 Pretty Good Privacy (PGP)

Phil Zimmermann wrote Pretty Good Privacy (PGP) to bring strong crytography to ordinary computer users. Version 1.0 was released publically on the Internet in June 1991. PGP soon became the de facto standard for encrypting electronic mail.

Zimmermann, for his efforts, was charged in 1993 by the United States government with violating export controls on strong cryptographic methods. The case was dropped after three years.

PGP is a proprietary product, currently developed and marketed by PGP Incorporated. In 1997, the Internet Engineering Task Force (IETF) formed the OpenPGP working group to define an open standard based on the original PGP program. The result was a proposed standard (RFC 2440) based on version 5 of PGP.

OpenPGP protocol defines standard formats for encryption and decryption of messages, digital signatures, and public-key certificates.

Chapter 27 is a tutorial on Gnu Privacy Guard or GPG. Anyone is free to write a software product to implement the OpenPGP standards. One of the most popular products is the Gnu Privacy Guard (GnuPG or GPG) from the Open Software Foundation. GPG is described in Chapter 27.

24.12 Security vs. Convenience

Anyone who has ever forgotten a password can attest that security and convenience are often at odds. The most secure computer system would be one that is switched off, unplugged, and locked away in a windowless chamber protected by trained attack dogs. Of course, such a system would not be very convenient to use.

The trade-off between security and convenience is obvious in the case of the `.rhosts` file discussed previously. The `.rhosts` certainly is convenient for the authorized user; unfortunately, it is also convenient for a cracker. To maintain security, many system administrators restrict or even forbid the use of `.rhosts` files.

If systems are to remain secure, users must practice secure computing, even when this is inconvenient. Simple steps—such as choosing good passwords, changing passwords frequently, and keeping passwords secret—can go a long way toward maintaining system security. Conversely, if the users themselves do not follow good security practices, the system will remain vulnerable.

24.13 Exercises

1. Be sure you can define the following terms:

information theft	intrusion	denial of service	hacker
cracker	phreakers	script kiddy	trap door
logic bomb	trojan horse	virus	worm
r-utilities	spoofing	cryptography	plaintext
ciphertext	algorithm	encryption key	secret key
public key	hash	message digest	one-time passwords
tokens	biometrics	firewalls	proxy servers

2. What do the following acronyms stand for?

IPSec	SSH	SSL	SHTML
S/MIME	TLS	VPN	PGP

# Chapter 25

TUTORIAL: USING SSH-1

Secure Shell (SSH) uses strong encryption to make secure network connections between computers, serving as a secure replacement for the rcp (remote file copy), rlogin (remote login), rsh (remote shell), ftp (file transfer program), and telnet utilities.

Note that SSH-1 is a protocol; SSH1 is a product that uses that protocol.

This chapter deals with the SSH1 product from SSH Communications Security Ltd. This product uses the original SSH protocol, called SSH-1. Other SSH-1 programs should behave similarly (if not identically).

If you are interested in SSH-2 rather than SSH-1, skip to the next chapter.

The SSH-1 protocol is no longer supported by its parent company, having been superseded by the SSH-2 protocol. However, many SSH-1 implementations are still in use, and many SSH-2 products are backwardly-compatible with SSH-1.

25.1 SSH Clients and Servers

SSH works according to a client-server model. The client sits on your local machine; the server sits on the remote host. The client and server need to speak according to the same protocol (although they need not be products created by the same company).

A daemon is a program that awaits in the background to perform a specific task.

On most UNIX systems, the SSH-1 server program is named sshd (for "Secure Shell Daemon") or sshd1. The SSH-1 client program is named either ssh or ssh1. As a user, you will rarely have any reason to be concerned about the server program; you will almost always use the client program.

25.2 Which SSH?

Your first step is to determine which version of SSH is installed on your system.

1. Check for versions of ssh in your search path. Use the which command:

§ which ssh1 ssh2 ssh (Return)

If any of these commands exists in your search path, you should see its pathname. Otherwise, you will be told that the command was not found. For example,

The pathnames may be
different on your system.

```
ssh1: command not found
/usr/local/bin/ssh2
/usr/local/bin/ssh
§
```

In this example, the ssh2 and ssh commands were found in the search path, but not ssh1. (Remember, your system may be set up differently.)

If you do find ssh in your search path, you still cannot be sure which version of SSH it represents. On some systems, the ssh command runs the SSH-1 client; on other systems, it is a symbolic link to the SSH-2 client.

2. **Check the ssh version number.** Use the -V option with the ssh command:

```
§ ssh -V (Return)
```

If your ssh client supports this option, it will print information on the client, including which protocol it uses:

In this example, ssh is a
SSH-1.5 client.

```
ssh: Secure Shell 1.2.31 [powerpc-ibm-aix4.3.3.0], protocol
version 1.5.
```

If the -V option does not work, you can still check to see whether the ssh command links to the ssh2 client.

3. **If necessary, check for links to ssh2.** Use the ls -l command with the pathname of the ssh command:

The pathname of ssh may
be different on your system.

```
§ ls -l /usr/local/bin/ssh (Return)
```

If ssh is a link to the ssh2 command, the ls -l command will tell you. For example, you might see something like

```
lrwxrwxrwx  1  root  other  4 Aug 1999  ssh -> ssh2
```

In this example, ssh is a symbolic link (->) to the ssh2 client. If you find ssh2 on your system, you may prefer to use it instead of ssh1. If so, skip this chapter and go on to the next chapter.

4. **Repeat Steps 1 through 3 for other commands to be used in this chapter.** Check the version numbers for scp, ssh-keygen, ssh-agent, and ssh-add.

25.3 Logging In Remotely

In this section you will see how to use the SSH-1 client to log into your account on a remote host.

1. **Start the SSH-1 client, specifying the remote host and your remote login name.** Type the following line, substituting your remote login in place of *your-login* and the name of the remote host in place of *remote-host*:

On some systems, the
command will be ssh.

```
§ ssh1 your-login@remote-host (Return)
```

Alternatively, you can specify the user by the -l option (like rlogin):

§ ssh1 *remote-host* -l *your-login* (Return)

The SSH client must do some extra set-up the first time it attempts a connection to a remote host that it has not previously dealt with. The client will print a message letting you know what it is doing; then it will ask whether you wish to continue. You might see something like this:

```
Host key not found from list of known hosts.
Are you sure you want to continue connecting (yes/no)?
```

2. Answer yes to continue. Type *yes* (all lowercase) and press (Return).

```
...continue connecting (yes/no)? yes (Return)
```

You should see a message such as

```
Host remote-host added to the list of known hosts.
Creating random seed file ~/.ssh/random_seed. This may take
a while.
```

Eventually, a password prompt should appear:

your-login@remote-host s password:

3. Enter the password that you use for the remote host. This need not be the same as the password used on your local host. As usual, the password will not be echoed on screen as you type.

Enter your password; it will
not appear on the screen.

password: ▓▓▓▓▓▓▓▓▓▓ (Return)

If you entered the correct password, you should see the shell prompt on your remote account:

We will use far§ to
represent the shell prompt
on the remote host.

far§

4. Run some UNIX commands on your remote account. For instance, try the ls command:

far§ ls (Return)

5. When you finish working on your remote account, log out from that account. One of the usual commands should work (see Chapter 3):

far§ logout (Return)

far§ exit (Return)

far§ (CONTROL)-(D)

You should now see your local host prompt:

§

25.4 Generating an RSA Key Pair

You can continue using your password to log in to your remote host, but a more secure way is to use public-key encryption. For this, you will need to generate a key pair, consisting of a private key and a public key.

1. **Run the key-generating program**. At the shell prompt on your local host, type

On some systems, use the
`ssh-keygen` command.

§ ssh-keygen1 (Return)

The client will tell you that it is generating a key pair:

```
Initializing random number generator...
Generating p:  ...++ (distance 16)
Generating q:  ..++ (distance 10)
Computing the keys...
Testing the keys...
```

Once `ssh-keygen` finishes generating the keys, it will ask you to name the file in which to store the key:

```
Key generation complete
Enter file in which to save the key (.ssh/identity):
```

Note the file name in parentheses. This is the default key file. Your key will go into this file unless you specify a different file name.

2. **Choose a file name.** To follow the examples in this chapter, accept the default file name. Simply press (Return):

§ (Return)

You will then be prompted for a passphrase:

```
Enter passphrase:
```

3. **Choose a passphrase.** The difference between a passphrase and a password is simple: a passphrase may include spaces, a password may not. A good passphrase is easy for you to remember but hard for someone else to guess. In general, a passphrase should be at least a dozen characters long, including spaces, letters, numbers, and punctuation. It should not be a grammatical sentence, although a sentence including deliberately misspelled words is good. Also, make your passphrase different from your password.

4. **Enter your passphrase.** Carefully type your chosen passphrase at the prompt. Note that the passphrase does not appear on screen as you type. Then press (Return):

Your passphrase will not
appear as you type.

```
Enter passphrase:             (Return)
```

You will be asked to enter the same passphrase again:

```
Enter the same passphrase again:
```

5. **Re-enter your passphrase.** Carefully enter your passphrase *exactly as before* and press ⟮**Return**⟯ :

Your passphrase will not appear as you type.

```
Enter the same passphrase again:▨▨▨▨▨▨ ⟮Return⟯
```

If you entered your passphrase correctly, your public key will appear on screen:

```
1024 35
136333986163806937786410849735179280730409214567928179706 56
441239311971264144325945014071550482179498677190082150618 45
428032769208867785223405797162409835977897200230223336042 66
116435212371375408675967700928586702961698014774199528257 84
106137128322899754978776444982552130287608416564560515337 76
20779414684593 your-login@local-host
```

```
Your public key has been saved in .ssh/identity.pub
§
```

25.5   Creating a Remote SSH Directory

To use RSA authentication, you will have to place a copy of your public key in the .ssh directory in your remote account.

1. **Start the SSH client on your local host and specify the remote account.**

On some systems, use the ssh command.

```
§ ssh1 your-login@remote-host ⟮Return⟯
```

You will receive a password prompt for the remote host:

your-login@remote-host s password:

2. **Enter your remote password.** As usual, you password will not appear on screen as you type:

Enter your password; it will not appear on the screen.

```
password:▨▨▨▨▨ ⟮Return⟯
```

If you entered the proper password, you should see the remote shell prompt:

```
far§
```

3. **Look for an existing** .ssh **directory.** Use the ls -a command to see whether the directory already exists:

```
far§ ls -a ⟮Return⟯
```

4. **If necessary, create a new** .ssh **directory.** If no .ssh exists in your remote home directory, create one using the mkdir command:

```
far§ mkdir .ssh (Return)
```

25.6 Suspending the SSH Client

If you have been following the tutorial closely, you should still be connected by
ssh to your remote account. Next you will suspend the SSH client process, putting
it in the background without severing the connection between the local host and
the remote host. This will allow you to work in your local account.

By default, the SSH client recognizes a tilde (~) as an *escape character* when it
occurs as the first character on a command line. (This is not to be confused with
the (Esc) key that is used with the vi editor.)

1. **List the ssh escape sequences.** On most systems, this is done by typing a tilde
(~) followed by a question mark (?):

```
far§ ~?
```

The ssh client will list the escape sequences that it recognizes:

```
~.      terminate connection
~C      open a command line
~^Z     suspend ssh
~#      list forwarded connections
~&      background ssh (while connections terminate)
~?      this message
~~      send the escape character by typing it twice
```

2. **Enter the "suspend" escape sequence.** On most systems, this will be the tilde
(~) followed by the (Control)-(Z) key combination:

```
far§ ~^Z
```

The shell will respond with a message that the process has been stopped or sent to
the background:

```
Stopped (user)
```

3. **If necessary, get a local shell prompt.** Pressing (Return) ought to do the trick:

(Return)

Your local shell should display a prompt:

§

Now you are ready to copy a file to the remote host.

25.7 Copying Files

In this section you will see how to use scp1 to copy a file from your local host to
a remote host on which you have an account.

Recall that
`identity.pub` holds
your public key.

1. Move to the `.ssh` directory and check that the `identity.pub` file exists.

§ `cd .ssh` (Return)
§ `ls` (Return)

You should see `identity.pub` in the file listing. (If you do not, you will need to find the file.

2. Copy the file. You have to specify (1) the file to copy, (2) the remote account, and (3) a name for the copy. A colon (:) is used to separate the account name from the file name of the copy.

Thus, to copy `identity.pub` to the account *your-login@remote-host*, and name the copy `key.pub`, you would type

On some systems, use the
`scp` command.

§ `scp1 identity.pub` *your-login@remote-host*`:key.pub` (Return)

You will receive the `password` prompt:

`password:`

3. Enter your remote password. As always, your password does not appear on screen as you type:

Enter your password; it will
not appear on the screen.

`password:`▨▨▨▨▨▨▨ (Return)

The `scp1` program will try to copy the specified file. If it is successful, you should see a message

`Transferring identity.pub ->` *your-login@remote-host*`:key.pub`
`|.....................................................|`
`333 bytes transferred in 0.08 seconds [3.77 kb/sec].`

If `scp1` cannot copy the file, it will print an appropriate warning:

`scp: warning: no such file or directory`

Either way, `scp1` will return you to the local shell:

§

25.8 Resuming Work on the Remote Host

At this point, the SSH-1 client should still be running in the background. Bringing it to the foreground will allow you to resume working on your remote account.

1. Check that the SSH-1 process is still running in the background. You can do this using the `jobs` command:

§ `jobs` (Return)

This will list each job and its status. In this case, there should be just one job:

Some shells say "Suspended."

```
[1] +  Stopped (user) ssh1 your-login@remote-host
```

2. Bring the SSH-1 client to the foreground.

§ `fg %1` (Return)

The shell will echo the command line:

`ssh1` *your-login@remote-host*

3. Press (Return)

You ought to see a prompt from the remote shell:

`far§`

Now you will be able to continue working in your remote home directory.

4. List your remote files.

`far§ ls` (Return)

Among your files you should see one named `key.pub` that you transferred from your local host. Next, you will use this file to set up RSA-authentication.

25.9 Creating an Authorized Keys File

To use RSA-authentication, your public key must be found in a file named `authorized_keys` in the `.ssh` directory.

1. Move to the `.ssh` **directory.**

`far§ cd .ssh` (Return)

2. Check for an existing `authorized_keys` **file.**

`far§ ls` (Return)

3. If `authorized_keys` **exists, append your public key to the file.**

`far§ cat ../key.pub >> authorized_keys` (Return)

4. If `authorized_keys` **does not exist, create it.** Move `key.pub` and rename it `authorized_keys`:

`far§ mv ../key.pub authorized_keys` (Return)

File modes and access privileges are discussed in Chapter 6.

5. Change the file access modes. The `.ssh` directory should be readable and executable by all, but writable only by the user. The `authorized_keys` file should be readable by all, but writable only by the user:

```
far§ chmod u=rwx,go=rx ~/.ssh (Return)
far§ chmod u=rw,go=r ~/.ssh/authorized_keys (Return)
```

The remote shell will respond with a prompt:

`far§`

6. Log out from your remote account. The usual command will work:

`far§ logout (Return)`

The SSH-1 client will close the connection and you will see a prompt from your local shell:

`Connection to remote-host closed.`
`§`

25.10 Logging In Using RSA Authentication

If you have set up your key files correctly, you should be able to

1. Start the SSH-1 client on your local host and specify the remote account.

On some systems, use the `ssh` *command.*

`§ ssh1 your-login@remote-host (Return)`

You will receive a `passphrase` prompt:

`Enter passphrase for RSA key: 'your-login@local-host':`

2. Enter your passphrase. As usual, your passphrase will not appear on screen as you type:

Enter your passphrase; it will not appear on screen.

`passphrase:▓▓▓▓▓▓▓ (Return)`

If you entered the proper password, you should see the remote shell prompt:
`far§`

3. Work on your remote account.

4. Logout when you finish.

`far§ logout (Return)`

The `ssh` client will close the connection and you will see a prompt from your local shell:

`Connection to remote-host closed.`
`§`

At this point, you may be wondering how RSA public-key authentication is an improvement over password authentication. Superficially, it would appear that the only difference is that you enter a passphrase instead of a password. That hardly seems worth the extra trouble of generating the key pair.

The principal advantage of RSA public-key authentication is that it is more secure than password authentication. Moreover, as we shall see in the next section, there is a way to make RSA authentication more convenient than password authentication.

25.11 Using an Agent

Having to enter your passphrase every time you run ssh or scp can be annoying. Fortunately, there is an easier way: use an SSH agent.

The SSH agent provides your passphrase whenever ssh or scp requests it. You still have to enter the passphrase when you start up the agent; once that is done, however, you will not be prompted for the passphrase as long as the SSH agent is running.

1. **Start the agent and specify a shell.** The ssh-agent1 (or ssh-agent) command starts the agent and a shell process:

The variable SHELL holds the name of your login shell.

§ `ssh-agent1 $SHELL` (Return)

or

§ `ssh-agent $SHELL` (Return)

The shell runs as a subshell or child of the agent, but otherwise behaves just like a normal login shell. It will display the usual shell prompt:

§

2. **Add your private key to the agent.** The ssh-add1 (or ssh-add) command does this:

On some systems, use the ssh-add command.

§ `ssh-add1 ~/.ssh/identity` (Return)

By default, ssh-add1 looks for your private key in the identity file inside your .ssh directory. (If your key is in a different file, specify that file.) The utility will prompt for the passphrase protecting that file:

```
Need passphrase for ~/.ssh/identity (your-login)
Enter passphrase:
```

3. **Enter your passphrase.** Type your passphrase and press (Return); as always, the passphrase remains hidden as you type:

Enter your passphrase; it will not appear on screen.

`passphrase:`▓▓▓▓▓▓▓▓ (Return)

The ssh-add1 utility will tell you that your "identity" has been added:

```
Identity added: ~/.ssh/identity (your-login)
```

If you have done everything correctly, you will be able to use ssh or scp without being prompted for a password or a passphrase. (Try it.)

4. Log out when you finish. When you log out from your local account, the agent will automatically terminate.

§ `logout` (Return)

Startup files are discussed in Chapter 28. Most users set up their login initialization file (`.profile` or `.login`) to start the ssh agent every time they log in. We leave this as an exercise for you.

25.12   Command Summary

Each of these commands is typed in after the UNIX prompt, and each is terminated by a (Return).

Remote Login Commands (UNIX shell prompt)

ssh1 *user@host*	connect to a remote account *user* on *host*
ssh1 *host* -1 *user*	connect to a remote account *user* on *host*
ssh *user@host*	connect to a remote account *user* on *host*
ssh *host* -1 *user*	connect to a remote account *user* on *host*

SSH-1 Escape Sequences

~.	terminate connection
~C	open a command line
~^Z	suspend ssh
~#	list forwarded connections
~&	background ssh (while connections terminate)
~?	list the escape sequences
~~	send the escape character by typing it twice

Remote Copy (UNIX shell prompt)

scp1 *user@host1*:*file1* *user@host2*:*file2*

    copy *file1* (on *host1*) to *file2* (on *host2*)

scp *user@host1*:*file1* *user@host2*:*file2*

    copy *file1* (on *host1*) to *file2* (on *host2*)

Key Pair Generation (UNIX shell prompt)

ssh-keygen1	generate an RSA key pair
ssh-keygen	generate an RSA key pair

SSH Agent (UNIX shell prompt)

`ssh-agent1 $SHELL` start an SSH agent and $SHELL subshell process

`ssh-add1 keyfile` add a private key (from `keyfile`) to the SSH agent

`ssh-agent $SHELL` start an SSH agent and $SHELL subshell process

`ssh-add keyfile` add a private key (from `keyfile`) to the SSH agent

25.13 Exercises

1. If you have an account on a remote UNIX machine, log into that account using `ssh`.

2. If you have not already done so, set up your local and remote accounts to permit RSA authentication.

3. After reading Chapter 28, modify your login initialization file (`.profile` or `.login`) to start the `ssh` agent whenever you log in. It is recommended that the command to start the agent be the last line in the file.

# Chapter 26

TUTORIAL: USING SSH-2

The previous chapter describes Secure Shell Version 1 (SSH-1). This chapter deals with remote access using the Secure Shell Version 2 (SSH-2). SSH-2 offers a number of improvements over SSH-1, including enhanced security and a wider choice of encryption algorithms.

Note that SSH-2 is a protocol; SSH2 is a product that uses that protocol.

The focus of this chapter is primarily on two of the most popular SSH-2 products: SSH2 from SSH Communications Security Ltd., and OpenSSH from the OpenBSD project. Other SSH-2 programs should behave similarly (if not identically).

26.1 SSH-2 Clients and Servers

SSH-2 works according to a client-server model. The client sits on your local machine; the server sits on the remote host. The client and server need to speak according to the same protocol (although they need not be written by the same company).

A daemon is a program that awaits in the background to perform a specific task.

On most UNIX systems, the SSH-2 server program is named `ssh` or `sshd2`—for "Secure Shell Daemon." The SSH-2 client program is named either `ssh` or `ssh2`. As a user, you will rarely have any reason to be concerned about the server program; you will almost always use the client program.

26.2 Which SSH?

A SSH-2 utility typically has a *2* appended to the command name to distinguish it from its SSH-1 counterpart:

Version 1: `ssh1`, `scp1`, `ssh-keygen1`, `ssh-agent1`, `ssh-add1`

Version 2: `ssh2`, `scp2`, `ssh-keygen2`, `ssh-agent2`, `ssh-add2`

This is not a hard and fast rule, however. OpenSSH commands may have no number attached:

OpenSSH: `ssh`, `scp`, `ssh-keygen`, `ssh-agent`, `ssh-add`

On some systems, the unnumbered commands (ssh, scp, ...) are linked to the Version 1 commands (ssh1, scp1, ...); on other systems, they are linked to the Version 2 commands (ssh2, scp2, ...).

Your first task is to determine which versions of SSH are installed on your system.

1. **Check for SSH clients in your search path.** Use the which command:

§ which ssh1 ssh2 ssh (Return)

If any of these commands exists in your search path, you should see its pathname. Otherwise, you will be told that the command was not found. For example,

The pathnames may be different on your system.

ssh1: command not found
/usr/local/bin/ssh2
/usr/local/bin/ssh
§

In this example, the ssh2 and ssh commands were found in the search path, but not ssh1. (Remember, your system may be set up differently.)

Even if you do find ssh in your search path, you still cannot be sure which version of SSH it represents. On some systems, the ssh command runs the SSH-1 client; on other systems, it is a symbolic link to the SSH-2 client.

2. **Check the ssh version number.** Use the -V option with the ssh command:

§ ssh -V (Return)

If your ssh client supports the -V option, it will print information on the client, including which protocol(s) it supports:

In this example, SSH-1.5 and SSH-2.0 are supported.

OpenSSH_3.4p1, SSH protocols 1.5/2.0, OpenSSL 0x0090602f

If the -V option does not work on your system, you can still check to see whether the ssh command links to the ssh2 client.

3. **If necessary, check for links to ssh2.** Use the ls -l command with the path-name of the ssh command:

The pathname of ssh may be different on your system.

§ ls -l /usr/local/bin/ssh (Return)

If ssh is a link to the ssh2 command, the ls -l command will show this. For example, you might see something like

lrwxrwxrwx 1 root other 4 Aug 1999 ssh -> ssh2

In this example, ssh is a symbolic link to the ssh2 client, so either command may be used.

4. **Repeat Steps 1 through 3 for other commands to be used in this chapter.** Check the version numbers for scp2 (or scp), ssh-keygen2 (or ssh-keygen), ssh-agent2 (or ssh-agent), and ssh-add2 (or ssh-add).

26.3 Logging In Remotely

In this section you will see how to use a SSH-2 client to connect to your account on a remote host.

1. Start the SSH-2 client, specifying the remote host and your remote login name. Type the following line, substituting your remote login in place of *your-login* and the name of the remote host in place of *remote-host*:

[SSH2]   § `ssh2` *your-login@remote-host* (**Return**)

[OpenSSH]   § `ssh` *your-login@remote-host* (**Return**)

Alternatively, you can specify the user by the `-l` option (like `rlogin`):

[SSH2]   § `ssh2` *remote-host* `-l` *your-login* (**Return**)

[OpenSSH]   § `ssh` *remote-host* `-l` *your-login* (**Return**)

The SSH-2 client must do some extra set-up the first time it attempts a connection to a remote host that it has not previously dealt with. The client will print a message letting you know what it is doing; then it will ask whether you wish to continue. You might see something like this:

```
The authenticity of host 'farhost.ed (198.45.24.239)' can't
be established.
```

See the sidebar
"Fingerprints Explained."
```
RSA key fingerprint is
f4:3c:ab:21:97:38:fb:68:ec:e1:2d:39:5b:4f:49:5f.
Are you sure you want to continue connecting (yes/no)?
```

2. Answer yes to continue. Type *yes* (all lowercase) and press (**Return**).

```
...continue connecting (yes/no)? yes (Return)
```

You should see a message such as

```
Warning: Permanently added 'remote-host, ###.##.##.##' (RSA) to
the list of known hosts.
```

Eventually, a password prompt should appear:

your-login@remote-host `s password:`

3. Enter the password that you use for the remote host. This need not be the same as the password used on your local host.

Enter your password; it will
not appear on the screen.
`password:`▓▓▓▓▓▓▓ (**Return**)

If you entered the correct password, you should see the shell prompt on your remote account:

Fingerprints Explained

A *key fingerprint* is a string of characters computed from a public key using a one-way hash function. Fingerprints are useful in checking the authenticity of a public key.

For example, suppose Alice and Bill are working on a project, and Bill needs access to files in Alice's account. She does not want to disclose her password to Bill; instead, they agree to use SSH and public-key authentication.

Alice asks Bill to send her an e-mail message containing his public key, so she can add it to her SSH authorization file. But there is a serious problem. Stan, an unfriendly third party, might intercept Bill's e-mail. Stan could then substitute his public key for Bill's, and send the message on to Alice. If she were to add this key to her SSH authorization file, Stan would be able to log into her account.

So how can Alice be sure she *really* has Bill's public key? She could call Bill on the telephone and read the key back to him; however, this would be quite tedious because the key is very long. This is where the fingerprint comes in.

Suppose Alice has stored what she thinks is Bill's public key in the file `bill.pub`. She can check the fingerprint for the key. If she is using SSH2, the command is `ssh-keygen2` with the `-F` option:

[SSH2]
```
§ ssh-keygen2 -F bill.pub (Return)
Fingerprint for key:
pitxr-aswjh-umlay-shrgw-beaes-wuaxs-suriv-vezos-lubtf-cspor-vwudr
```

Using OpenSSH, the command is `ssh-keygen` with the `-l` and `-f` options:

[OpenSHH]
```
§ ssh-keygen -l -f bill.pub (Return)
1024: f6:7c:4b:37:2c:67:53:57:a8:2c:43:2a:5c:e4:44:39  Bill@some
host.com
```

Because the fingerprint is much shorter than the key, Alice can easily read it to Bill over the telephone. He can verify that the fingerprints match.

We will use `far§` to represent the shell prompt on the remote host.

```
far§
```

4. Run some UNIX commands on your remote account. For instance, try the `ls` command:

```
far§ ls (Return)
```

5. When you finish working on your remote account, log out. One of the usual commands should work (see Chapter 3):

```
far§ logout (Return)
```

```
far§ exit (Return)
```

far§ (CONTROL)–(D)

You may be told that the connection has been closed, and you will see your local shell prompt:

Connection to *remote-host* closed.
§

26.4 Generating a DSA Key Pair

You can continue using your password to log in to your remote host, but a more secure way is to use public-key encryption. For this, you will need to generate a key pair, consisting of a private key and a public key. SSH-2 can handle a variety of public-key systems. In this chapter, we will see how to generate a DSA (Digital Signature Algorithm) key pair.

1. Run the key-generating program. At the shell prompt on your local host, start either the ssh-keygen or ssh-keygen2 utility. Specify the key type using either the -t ("type") or -d ("dsa") option. One of the following command lines should work:

[SSH2]   § ssh-keygen2 -t dsa (Return)

[OpenSSH]   § ssh-keygen -d (Return)

[Alternate]   § ssh-keygen -t dsa (Return)

The utility may tell you that it is generating a key pair:

Generating public/private dsa key pair.

The utility may display a *progress indicator*, something like

.oOo.oOo.oOo.oOo.oOo.

The utility may display nothing while it generates the key pair.

Once the key is generated, the utility may prompt for a file in which to store the key (not all utilities do):

Your system need not prompt for a file name.

Enter file in which to save the key (~/.ssh/id_dsa):

Note the file name in parentheses. This is the default file that will be used unless you specify another.

2. If you are given a choice, specify a file name. To follow the examples in this chapter, accept the default file name. Simply press (Return):

§ (Return)

You will be prompted for a passphrase:

Enter passphrase (empty for no passphrase):

The key-generation utility may refuse a passphrase that is too short.

3. Choose a passphrase. The difference between a passphrase and a password is simple: a passphrase may include spaces, but a password may not. A good passphrase is easy for you to remember but hard for someone else to guess. In general, a passphrase should be at least a dozen characters long, including spaces, letters, numbers, and punctuation. It should not be a grammatical sentence, although a sentence including deliberately misspelled words is good. Also, make your passphrase different from your password.

4. Enter your passphrase. At the prompt, carefully type your chosen passphrase and press `Return`:

Your passphrase will not appear as you type.

`Enter passphrase:`▓▓▓▓▓▓ `Return`

You will be asked to enter the same passphrase a second time:

`Enter same passphrase again:`

5. Re-enter your passphrase. Carefully type your passphrase *exactly as before* and press `Return`:

Your passphrase will not appear as you type.

`Enter the same passphrase again:`▓▓▓▓▓ `Return`

If you entered your passphrase correctly, you will be told that your identification (private key) and your public key have been saved:

`Your identification has been saved in ~/.ssh/id_dsa.`

`Your public key has been saved in ~/.ssh/id_dsa.pub.`

See the sidebar "Fingerprints Explained."

`The key fingerprint is:`
`af:97:3b:5f:a3:bb:88:5e:0f:95:4e:d2:9b:9c:ee:0c` *your-login@local-host*
§

26.5 Creating a Remote SSH Directory

To use DSA authentication, you will have to place a copy of your public key in the `.ssh2` or `.ssh` directory in your remote account.

1. Start the SSH-2 client on your local host and specify the remote account.

[SSH2]　§ `ssh2` *your-login@remote-host* `Return`

[OpenSSH]　§ `ssh` *your-login@remote-host* `Return`

You will receive a `password` prompt for the remote host:

your-login@remote-host`'s password:`

2. Enter your remote password.

Enter your password; it will not appear on the screen. ──── `password:`▓▓▓▓▓ (Return)

If you entered the proper password, you should see the remote shell prompt:

`far§`

3. Look for an existing SSH directory. The directory will probably be named `.ssh2` (for SSH2) or `.ssh` (OpenSSH). Enter the `ls -a` command:

`far§ ls -a`(Return)

4. If necessary, create a new SSH directory. If no `.ssh2` or `.ssh` directory exists in your remote home directory, create one using the `mkdir` command:

[SSH2]   `far§ mkdir .ssh2`(Return)

[OpenSSH]   `far§ mkdir .ssh`(Return)

26.6 Suspending the SSH Client

If you have been following the tutorial closely, you should still be connected by SSH-2 to your remote account. Next you will suspend the SSH-2 client process, putting it in background without severing the connection between the local host and the remote host. This will allow you to work in your local account.

By default, the SSH-2 client recognizes a tilde (~) as an *escape character* when it occurs as the first character on a command line. (This is not to be confused with the (Esc) key that is used with the `vi` editor.)

1. List the escape sequences. On most systems, this is done by typing a tilde (~) followed by a question mark (?):

`far§ ~?`

The SSH-2 client will list the escape sequences that it recognizes:

```
~.     terminate connection
~C     open a command line
~^Z    suspend ssh
~#     list forwarded connections
~&     background ssh (while connections terminate)
~?     this message
~~     send the escape character by typing it twice
```

2. Enter the "suspend" escape sequence. On most systems, this will be the tilde (~) followed by the (Control)-(Z) key combination:

far§ ~^Z

The shell will respond with a message that the process has been stopped or sent to the background:

Some shells say "Suspended."

Stopped (user)

3. If necessary, get a local shell prompt. Pressing (Return) ought to do the trick:

(Return)

Your local shell should display a prompt:

§

Now you are ready to copy a file to the remote host.

26.7 Copying Files with Secure Copy

In this section you will see how to use SCP-2 to copy a file from your local host to a remote host.

1. Move to the SSH hidden directory.

[SSH2]   § cd .ssh2 (Return)

[OpenSSH]   § cd .ssh (Return)

2. Check that the public-key identity file exists.

§ ls (Return)

You should see a file containing your private key and another containing your public key. (You may see other files as well.)

[SSH2]   id_dsa_1024_a   id_dsa_1024_a.pub

[OpenSSH]   id_dsa   id_dsa.pub

3. Copy the file to the remote host. You have to specify (1) the file to copy, (2) the remote account, and (3) a name for the copy. A colon (:) is used to separate the account name from the file name of the copy.

Hence, to copy id_dsa_1024_a.pub to *your-login@remote-host*, and name the copy key, you would type

[SSH2]   § scp2 id_dsa_1024_a.pub *your-login@remote-host*:key (Return)

Alternatively, to copy id_dsa.pub to *your-login@remote-host*, and name the copy key, you would type

[OpenSSH]   § scp id_dsa.pub *your-login@remote-host*:key (Return)

You will receive a password prompt:

password:

4. Enter your remote password. As always, your password does not appear on screen as you type:

Enter your password; it will not appear on the screen. ——

```
password:▓▓▓▓▓▓▓ (Return)
```

The Secure Copy program will try to copy the specified file. If it is successful, you should see a message:

```
Transferring id_dsa.pub -> your-login@remote-host:key
|.................................................|
333 bytes transferred in 0.08 seconds [3.77 kb/sec].
```

If scp2 cannot copy the file, it will print an appropriate warning:

```
scp: warning: no such file or directory
```

Either way, the local shell prompt will appear:

```
§
```

26.8 Resuming Work on the Remote Host

At this point, the SSH-2 client should still be running in the background. Bringing it to the foreground will allow you to resume working on your remote account.

1. Check that the SSH-2 process is still running in the background. You can do this using the jobs command:

```
§ jobs (Return)
```

This will list each job and its status. In this case, there should be just one job:

Some shells say "Suspended."

```
[1] +  Stopped (user) ssh2 your-login@remote-host
```

2. Bring the SSH-2 client to the foreground.

```
§ fg %1 (Return)
```

The shell will echo the command line:

```
ssh2 your-login@remote-host
```

3. Press (Return).

You ought to see a prompt from the remote shell:

```
far§
```

Now you will be able to continue working in your remote home directory.

4. List your remote files.

```
far§ ls (Return)
```

Among your files you should see one named key that you transferred from your local host. Next, you will use this file to set up DSA-authentication.

26.9 Creating an Authorized Keys File

For DSA-authentication, your public key must be in ~/.ssh/authorization or .ssh/authorized_keys on the remote host. (Your private key stays on your local host).

1. On the remote host, move to the .ssh2 or .ssh directory.

[SSH2]   far§ cd .ssh2 (Return)

[OpenSSH]   far§ cd .ssh (Return)

2. Check for an existing authorization or authorized_keys file.

far§ ls (Return)

3. If either authorization or authorized_keys exists, append your public key to the file.

[SSH2]   far§ cat ../key >> authorization (Return)

[OpenSSH]   far§ cat ../key >> authorized_keys (Return)

4. If necessary, create either authorization or authorized_keys. Move key and rename it:

[SSH2]   far§ mv ../key authorization (Return)

[OpenSHH]   far§ mv ../key authorized_keys (Return)

5. Change the file access modes. The .ssh2 or .ssh directory should be readable and executable by all, but writable only by the user. The authorization or authorized_keys file should be readable by all, but writable only by the user:

[SSH2]   far§ chmod u=rwx,go=rx ~/.ssh2 (Return)
far§ chmod u=rw,go=r ~/.ssh/authorization (Return)

[OpenSSH]   far§ chmod u=rwx,go=rx ~/.ssh (Return)
far§ chmod u=rw,go=r ~/.ssh/authorized_keys (Return)

The remote shell will respond with a prompt:

far§

6. Log out from your remote account. The usual command will work:

far§ logout (Return)

The ssh client will close the connection and you will see a prompt from your local shell:

```
Connection to remotehost closed.
§
```

26.10 Logging In Using DSA Authentication

If you have set up your key files correctly, you should be able to log into your remote account without a password (although you will still have to provide a passphrase).

1. **Start the SSH-2 client on your local host.** Specify the remote account:

[SSH2]   § ssh2 *your-login@remote-host* (**Return**)

[OpenSSH]   § ssh *your-login@remote-host* (**Return**)

You will receive a prompt for a passphrase:

```
Enter passphrase for DSA key:
```

2. **Enter your passphrase.** As usual, your passphrase will not appear on screen as you type:

Enter your passphrase; it will not appear on screen.

```
Enter passphrase for DSA key:              (Return)
```

If you entered the proper passphrase, you should see the remote shell prompt:

```
far§
```

3. **Work on your remote account.**

4. **Logout when you finish.**

```
far§ logout (Return)
```

The ssh client will close the connection and you will see a prompt from your local shell:

```
Connection to remotehost closed.
§
```

At this point, you may be wondering how public-key authentication is an improvement over password authentication. Superficially, it would appear that the only difference is that you enter a passphrase instead of a password. That hardly seems worth the extra trouble of generating the key pair.

The principal advantage of public-key authentication is that it is more secure than password authentication. Moreover, as we shall see in the next section, there is a way to make authentication more convenient than password authentication.

26.11 Using an Agent

Having to enter your passphrase every time you run SSH can be annoying. Fortunately, there is an easier way: use an SSH agent.

The SSH agent provides your passphrase whenever `ssh2` or `scp2` requests it. You still have to enter the passphrase when you start up the agent; once that is done, however, you will not be prompted for the passphrase as long as the SSH agent is running.

1. **Start the agent and specify a shell.**

[SSH2] § `ssh-agent2 $SHELL` (Return)

[OpenSSH] § `ssh-agent $SHELL` (Return)

The shell runs as a subshell or child of the agent, but otherwise behaves just like a normal login shell. It will display the usual shell prompt:

§

2. **Add your private key to the agent.** The `ssh-add2` (or `ssh-add`) command does this:

[SSH2] § `ssh-add2 ~/.ssh2/id_dsa_1024_a` (Return)

[OpenSSH] § `ssh-add ~/.ssh/id_dsa` (Return)

By default, `ssh-add` looks for your private key in one of the files `id_dsa_1024`, `id_dsa_1024_a`, or `identity` inside your `.ssh` directory. (If you keep your key in a different file, simply specify that file.) The utility will prompt for the passphrase protecting the file:

```
Need passphrase for ~/.ssh/id_dsa ( your-login )
Enter passphrase:
```

3. **Enter your passphrase.** Type your passphrase and press (Return); as always, the passphrase remains hidden as you type:

Enter your passphrase; it will not appear on screen.

`passphrase:`▓▓▓▓▓▓ (Return)

The utility will tell you that your "identity" has been added:

```
Identity added: ~/.ssh/id_dsa ('Your name')
```

If you have done everything correctly, you will be able to use SSH or Secure Copy without being prompted for a password or a passphrase. (Try it.)

4. **Log out when you finish.** When you log out from your local account, the agent will automatically terminate.

§ `logout` (Return)

Most users set up their login initialization file (.profile or .login) to start the agent every time they log in. We leave this as an exercise for you.

26.12 Command Summary

Each of these commands is typed in after the UNIX prompt, and each is terminated by a (Return).

Remote Login Commands (UNIX shell prompt)

ssh2 *user@host*	log into account named *user* on *host* (SSH2)
ssh2 *host* -l *user*	log into account named *user* on *host* (SSH2)
ssh *user@host*	log into account named *user* on *host* (OpenSSH)
ssh *host* -l *user*	log into account named *user* on *host* (OpenSSH)

SSH Escape Sequences

~.	terminate connection
~C	open a command line
~^Z	suspend ssh
~#	list forwarded connections
~&	background ssh (while connections terminate)
~?	list the escape sequences
~~	send the escape character by typing it twice

Remote Copy (UNIX shell prompt)

scp2 *user@host1*:*file1* *user@host2*:*file2*

                copy *file1* (on *host1*) to *file2* (on *host2*)

scp *user@host1*:*file1* *user@host2*:*file2*

                copy *file1* (on *host1*) to *file2* (on *host2*)

Key Pair Generation (UNIX shell prompt)

ssh-keygen2 -t dsa	generate a DSA key pair (SSH2)
ssh-keygen -d	generate a DSA key pair (OpenSSH)

SSH Agent (UNIX shell prompt)

ssh-agent2 $SHELL	start an SSH agent and $SHELL subshell (SSH2)
ssh-add2 keyfile	add a private key to the SSH agent (SSH2)
ssh-agent $SHELL	start an SSH agent and $SHELL subshell (OpenSSH)
ssh-add keyfile	add a private key to the SSH agent (OpenSSH)

26.13 Exercises

1. If you have an account on a remote UNIX machine, log into that account using SSH-2.

2. If you have not already done so, set up your local and remote accounts to permit DSA authentication.

3. After reading Chapter 28, modify your login initialization file (`.profile` or `.login`) to start the SSH-2 agent whenever you log in. It is recommended that the command to start the agent be the last line in the file.

Tutorial: Encryption Using GPG

This chapter deals with the use of Pretty Good Privacy (PGP) for the encryption of data files and electronic mail. Specifically, the chapter focusses on Gnu Privacy Guard (GPG), an open-source implementation of the OpenPGP standard.

27.1 Finding GPG

Your first task is to determine whether GPG is installed on your system.

1. Check for the gpg program in your search path. Use the `which` command:

```
§ which gpg (Return)
```

If the gpg command exists in your search path, you should see its pathname:

The pathname may be different on your system.

```
/usr/local/bin/gpg
§
```

If gpg is not found, some shells will simply display a prompt:

```
§
```

Other shells will tell you explicitly if the command is not found in the search path:

```
gpg: command not found
§
```

If gpg (or a similar program) is not available on your system, you may want to ask your system administrator to install it.

2. If gpg is installed, check its version number. Use the `--version` option with the gpg command:

Note that two hyphens are used here.

```
§ gpg --version (Return)
```

You should see the version information, something like this:

```
gpg (GnuPG) 1.2.4
Copyright (C) 2003 Free Software Foundation, Inc.
This program comes with ABSOLUTELY NO WARRANTY.
This is free software, and you are welcome to redistribute
```

```
it under certain conditions. See the file COPYING for
details.

Home: ~/.gnupg
Supported algorithms:
Pubkey: RSA, RSA-E, RSA-S, ELG-E, DSA, ELG
Cipher: 3DES, CAST5, BLOWFISH, AES, AES192, AES256, TWOFISH
Hash: MD5, SHA1, RIPEMD160, TIGER192, SHA256
Compression: Uncompressed, ZIP, ZLIB, BZIP2
§
```

27.2 Creating GPG Files and Directories

The gpg program looks in your home directory for a subdirectory named
.gnupg, which is supposed to contain a configuration file (named gpg.conf), a
secret keyring file (secring.gpg), and a public keyring file (pubring.gpg). If
you do not have these, gpg will create them for you.

1. **Start** gpg. You do not need to specify any options:

§ gpg (Return)

You should see some advisory messages similar to the following:

The messages you see may
be slightly different.

```
gpg: ~/.gnupg: directory created
gpg: new configuration file '~/.gnupg/gpg.conf' created
gpg: WARNING: options in '~/.gnupg/gpg.conf' are not yet
active during this run
gpg: keyring '~/.gnupg/secring.gpg' created
gpg: keyring '~/.gnupg/pubring.gpg' created
```

Some versions of gpg will tell you that you must restart the program, after which
you will see the shell prompt:

```
gpg: you have to start GnuPG again, so it can read the new
options file
§
```

If you see such a message, skip the rest of this section and go on to the next one.
Otherwise, you might see something like

```
gpg: Go ahead and type your message ...
```

2. **If necessary, enter a null message.** If you were prompted for a message, use ^D
to signal an end of file:

```
gpg: Go ahead and type your message ...    (CONTROL)-(D)
```

The program will terminate, after which you should see the shell prompt:

```
gpg: processing message failed: eof
§
```

27.3 Creating a Keypair

Next you must generate a keypair, consisting of a private key and a public key. Recall that text encrypted with your private key can be decrypted only with your public key, and vice versa.

1. Start gpg with the key-generation option. Enter the following command line

§ gpg --gen-key ⟨Return⟩

The gpg will print the usual legal information followed by several key options:

```
gpg (GnuPG) 1.2.4; Copyright (C) 2003 Free Software
Foundation, Inc.
This program comes with ABSOLUTELY NO WARRANTY.
This is free software, and you are welcome to redistribute
it under certain conditions. See the file COPYING for
details.
```

You may see different options.

```
Please select what kind of key you want:
    (1) DSA and ElGamal (default)
    (2) DSA (sign only)
    (4) RSA (sign only)
Your selection?
```

Here we see three options, strangely numbered (1), (2), and (4). The first creates two keypairs: a primary DSA keypair for making signatures, and a subordinate ElGamal keypair for encryption. (Your options may be different.)

2. Choose the kind of key(s) you prefer. Press ⟨Return⟩ to accept the default. Otherwise, enter the number of your choice. For most users, the default option is usually satisfactory.

```
Your selection? ⟨Return⟩
```

You will next be asked to select a key size:

```
DSA keypair will have 1024 bits.
About to generate a new ELG-E keypair.
              minimum keysize is  768 bits
              default keysize is 1024 bits
    highest suggested keysize is 2048 bits
What keysize do you want? (1024)
```

In this case, the DSA key size is automatically set at 1024 bits. However, you may select an ElGamal key size between 768 bits and 2048 bits. There is a trade-off here between security and convenience. All other things being equal, a longer key is usually more secure than a shorter one; but encryption and decryption are slower with a longer key. The default keysize is listed in parentheses (1024).

3. Specify the key size. For most users, the default is usually adequate:

```
What keysize do you want? (1024) (Return)
```

You will be asked to specify an expiration date.

```
Requested keysize is 1024 bits
Please specify how long the key should be valid.
        0 = key does not expire
      <n>  = key expires in n days
      <n>w = key expires in n weeks
      <n>m = key expires in n months
      <n>y = key expires in n years
Key is valid for? (0)
```

The default choice (0) is a key that does not expire, which is best for most users.

4. Choose an expiration date. The default (no expiration date) is usually the preferred choice:

```
Key is valid for? (0) (Return)
```

The gpg program will ask you to confirm your choice:

```
Key does not expire at all
Is this correct (y/n)?
```

5. Confirm the expiration date. Enter y for "yes":

```
Is this correct (y/n)? y (Return)
```

You will be prompted for a User-ID:

```
You need a User-ID to identify your key; the software
constructs the user id
from Real Name, Comment and Email Address in this form:
   "Heinrich Heine (Der Dichter) <heinrichh@duesseldorf.de>"
```

```
Real name:
```

This prompt is misleading; you do *not* enter your real name, comment (the text in parentheses), or e-mail address in the form indicated. Instead, you will enter each of these separately, without quotes, parentheses, or angle brackets.

6. Enter your real name. For example,

Enter your name, not John
Doe (unless that is your
your real name).

```
Real name: John Doe (RETURN)
```

Next you will be prompted for an e-mail address:

```
Email address:
```

7. Enter your e-mail address. Do not put angle brackets or parentheses around the address:

Enter your e-mail address, not `jdoe@podunk.edu`.

```
Email address: jdoe@podunk.edu RETURN
```

You will be prompted for a comment that describes you:

```
Comment:
```

8. Enter a comment. Do not put angle brackets or parentheses around the comment. For instance, if you are a student, you might enter

```
Comment: student Return
```

Next you will be given a chance to review your personal USER-ID:

```
You selected this USER-ID:
    "John Doe (student) <jdoe@podunk.edu>"

Change (N)ame, (C)omment, (E)mail or (O)kay/(Q)uit?
```

9. If necessary, correct your USER-ID. Check your User-ID carefully, because it cannot be changed once it has been created. To correct your name, comment, or e-mail, enter N, C, or E, respectively, at the prompt. If your USER-ID is correct, enter O (for "Okay").

When you okay the USER-ID, you will be prompted for a passphrase:

```
You need a Passphrase to protect your secret key.

Enter passphrase:
```

10. Enter your passphrase. Your passphrase is used to unlock your private key. A good passphrase, like a good password, should be easy for you to remember but difficult for someone else to guess. (The difference between a passphrase and a password is that the passphrase may be longer and it may contain spaces.)

Your passphrase will not appear as you type.

```
Enter passphrase:
```

You will be asked to enter your passphrase a second time:

```
Repeat passphrase:
```

11. Confirm your passphrase. Enter your passphrase exactly as before.

Your passphrase will not appear as you type.

```
Repeat passphrase:
```

The program will create the keypairs:

```
We need to generate a lot of random bytes. It is a good
```

idea to perform some other action (type on the keyboard, move the mouse, utilize the disks) during the prime generation; this gives the random number generator a better chance to gain enough entropy.

```
+++++++++.++++++++++++++...+++++++++++++++++++++++++++++++
+++++++++++++++++++++++++++++++++++.+++++...+++++..++++++++
++.++++++++++++++++++++>+++++.+++++.....................
.........................;l.k.............................
............................................t.e.st.......
...i..n.g..... ..o..ne +++++...............................
..............t.w..o...thr..ee.....Wh.at..is..th.is...do.in
g.?........+++++
```

Eventually, the program will finish. It will tell you that a key pair has been created:

```
gpg: ~/.gnupg/trustdb.gpg: trustdb created
public and secret key created and signed.
key marked as ultimately trusted.

pub   1024D/202C0A83 2004-08-17 John Doe (student)
<jdoe@podunk.edu>

Key fingerprint = 418D DCC4 DA3E 1ED5 15FE FD36 9176 8CD4
202C 0A83
sub   1024g/8A770E55 2004-08-17
§
```

27.4 Creating a Revocation Certificate

If you ever forget your passphrase or have reason to suspect that someone has learned your private key, you will want to *revoke* the keypair. A revoked public key cannot be used to encrypt new messages to you (although it may be used to verify old signatures and decrypt old messages). You will need to create a secure revocation certificate that you can publish to confirm to the world that your key has indeed been revoked.

1. **Run gpg with the --gen-revoke option.** You will need to specify your key, either by using its key ID or part of your USER-ID such as your last name or your e-mail address. Redirect the output into a file named revoke.asc:

Enter the key ID or part of your USER-ID (e.g., your name or e-mail address).

```
§ gpg --gen-revoke keyID > revoke.asc (Return)
```

You will be asked to confirm that you want a revocation certificate:

```
sec 1024D/202C0A83 2004-08-17 John Doe (student)
<jdoe@podunk.edu>

Create a revocation certificate for this key?
```

2. Agree to create the certificate. Enter y for yes at the prompt:

```
Create a revocation certificate for this key? y
```
(Return)

You will be asked to give a reason for revoking the key:

```
Please select the reason for the revocation:
  0 = No reason specified
  1 = Key has been compromised
  2 = Key is superseded
  3 = Key is no longer used
  Q = Cancel
(Probably you want to select 1 here)
Your decision?
```

3. Give a reason. Following the advice of the prompt, enter 1 at the prompt:

```
Your decision? 1
```
(Return)

You will be asked to enter a description.

```
Enter an optional description; end it with an empty line:
>
```

4. If desired, enter a description. This is optional; you may omit it by pressing (Return):

```
>
```
(Return)

You will be asked to confirm both the reason for revocation and the description:

```
Reason for revocation: Key has been compromised
(No description given)
Is this okay?
```

5. Confirm the reason and description. Enter y or n at the prompt:

```
Is this okay? y
```
(Return)

You will be prompted for your passphrase:

```
You need a passphrase to unlock the secret key for
user: "John Doe (student) <jdoe@podunk.edu>"
1024-bit DSA key, ID 202C0A83, created 2004-08-17
```

6. Enter your passphrase.

Your passphrase does not appear as you type.

```
Passphrase:
```

If you entered the correct passphrase, the program will create a revocation certificate:

ASCII armor is explained
later.

```
ASCII armored output forced.
Revocation certificate created.
```

Please move it to a medium which you can hide away; if
Mallory gets access to this certificate he can use it to
make your key unusable. It is smart to print this
certificate and store it away, just in case your media
become unreadable. But have some caution: The print
system of your machine might store the data and make it
available to others!

As noted in the message, you should store the revocation certificate somewhere
secure (such as a safe-deposit box) where it will be available in case you ever need
it. Do not allow anyone else access to your revocation certificate!

7. Examine your revocation certificate.

§ cat revoke.asc (Return)

You should see something like the following:

Your certificate will be
different.

```
----- BEGIN PGP PUBLIC KEY BLOCK -----
Version: GnuPG v1.2.4 (Darwin)
Comment: A revocation certificate should follow

iEkEiBECAAkFAkEtg5ECHQIACgkQOMhAxn7hn2Y+3gCfUMtp2k6x1IVxqsj
VvyhO+sAnOAA+S+tkF72Jp1b5XFDgOfo2AQc
=PdR
----- END PGP PUBLIC KEY BLOCK -----
§
```

27.5 Checking Your Keyring

Your public keys are stored in a special file called a keyring. You can list the keys
in your keyring using the --list-keys option.

■ **Run gpg with the --list-keys option.**

§ gpg --list-keys (Return)

The response will be a list of the keys on your public keyring:

```
~/.gnupg/pubring.gpg
---------------------------
pub 1024D/202C0A83 2004-08-17 John Doe (student)
<jdoe@podunk.edu>
sub  1024g/8A770E55 2004-08-17
```

■ **Compress and sign.** The `--sign` option compresses the document before adding a signature to the file. The result text is in binary form, and is not human-readable.

■ **Detach the signature.** The `--detach-sig` option creates a signature in a separate file from the document. The signature and document are both needed to verify the signature.

We will see how to clear-sign a document in the next section.

27.12 Clear-Signing a Document

Clear-signed documents may be sent as ordinary e-mail or published on a web page. The process of clear-signing is straightforward:

1. Start gpg with the appropriate options. Use the `--output` (or `-o`) option to specify an output file along with the `--clearsign` option and the name of the plaintext file:

§ `gpg --output plain.sig.asc --clearsign plain.txt` (Return)

You will be prompted for your passphrase:

```
You need a passphrase to unlock the secret key for user:
"John Doe (student) <jdoe@podunk.edu>"
1024-bit DSA key, ID 0F4867EB, created 2004-08-25

Enter passphrase:
```

2. Enter your passphrase.

`Enter passphrase:` ▓▓▓▓▓▓▓▓

The shell prompt will inform you that gpg has finished:

§

3. View the clear-signed file. Use the `cat` command:

§ `cat plain.sig.asc` (Return)

You should see the signed file:

```
-----BEGIN PGP SIGNED MESSAGE-----
Hash: SHA1

Time flies like the wind; fruit flies like bananas.
-----BEGIN PGP SIGNATURE-----
Version: GnuPG v1.2.4 (Darwin)

iD8DBQFBNTifq3YHg9IZ+sRAubYAJ9IJN1NEdbOiUMpnU9uDIFcGD1UjwCg
xc+i1bpp7Wj1k/CQfrS7BsiSyRU==1DI1
```

```
-----END PGP SIGNATURE-----
§
```

27.13 Verifying a Signature

You can verify the digital signature on a clear-signed document using gpg with
the --verify option. This requires that you possess the public key of the person
who signed the document. In this section, you will verify the document you
previously signed with your own private key.

1. Run gpg to verify the signature. Use the --verify option, taking the signed
file as an argument:

```
§ gpg --verify plain.sig.asc (Return)
```

You will be prompted for your passphrase:

```
You need a passphrase to unlock the secret key for user:
"John Doe (student) <jdoe@podunk.edu>"
1024-bit DSA key, ID 0F4867EB, created 2004-08-25

Enter passphrase:
```

2. Enter your passphrase.

```
Enter passphrase: ▓▓▓▓▓▓▓▓
```

You should see a message that the signature is good:

```
gpg: Signature made Mon Aug 30 19:01:46 2004 MDT using DSA
key ID 0F4867EB
gpg: Good signature from "John Doe (student)
<jdoe@podunk.edu>"
§
```

In contrast, if the file has been modified, you will be told that the signature is bad:

```
gpg: Signature made Mon Aug 30 19:01:46 2004 MDT using DSA
key ID 0F4867EB
gpg: BAD signature from "John Doe (student)
<jdoe@podunk.edu>"
§
```

27.14 Command Summary

GPG Options (following gpg command)

`--version`	check the version of gpg
`--gen-key`	generate a keypair
`--gen-revoke`	generate a key revocation certificate
`--list-keys`	list the keys on the keyring
`--armor`	apply ASCII armor (used with `--export`)
`--export` *keyID*	export the key identified by *keyID*
`--import` *file*	import a key from the file *file*
`--edit-key` *keyID*	edit the key identified by *keyID*
`-e`	encrypt (used with `-r` and `-o`)
`--encrypt`	encrypt
`-r` *Doe*	recipient *Doe*
`--recipient` *Doe*	recipient *Doe*
`-o` *file*	output to *file*
`--output` *file*	output to *file*
`--decrypt` *file*	decrypt *file*
`--clearsign` *file*	clear-sign *file*
`--verify` *file*	verify the signature on *file*

Edit Commands (Command> prompt)

`fpr`	get the key's fingerprint
`sign`	sign a key
`check`	check a signed key
`quit`	quit editing and return to the shell

27.15 Exercises

1. If you have not already done so, exchange public keys with a friend, co-worker, or classmate.

2. Sign and encrypt a message in ASCII armor and send it to someone who has your public key.

3. Read the man pages for gpg to learn about the `--sign` option. Run gpg with this option to sign and compress a document. Then run gpg with the `--decrypt` option to decrypt the file and verify the signature.

4. Read the man pages for gpg to learn about the `--detach-sig` option. Run gpg with this option to sign a document. Then run gpg with the `--verify` option to verify the signature.

PART VII
STARTUP FILES

# Chapter 28

STARTUP FILES

Tutorials related to this chapter are found in Chapters 29, 30, and 31.

A *startup file* contains commands for a shell to execute when it begins running. Startup files greatly increase the convenience and flexibility of the shell by performing routine tasks such as setting up your terminal, customizing the shell prompt, and reminding you of upcoming events.

28.1 Startup Files

In general, there are three types of startup files:

■ **System-wide startup files.** On many systems, the system administrator creates startup files containing commands that are to be used by login shells on the system. These files are typically found in the /etc directory.

■ **Login initialization files.** The login initialization file contains commands that are executed by the login shell when you log in. This file exists in your home directory.

■ **Shell initialization files.** Also called an *environment file*, this is a file in your home directory that contains commands to be executed by any new shell that starts up, whether or not it is the login shell.

28.2 System-wide Startup Files

When you log in, your login shell first looks for a system-wide or default startup file in the directory /etc. If such a file exists, it will have been created for you by the system administrator; you may not create or change it yourself. Different login shells use different system-wide startup files:

■ The Bourne Shell (sh), Korn Shell (ksh), and Bourne Again Shell (bash) look for the file /etc/.profile.

■ The C Shell (csh) typically looks for one of the following files:

/etc/.login

/etc/csh.login

/etc/csh.cshrc

■ The TC Shell (`tcsh`) typically looks for one of the following files:

`/etc/.login`

`/etc/tcsh.login`

`/etc/tcsh.tcshrc`

The system-wide startup file is optional; there is no requirement that your particular system have such a file.

28.3 Login Initialization Files

After executing the system-wide startup file (if there is one), your login shell looks for a *login initialization file* in your home directory. The name of this file varies, depending on which shell you are using as your login shell:

■ `sh` and `ksh` look in your home directory for a file named `.profile`.

■ `csh` and `tcsh` look for a file named `.login` in your home directory. (On some systems, the shell initialization file—described in the next section—may be executed before the `.login` file.)

■ `bash` looks for one of several possible files, in the following order:

`.bash_profile`

`.bash_login`

`.profile`

28.4 Shell Initialization Files

The third and last type of startup file is the *shell initialization file* or *environment file*, which contains commands to be executed when a new shell process is started. Keep in mind that a new shell process starts whenever you log in; it also happens when you start up a subshell. For example, you can run `ksh` as a subshell simply by entering the command line

§ `/bin/ksh` (Return)

A subshell is sometimes started for you by the login shell. For instance, when you run your own program or shell script, the login shell actually calls up a subshell to run the program. The same thing happens when you group several commands together using parentheses. In either case, the new subshell executes the commands it finds in the shell initialization file.

However a new shell process starts, it looks for commands in a shell initialization file. The name of this file depends on the shell:

■ `sh` does not use a shell initialization file.

Control Files

Note that startup files are hidden files—their names begin with a period (.)—meaning that they will not be listed by the simple `ls` command. (To list these files, use the `ls -l` command.) Most hidden files are used to control the way the system works. For this reason, they are sometimes called *control files*. Some of the more common control files are listed below, along with a description of their contents:

`.exrc`	Settings for the `vi` editor
`.forward`	Addresses to which e-mail is forwarded
`.logout`	Commands to be run when you log out
`.mailrc`	Mail aliases
`.mwmrc`	Commands to configure Motif Window Manager (`mwm`)
`.newsrc`	List of newsgroups and messages read
`.plan`	Information displayed by `finger` command
`.xinitrc`	Commands to configure the X Window System
`.dtprofile`	Commands to configure the CDE Desktop

The rc ending stands for "run command."

- `ksh` looks for `.kshrc` in your home directory.

- `csh` looks for `.cshrc` in your home directory.

- `tcsh` looks for `.tcshrc` in your home directory. If it cannot find such a file, `tcsh` then looks for the file `.cshrc`.

- `bash` looks for `.bashrc` in your home directory.

28.5 Variables

One of the most important uses for a startup file is to set the values of variables used by the shell. A *variable* is a named storage location that can hold a value. Three types of variables are commonly used by the shell:

- **Environment Variables.** Also called *special shell variables*, *keyword variables*, *predefined shell variables*, or *standard shell variables*, these variables hold information about the computer system that the shell needs to operate correctly.

- **User-created Variables.** You can name your own variables and assign them values. These are also called *personal variables*.

- **Positional Parameters.** These are used in shell programs.

Shell scripts are discussed in Chapters 30 and 31.

In this chapter we will discuss the environment and user-created variables. We will discuss positional parameters in greater detail when we take up shell scripts.

Variable	Contents
DISPLAY	Default display name
HOME	Pathname of your home directory
MAIL	Pathname of your system mailbox
PATH	Directories where shell is to look for commands
PWD	Your current working directory
SHELL	Pathname of shell (e.g., /bin/csh)
TERM	The termcap code for your terminal
USER	Your user name

Table 28-1
Some common environment variables.

28.6 Environment Variables

The environment shell variables provide information to the shell about the way your account is set up. Some of the more common environment variables are listed in Table 28-1.

28.7 Setting the Environment Variables

Some of the standard shell variables (such as HOME and SHELL) are set automatically when you log in. Others (such as TERM) you may have to set yourself. This is usually done in your login initialization file.

If your login shell is one of the Bourne family of shells (either sh, ksh, or bash), you can set the values of the shell variables using your login initialization file. For example, you could set the terminal type to be a vt100 by putting the following command line in your .profile (or .bash_profile):

There are no spaces around the equals sign.

TERM=vt100

This line would suffice to tell the login shell that you are working on a vt100, but you also need to get this information to any subshells that might be created. To do this, you must include the export command in your login initialization file:

export TERM

This will ensure that the subshells are given the value of TERM. If for some reason you did not want the subshells to know what kind of terminal you are using, you could simply omit the export command.

If your login shell is from the C Shell family (csh or tcsh), you can set the terminal type and "export" it all at once by putting the setenv ("set environment") command in your .login file:

setenv does not take an equals sign (=).

setenv TERM vt100

28.8 Listing the Environment Variables

There are several ways to examine the value of a standard shell variable once it is set. If you are using sh, ksh, or bash, the set command without arguments will list the values of all the environment variables:

(sh, ksh, or bash)   § set (Return)

If you are using csh or tcsh, the setenv command will do the same thing:

(csh or tcsh)   § setenv (Return)

You can also view the values of the individual variables one at a time with the echo command. For example, the following command line will display the current value of TERM:

§ echo $TERM (Return)
vt100

Note the dollar sign ($) preceding TERM; this is a special character that tells echo you want to see the contents of the variable TERM, not just its name. If you omitted the dollar sign, this is what you would see:

§ echo TERM (Return)
TERM

28.9 The Search Path

In Chapter 10, we summarized how the shell processes commands:

1. The shell displays a prompt symbol on the screen. The prompt tells you the shell is ready to receive your commands.

2. You type in a command. As you type, the shell stores the characters and also echoes them back to the terminal screen.

3. You type (RETURN). This is the signal for the shell to interpret the command and start working on it.

4. The shell interprets your command. In most cases, the shell looks for the appropriate software to run your command. If the shell can't find the right software, it gives you an error message; otherwise, the shell asks the kernel to run it.

5. The kernel runs the requested software. While the command is running, the shell "goes to sleep." When the kernel finishes, it "wakes up" the shell.

6. The shell displays a prompt symbol. This indicates that the shell is once again ready to receive your commands.

In Step 4, the shell examines the value of the environment variable PATH. This variable holds the *search path,* which is a list of pathnames telling the shell where to look.

If you are using either sh, ksh or bash, the pathnames of the search path are separated by colons (:). The PATH variable can be set like this:

sh, ksh and bash use
colons between pathnames.

```
PATH=/bin:/usr/bin:/usr/your-login/bin:
export PATH
```

This tells the shell to look first in the /bin directory. If it cannot find the right software in that directory, it is to search /usr/bin, then /usr/*your-login*/bin, and finally, the current directory. (Placing a colon by itself at the beginning or end of the path, or two colons in a row within the path, tells the shell to search the current directory.)

A csh or tcsh search path uses spaces instead of colons to separate the directory pathnames, and it uses the setenv command to set the value of PATH:

csh and tcsh use spaces
to separate pathnames.

```
setenv PATH ( /bin /usr/bin /usr/your-login/bin . )
```

This tells the shell to search /bin, then /usr/bin, then /usr/*your-login*/bin, and finally, the current directory (.).

28.10 User-Defined Variables

In addition to the standard shell variables, you can define your own variables. This is done by giving the variable a name and a value. Suppose, for example, that you were to use a long directory name such as /usera/george/bin/stuff and would prefer not to have to type it out each time.

If you are using sh, ksh, or bash, you could place the following line in your .profile (or .bash_profile) to define a variable to hold the pathname:

sh, ksh, and bash require
that no spaces appear
around the equals sign.

```
stuff=/usera/george/bin/stuff
```

This creates a variable named stuff, and gives it the pathname as a value. This variable will be known only to the login shell; if you also want it to be available to any subshells, you will have to "export" it:

```
export stuff
```

If you are a ksh or bash user, you could also make stuff available to the subshells by defining it in the shell initialization file (.kshrc or .bashrc).

csh and tcsh handle user-defined variables somewhat differently. To create the variable stuff you could use the set command in your .login file:

csh and tcsh allow spaces
around the equals sign.

```
set stuff = /usera/george/bin/stuff
```

This would define stuff for the login shell, but the definition would not carry over to any subshells. If you want your subshells to be able to use this variable, you have two choices. First, you could use the setenv command in your .login file:

Do not use an equals sign
with setenv.

```
setenv stuff /usera/george/bin/stuff
```

Or you could use the `set` command in your shell initialization file (`.cshrc` or `.tcshrc`):

```
set stuff = /usera/george/bin/stuff
```

Remember, commands in your shell initialization file are run each time a new shell process is started, including subshells.

Having defined the variable `stuff` and given it a value, you can use it to save keystrokes. For example, you could list the files in `/usera/george/bin/stuff` with the following command line:

Note the dollar sign preceding the variable name.

§ `ls $stuff` (Return)

Traditionally, user-defined variable names are spelled in lowercase letters, to distinguish them from the standard shell variables.

28.11 The calendar Utility

Do not confuse this with the `cal` *utility, which displays a calendar on the screen.*

Most UNIX systems offer the `calendar` utility, a kind of electronic datebook that can remind you of important assignments, appointments, project deadlines, and so on. To use `calendar`, include the following line in your login initialization file:

```
calendar
```

This command tells UNIX to search through a file named `calendar` for any lines that contain today's date or tomorrow's date; it then displays those lines on the screen. (On weekends, it also displays Monday's messages.) Suppose you wanted to remember to call Adam Smith on April 12. You might put the following line in `calendar`, which will be displayed when you log in on April 11:

```
Call Adam Smith April 12
```

The same line will be displayed when you log in on April 12. Any of the following messages would have the same effect:

```
Call Adam Smith on 4/12
```

```
April 12: call Adam Smith
```

```
Call Adam Smith on Apr 12
```

The date may appear anywhere on the line, and it may be spelled out (April 12), abbreviated (Apr 12), or written in numerals (4/12). However, you must put the month before the date. (Do not write 12 April, 12 Apr, or 12/4). If you include the year, it will be ignored; `calendar` always assumes the current year.

28.12 The history Mechanism

The Bourne Shell does not have a history mechanism.

Recall that the history feature (offered by ksh, bash, csh, and tcsh) records the most recent commands you have issued and gives you a quick way to repeat those commands.

You can specify how many commands you want history to remember for you. If you are a csh or tcsh user, you can set history to remember the last ten commands by putting the following line in your shell initialization file (.cshrc or .tcshrc):

csh and tcsh allow spaces around the equals sign.

```
set history = 10
```

To set ksh and bash to remember the last ten commands, you would put the following line in your .kshrc or .bashrc file to set the value of the variable HISTSIZE:

ksh and bash do not allow spaces around the equals sign.

```
HISTSIZE=10
```

If you do not set the HISTSIZE variable, ksh will remember 128 commands by default; bash remembers 500 commands.

28.13 Command Aliases

All of the common shells except the original Bourne Shell allow you to rename UNIX commands. A renamed command —called an *alias*—may be used to shorten long commands or to protect you from accidentally deleting an important file. Most users set up a list of aliases in their shell initialization file (.kshrc, .bashrc, .cshrc, or .tcshrc), so that the aliases are defined automatically each time a new shell is started.

The alias command is used to define aliases in csh or tcsh. Placing the following line in the .cshrc or .tcshrc file tells the shell to treat m as an alias for the mailx command:

(csh or tcsh)

```
alias m mailx
```

The alias command works a bit differently with ksh and bash. The following line may be placed in the shell initialization file to create an alias for the mailx command:

(ksh or bash)

```
alias m=mailx
```

Once the alias is set, you could send mail to the user bfranklin with the command line

§ m bfranklin (Return)

You can remove an alias with the unalias command:

§ unalias m (Return)

28.14 Protecting Existing Files

One of the common uses of command aliases is to protect files from being deleted accidentally. When you specify the i ("interactive") option with the cp, mv, or rm command, you will be asked to confirm your intentions if you try to do something that would destroy an existing file. For example, suppose you tried to remove a file named oldfile using the rm -i command:

§ rm -i oldfile (Return)

The command will prompt you to confirm that this is what you want:

rm: remove oldfile?

If you enter a *y* (for "yes"), the file will be removed. Otherwise, no action will be taken. The -i option works similarly with the cp or mv commands, should you try to overwrite an existing file.

If you are a csh or tcsh user, you can create a "safe" alias for rm by placing the following line in the .cshrc or .tcshrc file:

(csh or tcsh)   alias rm 'rm -i'

If you use ksh or bash, you would put this line in your .kshrc or .bashrc file:

(ksh or bash)   alias rm='rm -i'

The single quotes are required because of the space between rm and -i.

Alternatively, you could put the alias command in your .profile or .bash_profile, using the -x option to export the command to all subshells:

The -x option exports the alias (ksh or bash).   alias -x rm='rm -i'

Incidentally, the alias command without arguments lists any aliases you have defined:

§ alias (Return)

28.15 Comment Lines

A *comment* is a line of text in a startup file that is ignored by the shell when the file is executed. Comments are useful for reminding you of the file's purpose. In shell startup files, a comment begins with a pound sign (#). For example,

This is a comment line

28.16 Exercises

1. Be sure you can define the following terms:

startup file   login initialization file   shell initialization file

subshell   variable   special shell variable

environment variable   alias

2. Be sure you can explain the function or contents of each of the following files:

.cshrc	.exrc	.forward	.kshrc
.login	.logout	.mailrc	.mwmrc
.newsrc	.plan	.profile	.xinitrc
.dtprofile	.tcshrc	.bashrc	

3. Be sure you can explain the purpose of each of the following variables:

HOME	MAIL	PATH
PWD	SHELL	TERM

4. Suppose a sh user wanted to create a variable named myhome to hold the pathname of his or her home directory.

a. What command(s) should be put in the login initialization file so that myhome will be usable by the login shell only?

b. What command(s) will ensure that myhome will be available to all subshells? (The variable HOME contains the pathname of the home directory.)

5. Suppose a ksh or bash user wanted to create a variable named myhome to hold the pathname of his or her home directory.

a. What command(s) should be put in the login initialization file so that myhome will be usable by the login shell only?

b. What command(s) will ensure that myhome will be available to all subshells? (The variable HOME contains the pathname of the home directory.)

6. Suppose a csh or tcsh user wanted to create a variable named myhome to hold the pathname of his or her home directory. What command should be put in the login initialization file so that myhome will be available to all subshells? (The variable HOME contains the pathname of the home directory.)

# Chapter 29

TUTORIAL:
USING SH & KSH STARTUP FILES

Skip this chapter if you are not using sh or ksh.

In this chapter, you will learn how to create and modify startup files used by the Bourne Shell (sh) and Korn Shell (ksh).

29.1 Review of sh and ksh Startup Files

The Bourne Shell uses two startup files: a system-wide startup file and a login initialization file. If sh is your login shell, it executes the commands in the following files:

[sh]
```
/etc/profile
.profile
```

The shell executes the commands in these files just once each time you log in.

The Korn Shell uses three startup files: a system-wide startup file, a login initialization file, and a shell initialization file. When you log in using ksh as your login shell, it executes the files in the following order:

[ksh]
```
/etc/profile
.profile
.kshrc
```

After that, every ksh subshell executes the commands in .kshrc.

29.2 Listing the Variables with set

■ **List the current settings of the environment variables.** This is done with the set command, used without arguments:

The $ is the default prompt for sh and ksh, and will be used in this chapter.

```
$ set Return
```

The shell will display a list of variables and their current settings. Some variables you might see are shown in Table 29-1.

Table 29-1

Some common environment variables.

Variable	Contents
HOME	Pathname of your home directory
MAIL	Pathname of your system mailbox
PATH	Directories where shell is to look for commands
PS1	"Prompt string 1"—primary prompt (default: $)
PS2	"Prompt string 2"—secondary prompt (default: >)
PWD	Your current working directory
SHELL	Pathname of shell (/bin/sh or /bin/ksh)
TERM	The termcap code for your terminal
USER	Your user name

29.3 Showing the Value of a Variable with echo

You can examine the values of the environment variables one at a time using the echo command.

■ **Enter the echo command, specifying the variable you wish to examine.** You must enter a dollar sign ($) as a prefix to the variable name. Thus, to view the contents of the PS2 variable, type

```
$ echo $PS2 (Return)
```

The secondary prompt is discussed in the next section.

PS2 contains the secondary prompt. Its default value is

```
>
```

If you omit the dollar sign prefix, the name of the variable, not its contents, will be displayed:

```
$ echo PS2 (Return)
PS2
```

29.4 The Secondary Prompt

The secondary prompt is a symbol that indicates that the shell is waiting for you to finish an incomplete command line. In this section, you will see how this works.

1. Enter an incomplete command line. Try the following line, making sure not to type any closing quotes:

```
$ echo "This is an (Return)
```

Because you did not provide the closing quotes, the shell assumes that there is more to come, and it displays the secondary prompt stored in PS2:

```
>
```

2. Enter the rest of the command line. Be sure to finish it off with double quotes, before pressing (Return):

```
>incomplete command line." (Return)
```

The shell will echo back the entire message:

```
This is an
incomplete command line.
```

29.5 Making Backups of the Startup Files

The first step in creating a .profile is to see whether you already have such a file. If so, you should prepare a backup copy.

1. If necessary, go to your home directory. Remember, the cd command without arguments will take you to your home directory:

```
$ cd (Return)
```

2. List all files in your home directory. Enter the ls   a ("list -all") command:

```
$ ls -a (Return)
```

If you see a file named .profile, it was placed in your home directory when your account was created. Do not edit this file; copy it and work on the copy instead. (If you are a ksh user, also note whether you already have a .kshrc file.)

3. Make a backup copy of the existing startup file(s).

```
$ cp .profile .profile.BAK (Return)
$ cp .kshrc .kshrc.BAK (Return)
```

29.6 A Login Message

In this section you will create a .profile file (or edit an existing file) to display a message on the screen every time you log in. You will use the echo command to do this.

1. Try out the login message. Type

```
$ echo "Your wish is my command, Oh Great One." (Return)
```

The shell should respond with the appropriate message:

```
Your wish is my command, Oh Great One.
```

2. Use your text editor to open the .profile file.

```
$ vi .profile (Return)
```

3. Insert a comment showing the modification date. Put the following line at the top of .profile:

```
# This file was last modified on [enter today's date here].
```

The # at the beginning of the line makes this a comment. This shows a typical use of comments, which is to tell you when the file was last edited.

4. Add the message command to the file.

```
echo "Your wish is my command, Oh Great One."
```

5. Write the file and quit the editor.

29.7 Running the Startup File

At this point, you could log out and log back in again to see if your .profile works. However, there is an easier way: Use the "dot" command.

■ **Run the "dot" command.** Type a period, a space, and the name of the file:

```
$ . .profile (Return)
```

This will cause the shell to execute the commands in .profile, as if you had just logged in. You should see the login message:

```
Your wish is my command, Oh Great One.
```

The shell will display this message each time you log in, unless you change it or delete it from your .profile.

29.8 Changing the Prompt Symbol

The default primary prompt symbol for sh or ksh is the dollar sign ($). You can change the prompt symbol by changing the value of the variable PS1. In this section, you will try out various prompts, then edit .profile to display one of the new prompts.

1. Change the value of the PS1 variable. Type the following line, making sure not to put spaces around the equals sign:

```
$ PS1=# (Return)
```

This will change your shell prompt to the pound sign:

```
#
```

2. Try out another prompt. You can include spaces and special characters in the prompt string if you quote it:

```
# PS1="Your Majesty? " (Return)
```

The prompt will change to the new string:

```
Your Majesty?
```

3. Include shell variables in your prompt. Some users like to display the pathname of their home directory as part of their prompt. Remember, your home directory's pathname is stored by the shell in a variable named HOME. Try the following command (don't type Your Majesty?—it is the prompt):

Your Majesty? PS1="$HOME > " (Return)

Without the dollar sign, the word HOME would appear instead of the pathname.
The dollar sign placed in front of HOME tells the shell to put the contents of HOME in the prompt. Now your prompt should show the absolute pathname of your home directory, followed by an arrow (>). For example, if the absolute pathname of your home directory were /home/you, the prompt would now be

/home/you >

Let's put this prompt into your .profile.

4. Use the text editor to edit the startup file. Add the following to .profile:

```
PS1="$HOME > "
export PS1
```

5. Write to the file and quit the editor.

6. Use the "dot" command to run the commands in .profile.

/home/you > . .profile (Return)

Your prompt should now consist of your home directory's pathname, followed by an arrow. Thus, if your home directory were /home/you, you would see your login message, then the prompt

/home/you >

29.9   Setting the Terminal Type

Having to set your terminal type each time you log in is a nuisance—especially if you use the same kind of terminal all of the time. You can set the terminal in your .profile file.

1. Edit your .profile to set the terminal type. Insert the following lines, substituting your terminal's termcap code for vt100:

```
TERM=vt100
export TERM
echo "Terminal set to $TERM"
```

2. Write and quit the editor.

3. Apply the "dot" command to .profile:

/home/you > . .profile (Return)

Your login message should appear, then the message about the terminal type:

Terminal set to vt100

29.10 Making a calendar File

Skip this section if
calendar is not available
on your system.

The calendar utility will remind you of upcoming events. This requires that you have a calendar file in your home directory, and that you modify .profile to read the calendar file.

1. Edit your .profile **with the text editor.** Add the following line:

```
calendar
```

2. Write the change into the file and quit the editor.

3. Use the text editor to create a calendar **file.** Be sure to use this exact spelling of calendar, in lowercase letters. Otherwise, the shell won't recognize the file.

4. Add a message to the calendar **file.** Include today's date in the message. For example, if today is April 12, type

Write the date in the form
April 12, Apr 12, or 4/12.

```
This is a test for April 12
```

5. Write the changes into the calendar **file and quit the editor.**

6. Use the "dot" command to run the .profile **file.**

```
/home/you > . .profile Return
```

You should see your login message, the message about your terminal type, and the calendar message:

```
Your wish is my command, Oh Great One.
Terminal set to vt100
This is a test for April 12
$
```

29.11 Creating a .kshrc File (ksh only)

If you are a ksh user, you may create a shell initialization file named .kshrc. This file is typically used for setting up command aliases and the history mechanism. Before doing this, however, you need to edit .profile:

1. Use the text editor to edit .profile. Add the following lines to the file:

```
ENV=$HOME/.kshrc
export ENV
```

This tells ksh that it should look for .kshrc in your home directory. If the ENV variable is not set, ksh will not execute .kshrc.

2. Write and quit the editor.

3. Use the text editor to edit the .kshrc **file.** Start by inserting a comment line giving today's date:

```
# This file was last modified on [today's date]
```

29.12 Creating an Alias (ksh)

One of the uses for .kshrc is to create aliases. In this section, you will create a one-letter alias for the history command.

1. Use the text editor to edit the .kshrc file. Add the following line to the file to create an alias for the history command:

Spaces are not allowed around the equals sign.

```
alias -x h=history
```

The -x option tells alias to export the alias to all subshells.

2. Write the changes to the file and quit the editor.

3. Use the "dot" command to run the .kshrc file.

```
/home/you > . .kshrc (Return)
```

At this point, the alias should be set. In the next section, you will see how to use the alias to run the history command.

29.13 Using the history Mechanism (ksh)

sh does not have a history mechanism.

The history mechanism keeps a list of the commands you have used most recently, and it allows you to view and repeat commands on the list.

1. Run the history command using its alias. Type h followed by (Return) to run the history command:

```
/home/you > h (Return)
```

By default, ksh remembers 128 commands. See Exercise 7.

If you correctly set up the alias for history, you should see a numbered list of the most recently executed commands. Note that the history command itself will appear as the last item on the list:

```
1   set
2   echo $PS2
3   echo PS2
4   echo "This is an incomplete command line."
5   ls -a
6   echo "Your wish is my command, Oh Great One."
7   vi .profile
8   . .profile
9   PS1=#
10  PS1="Your Majesty? "
11  PS1="$HOME >"
12  vi .profile
13  . .profile
14  vi .profile
15  . .profile
16  vi .profile
17  vi calendar
18  vi .kshrc
```

```
19  .  .kshrc
20  h
```

2. Repeat the most recent command on the list. Remember, this is done by typing an r at the prompt. Try it:

```
/home/you > r (Return)
```

You should see another listing of commands, as before:

```
1    set
2    echo $PS2
3    echo PS2
4    echo "This is an incomplete command line."
5    ls -a
6    echo "Your wish is my command, Oh Great One."
7    vi .profile
8    .  .profile
9    PS1=#
10   PS1="Your Majesty? "
11   PS1="$HOME >"
12   vi .profile
13   .  .profile
14   vi .profile
15   .  .profile
16   vi .profile
17   vi calendar
18   vi .kshrc
19   .  .kshrc
20   h
21   h
```

3. Repeat a command by number. Thus, to repeat the sixth command on the list, type

```
/home/you > r  6 (Return)
```

The command line will appear on the screen, and the command will be run.

```
echo "Your wish is my command, Oh Great One."
Your wish is my command, Oh Great One.
```

4. Repeat a command by entering the first letter(s) of the command line. Thus, to repeat a command line that starts with the letter s, type

```
/home/you > r  s (Return)
```

The most recent command beginning with s is the set command; it should list the values of the environment variables.

```
set
```

29.14 Command Summary

Checking the Values of Variables

`set`	list the values of all variables
`echo $`*var*	print value of variable *var*

Setting Values of Variables

var=value	set variable *var* to the value *val*
var="a string"	store string *a string* in variable *var*
`export` *var*	export contents of *var* to all subshells

Executing a Startup File

`. .profile`	execute `.profile`

Changing Prompts

`PS1="`*string*`"`	set primary prompt to *string*
`export PS1`	export contents of PS1 to all subshells

Creating Command Aliases (`ksh`)

`alias` *c=command*	define *c* as an alias for *command*
`alias -x` *c=command*	define and export *c* as an alias for *command*
`unalias` *c*	remove *c* as an alias for *command*

Using the history Mechanism (`ksh`)

`history`	print `history` list
`r`	repeat the most recent event on `history` list
`r` *n*	repeat the *n*th event on `history` list
`r` *abc*	repeat the most recent event starting with letters *abc*

29.15 Exercises

1. The `date` command prints the date and current time. Add the following line to your `.profile`, making sure to use backquotes around `date`:

```
echo "The date and time are `date`."
```

Exit the editor and run the `.profile` using the "dot" command. What happens?

2. The backquotes were needed in the previous exercise to tell the shell that `date` was to be interpreted as a command, not as a word. What happens if the backquotes are omitted? Try it. Open `.profile` and remove the backquotes from `date`:

```
echo "The date and time are date"
```

Exit the editor and run the `.profile` using the "dot"command. What happens? (Now open up the file and replace the backquotes.)

3. What is your search path (PATH)?

4. What is the complete pathname for your shell?

5. The `rm`, `cp`, and `mv` commands are dangerous because they can overwrite or remove existing files. The `i` ("interactive") option will ask you to confirm that this is what you want. If this option is available to you, add the following lines to your `.kshrc` file:

```
alias -x rm='rm -i'

alias -x cp='cp -i'

alias -x mv='mv -i'
```

Note that quotes are required around a command that contains a space.

6. Explain what the following lines would do if they were placed in your `.kshrc` file:

```
alias -x m=more

alias -x f=finger

alias -x ls='ls -R'
```

7. Most users set up their `history` mechanism to remember about 100 commands. To do this yourself, open your `.kshrc` file and insert this line:

```
HISTSIZE=100
```

If you neglect to set the `HISTSIZE` variable, `ksh` will remember the most recent 128 commands by default.

# Chapter 30

TUTORIAL: USING CSH & TCSH STARTUP FILES

Skip this chapter if you are not using csh or tcsh.

In this chapter, you will learn how to create and modify startup files used by the C Shell (csh) and TC Shell (tcsh).

30.1 Review of csh & tcsh Startup Files

The C Shell uses three startup files: a system-wide startup file, a login initialization file, and a shell initialization file. When you log in using csh as your login shell, it looks for the files in the following order:

[csh]   /etc/.login (alternatively, /etc/csh.login or /etc/csh.cshrc)

.login

.cshrc

The commands in these files are executed once each time you log in; thereafter, the commands in the file .cshrc are executed when a new csh process is started. (On some systems, .cshrc is executed before .login when you log in.)

The TC Shell also uses three startup files: a system-wide startup file, a login initialization file, and a shell initialization file. When you log in using tcsh as your login shell, it looks for the files in the following order:

[tcsh]   /etc/.login (alternatively, /etc/tcsh.login or /etc/tcsh.tcshrc)

.login

.tcshrc (if it exists; .cshrc otherwise)

The commands in these files are executed once each time you log in; thereafter, the commands in the file .tcshrc are executed whenever a new tcsh process is started. (On some systems, .tcshrc is executed before .login when you log in.)

Table 30-1
Some csh and tcsh
environment variables.

Variable	Contents
HOME	Pathname of your home directory
MAIL	Pathname of your system mailbox
PATH	Directories where shell is to look for commands
PWD	Your current working directory
SHELL	Pathname of shell (/bin/csh or /bin/tcsh)
TERM	The termcap code for your terminal
USER	Your user name

30.2 Listing the Environment Variables

■ **List the current settings of the environment variables.** This is done with the setenv command, used without arguments:

The percent sign is the usual default prompt for csh and tcsh, and will be used in this chapter.

% setenv (Return)

The shell will display a list of variables and their current settings (see Table 30-1).

You can examine the values of these variables one at a time using the echo command.

■ **Enter the echo command, specifying the variable you wish to examine.** You must enter a dollar sign ($) as a prefix to the variable name. Thus, to view the contents of the SHELL variable, type

% echo $SHELL (Return)

This will display the absolute pathname of csh or tcsh:

/bin/csh

/bin/tcsh

If you omit the dollar sign prefix, the name of the variable, not its contents, will be displayed:

% echo SHELL (Return)
SHELL

Variable	Contents
cwd	Pathname of current working directory
history	Size of history list
home	Pathname of your home directory
path	Directories where shell is to look for commands
prompt	Current prompt symbol (default: %)
shell	Pathname of shell (/bin/csh or /bin/tcsh)
term	The termcap code for your terminal
user	Your user name

Table 30-2
Some special csh and tcsh variables. These variables are not used by sh or ksh.

30.3 Checking the Special Variables

The C Shell and TC Shell use the same environment variables as the Bourne Shell and Korn Shell; but csh and tcsh also have some special shell variables of their own. You can check the settings of these variables using the set command.

■ **Enter the set command without arguments.**

% set (Return)

This will list the special shell variables and their current settings; some of these are shown in Table 30-2. Note that csh and tcsh special variables are written in lowercase letters to distinguish them from the environment variables.

30.4 Setting the Special Variables

The set command is used to assign a value to a variable.

1. Enter the set command. For example, to set the value of the history variable, type the following:

% set history = 100 (Return)

2. Check the setting with echo.

Do not omit the $ sign.   % echo $history (Return)

This should show the value stored in history:

100

The variables home, path, shell, term, and user have a special relationship with their uppercase counterparts. When you change the value of the lowercase variable, the uppercase variable is changed as well. If you change the value of term, for example, the value of TERM is changed automatically to match.

30.5 Making Backups of the Startup Files

The first step in creating or editing .login, .cshrc or .tcshrc is to see whether you already have such files. If so, you should prepare backup copies.

1. If necessary, go to your home directory. Remember, the cd command without arguments will take you to your home directory:

% cd (Return)

2. List all files in your home directory. Enter the ls -a ("list -all") command:

% ls -a (Return)

If you see files named .login and .cshrc or .tcshrc, these were probably placed in your home directory when your account was created. You may want to consult with your instructor or system administrator before editing them.

3. Make a backup copy of the existing startup file(s). Use the cp command, and name the copies with the .BAK suffix to indicate that these are backups:

% cp .login .login.BAK (Return)
% cp .cshrc .cshrc.BAK (Return)
% cp .tcshrc .tcshrc.BAK (Return)

30.6 A Login Message

In this section you will create a .login file (or edit an existing file) to display a message on the screen every time you log in.

1. Try out the login message. Type

% echo "Your wish is my command, Oh Great One." (Return)

The shell should respond with the appropriate message:

Your wish is my command, Oh Great One.

2. Use your text editor to open the .login file.

% vi .login (Return)

3. Insert a comment showing the modification date. Put the following line at the top of .login:

This file was last modified on [*insert today's date*].

The # at the beginning of the line makes this a comment. This shows a typical use of comments, which is to tell you when the file was last edited.

4. Add the message command to the file.

echo "Your wish is my command, Oh Great One."

5. Write the file and quit the editor.

30.7 Running the Startup File

At this point, you could log out and log back in again to see if your `.login` works. However, there is an easier way: Use the `source` command.

■ **Run the `source` command on the file.** Thus, to run the commands in `.login`, type:

```
% source .login (Return)
```

This will cause the shell to execute the commands in `.login`, as if you had just logged in. You should see the login message:

```
Your wish is my command, Oh Great One.
```

The shell will display this message each time you log in, unless you change it or delete it from your `.login`.

30.8 Changing the Prompt Symbol

The default primary prompt symbol for `csh` and `tcsh` is the percent sign (%). You can change the prompt symbol by changing the value of the variable `prompt`. In this section, you will try out various prompts, then edit `.login` to display one of the new prompts.

1. **Change the value of the `prompt` variable.** Type the following line:

```
% set prompt = # (Return)
```

This will change your shell prompt to the pound sign:

```
#
```

2. **Try out another prompt.** You can include spaces and special characters in the prompt string if you quote it:

```
# set prompt = 'Your Majesty? ' (Return)
```

The prompt will change to the new string:

```
Your Majesty?
```

3. **Include shell variables in your prompt.** Some users like to display the pathname of their home directory as part of their prompt. Remember, your home directory's pathname is stored by the shell in a variable named `home`. Try the following command (don't type `Your Majesty?`—it is the prompt):

```
Your Majesty? set prompt = "$home > " (Return)
```

The dollar sign placed in front of `home` tells the shell to put the contents of `home` in the prompt. Now your prompt should show the absolute pathname of your home directory, followed by an arrow (>). For example, if the absolute pathname of your home directory were `/home/you`, the prompt would now be

```
/home/you >
```

Let's put this prompt into your `.login`.

4. Use the text editor to edit the startup file. Add the following to `.login`:

```
set prompt = "$home > "
```

5. Write to the file and quit the editor.

6. Use the `source` command to run the commands in `.login`.

```
/home/you > source .login (Return)
```

Your prompt should now consist of your home directory's pathname, followed by an arrow. Thus, if your home directory were `/home/you`, you would see your login message, then the prompt

```
/home/you >
```

30.9 Setting the Terminal Type

Having to set your terminal each time you log in is a nuisance—especially if you use the same kind of terminal all of the time. You can set the terminal in your `.login` file.

1. Edit your `.login` to set the terminal type. Insert the following lines, substituting your terminal's termcap code for `vt100`:

```
set term = vt100
echo "Terminal set to $term"
```

2. Write and quit the editor.

3. Apply the `source` command to `.login`:

```
/home/you > source .login (Return)
```

Your login message should appear, then the message:

```
Terminal set to vt100
```

30.10 Making a calendar File

The `calendar` utility will remind you of upcoming events. This requires that you have a `calendar` file in your home directory and that you modify `.login` to read the `calendar` file.

1. Edit your `.login` with the text editor. Add the following line:

```
calendar
```

2. Write the change into the file and quit the editor.

3. **Use the text editor to create a** `calendar` **file.** Be sure to use this exact spelling of `calendar`, in lowercase letters. Otherwise, the shell won't recognize the file.

4. **Add a message to the** `calendar` **file.** Include today's date in the message. For example, if today is April 12, write:

Write the date in the form April 12, Apr 12, or 4/12.

```
This is a test for April 12
```

5. **Write the changes into the** `calendar` **file and quit the editor.**

6. **Use the** `source` **command to run the** `.login` **file.**

```
/home/you > source .login (Return)
```

You should see your login message, the message about the terminal type, and the `calendar` message:

```
Your wish is my command, Oh Great One.
Terminal set to vt100
This is a test for April 12
```

30.11   Editing a .cshrc or .tcshrc File

Always work on a copy of the file—see Section 30.5.

The shell initialization file (`.cshrc` or `.tcshrc`) is typically used for setting up command aliases and the `history` mechanism. In this section, you will create a one-letter alias for the `history` command.

1. **Use the text editor to edit the** `.cshrc` **or** `.tcshrc` **file.** Start by inserting a comment line giving today's date:

```
# This file was last modified on [today's date]
```

2. **Use the text editor to define an alias.** Add the following line to the file to create an alias for the `history` command:

```
alias h history
```

3. **Write the changes to the file and quit the editor.**

4. **Use the** `source` **command to run the file.** If you are using `csh` (or `tcsh` with a `.cshrc` file) type

```
/home/you > source .cshrc (Return)
```

If you are using `tcsh` with a `.tcshrc` file, type

```
/home/you > source .tcshrc (Return)
```

At this point, the alias should be set. In the next section, you will see how to use the alias to run the `history` command.

30.12 Using the history Mechanism

Recall that the history mechanism keeps a list of the commands you have used most recently, and it allows you to view and repeat commands on the list.

1. Run the history command using its alias. Type h followed by (Return) to run the history command:

/home/you > h (Return)

If you correctly set up the alias for history, you should see a numbered list of the most recently executed commands. Note that the history command itself will appear as the last item on the list:

```
1    set history = 100
2    echo $history
3    cd
4    ls -a
5    cp .login .login.BAK
6    cp .cshrc .cshrc.BAK
7    echo "Your wish is my command, Oh Great One."
8    vi .login
9    source .login
10   set prompt = #
11   set prompt = 'Your Majesty? '
12   vi .login
13   source .login
14   vi .login
15   source .login
16   vi calendar
17   source .login
18   vi .cshrc
19   . .cshrc
20   h
```

2. Repeat the most recent command on the list. This is done by typing two exclamation marks at the prompt. Try it:

/home/you > !! (Return)

You should see another listing of commands, as before.

3. Repeat a command by number. Thus, to repeat the seventh command, type

/home/you > !7 (Return)

The command line will appear on the screen, and the command will be run.

```
echo "Your wish is my command, Oh Great One."
Your wish is my command, Oh Great One.
```

4. Repeat a command by the first letter(s) of the command line. Thus, to repeat a command line that starts with the letter *s*, type

```
/home/you > !s Return
```

The most recent command beginning with *s* is the `source` command:

```
source .login
```

30.13 Command Summary

Checking the Values of Variables

`setenv`	list the values of environment variables
`set`	list the values of special `csh` variables
`echo $var`	print value of variable *var*

Setting Values of Variables

`set var = value`	set variable *var* to *value*
`set var = "a string"`	store string *a string* in variable *var*
`setenv VAR value`	set environment variable *VAR* to *value*

Executing a Startup File

`source .login`	execute `.login`

Changing Prompts

`set prompt = "str"`	set prompt to *str*

Creating Command Aliases

`alias c command`	make *c* an alias for *command*
`unalias c`	remove *c* as an alias for *command*

Using the history Mechanism

`history`	print `history` list
`!!`	repeat most recent event on `history` list
`!n`	repeat the *n*th event on `history` list
`!abc`	repeat the most recent event starting with letters *abc*

30.14 Exercises

1. The `date` command prints the date and current time. Add the following line to your `.login`, making sure to use backquotes around `date`:

```
echo "The date and time are `date`."
```

Exit the editor and run the `.login` using the `source` command. What happens?

2. The backquotes were needed in the previous exercise to tell the shell that `date` was to be interpreted as a command, not as a word. What happens if the back-quotes are omitted? Try it. Open up your `.login` and remove the backquotes from `date`:

```
echo "The date and time are date"
```

Exit the editor and run the `.login` using the `source` command. What happens? (Now open up the file and replace the backquotes.)

3. What are your search paths (`path` and PATH)?

4. What is the complete pathname for your shell?

5. Change your prompt so that it always displays the current working directory.

6. The `rm`, `cp`, and `mv` commands are dangerous because they can overwrite or remove existing files. The i ("interactive") option will ask you to confirm that this is what you want. If the i option is available to you, put the following lines in your shell initialization file:

```
alias rm 'rm -i'
```

```
alias cp 'cp -i'
```

```
alias mv 'mv -i'
```

7. Explain what the following lines would do if they were placed in your shell ini-tialization file:

```
alias m more
```

```
alias f finger
```

```
alias ls 'ls -R'
```

8. To prevent files from being overwritten by the redirection operation, place the following line in your `.cshrc` or `.tcshrc`:

```
set noclobber
```

Does this work as expected?

# Chapter 31

TUTORIAL:
USING BASH STARTUP FILES

Skip this chapter if you are not using bash.

In this chapter, you will learn how to create and modify startup files used by the Bourne Again Shell (bash).

31.1 Review of bash Startup Files

The Bourne Again Shell uses three startup files, a system-wide startup file, a login initialization file, and a shell initialization file. When you log in using bash as your login shell, it first looks for the system-wide startup file created by your system administrator:

```
/etc/.profile
```

Next, bash looks in your home directory for one of the following login initialization files:

bash looks for the files in the order shown; it reads only the first one it finds.

```
.bash_profile
```

```
.bash_login
```

```
.profile
```

Finally, bash looks in your home directory for the shell initialization file:

```
.bashrc
```

After that, every interactive bash subshell executes the commands in .bashrc.

31.2 Listing the Variables with set

■ **List the current settings of the environment variables.** This is done with the set command, used without arguments:

The default bash prompt consists of the shell name and version number, followed by the > symbol. This prompt will be used in this chapter.

```
BASH 2.0 > set (Return)
```

The shell will display a list of variables and their current settings. Some variables you might see are shown in Table 31-1.

Table 31-1
Some common
environment variables.

Variable	Contents
HOME	Pathname of your home directory
MAIL	Pathname of your system mailbox
PATH	Directories where shell is to look for commands
PS1	"Prompt string 1"—primary prompt (default: BASH 2.0 >)
PS2	"Prompt string 2"—secondary prompt (default: >)
PWD	Your current working directory
SHELL	Pathname of login shell (e.g. /bin/bash or /usr/bin/bash)
TERM	The termcap code for your terminal
USER	Your user name

31.3 Showing the Value of a Variable with echo

You can examine the values of the environment variables one at a time using the echo command.

■ **Enter the echo command, specifying the variable you wish to examine.** You must enter a dollar sign ($) as a prefix to the variable name. Thus, to view the contents of the PS2 variable, type

BASH 2.0 > echo $PS2 (Return)

The secondary prompt is discussed in the next section.

PS2 contains the secondary prompt. Its default value is

>

If you omit the dollar sign prefix, the name of the variable, not its contents, will be displayed:

BASH 2.0 > echo PS2 (Return)
PS2

31.4 The Secondary Prompt

The secondary prompt is a symbol that indicates that the shell is waiting for you to finish an incomplete command line. In this section, you will see how this works.

1. **Enter an incomplete command line.** Try the following line, making sure not to type any closing quotes:

BASH 2.0 > echo "This is an (Return)

Because you did not provide the closing quotes, the shell assumes that there is more to come, and it displays the secondary prompt stored in PS2:

>

2. Enter the rest of the command line. Be sure to finish it off with double quotes, before pressing (Return):

```
>incomplete command line." (Return)
```

The shell will echo back the entire message:

```
This is an
incomplete command line.
```

31.5   Making Backups of the Startup Files

The first step in creating or editing a startup file is to see whether you already have such a file. If so, you should prepare a backup copy.

1. If necessary, go to your home directory. Remember, the cd command without arguments will take you to your home directory:

```
BASH 2.0 >   cd (Return)
```

2. List all files in your home directory. Enter the ls   a ("list -all") command:

```
BASH 2.0 >   ls -a (Return)
```

If you see a file named .profile, .bash_profile, .bash_login, or .bashrc, it was probably placed in your home directory when your account was created. You may want to consult with your instructor or system administrator before editing this file.

3. Make a backup copy of the existing startup file(s). Use the cp command, and name the copies with the .BAK suffix to indicate that these are backups:

```
BASH 2.0 >   cp .profile .profile.BAK (Return)
BASH 2.0 >   cp .bash_profile .bash_profile.BAK (Return)
BASH 2.0 >   cp .bash_login .bash_login.BAK (Return)
BASH 2.0 >   cp .bashrc .bashrc.BAK (Return)
```

31.6   A Login Message

In this section you will create a .bash_profile file (or edit an existing file) to display a message on the screen every time you log in. You will use the echo command to do this.

1. Try out the login message. Type

```
BASH 2.0 >   echo "Your wish is my command, Great One." (Return)
```

The shell should respond with the appropriate message:

```
Your wish is my command, Great One.
```

2. Use your text editor to open the .bash_profile **file.**

```
BASH 2.0 >  vi .bash_profile (Return)
```

3. Insert a comment showing the modification date. Put the following line at the top of `.bash_profile`:

```
# This file was last modified on [today's date].
```

The # at the beginning of the line makes this a comment. This shows a typical use of comments, which is to tell you when the file was last edited.

4. Add the message command to the file.

```
echo "Your wish is my command, Great One."
```

5. Write the file and quit the editor.

31.7 Running the Startup File

At this point, you could log out and log in again to see if your `.bash_profile` works. However, there is an easier way: Use the "dot" command.

■ **Run the "dot" command.** Type a period, a space, and the name of the file:

```
BASH 2.0 >  . .bash_profile (Return)
```

This will cause the shell to execute the commands in `.bash_profile`, as if you had just logged in. You should see the login message:

```
Your wish is my command, Great One.
```

The shell will display this message each time you log in, unless you change it or delete it from your `.bash_profile`.

31.8 Customizing the Prompt

Older versions of bash use the dollar sign ($) as the default prompt.

The default primary prompt symbol for bash consists of the shell name (BASH) followed by the version number (e.g., 2.0) and the "greater-than" symbol (>). You can change the prompt symbol by changing the value of the variable PS1. In this section, you will try out various prompts, then edit `.bash_profile` to display one of the new prompts.

1. Change the value of the PS1 variable. Type the following line, making sure not to put spaces around the equals sign:

```
BASH 2.0 > PS1=# (Return)
```

This will change your shell prompt to the pound sign:

```
#
```

2. Try out another prompt. You can include spaces and special characters in the prompt string if you quote it:

```
# PS1="Your Majesty? " (Return)
```

The prompt will change to the new string:

`Your Majesty?`

3. Include shell variables in your prompt. Some users like to display the path-name of their home directory as part of their prompt. Remember, your home directory's pathname is stored by the shell in a variable named HOME. Try the following command (don't type `Your Majesty?`—it is the prompt):

`Your Majesty? PS1="$HOME > "` (Return)

The dollar sign placed in front of HOME tells the shell to put the contents of HOME in the prompt. Now your prompt should show the absolute pathname of your home directory, followed by an arrow (>). For example, if the absolute pathname of your home directory were /home/you, the prompt would now be

> Without the dollar sign, the word HOME would appear instead of the pathname.

`/home/you >`

4. Include prompt commands in your prompt string. Table 31-2 lists some of the commands that can be used to customize your prompt string. Suppose, for example, that you wanted to include the current working directory in your prompt. The \w command can do this:

`/home/you > PS1="\w > "` (Return)

The prompt will change to show your current working directory, followed by the > symbol. Thus, if you are working in the directory /home/you, you should see somthing like this:

`/home/you >`

Let's put this prompt into your `.bash_profile`.

5. Use the text editor to edit the startup file. Add the following lines to your `.bash_profile`:

```
PS1="\w > "
export PS1
```

6. Write to the file and quit the editor.

7. Use the "dot" command to run the commands in `.bash_profile`.

`/home/you > . .bash_profile` (Return)

Your prompt should now consist of your working directory's pathname, followed by an arrow. Thus, if your working directory were /home/you, you would see your login message, then the prompt

`/home/you >`

	Command	Meaning
Table 31-2 Commands for customizing prompt strings.	\a	audible bell (ASCII code 007)
	\d	date in "Weekday Month Day" format
	\e	escape character (ASCII code 033)
	\H	Hostname (long)
	\h	hostname (short)
	\n	newline (i.e., a carriage return followed by a line feed)
	\s	shell name
	\T	Time in 12-hour "HH:MM:SS" format
	\t	time in 24-hour "HH:MM:SS" format
	\@	time in 12-hour "am/pm" format
	\u	user name
	\V	version of bash (long listing—includes "patch level")
	\v	version of bash (short listing)
	\W	working directory (including basename)
	\w	working directory
	\#	number of current command
	\!	history number of current command
	\$	# for superuser (UID of 0); $ otherwise
	\\	backslash
	\nnn	ASCII character code (in octal)
	\[	start of non-printing character sequence
	\]	end of non-printing character sequence

31.9 Setting the Terminal Type

Having to set your terminal type each time you log in is a nuisance—especially if you use the same kind of terminal all of the time. You can set the terminal in your .bash_profile file.

1. **Edit your .bash_profile to set the terminal type.** Insert the following lines, substituting your terminal's termcap code for vt100:

```
TERM=vt100
export TERM
echo "Terminal set to $TERM"
```

2. **Write and quit the editor.**

3. Apply the "dot" command to `.bash_profile`:

`/home/you > . .bash_profile` (Return)

Your login message should appear, then the message about the terminal type:

`Terminal set to vt100`

31.10   Making a calendar File

Skip this section if `calendar` is not available on your system.

The `calendar` utility will remind you of upcoming events. This requires that you have a `calendar` file in your home directory, and that you modify `.bash_profile` to read the `calendar` file.

1. Edit your `.bash_profile` **with the text editor.** Add the following line:

`calendar`

2. Write the change into the file and quit the editor.

3. Use the text editor to create a `calendar` **file.** Be sure to use this exact spelling of `calendar`, in lowercase letters. Otherwise, the shell won't recognize the file.

4. Add a message to the `calendar` **file.** Include today's date in the message. For example, if today is April 12, type

`This is a test for April 12`

Write the date in the form April 12, Apr 12, or 4/12.

5. Write the changes into the `calendar` **file and quit the editor.**

6. Use the "dot" command to run the `.bash_profile` **file.**

`/home/you > . .bash_profile` (Return)

You should see your login message, the message about your terminal type, and the `calendar` message:

```
Your wish is my command, Great One.
Terminal set to vt100
This is a test for April 12
```

31.11   Creating a .bashrc File

The shell initialization `.bashrc` is typically used for setting up command aliases and the `history` mechanism. Before doing this, however, you need to edit `.bash_profile`:

1. Use the text editor to edit `.bash_profile`. Add the following lines to the file:

```
ENV=$HOME/.bashrc
export ENV
```

This tells bash that it should look for .bashrc in your home directory. If the ENV variable is not set, bash will not execute .bashrc.

2. Write and quit the editor.

3. Use the text editor to edit the .bashrc **file.** Start by inserting a comment line giving today's date:

```
# This file was last modified on [today's date]
```

31.12 Creating an Alias

One of the uses for .bashrc is to create aliases. In this section, you will create a one-letter alias for the history command.

1. Use the text editor to edit the .bashrc **file.** Add the following line to the file to create an alias for the history command:

```
alias -x h=history
```

The -x option tells alias to export the alias to all subshells.

2. Write the changes to the file and quit the editor.

3. Use the "dot" command to run the .bashrc **file.**

```
/home/you > . .bashrc (Return)
```

At this point, the alias should be set. In the next section, you will see how to use the alias to run the history command.

31.13 Using the history Mechanism

Recall that the history mechanism keeps a list of the commands you have used most recently, and it allows you to view and repeat commands on the list.

1. Run the history **command using its alias.** Type h followed by (Return) to run the history command:

```
/home/you > h (Return)
```

By default, bash remembers 500 commands.

If you correctly set up the alias for history, you should see a numbered list of the most recently executed commands. Note that the history command itself will appear as the last item on the list.

```
1   set
2   echo $PS2
3   echo PS2
4   echo "This is an incomplete command line."
5   ls -a
6   echo "Your wish is my command, Great One."
7   vi .bash_profile
8   . .bash_profile
```

```
 9  PS1=#
10  PS1="Your Majesty? "
11  PS1="$HOME > "
12  PS1="\w > "
13  vi .bash_profile
14  . .bash_profile
15  vi .bash_profile
16  . .bash_profile
17  vi .bash_profile
18  vi calendar
19  vi .bashrc
20  . .bashrc
21  h
```

2. Repeat the most recent command on the list. This is done by typing two exclamation points (! !) at the prompt. Try it:

/home/you > !! (Return)

You should see another listing of commands, as before:

```
 1  set
 2  echo $PS2
 3  echo PS2
 4  echo "This is an incomplete command line."
 5  ls -a
 6  echo "Your wish is my command, Great One."
 7  vi .bash_profile
 8  . .bash_profile
 9  PS1=#
10  PS1="Your Majesty? "
11  PS1="$HOME > "
12  PS1="\w > "
13  vi .bash_profile
14  . .bash_profile
15  vi .bash_profile
16  . .bash_profile
17  vi .bash_profile
18  vi calendar
19  vi .bashrc
20  . .bashrc
21  h
22  h
```

3. Repeat a command by number. Thus, to repeat the sixth command on the list, type

/home/you > !6 (Return)

The command line will appear on the screen, and the command will be run.

```
echo "Your wish is my command, Great One."
Your wish is my command, Great One.
```

4. Repeat a command by the first letter(s) of the command line. Thus, to repeat a command line that starts with the letter *s*, type

```
/home/you > !s (Return)
```

The most recent command beginning with *s* is the `set` command; it should list the values of the environment variables.

```
set
```

31.14 Command Summary

Checking the Values of Variables

`set`	list the values of all variables
`echo $var`	print value of variable *var*

Setting Values of Variables

var=value	set variable *var* to *value*
`var="A string"`	store string *A string* in variable *var*
`export var`	export contents of *var* to all subshells

Executing a Startup File

`. .bash_profile`	execute `.bash_profile`

Changing Prompts

`PS1="String"`	set primary prompt to *String*
`export PS1`	export prompt string

Creating Command Aliases

`alias c=command`	define *c* as an alias for *command*
`alias -x c=command`	define and export *c* as an alias for *command*
`unalias c`	remove *c* as an alias for *command*

Using the history Mechanism

`history`	print `history` list
`!!`	repeat the most recent event on `history` list
`!n`	repeat the *n*th event on `history` list
`!abc`	repeat the most recent event starting with letters *abc*

31.15 Exercises

1. The date command prints the date and current time. Add the following line to your .bash_profile, making sure to use backquotes around date:

```
echo "The date and time are 'date'."
```

Exit the editor and run the .bash_profile using the "dot" command. What happens?

2. The backquotes were needed in the previous exercise to tell the shell that date was to be interpreted as a command, not as a word. What happens if the backquotes are omitted? Try it. Open .bash_profile and remove the backquotes from date:

```
echo "The date and time are date"
```

Exit the editor and run the .bash_profile using the "dot" command. What happens? (Now open up the file and replace the backquotes.)

3. What is your search path (PATH)?

4. What is the complete pathname for your shell?

5. The rm, cp, and mv commands are dangerous because they can overwrite or remove existing files. The -i ("interactive") option will ask you to confirm that this is what you want. If this option is available to you, add the following lines to your .bashrc file:

```
alias -x rm='rm -i'
```

```
alias -x cp='cp -i'
```

```
alias -x mv='mv -i'
```

Note that quotes are required around a command that contains a space.

6. Explain what the following lines would do if they were placed in your shell initialization file:

```
alias m=more
```

```
alias f=finger
```

```
alias ls 'ls -R'
```

7. Most users set up their history mechanism to remember about 100 commands. To do this yourself, open your .bashrc file and insert this line:

```
HISTSIZE=100
```

If you neglect to set the HISTSIZE variable, bash will remember the most recent 128 commands by default.

PART VIII
SCRIPTING LANGUAGES

# Chapter 32

SCRIPTING LANGUAGES

Tutorials related to this
chapter are found in
Chapters 33 through 35.

Although UNIX systems offer an impressive set of powerful utilities, there may come the time that you need to write your own software. For this you have a wide choice of programming languages, which we will classify into scripting languages (such as awk, Perl, and the shell) and systems languages (such as C, C++, Fortran, and Java). In this chapter, we will discuss what is meant by a programming language, then examine the characteristics of scripting languages.

32.1 Programming Languages

A *computer program* is a set of coded instructions that tell the computer how to perform some task. Computers do not (yet) understand English or any other human language. Instead, computers respond to what is called *machine language* (also called *object code*), in which everything is represented by binary numbers—combinations of 0s and 1s. Consider, for example, how a segment of a program might appear in binary form:

```
00000000011000110000000000011000
00000000000000000011100000010010
00000000111000100001000000100000
00100000110001100000000000000001
```

Obviously, it would be tedious to program in a binary code such as this. A better alternative would be to program in *assembly language*, which represents each of the machine's binary instructions symbolically. For example, the previous four lines of binary code might be represented by the following four lines of assembly language:

```
mult $6, $6
mflo $7
add $2, $7, $2
addi $6, $6, 1
```

Assembly language is clearly a step up from binary, but it is still fairly difficult to master. Fortunately, high-level programming languages are available that make programming much easier. For example, the previous assembly-language code could be written in Perl like this:

```
sum = sum + i * i;
i = i + 1;
```

Not only is this much easier to write and understand than the assembly-language code; it is also much more portable because Perl scripts can be written and run on nearly any kind of computer.

32.2 Source Code

Listing 32-1 shows how the traditional first program might appear when written as a Bourne shell script; Listing 32-2 shows how it might be written in awk; and Listing 32-3 shows how it might be written in Perl.

Listing 32-1
The Bourne shell
script hello.sh.

```
#!/bin/sh

echo "Hello, world!"
```

Listing 32-2
The awk script
hello.awk.

```
#!/usr/bin/awk -f

BEGIN { print "Hello, world!" }
```

Listing 32-3
The Perl script
hello.pl.

```
#!/usr/bin/perl -w

print "Hello, world! \n";
```

A program written in a high-level language is called *source code*. Typically, you will use a text editor such as vi to prepare a file containing the source code. The names for files containing source code will carry a suffix or *extension* that indicates the language in which they are written:

.awk	(awk source code)
.c	(C source code)
.cpp or .C	(C++ source code)
.f	(Fortran source code)
.java	(Java source code)
.ksh	(Korn shell source code)
.pl	(Perl source code)
.sh	(Bourne shell source code)

File extensions are usually optional for script files, but may be required for source code written in other languages.

32.3 Translation

Once the source code is written, it must be translated into machine language. Translation can be done either by an interpreter or a compiler.

An *interpreter* is a program that executes other programs. The interpreter steps through the source code, translating and executing each instruction as it encounters it.

In contrast, a *compiler* translates source code into machine language, which is stored in a file for later execution. The resulting object code can then be run independently of the compiler.

To understand the difference between an interpreter and a compiler, suppose that your favorite local restaurant has hired a new cook. The cook is fast, efficient, and indefatigable. However, he neither speaks nor reads English, but only his native language of Ugaritic. The restaurant owner wants the cook to prepare dishes according to the usual recipes, which are written in English.

The restaurant owner could hire a Ugaritic interpreter to do simultaneous interpretation. The interpreter would read an instruction from the cookbook, translate it aloud into the cook's language and wait until the cook has understood and completed the required task. Step-by-step, the interpreter would translate the recipe as the cook works through it.

Alternatively, the restaurant owner could hire someone to translate the entire English cookbook into Ugaritic. This way, the translator would compile a Ugaritic cookbook which the cook could then read for himself.

Each approach has its advantages and disadvantages. Using an interpreter, the cook could get started right away, without waiting for the entire cookbook to be translated and compiled. Changes in the recipe and additional instructions from the boss could be communicated immediately to the cook. Recipes that are not used are not interpreted. However, if the Ugaritic cook never remembers anything or writes anything down, he will need an interpreter to repeat the translation every time a particular recipe is reused.

On the other hand, once the Ugaritic cookbook is compiled, there is no need to have an interpreter standing by to translate for the cook. It most cases, it is faster for the cook to read the recipes himself. The translated cookbook can be used by other Ugaritic cooks without further translation (although it would not be much use to non-Ugaritic cooks). However, it takes some time to translate the entire cookbook.

Most scripting languages are interpreted, not compiled.

Traditionally, scripting languages have been interpreted, while systems programming languages have been compiled.

However, the distinction between interpreting and compiling has been blurred in scripting languages like Perl. Such languages typically compile their programs into a intermediate form called *byte code*, which is then interpreted. (Imagine that the English cookbook were first compiled into Hebrew before being read by an interpreter to the Ugaritic cook.) Even so, Perl acts as if it were interpreted because a single command causes compilation and execution to occur.

Compilation is discussed in Chapter 36. In contrast, most compiled languages require that you start the compiler with one command, then execute the resulting object code with another command. Some also require that extensive libraries be linked into the object code.

32.4 Variables and Data Types

A *variable* is a named storage location for data. Some of the data types encountered in programming are the following:

■ **Character.** A character is a symbol, typically including letters (`'A'`, `'B'`, …), numerals (`'0'`, `'1'`, `'2'`, …), and punctuation marks (`'!'`, `'?'`, …).

■ **Integer.** Integers are whole numbers (…, −2, −1, 0, 1, 2,…) used for counting.

■ **Logical.** Logical data can be either TRUE or FALSE. Logical types are often called Boolean types, named for the nineteenth century mathematician George Boole.

■ **Pointer.** Pointers are references to addresses in memory.

■ **Real.** Real numbers are rational numbers, usually represented in decimal form, that are used for measuring and computing.

■ **String.** A string is a sequence of characters (`"This is a string"`).

Not all languages have all of these data types; some languages have other types.

In a *typeless* or *weakly typed* language, a variable has no specified type. A variable can hold any data type available in that language. For instance, the variable x may hold a real number such as 3.14159 one moment, then a string such as `"Aardvark"` the next.

In a *strongly typed* language, a variable's type must be specified or declared. A variable is not allowed to hold the "wrong" type of data. Thus, a variable x that has been declared as a real type cannot store a string.

To continue our cooking analogy, a weakly typed language is like a cook who stores ingredients wherever they may fit in the kitchen. The same cabinet may hold flour one day and potatoes the next. This is quick and flexible, but not always the best use of space. (It may not be a good idea to keep fresh fruit in the freezer.)

In contrast, a strongly typed language is like a cook who carefully separates different kinds of ingredients and stores each in its proper place. Spices are never put in the breadbox; vegetables are never kept among the canned goods. This permits the cook to check that everything is being stored correctly, but it is not a flexible arrangement.

Strongly typed languages also limit what kinds of operations can be performed on a particular data type. For example, in most cases it makes little sense to divide a string by another string, so a strongly typed language will not permit it. A weakly typed language may allow such an operation, often with surprising results.

Most scripting languages are weakly typed, whereas most system programming languages are strongly typed.

32.5   Software Components and Reuse

Typeless languages encourage the reuse of software, even software written in different languages. We have already seen how the UNIX shell's pipes can be used to connect several commands. For instance, the following will count the files in the current directory and its subdirectories:

§ ls -aR | wc -l   (Return)

The output from the ls -aR ("list-all recursively") command is piped to the wc -l ("word count—lines only") command. This works because the output from ls and the input to wc are plain ASCII text—there is no need to convert from one data type to another.

Scripting languages take the pipe concept a step further. A language such as Perl can communicate with several files and processes at the same time. This makes it ideal for connecting existing software components (often written in a systems programming language such as C) to build complicated programs. For this reason, scripting languages are sometimes called "glue" languages. They have become increasingly important for Internet applications.

32.6   Data Structures

Most high-level languages allow the programmer to organize the basic data types into ordered collections called *data structures*.

The most common data structure is the *array*, which consists of one or more variables sharing the same name. In Perl, for instance, we might have an array named marsupial that holds the names of various marsupials

```
$marsupial[0] = "kangaroo";
$marsupial[1] = "opossum";
$marsupial[2] = "wombat";
$marsupial[3] = "bandicoot";
$marsupial[4] = "quoll";
```

In this example, the `marsupial` array comprises five variables, called *elements*. The elements are distinguished from each other by an integer *index* (0 through 4 in this case).

Other common data structures include multidimensional arrays, records, stacks, queues, linked lists, trees, graphs, and hashes.

Early scripting languages offered only the simplest data structures, usually arrays. (although the Bourne shell does not even have arrays). Systems programming languages tended to have a greater variety of data structures. Again, however, this distinction has become blurred because newer scripting languages provide a greater selection of data structures.

32.7 Specialized Tools

Scripting languages were originally developed to perform special tasks such as processing ASCII text files. It is not surprising that scripting languages are equipped with specialized tools for completing these tasks.

<aside>Regular expressions are discussed in Appendix D.</aside>

For instance, the most popular scripting languages include built-in support for regular expressions. A *regular expression* is a compact notation for describing strings of characters. Regular expressions are a powerful tool for text processing.

32.8 Performance

It is often said that scripting languages allow fast development while systems languages allow rapid execution. In other words, it is faster to write and debug a script, but a script will generally not run as fast as a compiled program.

There are a number of reasons why development tends to be faster with a scripting language.

■ Scripting languages tend to be simpler than systems languages.

■ Scripting languages encourage the use of existing software components, which in most cases is quicker than writing software from scratch.

■ Scripting languages are interpreted, not compiled. An interpreted language avoids the time required to compile.

32.9 Exercises

1. Be sure you can define each of the following terms:

program	machine language	object code
binary number	assembly language	pseudocode
source code	filename extension	translation
interpreter	compiler	byte code

variable	weakly typed	strongly typed
array	array element	array index
marsupial	regular expressions	scripting language
system language		

2. Write the usual filename extension for each of the following:

awk source code

C source code

C++ source code

Fortran source code

Java source code

Korn shell source code

Perl source code

Bourne shell source code

3. Describe each of the following data types:

character	integer	logical (Boolean)
pointer	real	string

# Chapter 33

Tutorial: Shell Scripting

Until now, you have been giving commands to the UNIX shell by typing them on the keyboard. When used this way, the shell is said to be a command interpreter. The shell can also be used as a high-level programming language. Instead of entering commands one at a time in response to the shell prompt, you can put a number of commands in a file, to be executed all at once by the shell. A program consisting of shell commands is called a *shell script*.

33.1 A Simple Shell Script

Suppose you were to make up a file named commands as shown in Listing 33-1.

```
① # A simple shell script
② cal
  date
  who
```

Listing 33-1
The commands script.

Let's dissect the commands script:

```
① # A simple shell script
```

The first line in this file begins with a # symbol, which indicates a *comment line*. Anything following the #, up to the end of the line, is ignored by the shell.

```
② cal
  date
  who
```

The remaining three lines are shell commands: the first produces a calendar for the current month, the second gives the current date and time, and the third lists the users currently logged onto your system.

We can get the Bourne Shell (sh) to run these commands by typing

§ sh < commands (Return)

The redirection operator (<) tells the shell to read from the file `commands` instead of from the standard input. It turns out, however, that the redirection symbol is not really needed in this case. Thus, you can also run the `commands` file by typing

§ `sh commands` (Return)

Is there any way to set up `commands` so that you can run it without explicitly invoking the shell? In other words, can you run `commands` without first typing `sh`? The answer is yes, but you first have to make the file *executable*. The `chmod` utility does this:

chmod is described in Chapter 6.

§ `chmod u+x commands` (Return)

The argument `u+x` tells `chmod` that you want to add (+) permission for the user (u) to execute (x) the shell script in the file. Now all you need do is enter the file name

§ `commands` (Return)

The search path is the list of directories where the shell is to look for executable files.

If your search path is set up to include the current directory, the shell will run the commands in the file. If it is not, the shell will complain that it cannot find the file you want it to execute:

`commands not found`

If this happens, you can still get the shell to run your commands this way:

§ `./commands` (Return)

Remember, "dot" (`.`) stands for the current working directory.

33.2 Subshells

The new shell process is a subshell or child of the original shell.

When you tell the shell to run a script such as the `commands` file, your login shell actually calls up another shell process to run the script. (Remember, the shell is just a program, and UNIX can run more than one program at a time.) The parent shell waits for its child to finish, then takes over and gives you a prompt:

§

Incidentally, a subshell can be different from its parent shell. For example, you can have `ksh`, `csh`, `tcsh` or `bash` as your login shell, but use `sh` to run your shell scripts. Many users in fact do this. When it comes time to run a script, the login shell simply calls up `sh` as a subshell to do the job.

We will always use `sh` for running shell scripts. To make sure that `sh` is used, regardless of your login shell, include the following line at the top of each shell script file:

`#!/bin/sh`

The origins of the term "shebang" in this connection are obscure.

A pound sign and an exclamation point entered together (#!) as the first characters in the file are called the "shebang." Thus, we can modify our commands file as shown in Listing 33-2.

```
#!/bin/sh
# A simple shell script
cal
date
who
```

Listing 33-2
The modified commands script.

This modified script can be run by entering its name at the shell prompt:

§ ./commands (Return)

33.3　The Shell as a Scripting Language

The sample script commands is almost trivial—it does nothing more than execute three simple commands that you could just as easily type into the standard input. The shell can actually do much more. It is, in fact, a sophisticated scripting language, with many of the same features found in other scripting languages, including

- Variables

- Input/output functions

- Arithmetic operations

- Conditional expressions

- Selection structures

- Repetition structures

We will discuss each of these in this chapter.

33.4　Variables

Three kinds of variables are commonly used in shell scripts:

- **Environment Variables.** Sometimes called special shell variables, keyword variables, predefined shell variables, or standard shell variables, they are used to tailor the operating environment to suit your needs. Examples include TERM, HOME, and MAIL.

- **User-created Variables.** These are variables that you create yourself.

- **Positional Parameters.** These are used by the shell to store the values of command-line arguments.

Of these, the environment variables have been introduced already, and the user-defined variables will be discussed later in this chapter. The positional parameters, which are very useful in shell programming, will be examined in this section.

The positional parameters are also called *read-only variables*, or *automatic variables*, because the shell sets them for you automatically. They "capture" the values of the command-line arguments that are to be used by a shell script. The positional parameters are numbered 0, 1, 2, 3, ... , 9. To illustrate their use, consider the following shell script, and assume that it is contained in an executable file named `echo.args`:

```
#!/bin/sh
# Illustrate the use of positional parameters
echo $0 $1 $2 $3 $4 $5 $6 $7 $8 $9
```

Suppose you run the script by typing the command line

§ echo.args We like UNIX. (Return)

The shell stores the name of the command ("`echo.args`") in the parameter $0; it puts the argument "We" in the parameter $1; it puts "like" in the parameter $2, and "UNIX." in parameter $3. Since that takes care of all the arguments, the rest of the parameters are left empty. Then the script prints the contents of the variables:

echo.args We like UNIX.

What if the user types in more than nine arguments? The positional parameter $* contains all of the arguments $1, $2, $3, ... $9, and any arguments beyond these nine. Thus, we can rewrite `echo.args` to handle any number of arguments:

```
#!/bin/sh
# Illustrate the use of positional parameters
echo $*
```

The shell also counts the arguments that the user typed; this number is stored in the parameter $#. We can modify the script `echo.args` to use this parameter:

```
#!/bin/sh
# Illustrate the use of positional parameters
echo You typed $# arguments: $*
```

Suppose we were then to type the command line

§ echo.args To be or not to be (Return)

The computer would respond with

You typed 6 arguments: To be or not to be

§

$* does not contain $0, so `echo.args` is neither counted nor printed.

33.5   Making a File Executable: chex

If you are planning to write a lot of shell scripts, you will find it convenient to have a script that makes files executable. If we were to write a shell script for this, it might resemble Listing 33-3.

```
#!/bin/sh
# Make a file executable

① chmod u+x $1
② echo $1 is now executable:
   ls -l $1
```

Listing 33-3
The chex script.

Let's examine the interesting new features of the **chex** script:

① `chmod u+x $1`

Recall that the **chmod** utility changes file permissions. The utility takes two arguments. The first (u+x) adds execution privileges to the user. The second ($1) is a positional parameter that contains the name of the file.

② `echo $1 is now executable:`
   `ls -l $1`

The script confirms that the file permissions have been changed.

Next, we need to make the **chex** file executable. The easiest way to do this is to tell the shell to run **chex** on itself. Try this command line:

§ `sh chex chex` (Return)

This tells the shell to run **chex**, taking the **chex** file as the argument. The result is that **chex** makes itself executable. The output from this command will look something like this:

```
chex is now executable:
-rwxr-xr-x     1     yourlogin  59     Date time   chex
```

Now you can use **chex** to make other files executable.

33.6   The set Command

The positional parameters are sometimes called *read-only variables* because the shell sets their values for you when you type arguments to the script. However, you can also set their values using the **set** command. To see how this command works, consider the shell script shown in Listing 33-4, which we will assume is in the file `setdate`.

```
#!/bin/sh
# Demonstrate the set command

① set `date`
② echo "Time: $4 $5"
  echo "Day: $1"
  echo "Date: $3 $2 $6"
```

Listing 33-4
The setdate script.

This script introduces some new features:

① set `date`

The backquotes cause the date command to be run, with its output being captured by the set command and stored in the positional parameters $1 through $5.

② echo "Time: $4 $5"
  echo "Day: $1"
  echo "Date: $3 $2 $6"

Here is how we print out the values of the positional parameters.

Once setdate has been made executable by the chmod utility or the chex script, we can run the script by typing the command

§ ./setdate (Return)

The output will show the current time, day, and date:

Time: 10:56:08 EST
Day: Fri
Date: 20 Aug 2004

To understand what the script does, consider the command line

set `date`

The backquotes run the date utility, which produces output something like this:

Fri Aug 20 10:56:08 EST 2004

This does not appear on the screen. Instead, the set command catches the different parts of the output and stores them in the positional parameters $1 through $6:

$1 *contains* Fri
$2 *contains* Aug
$3 *contains* 20
$4 *contains* 10:56:08
$5 *contains* EST
$6 *contains* 2004

33.7 Labeling the Output from wc: mywc

The wc ("word count") filter counts the words, lines, and characters in a file. For example, try running wc on the chex file:

```
§ wc chex (Return)
5    17    84     chex
§
```

The output tells us that there are 5 lines, 17 words, and 84 characters in the file chex. This can be very useful information, but it would be a bit more convenient to use if the output were labeled. Listing 33-5 shows a shell script that does this.

Listing 33-5
The mywc script.

```
   #!/bin/sh
   # Label the output from wc

①  set `wc $1`
②  echo "File: $4"
   echo "Lines: $1"
   echo "Words: $2"
   echo "Characters: $3"
```

This script is similar to the previous one:

```
① set `wc $1`
```

The wc $1 command is run inside the backquotes. The output from this command is then captured and stored in positional parameters $1 through $4. Note that $1 initially receives the file name when the mywc script is run; then it receives the number of lines counted by the wc utility.

```
② echo "File: $4"
   echo "Lines: $1"
   echo "Words: $2"
   echo "Characters: $3"
```

As shown here, the values of the positional parameters are printed, properly labeled.

Run the chex script to make mywc executable. Then run mywc on an ASCII file. You might try the chex file:

```
§ ./mywc chex (Return)
```

```
File: chex
Lines: 5
Words: 17
Characters: 84
```

33.8 User-Defined Variables

You can create your own shell variable by writing its name. A variable name may include uppercase letters (A through Z), lowercase letters (a through z), numerals (0 through 9), and the underscore character (_). A variable name may not contain spaces or begin with a numeral.

There is no need to declare a variable's data type because the shell only works on character strings.

A string can be put into a variable using the assignment operator. For example, the assignment

```
first_var="This is a string"
```

This assignment stores the string This is a string in the variable first_var, overwriting any string that may already be in the variable. Note that no spaces are allowed around the assignment operator. Once the assignment is done, the value can be assigned to another variable:

```
second_var=$first_var
```

This assignment copies the string This is a string from first_var into second_var. As a result, both variables contain the same value. The dollar sign prefix $ indicates that the value of the variable is to be used. Suppose we were to omit the dollar sign:

```
second_var=first_var
```

This assignment copies the string first_var into second_var.

33.9 Input Using the read Statement

The positional parameters are useful for capturing command-line arguments but they have a limitation: once the script begins running, the positional parameters cannot be used for obtaining more input from the standard input. For this you have to use the read statement and a user-defined variable. Listing 33-6 shows how this is done.

```
#!/bin/sh
# Use positional parameters, user-defined variables, and
# the read command

① echo 'What is your name?'
② read name
③ echo "Well, $name, you typed $# arguments:"
④ echo $*
```

Listing 33-6
The echo.args script.

Let's examine the interesting features of this script:

① echo 'What is your name?'

In this script, the echo command prints a prompt on the standard input.

② `read name`

The read command obtains the user's response and stores it in the user-defined variable name.

③ `echo "Well, $name, you typed $# arguments:"`

To obtain the contents of the variable name, we use a dollar sign prefix ($). The positional parameter $# contains the count of command-line arguments that are entered when the script is executed.

④ `echo $*`

The positional parameter $* contains the command-line arguments that are entered when the script is executed

The script echo.args works something like this:

§ `echo.args To be or not to be` (Return)

The shell script would respond by prompting you for your name:

`What is your name?`

Suppose you were to type

`Rumpelstiltskin` (Return)

The computer would respond with

```
Well, Rumpelstiltskin, you typed 6 arguments:
To be or not to be
```

33.10   Arithmetic Operations Using the expr Utility

The shell is not intended for numerical work—if you need to do many calculations, you should consider a scripting language such as Perl or a programming language such as C, C++, Fortran, or Java. Nevertheless, the expr utility may be used to perform simple arithmetic operations on integers. (expr is not a shell command, but rather a separate UNIX utility; however, it is most often used in shell scripts.) To use it in a shell script, you simply surround the expression with backquotes. For example, let's write a simple script called add that adds two integers typed as arguments (Listing 33-7).

Listing 33-7
The add script.

```
#!/bin/sh
# Add two numbers

① sum=`expr $1 + $2`
② echo $sum
```

This script has two executable lines:

① `sum=`expr $1 + $2``

Here we defined a variable `sum` to hold the result of the operation. (Note that spaces are required around the plus sign, but are not allowed around the equals sign.) The backquotes cause the `expr` utility to be run, adding the contents of the parameters $1 and $2.

② `echo $sum`

The `echo` command is used to print the value of `$sum`. Note that the dollar sign prefix ($) is needed.

Make the `add` script executable, then type the following line:

§ `add 4 3` (Return)

The first argument (4) is stored in $1, and the second (3) is stored in $2. The `expr` utility then adds these quantities and stores the result in `sum`. Finally, the contents of `sum` are echoed on the screen:

```
7
§
```

Next try the following line:

§ `add 0.5 0.5` (Return)

The values 0.5 and 0.5 will not be recognized as numbers because they contain decimal points. You might see something like this:

`expr: non-numeric argument`

The `expr` utility only works on integers (i.e., whole numbers). It can perform addition (+), subtraction (-), multiplication (*), integer division (/), and integer remainder (%).

33.11 Control Structures

Normally, the shell processes the commands in a script sequentially, one after another in the order they are written in the file. Often, however, you will want to change the way that commands are processed. You may want to choose to run one command or another, depending on the circumstances; or you may want to run a command more than once.

To alter the normal sequential execution of commands, the shell offers a variety of control structures. There are two types of *selection structures*, which allow a choice between alternative commands:

■ `if-then-elif ... else/fi`

■ `case`

There are three types of *repetition* or *iteration structures* for carrying out commands more than once:

- `for`
- `while`
- `until`

33.12 The if Statement and test Command

The `if` statement lets you choose whether to run a particular command (or group of commands), depending on some condition. The simplest version of this structure has the general form

```
if condition
then
    command(s)
fi
```

When the shell encounters a structure such as this, it first checks to see whether the *condition* is true. If so, the shell runs any *command(s)* that it finds between the `then` and the `fi` (which is just *if* spelled backwards). If the *condition* is not true, the shell skips the *command(s)* between `then` and `fi`. A shell script that uses a simple `if` statement is shown in Listing 33-8.

```
   #!/bin/sh

①  set `date`

②  if test $1 = Fri
   then
       echo "Thank goodness it's Friday!"
   fi
```

Listing 33-8
The `friday` script.

The `friday` script has some interesting features:

① `set `date``

The `date` command is run (note the backquotes) and its output is captured by the `set` command.

```
② if test $1 = Fri
   then
       echo "Thank goodness it's Friday!"
   fi
```

Here we have used the `test` command in our conditional expression. The expression

```
test $1 = Fri
```

Table 33-1
Some arguments to the
test command. Here,
file represents the
pathname of a file.

Argument	Test is true if . . .
-d *file*	*file* is a directory
-f *file*	*file* is an ordinary file
-r *file*	*file* is readable
-s *file*	*file* size is greater than zero
-w *file*	*file* is writable
-x *file*	*file* is executable
! -d *file*	*file* is not a directory
! -f *file*	*file* is not an ordinary file
! -r *file*	*file* is not readable
! -s *file*	*file* size is not greater than zero
! -w *file*	*file* is not writable
! -x *file*	*file* is not executable
n1 -eq *n2*	integer *n1* equals integer *n2*
n1 -ge *n2*	integer *n1* is greater than or equal to integer *n2*
n1 -gt *n2*	integer *n1* is greater than integer *n2*
n1 -le *n2*	integer *n1* is less than or equal to integer *n2*
n1 -ne *n2*	integer *n1* is not equal to integer *n2*
n1 -lt *n2*	integer *n1* is less than integer *n2*
s1 = *s2*	string *s1* equals string *s2*
s1 != *s2*	string *s1* is not equal to string *s2*

checks to see if the parameter $1 contains Fri; if it does, the test command reports that the condition is true, and the message is printed.

The test command can carry out a variety of tests; some of the arguments it takes are listed in Table 33-1.

33.13 The elif and else Statements

We can make the selection structures much more elaborate by combining the if with the elif ("else if") and else statements. The important thing to note about such structures is that no more than one of the alternatives may be chosen each time the selection structure is executed; as soon as one is, the remaining choices are skipped.

Listing 33-9 shows a script using an if-then-elif...else-fi structure.

```
  #!/bin/sh

  set ‘date‘
① if test $1 = Fri
  then
      echo "Thank goodness it's Friday!"
② elif test $1 = Sat  || test $1 = Sun
  then
      echo "You should not be here working."
      echo "Log off and go home."
③ else
      echo "It is not yet the weekend."
      echo "Get to work!"
  fi
```

Listing 33-9
The weekend script.

The weekend script shows a three-part selection structure:

```
① if test $1 = Fri
  then
      echo "Thank goodness it's Friday!"
```

Here, the first conditional expression is tested to see if the day is a Friday. If it is, the message "Thank goodness it's Friday!" is printed, and the shell script is finished.

```
② elif test $1 = Sat  || test $1 = Sun
  then
      echo "You should not be here working."
      echo "Log off and go home."
```

If the first conditional is false, the second conditional expression is tested. Note that we have used the OR operator (||) in this expression to test whether the day is a Saturday or Sunday, in which case the second set of messages will be printed, and the script is finished.

```
③ else
      echo "It is not yet the weekend."
      echo "Get to work!"
  fi
```

The else clause has no conditional; it is the *default case*, which is selected if no other pattern is matched. Thus, the third set of messages are printed if the other conditions are false. Note that the keyword fi terminates the selection structure.

We could make even more elaborate selection structures by including more elif clauses. Regardless of the number of alternatives in an if-then-elif...else-fi structure, no more than one will be selected each time the structure is executed. And once a choice is made, the remaining choices are skipped.

33.14 The case Statement

The shell provides another selection structure that may run faster than the `if` statement on some UNIX systems. This is the `case` statement, and it has the following general form:

```
case variable in
pattern1)   command(s) ;;
pattern2)   command(s) ;;
...
patternN)   command(s) ;;
esac
```

The `case` statement compares the value of *variable* with *pattern1*; if they match, the shell runs the *command(s)* controlled by that pattern. Otherwise, the shell checks the remaining patterns, one by one, until it finds one that matches the *variable*; it then runs the corresponding *command(s)*.

Listing 33-10 shows a simple shell script that uses the `case` statement instead of an `if-then-elif-else` structure.

```
#!/bin/sh

set `date`

① case $1 in
  Fri) echo "Thank goodness it's Friday!";;
② Sat | Sun) echo "You should not be here working";
            echo "Log off and go home!";;
③ *)    echo "It is not yet the weekend.";
        echo "Get to work!";;
  esac
```

Listing 33-10
The weekend2 script.

This script employs a three-part case structure:

```
① case $1 in
  Fri) echo "Thank goodness it's Friday!";;
```

If `$1` contains `Fri`, the message "Thank goodness it's Friday!" is printed, and the shell script is finished. The commands are separated by semicolons (`;`), and the end of a group of commands is indicated by two semicolons (`;;`).

```
② Sat | Sun) echo "You should not be here working";
            echo "Log off and go home!";;
```

We have used the OR operator (`|`) in this expression to test whether `$1` contains `Sat` or `Sun`, in which case the second set of messages will be printed, and the script is finished. Note that the OR symbol used in `case` statements is a single vertical line (`|`), not the double vertical lines (`||`) used in the `if` statement.

```
③ *)   echo "It is not yet the weekend.";
       echo "Get to work!";;
  esac
```

The pattern *) marks the *default case*, which is selected if no other pattern is matched. Thus, the third set of messages are printed if the other conditions are false.

33.15 for Loops

Sometimes we want to run a command (or group of commands) over and over. This is called *iteration*, *repetition*, or *looping*. The most commonly used shell repetition structure is the for loop, which has the general form

```
for variable in list
do
    command(s)
done
```

Here, *variable* is a user-defined variable—called the *control variable*—and *list* is a sequence of character strings separated by spaces. For each repetition of the loop, the control variable takes the value of the next item in the list and the *command(s)* in the body of the loop are executed. Here is a simple application of the for loop:

```
#!/bin/sh
#
for name in $*
do
    finger $name
done
```

Each time through the for loop, the control variable name takes on the value of the next argument in the list $*. This is then used as the argument to the finger command. Assuming this script is contained in the executable file fingerall, it would be run by typing the name of the file, followed by the login names you wish to finger:

§ fingerall johnp maryl frederick (Return)

33.16 while Loops

The general form of the while loop is

```
while condition
do
    command(s)
done
```

As long as the *condition* is true, the *command(s)* between the do and the done are executed. Here is an example of a shell script that uses the expr utility with the while loop to echo the keyboard entry ten times:

```
#!/bin/sh
# Print a message ten times
count=10
while test $count -gt 0
do
    echo $*
    count=`expr $count - 1`
done
```

33.17 until Loops

Another kind of iteration structure is the until loop. It has the general form

```
until  condition
do
     command(s)
done
```

This loop continues to execute the *command(s)* between the do and done until the *condition* is true. We can rewrite the previous script using an until loop instead of the while loop:

```
#!/bin/sh
# Print a message ten times
count=10
until test $count -eq 0
do
    echo $*
    count=`expr $count - 1`
done
```

33.18 Removing Files Safely

The rm command can be very dangerous because it allows you to remove a file, but does not give you a way of getting back a file you may have removed accidentally. Most shells allow you to create an alias for the rm with the -i ("interactive") option; it will ask you if you are sure you want to remove the file in question. But sh does not allow aliases. Listing 33-11 shows a script that will duplicate the effect of the rm -i command. The script will also tell what action has been taken.

```
  #!/bin/sh
  # Delete a file interactively

① if test ! -f $1
  then
      echo "There is no file \"$1\"."
② else
      echo "Do you want to delete \"$1\"?"
      read choice

③    if  test  $choice = y
      then
          rm $1
          echo "\"$1\" deleted."
④    else
          echo "\"$1\" not deleted."
⑤    fi
  fi
```

Listing 33-11
The del script.

The del script has a selection structure nested within another selection structure:

```
① if test ! -f $1
  then
      echo "There is no file \"$1\"."
```

The script is designed take one command-line argument, the name of the file to be deleted. This file name is stored in the postitional parameter $1. The test

```
test ! -f $1
```

is true if the file named in $1 does *not* exist. In that case, the user is informed that there is no file by that name, and the script quits.

```
② else
      echo "Do you want to delete \"$1\"?"
      read choice
```

The default alternative is chosen when the file exists. In that case, the user is asked to confirm that he or she really wants to delete the file. The user's choice is read into the variable choice.

```
③    if  test  $choice = y
      then
          rm $1
          echo "\"$1\" deleted."
```

If the user's choice is y, the script calls the rm utility to remove the file, then prints an appropriate message.

```
④    else
          echo "\"$1\" not deleted."
```

If the user's choice is anything but y, the script takes no action other than printing an appropriate message.

⑤   `fi`
  `fi`

The first `fi` closes the inner selection structure; the second `fi` closes the outer structure.

33.19 An Improved Spelling Script

The `spell` utility is very useful, but it has a serious limitation: it lists the (possibly) misspelled words in a file, but does not tell you where in the file the misspelled words reside. Listing 33-12 describes a script that will correct this problem by labelling the output from the `spell` program.

```
#!/bin/sh
# An improved spelling-checker

① for word in `spell $1`
   do
②      line=`grep -n $word $1`
        echo "       "
        echo "Misspelled word: $word"
③      echo "$line"
   done
```

Listing 33-12
The `myspell` script.

If `spell` is not available, try `ispell` intead. Check the `man` pages for `ispell`.

The `myspell` script illustrates the use of a `for` loop:

① `for word in `spell $1``

The `spell` utility is run on the file (note the backquotes), producing a list of (possibly) misspelled words. The loop variable `word` takes each of these misspelled words, one at a time.

② `line=`grep -n $word $1``

Here, `grep` is run on the file to find any lines containing the current misspelled word. The `-n` option causes `grep` to print the line number when a match is found.

③ `echo "$line"`

This command prints the contents of the variable `line`, which shows the current misspelled word in context.

33.20 Exercises

1. Be sure you can define each of the following terms:

shell script	comment	subshell
child process	positional parameter	selection structure
default case	repetition structure	iteration
loop	variable	

2. If you haven't already done so, write and run the sample shell scripts in this chapter.

3. Read about the chmod utility in Chapter 6. Suppose you have a text file named myfile. Write the commands you would use to accomplish the following:

a. Make myfile executable (but not readable or writable) by everyone.

b. Allow the owner to read, write, or execute myfile; allow the group to read or execute the file; allow everyone else to execute the file only.

c. Add write permissions for members of the group.

d. Remove all permissions from everyone. (Why might you want to do this?)

4. Write a shell script named chnoex that reverses the effects of chex by removing the execution permissions on a file.

5. Write a shell script named private that uses chmod to change the access permissions on a file so that only the owner may read, write, or execute it. Be sure to label the output to show what was done to the file.

6. Write a shell script named public that reverses the effect of the private script you wrote in the previous exercise.

7. Modify the del script so that it detects whether the user has specified a directory to be deleted, in which case the script should call the rmdir command. (Hint: use test with the -d option to test for a directory.)

8. The calendar utility will remind you of important events. One limitation of calendar is that you have to enter each event individually, along with its date. This can be a problem for routine events that happen every day or every week. For reminding yourself of such events, write a script named tickle that can be run from your shell startup file when you log in. Have the script run the date utility to determine the day of the week. Use a case structure to select the appropriate message for each day of the week.

9. Rewrite tickle to use an if/then/elif.../fi structure.

10. The standard echo command echoes its arguments just once. Write a script echo.by that echoes its arguments as many times as the user chooses. For example, if the user enters the command line

§ echo.by 5 Play it again, Sam. (Return)

the script should print

```
Play it again, Sam.
Play it again, Sam.
Play it again, Sam.
Play it again, Sam.
Play it again, Sam.
```

(Hint: Use a `while` loop.)

11. Rewrite `echo.by` to use an `until` loop.

TUTORIAL:
SCRIPTING WITH AWK

Awk is a pattern-matching language that is especially useful for processing files containing plain (ASCII) text. POSIX-compliant UNIX systems include awk as one of the standard utilities.

34.1 Versions of Awk

The unusual name awk stands for Aho, Weinberger, and Kernighan, the creators of awk.

The original version of awk was written for UNIX Version 7 (1978) by Alfred Aho, Brian Kernighan, and Peter Weinberger at AT&T Bell Laboratories. On some systems, this version is still available, often under the name oawk ("old awk").

A major upgrade of awk was included in UNIX System V Release 3.1 (SVR3.1) in 1987. Further improvements were made for System V Release 4 (SVR4) in 1989. These versions are sometimes available under the name nawk ("new awk").

The Free Software Foundation released Version 1.0 of gawk ("GNU awk") in 1986, written by Paul Rubin and Jay Fenlason.

The Portable Operating System (POSIX) standard P1003.2 defined a version of awk in 1992. POSIX awk borrowed features from nawk and gawk.

The later versions of awk (nawk, gawk, and POSIX awk) are similar in their basic syntax and functionality, differing mostly in their advanced features.

34.2 Data Files, Records, and Fields

Awk is designed to work on plain text (ASCII data), obtained from the standard input or from a file.

Awk reads and processes data in units called *records*. By default, a record is a single line of text, terminated by a newline character. (Other characters can be used to separate records.)

Awk reads the input one record at a time, dividing each record into *fields*. By default, fields are groupings of text separated by spaces. (The field separator can be changed.)

The file `solar.system` is available from the *Just Enough Unix* website.

The examples in this chapter use the sample data file `solar.system`, which contains data on the major natural satellites in the solar system. In this file, records are separated by newlines (the default) and fields are separated by whitespace (also the default). For example, the first record in the file is for Adrastea, one of the moons of Jupiter:

```
Adrastea XV Jupiter 129000 0.30 0.00 0.00 Jewitt 1979
```

This record consists of nine fields, which we will designate $1 through $9:

$1 Name of the planet or moon (Adrastea)

$2 Number of the moon or planet (XV)

$3 Name of the object around which the satellite orbits (Jupiter)

$4 Orbital radius (semimajor axis) in kilometers (129000)

$5 Orbital period in days (0.30)

$6 Orbital inclination in degrees (0.00)

$7 Orbital eccentricity (0.00)

$8 Discoverer (Jewitt)

$9 Year of discovery (1979)

The file `solar.system` contains 88 lines of the same format. The lines are arranged in alphabetical order according to the name of the planet or moon.

34.3 Running Awk

You have several options for running an awk program. A short awk program can be entered at the command line. For example, the command

§ awk '{ print }' solar.system ⟨RETURN⟩

will print all of the lines in the data file, mimicking the `cat` utility. Note the single quotes: these are required to prevent the shell from trying to interpret the awk program.

More generally,

§ awk '*program*' *datafile(s)* ⟨RETURN⟩

where *program* represents the statement(s) making up the awk program and *datafile(s)* represents one or more data files.

Command-line entry is fine for simple, one-line awk programs. You will find it more convenient to put longer awk programs in a file. Listing 34-1 shows one way to do this.

Listing 34-1
The cat.awk script.

```
① # Print all of the lines in the standard input
② { print }
```

Listing 34-1
The cat.awk script.

The file contains two lines:

```
① # Print all of the lines in the standard input
```

Comments are for the benefit of human readers; they are ignored by awk.

The pound sign (#) marks this as a *comment*. With one exception (to be discussed shortly), any text appearing between a pound sign and the end of the same line is ignored by awk. Comments are intended to be informative to the programmer (or any other person) who may read the script at a later date.

```
② { print }
```

The second line of the file contains the same awk program we used before, consisting of a single print statement enclosed in braces.

To run the program, type the following at the command line:

```
§ awk -f cat.awk solar.system (RETURN)
```

The -f option tells awk that what immediately follows is a file containing the program. The result should be the same as before.

Yet another way to run an awk program is to turn it into an executable file, as shown in Listing 34-2. Such a script can be run simply by entering the names of the executable file and the data file.

```
① #!/usr/bin/awk -f

# Print all of the lines in the standard input
{ print }
```

Listing 34-2
The cat2.awk script.

The pathname may be different on your system.

The first line of the cat2.awk file starts with the *shebang*, consisting of a pound sign and an exclamation point together (#!). This is followed by the pathname of the program (i.e., awk) that is to run the script:

```
① #!/usr/bin/awk -f
```

The -f option specifies that what follows is the file containing the script. Note that in this situation a pound sign (#) does not mark the beginning of a comment.

The chmod utility is used to make the file executable:

The chmod utility is discussed in Section 6.17.

```
§ chmod a+x cat2.awk (RETURN)
```

How you run the program depends on whether the current working directory is included in the search path. If not, type the following at the command line:

```
§ ./cat2.awk solar.system (RETURN)
```

On the other hand, if the current directory is included in the search path, type

§ `cat2.awk solar.system` (RETURN)

34.4 Patterns and Actions

A typical awk program is designed to search through a file looking for one or more *patterns*; when it finds a record containing the pattern, the program then performs a specified action. For example, the command

§ `awk '/Mars/ {print}' solar.system` (RETURN)

produces the output

```
Mars IV Sun 227940000 686.98 1.85 0.09 - -
Phobos I Mars 9000 0.32 1.00 0.02 Hall 1877
Deimos II Mars 23000 1.26 1.80 0.00 Hall 1877
```

A regular expression is a compact formula for describing text. Regular expressions are described in Appendix D.

In this example, the awk program consists of one pattern and one action. The pattern is `/Mars/` and the action is `{print}`. This program directs awk to get an input record and examine it for the regular expression `Mars`. If the pattern is found, the line is printed on the standard output; otherwise, nothing is done. Then awk gets the next input record and processes it the same way.

More generally, an awk pattern-action statement has the form

pattern { *action* }

Note that the action is enclosed in curly braces to distinguish it from the pattern. (Curly braces are also used for grouping related awk statements.)

Either the pattern or the action (but not both) may be omitted. If a pattern is provided without an action, awk simply prints all of the lines that match the pattern. For example, the command line

§ `awk '/Mars/' solar.system` (RETURN)

produces the output

```
Mars IV Sun 227940000 686.98 1.85 0.09 - -
Phobos I Mars 9000 0.32 1.00 0.02 Hall 1877
Deimos II Mars 23000 1.26 1.80 0.00 Hall 1877
```

If an action is specified without a pattern, that action is applied to all of the lines in the input. For example, the command

§ `awk '{print}' solar.system` (RETURN)

prints all of the lines in the file (much like the cat utility).

If a script contains more than one pattern-action pair, each input line is compared with all of the patterns before the next input line is read. In other words, an input line is read just once.

34.5 BEGIN and END Patterns

Two special "patterns," BEGIN and END, are not intended to match any input records. BEGIN specifies actions that are to be done before any records are read. Likewise, END specifies actions that are to be done after all of the records have been read.

Because neither BEGIN nor END matches an input line, we can use them without an input file. For example,

§ awk 'BEGIN { print "Hello, world." }' (RETURN)

will produce the cheerful traditional greeting

Hello, world.

We will see more uses for BEGIN and END later.

The original version of awk permitted only a single BEGIN pattern at the beginning of the script and a single END pattern at the end. The POSIX standard now allows multiple BEGIN and END patterns, which may be intermixed with other pattern-action pairs. For readability, it is still a good idea to put BEGIN statements at the beginning of a script and END patterns at the end.

34.6 Script Layout

Although awk allows considerable flexibility in the layout of scripts, there are a few rules you must observe:

■ **Patterns and Actions.** When writing a pattern-action pair, place the opening brace of the action on the same line as the pattern. Statements following the opening brace may be placed on the same line, separated by semicolons. Or they may be placed on separate lines, separated by newlines.

■ **Allowable whitespace.** Blank lines may be inserted before and after any statement. Spaces and tabs may be inserted around operators, after opening braces and parentheses, and before closing braces and parentheses.

■ **Variables and Functions.** The name of a variable or function may not contain spaces. Nor may spaces be inserted between a function's name and its argument list.

■ **Line Breaking.** A newline may be inserted after a statement, a comma, a semicolon, or any of the following:

{ || &&   do   else

■ **Continuation.** A long statement may be continued from one line to the next by placing a backslash character (\) before the newline.

It is a good idea to use blank lines, spaces, and tabs to enhance readability for the human reader.

34.7 Constants

Awk recognizes just two kinds of data: numbers and character strings. (The file `solar.system` contains both kinds of data.)

An awk number may be written as an integer (such as 123), as a decimal fraction (such as -47.9), or in *e-notation* (such as 6.02e+23). The latter is a way of representing scientific notation without using superscripts. Hence,

The e may be capitalized: this is called E-notation.

$6.02e+23$ and $6.02E+23$ mean 6.02×10^{23}

$9.11e-31$ and $9.11E-31$ mean 9.11×10^{-31}

$-1.2e-09$ and $-1.2E-09$ mean -1.2×10^{-9}

Regardless of how it is written, every numeric quantity is stored by awk as a floating point number. (Floating point may be considered as a variation of scientific notation for binary numbers.)

An awk string constant is written as plain (ASCII) text enclosed in double quotes:

```
"This is a string."
```

```
"So is this."
```

```
"123"
```

```
" "
```

The null string contains no characters.
```
""
```

Note the difference between 123 and "123"; the former is a number, the latter a string.

Also note the difference between " " and ""; the former is a string containing a single space (ASCII value 32), the latter is the *null string* containing no characters.

The double quotes surrounding a string constant are not considered part of the string. To include double quotes in a string, "quote" them using backslashes:

```
"\"Play it again,\" he said."
```

An awk string may contain *escape sequences* to represent special characters. Table 34-1 lists the escape sequences recognized by awk. Some of these—the alert (\a), backspace (\b), carriage return (\r), formfeed (\f), horizontal tab (\t), newline (\n), and vertical tab (\v)—are said to be *nonprinting* because they affect the spacing of text in the output, but otherwise do not cause anything to be printed.

	Sequence	Meaning
Table 34-1 Escape sequences.	\a	Alert (audible alarm)
	\b	Backspace
	\f	Form feed
	\n	Newline
	\r	Carriage return
	\t	Horizontal tab
	\v	Vertical tab
	\\	Backslash (\)
	\'	Single quote or apostrophe (')
	\"	Double quote (")

34.8 Built-in Variables

In awk, as in most programming languages, a *variable* is a named storage location for data. Awk provides a number of pre-defined variables, called *built-in variables*, some of which are listed in Table 34-2.

Some built-in variables—ARGC, ARGV, ENVIRON, FILENAME, FNR, NF, and NR—are updated for you automatically.

Operators are discussed in Section 34.13.

Other built-in variables—CONVFMT, FS, OFMT, OFS, ORS, and RS—have default values that you can change using the *assignment operator*, which looks exactly like an equals sign (=). For example, the variable ORS contains the output record separator, which by default is the newline ("\n"). However, any string can be used as a record separator. Thus the assignment

```
ORS = "\n\n"
```

stores the string "\n\n" as the output record separator. To see what this does, try the following command line:

```
§ awk 'BEGIN{ ORS = "\n\n" }; {print}' solar.system  RETURN
```

This command should print the contents of the solar.system file, double-spacing the output lines.

Table 34-2
Selected built-in awk
variables.

Variable	Value or Meaning
ARGC	Number of command-line arguments
ARGV	Array of command-line arguments
CONVFMT	Format for conversion of numbers to strings
ENVIRON	Array of environmental variables
FILENAME	Name of the current input file
FNR	Number of the current record
FS	Input field separator (default is whitespace)
NF	Number of fields in the current input record
NR	Number of records processed thus far
OFMT	Output format for numbers (default is "%.6g")
OFS	Output field separator (default is " ", a single space)
ORS	Output record separator (default is "\n", a newline)
RLENGTH	Length of the substring matched by the match function
RS	Record separator for input data (default is "\n", a newline)
RSTART	Start index in a substring matched by match function
SUBSEP	Subscript separator for multidimensional array indices

34.9 Field Variables

The dollar sign ($) is called
the field operator.

Awk provides a set of *field variables*, denoted $0, $1, $2, $3, ... , which receive the current record and its fields as they are read:

$0 holds the current record;

$1 holds the first field of the current record;

$2 holds the second field of the current record;

$3 holds the third field of the current record;

and so on. Because the built-in variable NF contains the number of fields in the current record, $NF is the last field of the record.

The values of the field variables are updated automatically every time a new record is read.

You can use field variables just as you would any other variable. You can even assign a new value to a field variable, if that should ever be necessary.

Listing 34-3 shows an awk script that uses field variables in both the pattern and the action.

```
#!/usr/bin/awk -f

# List the planets and their orbital distances
① $3 == "Sun" { print $1, $4 }
```

Listing 34-3
The planets.awk
script.

The script consists of a single executable line:

```
① $3 == "Sun" { print $1, $4 }
```

Note that the equality
operator (==) consists of
two equals signs together.
This operator is discussed in
Section 34.13 below.

The pattern checks whether the third field ($3) equals (==) the text *Sun* (represented by the string constant "Sun"—the double quotes are not part of the string). If *Sun* occurs as the third field, the record describes a planet. In that case, the action is to print from the first field ($1) the name of the planet and from the fourth field ($4) the orbital distance.

When executed using the solar.system file, the planets.awk script lists the planets (in alphabetical order) and their distances from the Sun:

```
Earth 149600000
Jupiter 778330000
Mars 227940000
Mercury 57910000
Neptune 4504300000
Pluto 5913520000
Saturn 1429400000
Uranus 2870990000
Venus 108200000
```

34.10 User-Defined Variables

You can create your own variables. In most conventional programming languages, a variable must be *declared* (or *dimensioned*) before it can be used. This means that the variable's name and data type must be specified beforehand.

In awk, variables are not declared. To use a variable, you need only to write its name. You do not have to specify a variable's type. In fact, an awk variable has no permanent data type; its type depends on the kind of data that it happens to be holding.

A value can be put into a variable using the assignment operator. For example, the assignment

```
FirstVar =  3.14159
```

stores the constant value 3.14159 in the variable FirstVar, overwriting any value already in the variable. Once this is done, the value can be assigned to another variable:

```
SecondVar =  FirstVar
```

This assignment copies the value 3.14159 from FirstVar into SecondVar. As a result, both variables contain the same value.

As we said, an awk variable does not have a permanent type. Thus it is possible to assign a string to a variable that previously held a number:

```
FirstVar =  "This is a string."
```

Although the same variable may be used to hold numbers and strings, it is generally not good programming practice to do so. (It can be confusing.)

A valid name or identifier for a user-defined variable may include uppercase letters (A through Z), lowercase letters (a through z), numerals (0 through 9), and the underscore character (_). A variable name may not contain spaces or begin with a numeral. It should differ from an identifier that already has a meaning in awk, such as BEGIN and END or the names of awk's built-in variables and functions (discussed below).

Listing 34-4 shows a simple awk script that counts the records containing the pattern /Jupiter/.

```
#!/usr/bin/awk -f

# Count the records containing "Jupiter"

① BEGIN { count = 0 } # Initialize count (not necessary)

② /Jupiter/ { count = count + 1 }

③ END { print count }
```

Listing 34-4
The executable file
count.jupiter.awk.

There are several interesting features to consider in count.jupiter.awk:

① BEGIN { count = 0 } # Initialize count (not necessary) |

This BEGIN statement sets the value of the variable count to zero before any lines are read. As the comment indicates, this step is not really necessary: by default, awk initializes variables to the numeric value 0 and the null string (""). Nevertheless, it is good programming practice to initialize all variables explicitly.

② /Jupiter/ { count = count + 1 } |

Every time a record is found that matches /Jupiter/, 1 is added to count.

③ END { print count } |

An END statement is used to print the final count.

34.11   Built-in Mathematics Functions

A *function* is a self-contained group of statements that may be called upon as needed to perform some task. Table 34-3 lists awk's built-in functions for performing mathematical calculations. Some points to note about these functions:

■ **Arguments.** Most of the built-in mathematical functions take one or more *arguments,* which are expressions enclosed in parentheses following the function name. Consider, for example, the cos function:

```
cos(x)
```

Do not put any space between the function name and the left parenthesis.

Here, the variable x is the argument. Any constant, variable, or formula may be used as an argument in place of x. Thus, if z is a numerical variable, we may write

```
cos(14.5+log(z))
```

The argument in this example is the expression 14.5+log(z).

■ **Return value.** A mathematical function acts somewhat—but not exactly—like a variable that computes its own value. It may appear anywhere a variable may, except on the left side of an assignment. Thus you may write

```
y = cos(x)
```

but not

```
cos(x) = y     # Error!
```

The value computed by a function is called its *return value*. This value does not persist; you must assign it to a variable if you want to use it later in the program.

■ **Call by value.** None of the functions listed in Table 34-3 can change its argument(s) except by assignment. For example, the int function takes the numeric value of its argument, cuts off (truncates) the fractional part, and returns the integral part. It does this to the value of the argument, not on the argument itself. You can see the result yourself by running the following command:

§ awk 'BEGIN{a = 3.14159; b = int(a); print a, b}' (RETURN)

The output will show that the argument a is unchanged:

```
3.14159   3
```

If you want int to change the value stored in a, you must use the assignment operator:

§ awk 'BEGIN{a = 3.14159; a = int(a); print a}' (RETURN)

The output will show that the argument a has been changed:

```
3
```

Function	Return Value (and Side Effect)
`atan2(y,x)`	Arctangent of y/x, in radians
`cos(x)`	Cosine of x, where x is in radians
`exp(x)`	Exponential of x, e^x, where $e = 2.7183...$
`int(x)`	Integer part of x, truncating the fractional part
`log(x)`	Natural or base-e logarithm of a positive number x
`rand()`	Pseudo-random number uniformly distributed between 0 and 1
`sin(x)`	Sine of x, where x is in radians
`srand(x)`	Previous seed (seeds `rand` using x)
`srand()`	Previous seed (seeds `rand` using date and time)
`sqrt(x)`	Square root of non-negative number x

Table 34-3
Built-in awk mathe-
matics functions.

■ **Empty argument list.** The `rand` function differs from the other math functions in that it takes no arguments. Nevertheless, the parentheses are still required after the function name whenever `rand` or any function is called:

Do not omit the parentheses, even when there are no arguments.

```
y = rand()

y = rand     # Error!
```

Although `rand` is sometimes called a "random number generator," it really produces *pseudo-random* numbers. A sequence of pseudo-random numbers appears to be random, but is computed from a starting value—called a "seed"—using a well-defined formula. For a given seed, `rand` produces exactly the same sequence of numbers. This is not random, but it can be helpful in debugging a program.

■ **Optional arguments.** The seed value for `rand` is set using `srand`, which may be called with or without an argument. If an argument is present, it is used as a seed. Otherwise, `srand` computes a seed from the current date and time:

```
srand(n)    # Use n as the seed for rand

srand()     # Use the date and time to compute a seed
```

Note that `srand` does return a value, which is the previous seed value. However, this value is rarely used. We are usually more interested in the "side effect" of seeding the `rand` function.

34.12 Built-in String Functions

Awk is intended for processing files containing text. Therefore, it should not be surprising that awk is equipped with a set of built-in functions for manipulating text strings. These are listed in Table 34-4.

Table 34-4
Built-in awk string
functions.

Function	Return Value (and Side Effects)
gsub(*old*, *new*)	Number of substitutions made (*new* replaces *old* everywhere in $0)
gsub(*old*, *new*, *str*)	Number of substitutions made (*new* replaces *old* everywhere in string *str*)
index(*str*, *substr*)	Index of the substring *substr* in a string *str*; 0 if *substr* not found
length(*str*)	Number of characters in the string *str*
match(*str*, *regex*)	Index showing where the string *str* matches the regular expression *regex*; 0 if no match
split(*str*, *arr*, *sep*)	Number of fields in *str* (splits string *str* at the field separator *sep*, puts the fields into array *arr*)
sprintf(*fmt*, *ex1*,)	String that printf would print using format *fmt* and data *ex1*, ...
sub(*regex*, *new*)	Number of substitutions made (*new* replaces leftmost substring of $0 matched by *regex*)
sub(*regex*, *new*, *str*)	Number of substitutions made (*new* replaces leftmost substring of *str* matched by *regex*)
substr(*str*, *i*)	Substring starting at index *i* of string *str*
substr(*str*, *i*, *n*)	Substring having *n* characters starting at index *i* of string *str*
tolower(*str*)	Copy of string *str* with uppercase letters converted to lowercase, other characters unchanged
toupper(*str*)	Copy of string *str* with lowercase letters converted to uppercase, other characters unchanged

Note that some of the string functions—namely gsub, split, and sub—have side effects. That is, these functions can change the value stored in a string variable. For instance, if the variable name contains the string "Anderson", the function call

```
gsub("o","e", name);
```

will change the contents of name to "Andersen".

The wc utility is discussed in
Section 11.4.

Listing 34-5 shows an awk script named wc.awk that mimics the wc (word-count) utility, which prints the number of lines, words, and characters in a file. This script uses the length function.

```
#! /usr/bin/awk -f
# Mimic the Unix wc (word count) utility

BEGIN{words = 0; chars = 0}

①    { words = words + NF }  # Count each field as a word
②    { chars = chars + length($0) + 1}  # Add 1 for "\n"

③ END { print "\t", NR, "\t",words,"\t", chars, FILENAME }
```

Listing 34-5
The wc.awk script.

The script includes several interesting statements of note:

①   `{ words = words + NF }  # Count each field as a word`

The variable words contains the count of the words. Each time a line is read from the file, the built-in variable NF is updated to hold the number of fields in the line. This number is added to the number in the words variable, and the result is put back into words.

②   `{ chars = chars + length($0) + 1}  # Add 1 for "\n"`

The variable chars contains the count of the characters in the file. When a line is read from the file, the entire line (except for the newline character) is stored in the field variable $0. The built-in function length computes the number of characters in a string; we add 1 to account for the newline character. This is added to the number in the chars variable, and the result is put back into chars.

③ `END { print "\t", NR, "\t",words,"\t", chars, FILENAME }`

Finally, the results are printed using the END statement. Here we have used the tab character (\t) to space the output. Once all of the lines have been processed, the built-in variable NR contains the number of records that have been read. The built-in variable FILENAME contains the name of the data file.

When run from the command line using solar.system as the data file, the wc.awk script produces the output

           88   792   4628 solar.system

34.13 Expressions and Operators

An *expression* is a formula for representing or computing some value. The simplest expression is a single constant, variable, or function. From such building blocks, more complicated expressions can be created using symbols called *operators*.

Table 34-5
Operators.

Operator and Name		Example	Value (and Side Effect)
$	Field selection	$m	mth field of the current record
++	Increment	++x	x + 1 (result stored in x)
--	Decrement	--x	x – 1 (result stored in x)
^	Exponentiation	x^y	x raised to the power y
!	Logical NOT	!x	1 if x is false, 0 otherwise
+	Unary plus	+x	x
–	Unary minus	–x	negative of x
*	Multiplication	x * y	product of x and y
/	Division	x / y	quotient of x and y
%	Modulus	x % y	remainder from x / y
+	Addition	x + y	sum of x and y
–	Subtraction	x – y	difference of x and y
	String concatenation	"ab" "z"	"abz"
<	Less than	x < y	1 if x is less than y, 0 otherwise
<=	Less than or equal	x <= y	1 if x is less than or equal to y, 0 otherwise
==	Equality	x == y	1 if x is equal to y, 0 otherwise
!=	Non-equality	x != y	1 if x does not equal y, 0 otherwise
>=	Greater than or equal	x >= y	1 if x exceeds or equals y, 0 otherwise
>	Greater than	x > y	1 if x is greater than y, 0 otherwise
~	Matching	$n~/ab/	1 if field n contains ab, 0 otherwise
!~	Nonmatching	$n!~/ab/	1 if field n does not contain ab, 0 otherwise
in	Array membership	i in arr	1 if arr[i] exists, 0 otherwise
&&	Logical AND	x && y	1 if both x and y are true, 0 otherwise
||	Logical OR	x || y	1 if either x or y is true, 0 otherwise
?:	Conditional	x?y:z	y if x is true, z otherwise
=	Assignment	y = x	x (result stored in y)
+=	Add-assignment	y += x	sum y+x (result stored in y)
-=	Subtract-assignment	y –= x	difference y–x (result stored in y)
*=	Multiply-assignment	y *= x	product y*x (result stored in y)
/=	Divide-assignment	y /= x	quotient y/x (result stored in y)
%=	Modulus-assignment	y %= x	remainder of y/x (result stored in y)
^=	Power-assignment	y ^= x	power y^x (result stored in y)

We have already seen how to use operators to create expressions. For example, Listing 34-5 includes the following expression involving the user-defined variable char, the built-in function length, the field variable $0, and the numerical constant 1:

```
chars = chars + length($0) + 1
```

Four operators appear in this expression: an assignment operator (=), two addition operators (+) and a field operator ($).

Table 34-5 lists the operators available in awk, along with examples of how they are used. Several points should be noted about the information in the table:

School children are taught the mnemonic "Please Excuse My Dear Aunt Sally" for the precedence of arithmetic operations: Parentheses, Exponents, Multiplication and Division, Addition and Subtraction.

■ **Precedence.** Precedence refers to the order in which two operations are performed when they occur near each other in an expression. For example, multiplication and division have a higher precedence than addition and subtraction. Consequently, 3 + 9 * 2 equals 21, not 24. In Table 34-5, operators having the same precedence are grouped together between horizontal lines. Groups are listed in order of precedence, those near the top of the table having priority over those further down.

Use parentheses to enforce the precedence you want!

Precedence can be altered using parentheses: (3 + 9) * 2 equals 24. Indeed, you should always use parentheses to indicate the desired order of operations; do not rely on your memory of the precedence rules.

■ **Associativity.** When two operations of the same precedence (such as addition and subtraction) occur near each other in an expression, the operation on the left is performed first. Thus, x + y - z is equivalent to (x + y) - z. We say that the operations *associate* left-to-right, or that they have *left-to-right associativity*. The exceptions to this rule are the exponentiation operator (∧), the conditional operator (?:), and the assignment operators (=, +=, -=, etc.), which associate right-to-left.

Zero or null is false; nonzero or non-null is true.

■ **True and false.** The logical operators (!, &&, ||), relational operators (>, >=, ==, !=, <=, <), and conditional operator (?:) are used to make decisions depending on whether an expression is true or false. In awk, both the numerical value zero (0) and the null string ("") are considered "false." Any nonzero number (such as 1) or non-null string is considered "true." Note that the string constant "0" is true because it is non-null!

■ **Side effects.** The primary effect of any operation is to obtain or compute a value. In addition, some operators also have the side effect of modifying a stored value. For instance, the primary effect of the increment operation ++z is to add 1 to the value taken from the variable z. The side effect is that the incremented value is put back into z. (In the case of the assignment operator =, the "side effect" is usually what interests us.)

■ **Concatenation.** The only string operation is concatenation, the process of putting two strings together to make a single string. There is no symbol for this operation. To concatenate, simply write the strings next to each other.

■ **Relational Operations.** The relational operators (>, >=, ==, !=, <=, <) will work on either numbers or strings. If two numbers are compared, the results are what you would expect. Thus, 1999 < 2 is false (equals 0).

Comparison of two strings is more complicated. The strings are examined character by character, starting with their first (leftmost) characters. On most systems, characters are compared according to their places in the ASCII table:

"1999" < "2" is true (equals 1) because 1 precedes 2 in ASCII;

"ba" < "wa" is true (equals 1) because b precedes w in ASCII;

"Aw" < "aw" is true (equals 1) because A precedes a in ASCII;

"ab" < "ax" is true (equals 1) because b precedes x in ASCII.

■ **Equality and Matching.** Both the equality operator (==) and the matching operator (~) may be applied to strings. However, the two operations are not the same. The equality operation

```
$0 == "A fine kettle of fish!"
```

is true (has the value 1) only if $0 is *precisely* equal to the string "A fine kettle of fish!" (without the double quotes, of course). In contrast, the matching operation

```
$0 ~ "fin"
```

is true (has the value 1) if $0 contains a substring that matches fin. Any of the following records would be matched by this pattern:

```
A fine kettle of fish!
The finest selection in town.
The judge fined the fisherman.
Define the problem.
```

The righthand side of the matching operator (~) may be any expression, including a regular expression. Thus

Slashes delimit regular
expression literals.

```
$0 ~ /fine/
```

Similar remarks apply to the non-equality (!=) and non-matching (!~) operators.

34.14   Formatted Output

The print command is adequate for quick and simple output. For fancier output, awk offers the printf ("print-formatted") command. It has the form

```
printf(fmt, exp1, exp2, ...)
```

where *fmt* is a string describing the format of the output, and *exp1*, *exp2*, ... are expressions to be printed according to this format.

For example, assume that x contains the value 5. The printf statement

```
printf("The square root of %f is %f.\n", x, sqrt(x))
```

will produce the output

```
The square root of 5.000000 is 2.236068.
```

The formats used by printf are discussed in greater detail in Appendix E.

Listing 34-6 shows an awk script that uses printf to format output.

Listing 34-6
The orbits.1.awk
script.

```
#! /usr/bin/awk -f

① BEGIN { printf("\t  Orbital Radius\n")
          printf("PLANET\t      (km)\t(AU)\n") }

② $3 == "Sun"{ printf("%-9s %8.3e %8.3f \n",
               $1, $4, $4/1.496e+08)}
```

This script includes two pattern-action statements:

```
① BEGIN { printf("\t  Orbital Radius\n")
          printf("PLANET\t      (km)\t(AU)\n") }
```

The BEGIN statement prints the column headings. Remember that the BEGIN statement is executed before any records are read.

```
② $3 == "Sun"{ printf("%-9s %8.3e %8.3f \n",
               $1, $4, $4/1.496e+08)}
```

A record having the string "Sun" in the third field refers to a planet. The printf statement prints the name of the planet as a left-justified string (%-9s), the orbital radius in kilometers in e-notation (%8.3e), and the radius in Astronomical Units as a decimal fraction (%8.3f).

When run using solar.system as the data file, the output is

```
          Orbital Radius
PLANET       (km)       (AU)
Earth     1.496e+08    1.000
Jupiter   7.783e+08    5.203
Mars      2.279e+08    1.524
Mercury   5.791e+07    0.387
Neptune   4.504e+09   30.109
Pluto     5.914e+09   39.529
Saturn    1.429e+09    9.555
Uranus    2.871e+09   19.191
Venus     1.082e+08    0.723
```

34.15 Pipes

The `orbits.1.awk` script shown in the previous section (Listing 34-6) prints the orbital data in alphabetical order according to the name of the planet because that is how the data are listed in `solar.system`. We may prefer to have the data listed in order of distance from the Sun. One way to do this is to sort the file before piping it to the `orbits.1.awk` script:

§ sort -n +3 solar.system | orbits.1.awk RETURN

The Unix `sort` utility is described in Section 11.6

Here we have used the Unix `sort` command to perform a numerical sort (-n) on the fourth field (+3) of the `solar.system` file. The output of the sort is then piped to the `orbits.1.awk` script for formatting and printing. The output is

```
            Orbital Radius
PLANET        (km)        (AU)
Mercury   5.791e+07     0.387
Venus     1.082e+08     0.723
Earth     1.496e+08     1.000
Mars      2.279e+08     1.524
Jupiter   7.783e+08     5.203
Saturn    1.429e+09     9.555
Uranus    2.871e+09    19.191
Neptune   4.504e+09    30.109
Pluto     5.914e+09    39.529
```

It is possible to accomplish the same thing from within the `awk` script itself, as shown in Listing 34-7.

```
#! /usr/bin/awk -f

BEGIN { printf("\t  Orbital Radius\n")
        printf("PLANET\t      (km)\t(AU)\n") }

① $3 == "Sun"{ printf("%-9s %8.3e %8.3f \n",
                $1, $4, $4/1.496e+08) | "sort -n +2" }
```

Listing 34-7
The `orbits.2.awk`
script.

The only change is to the last line:

```
① $3 == "Sun"{ printf("%-9s %8.3e %8.3f \n",
                $1, $4, $4/1.496e+08) | "sort -n +2" }
```

The sort will be done on the third field of the output from `printf`, not the third field of the input file.

The pipe symbol (|) directs the output from the `printf` statement to the UNIX `sort` utility. Note the arguments to the `sort` command: -n specifies a numerical sort, and +2 specifies that the sort be done on the third field. (In other words, +2 means skip the the first two fields.) The double quotes around the `sort` call are required.

34.16 Output Redirection

Output from the print and printf statements can also be redirected into a data file using the redirection arrows (> or >>). Listing 34-8 shows how the orbits.2.awk script can be modified to do this.

```
   #! /usr/bin/awk -f

① BEGIN { printf("\t  Orbital Radius\n") > "output"
②          printf("PLANET\t      (km)\t(AU)\n") >> "output"}

   $3 == "Sun" { printf("%-9s %8.3e %8.3f \n",
③                 $1, $4, $4/1.496e+08) \
④                 | "sort -n +2 >> output" }
```

Listing 34-8
The orbits.3.awk
script.

Let's examine the script in detail:

① BEGIN { printf("\t Orbital Radius\n") > "output"

The output from the first printf statement is redirected into the file named output. If the file already exists, this operation writes over the existing data in the file. If the file does not already exist, the redirection operation creates it.

②   printf("PLANET\t   (km)\t(AU)\n") >> "output"}

The second redirection uses the append operator (>>) to add a line of text to the bottom of the output file.

③ $1, $4, $4/1.496e+08) \

The backslash (\) at the end of this line indicates that the statement is continued on the next line.

④ | "sort -n +2 >> output" }

The body of the table is sorted using the sort utility before being appended to the output file. As before, the double quotes are required.

34.17 Type Conversions

We have noted that awk only has two types of data, numbers and strings. At times, it may be necessary to convert data from one type to the other.

■ **Numeric value of a string.** Sometimes, you may wish to use a string where a number would be expected, such as in an arithmetic operation or as an argument to one of the mathematical functions listed in Table 34-3. When this happens, the "numeric value" of the string is used. If the string begins with some combination of characters that resembles a number, this becomes the numeric value of the string. Otherwise, the string has the numeric value 0. Thus,

"221B Baker Street" has the numeric value 221;

"3.048e-01meters/foot" has the numeric value 3.048e-01;

"Answer=47" has the numeric value 0.

■ **String value of a number.** You may wish to use a number where a string would be expected, such as in a concatenation operation or as an argument to one of the string functions listed in Table 34-4. When this happens, the "string value" of the number is used. This is simply the number as it would be printed by printf. A number can be represented as an integer, as a decimal fraction, or in e-notation. The format of the string value is determined by the value of the CONVFMT variable. The default is "%.6g".

■ **Mixed comparisons.** As we noted previously, the relational operators (>, >=, ==, !=, <=, <) work on either numbers or strings. For the comparison of a number and a string, the number is first converted to its string value according to the format stored in the CONVFMT variable.

Incidentally, you can force a string to be treated as a number by adding zero to it. Likewise, you can force a number to be treated as a string by concatenating the null string ("") to it.

34.18 Selection Structures

Thus far, we have seen that the statements in an awk action are executed from top to bottom, one after another. However, it is possible to change the normal order of execution according to conditions.

The simple if structure can be written in the form

The braces may be omitted when the body is a single statement.

```
if (condition) {
    body
}
```

where *condition* can be any expression, and the *body* of the loop consists of one or more awk statements. The braces are required only if there is more than one statement in the *body*. However, it is good programmming practice always to use the braces.

Nonzero numbers and non-null strings are "true."

The if structure follows the rule "Do if true." If the *condition* is true, the *body* statements are run in the order they are written; if the *condition* is false, the *body* is skipped entirely.

The if-else structure is used to make choices between two alternatives, one of which must be selected:

```
if (condition) {
    first body
}
else {
    alternative body
}
```

If the *condition* is true, the *first body* is chosen; if the *condition* is false, the *alternative body* is chosen.

Finally, an extended if-else structure can be used with multiple alternatives:

```
if (condition1) {
    body1
}
else if (condition2) {
    body2
}
else if (condition3) {
    body3
}

...

else {
    default body
}
```

Starting at the top of the if structure, *condition1* is examined first. If it is true, *body1* is run and the remaining alternatives are skipped. Otherwise, *condition2* is checked, then *condition3*, and so on. If a condition is found to be true, its body code is run and the remaining conditions and body statements are skipped. No more than one body may be run.

The very last else is not accompanied by an if or a condition. This is the *default case*, which is executed if none of the previous conditions is true. The default else is optional and may be omitted.

34.19 Repetition Structures

Like most programming languages, awk is able to perform tasks over and over using a *looping or repetition structure*. Awk offers three such structures which are similar to their counterparts in the C programming language: the while loop, the do-while loop, and the for loop.

The while loop has the general form

```
while (condition) {
    body
}
```

The while loop behaves as an if structure that can be executed more than once. Like the if structure, the while loop follows the rule "Do if true." When the while statement is encountered, its *condition* is tested. If it is true, the statements in the *body* are executed in the order they are written, then the *condition* is checked again. If the *condition* is true, the loop is repeated; otherwise, the *body* of the loop is skipped entirely.

The do-while loop is similar, except that the condition is checked after the statements in the loop are executed:

```
do {
    body
} while (condition)
```

The for loop has the form

```
for (Initialize; Test condition; Update) {
    body
}
```

The operation of the for loop may be summarized this way:

1. *Initialize* the loop

2. *Test condition*: if true, run the *body*; otherwise skip to Step 5

3. *Update* the counter

4. Repeat Steps 2 and 3.

5. Continue beyond the loop.

The for loop is sometimes called a *counter-controlled loop* because it is often used in situations in which we count the repetitions.

34.20 The ARGV Array

An *array* is a collection or list of variables that share the same name. The individual variables of an array—called *elements*—are distinguished from each other by an *index*. Most commonly, the indices of an array are positive integers.

One of the built-in variables listed in Table 34-2 is an array named ARGV (short for "argument vector"). This array receives the arguments when an awk program is executed from the command line. A related variable is ARGC, which contains the number of arguments. Listing 34-9 shows an awk script that uses ARGV and ARGC.

Listing 34-9
The print.args.awk script.

```
#! /usr/bin/awk -f

# Print the command-line arguments

BEGIN {
    printf("You entered: \n")
①   for (i = 0; i < ARGC; i++) {
        printf("ARGV[%d]: %s \n", i, ARGV[i])
    }
}
```

The interesting part of this script is the `for` loop:

```
①      for (i = 0; i < ARGC; i++) {
            printf("ARGV[%d]: %s \n", i, ARGV[i])
        }
```

Arrays are often processed using loops. Note that the array numbering begins with element 0. This is a convention inherited from the C programming language. Thus, ARGV[0] is the first element and ARGV[ARGC-1] is the last element.

Once the script is made executable, the command line

```
§ print.args.awk first 2nd "third" /fourth/ 'fifth'   (RETURN)
```

will produce the output

```
You entered:
ARGV[0]: awk
ARGV[1]: first
ARGV[2]: 2nd
ARGV[3]: third
ARGV[4]: /fourth/
ARGV[5]: fifth
```

In this example, ARG[0] contained the string "awk" because the script was run by the awk utility. On some systems, ARG[0] would contain instead the name of the executable awk file (e.g., `print.args.awk`).

34.21 User-Defined Arrays

You can create your own array by writing its name. There is no need to declare an array or specify its size before using it. Awk arrays are dynamic, meaning they grow as needed.

Although the elements of ARGV are numbered starting at 0, user-defined arrays may start from any index. Listing 34-10 shows `reverse.awk`, which prints the records of a file in the reverse order (last record first).

Listing 34-10
The executable file
reverse.awk.

```
#! /usr/bin/awk -f

# Print records in reverse order (last record first)

①      { record[NR] = $0 }

② END {
            i = NR
            while (i > 0){
                print record[i]
                --i
            }
      }
```

This script is fairly straightforward:

```
①      { record[NR] = $0 }
```

The first executable line of the script assigns the current record to the array named record. Because there is no pattern, the action is applied to every record. When a record is read, the variable NR is updated and the record is stored in the array element record[NR]. This causes the elements of record to be numbered beginning at 1, not 0.

```
② END {
      i = NR
      while (i > 0){
          print record[i]
          --i
      }
}
```

This loop counts down from NR (the number of the last record read) to 1 (the number of the first record), printing the contents of record[i] as it does. We could have accomplished the same thing with a for loop:

```
END {
    for (i = NR; i > 0; --i)
    print record[i]
}
```

Make the script executable, then enter the command line

§ reverse.awk (RETURN)

If no input file is specified, the program reads from the standard input. Enter some text, followed by an end-of-file signal:

```
Rock-a-bye baby in the tree top,
When the wind blows the cradle will rock.
When the bough breaks the cradle will fall,
And soon come the lawyers with lawsuits for all.
```
(Control)-(D)

You should see the same lines but in reversed order:

```
And soon come the lawyers with lawsuits for all.
When the bough breaks the cradle will fall,
When the wind blows the cradle will rock.
Rock-a-bye baby in the tree top,
§
```

34.22 Associative Arrays

Unlike many traditional programming languages, awk uses *associative arrays* (also known as *maps*, *hashes*, *lookup tables*, or *dictionaries*). An associative array consists of pairs of indices and elements, each index being associated with a particular element.

Whereas conventional arrays employ integers as indices, associative arrays may use any number or string as an index. (In fact, awk treats all array indices as strings, even those that look like numbers.)

Awk has a special for loop that is intended for processing associative arrays:

```
for (var in array) {
    body
}
```

Here, *var* represents the loop-control variable and *array* represents an array. For each iteration of the loop, *var* takes the value of an index of *array*. This is repeated until all of the elements have been processed.

Listing 34-11 shows how an associative array may be used to count and list the words in a file.

```
    #!/usr/bin/awk -f

    # Count the occurrence of each word in a file

        {
①           gsub(/[^a-zA-Z ]/, "")

②           for (field = 1; field <= NF; ++field) {
③               word = tolower($field)      #lowercase only
④               ++count[word]
              }
        }

⑤   END {
            for (word in count)
                print word, count[word] | "sort "
⑥           for (word in count)
                print word, count[word] | "sort -rn +1"
        }
```

Listing 34-11
The executable file
count.words.awk.

The count.words.awk script illustrates a number of important points:

①   gsub(/[^a-zA-Z]/, "") |

Here we have used the gsub ("global substitution") function to remove the punctuation and numbers from the input file. The gsub function works on text in the variable $0, which contains the current input record. The function substitutes the text of its second argument for any text in $0 that is matched by its first argument. In this case, the first argument is a regular expression matching any character that is not a lowercase letter (a through z), an uppercase letter (A through Z), or a space. The second argument is a null string. Thus, this function call replaces punctuation and numbers with null strings.

②   `for (field = 1; field <= NF; ++field) {`

A counter-controlled `for` loop is used to step through the input fields. The user-defined variable `field` serves as a counter; it is initialized to 1. Here we have used the increment operator (++) to update the counter.

③   `word = tolower($field)    #lowercase only`

The `tolower` function converts the uppercase letters to lowercase, leaving the other characters unchanged. The resulting string is assigned to the user-defined variable `word`.

④   `++count[word]`

The associative array `count` uses the string `word` as an index.

⑤ `END {`
      `for (word in count)`
         `print word, count[word] | "sort "`

Once all of the input lines have been processed, the words and their counts are sorted and printed. The `for` loop steps through the indices of the `count` array. The words and their counts are sorted alphabetically and printed on screen.

⑥   `for (word in count)`
         `print word, count[word] | "sort -rn +1"`

This for loop causes the words and counts to be printed, this time sorted by frequency.

34.23   User-Defined Functions

Awk allows you to define your own functions using statements of the general form

`function` *name(parameter-list)*
`{`
   body
`}`

where *name* is the function name, *parameter-list* is a sequence of variable names separated by commas, and the *body* consists of one or more awk statements. A function definition may appear anywhere that a pattern-action statement may.

Listing 34-12 shows the code for a program `trig.table.awk` that prints a table of the sine and cosine functions for angles from 0° to 360° in increments of 10°. The program calls the two built-in functions `sin` and `cos`, and two user-defined functions named `toRadians` and `pi`.

Because the built-in trigonometric functions take their arguments in radians, the program must convert from degrees to radians. The `toRadians` function performs this conversion according to the formula

$$\text{radians} = \text{degrees} \cdot \frac{\pi \text{ radians}}{180 \text{ degrees}}$$

The `pi ()` function approximates the value of $\pi = 3.14158\ldots$ using Machin's formula:

$$\frac{\pi}{4} = 4 \cdot \text{atan}\left(\frac{1}{5}\right) - \text{atan}\left(\frac{1}{239}\right)$$

```
#!/usr/bin/awk -f

# Print a table of trigonometric functions

BEGIN {
        printf("Degrees  Radians      Sine      Cosine\n")

        for(degrees = 0; degrees <= 360; degrees += 10) {
            x = toRadians(degrees)
            printf("%7.1f  %7.4f   %7.4f   %7.4f\n",
                degrees, x, sin(x), cos(x))
        }
}

function toRadians(x)
{
    return ( x * pi()/180.0 )
}

function pi()
{
    return (4 * (4 * atan2(1, 5) - atan2(1, 239)))
}
```

Listing 34-12
The `trig.table.awk` script.

This program introduces a number of awk features:

①   `for(degrees = 0; degrees <= 360; degrees += 10) {` |

We have used the addition-assignment operator (+=) to update the value of degrees.

②   x = toRadians(degrees)

An argument may be any expression, including a constant, a variable, a formula or a function call.

The `toRadians` function is called to convert from degrees to radians. The argument to the function is the variable `degrees`. The value of the argument is passed to the `toRadians` function, which calculates and returns its own value. The result is then assigned to the variable `x`. The argument `degrees` is unchanged by the function call.

③ `function toRadians(x)`

The first line of the function definition names the function and lists its parameters. The `toRadians` function has a single parameter named `x`. This parameter receives the argument value when the function is called. Any variable named in the parameter list is *local* to the function; the rest of the awk program does not have access to it. That means you can use the same variable name for other purposes elsewhere in the file. In this case, there are two different variables named `x`, one of which is restricted to the `toRadians` function.

④   `return ( x * pi()/180.0 )`

This statement converts degrees to radians, and returns the result to the place where the `toRadians` function was called. One awk function may call another: thus, `toRadians` calls `pi` to compute the value of π. Although `pi` takes no arguments, the parentheses are still required after the function name.

⑤ `function pi()`

Here the parameter list is empty because the `pi` function takes no arguments.

⑥   `return (4 * (4 * atan2(1, 5) - atan2(1, 239)))`

The `return` statement computes the approximation and causes this value to be returned to the place where the `pi` function was called.

Note the distinction between an argument and a parameter. An argument may be any expression (a constant, variable, formula, etc.), the value of which is passed to a function through the argument list. Thus, in the function call

`x = toRadians(degrees)`

the argument is the variable `degrees`. The value of `degrees` is passed to the `toRadians` function:

```
function toRadians(x)
{
    return ( x * pi()/180.0 )
}
```

According to the function definition, the value from the argument is stored in the parameter `x`.

In short, the argument produces a value that is passed to the function; the parameter stores that value inside the function.

Keep in mind that any variable named in a function parameter list is local to that function, so that the other functions and pattern-action statements cannot see it or use it. Thus, the parameter x used inside the function toRadians is not the same as the variable x used outside the function. All variables not named in a function's parameter list are *global*, meaning that they are accessible to any function or statement in the same file.

34.24 Optional Arguments

It is not necessary that an argument be supplied for every parameter in a function. For example, Listing 34-13 shows a function that computes the logarithm to an arbitrary base B. It may take two arguments; however, the second argument is optional.

```
# Base-B logarithm (B is a positive number)
# Base 10 assumed if B is not given in the function call

① function logB(x, B)
  {
②     if (B == 0) {
           B = 10
      }
③     return (log(x)/log(B))
  }
```

Listing 34-13
The logB function.

Let's dissect this function:

```
① function logB(x, B)
```

The first line of the function definition gives the name of the function and its parameters. Two parameters are defined (x and B), so the function may take as many as two arguments. If just one argument value is provided, it will be assigned to the parameter x, and B will contain the default value 0.

```
②     if (B == 0) {
           B = 10
      }
```

If the calling program does not provide a value for B, the function assigns the value 10 to B. In that case, the function computes the common logarithm.

③   `return (log(x)/log(B))` |

This `return` statement computes the logarithm and returns the result.

34.25 Exercises

1. Write a one-line awk program to accomplish each of the following tasks for the data file `solar.system`:

a. Print all records that do not list a discoverer in the eighth field.

b. Print every record after erasing the second field.

c. Print the records for satellites that have negative orbital periods. (A negative orbital period simply means that the satellite orbits in a counterclockwise direction.)

d. Print the data for the objects discovered by the Voyager2 space probe.

e. Print each record with the orbital period given in seconds rather than days.

2. The *periapsis* is the point of closest approach between a satellite and the object around which it orbits; the *apoapsis* is the point of greatest separation between the two. The periapsis distance P and the apoapsis distance A can be computed from the formulas

$$P = a(1 - \varepsilon)$$

$$A = a(1 + \varepsilon)$$

where a is the *semimajor axis* and ε is the *eccentricity* of the orbit. For a perfect circle, $\varepsilon = 0$; for an ellipse, $0 < \varepsilon < 1$. Print each record from `solar.system` with the values of P and A inserted between the orbital radius and the orbital period.

3. Modify the program shown in Listing 34-12 so that it also prints the value of the tangent. Write a function named `tan` to compute the tangent of an argument given in radians.

4. Write a script to test the logarithm function `logB` shown in Listing 34-13.

5. Awk has just one inverse trigonometric function, `atan2`. Use this function to write the other inverse trig functions according to the formulas

`asin(x) = atan2(x, sqrt(1-x*x))`

`acos(x) = atan2(sqrt(1-x*x), x)`

`atan(x) = atan2(x, 1)`

6. Write an awk script named `test.regexp.awk` to determine whether a given string matches a regular expression. If the user types the command line

§ `test.regexp.awk /Ma/ Mars` (RETURN)

the script should print

```
Match: /Ma/ matches "Mars"
```

7. The rand function computes pseudo-random numbers uniformly distributed between 0 and 1. Write a function rand2 that computes a pseudo-random number x evenly distributed between two limits low and high, according to the formula

```
x = rand()*(high - low) + low
```

8. Write a function randint that computes a pseudo-random integer x evenly distributed between two limits 1 and high, according to the formula

```
x =  int(high * rand()) + 1
```

9. Write an awk script that computes a student's grade mygrade.awk, given a score between 0 and 100. Thus, the command line

```
§ mygrade.awk 90.1 (RETURN)
```

should produce the output

```
You have an A!
```

Account for the following cases:

$100 < \text{score} \Rightarrow$ error message (scores may not exceed 100%)

$90 \leq \text{score} \leq 100 \Rightarrow$ A

$80 \leq \text{score} < 90 \Rightarrow$ B

$70 \leq \text{score} < 80 \Rightarrow$ C

$60 \leq \text{score} < 70 \Rightarrow$ D

$0 \leq \text{score} < 60 \Rightarrow$ F

$\text{score} < 0 \Rightarrow$ error message (scores may not be less than 0%)

# Chapter 35

TUTORIAL:
SCRIPTING WITH PERL

Perl was originally developed to replace tools such as sed, awk, and C for text processing. Perl has since developed into a general-purpose scripting language that is now used for system administration, GUI development, and network programming. Perl has become especially important on the Internet: it is said that Perl is the "glue that holds the Web together."

Although the POSIX standards do not require that Perl be included among the UNIX utilities, it is found on most UNIX systems. Perl is open-source software, available without charge from the Free Software Foundation.

Incidentally, it is common to write Perl when referring to the language, and perl when referring to the command that interprets Perl scripts.

35.1 Versions of Perl

Perl is also said to stand for "Pathologically Eclectic Rubbish Lister."

Perl is said to stand for "Practical Extraction and Report Language." Perl was written by Larry Wall, who also wrote the rn news reader and the patch command. The first version of Perl was released publicly in 1987. You can read about the subsequent development of Perl by entering the command

§ man perlhist (RETURN)

To determine the current version of Perl available on your system, enter the perl command with the -v ("version") option:

§ perl -v (RETURN)

The result should be a listing similar to the following:

```
This is perl, v5.8.1-RC3 built for darwin-thread-multi-
2level (with 1 registered patch, see perl -V for more
detail)

Copyright 1987-2003, Larry Wall

Perl may be copied only under the terms of either the
Artistic License or the GNU General Public License, which
```

may be found in the Perl 5 source kit.

Complete documentation for Perl, including FAQ lists, should be found on this system using 'man perl' or 'perldoc perl'. If you have access to the Internet, point your browser at http://www.perl.com/, the Perl Home Page.

You will need to know the pathname of the perl program, which you can determine using the Unix which or whereis utility:

§ which perl (RETURN)

or

§ whereis perl (RETURN)

Typically, the pathname will be /usr/bin/perl or /usr/local/bin/perl.

35.2 A Sample Data File

The file solar.system *is available from the* Just Enough Unix *website.*

The examples in this chapter use the same sample data file solar.system that was used in the previous chapter. Recall that this file contains data on the major natural satellites in the solar system. The first line of the file describes Adrastea, one of the moons of Jupiter:

Adrastea XV Jupiter 129000 0.30 0.00 0.00 Jewitt 1979

This line consists of nine fields:

1. Name of the planet or moon (Adrastea)

2. Number of the moon or planet (XV)

3. Name of the object around which the satellite orbits (Jupiter)

4. Orbital radius (semimajor axis) in kilometers (129000)

5. Orbital period in days (0.30)

6. Orbital inclination in degrees (0.00)

7. Orbital eccentricity (0.00)

8. Discoverer (Jewitt)

9. Year of discovery (1979)

The file solar.system contains 88 lines of the same format. The lines are arranged in alphabetical order according to the name of the planet or moon.

35.3 Running Perl

You have several options for running a Perl program. A short program can be entered at the command line. For example, the command

§ perl -n -e 'print' solar.system (RETURN)

Command-line options are often called "switches."

will print all of the lines in the data file, mimicking the cat utility. The -n option causes the program to be applied to every line of the input file. The -e option tells Perl that executable code follows. The Perl code itself is surrounded by single quotes, which prevent the shell from trying to interpret the Perl program.

This kind of action— printing the lines of a data file—occurs often enough that the -p option is provided to do this automatically:

§ perl -p -e '' solar.system (RETURN)

Here, the single quotes are required because code is always expected after the -e option; however, there is no need to include a print statement inside the quotes.

Command-line entry is fine for simple one-line Perl programs. You will find it more convenient to put longer Perl programs in a file. Listing 35-1 shows one way to do this.

Listing 35-1
The cat.pl script.

```
① # Print a line from the standard input
② print;
```

The file contains just two lines:

```
① # Print a line from the standard input
```

Comments are for the benefit of human readers; they are ignored by Perl.

The pound sign (#) marks this as a *comment*. With two exceptions (to be discussed shortly), text appearing between a pound sign and the end of the same line is ignored by Perl. Comments are intended to be informative to the programmer (or any other person) who may read the script at a later date.

```
② print;
```

The second line of the file contains the same Perl program we used before, consisting of a single print statement.

To run the program, type the following at the command line:

§ perl -n cat.pl solar.system (RETURN)

As before, the -n option tells Perl to apply the program to every line in the file. The result should be the same as before.

Yet another way to run a Perl program is to turn it into an executable file, as shown in Listing 35-2. Such a script can be run simply by entering the names of the executable file and the data file.

```
① #!/usr/bin/perl -w -n

# Print all of the lines in the standard input
print;
```

Listing 35-2
The cat2.pl script.

This script introduces one new wrinkle:

① `#!/usr/bin/perl -w -n`

The origins of the term "shebang" in this connection are obscure.

The first line of the cat2.pl file starts with a "shebang," consisting of a pound sign and an exclamation point together (#!). (Note that in this situation a pound sign does not mark the beginning of a comment.) The shebang is followed by the pathname of the perl program. The -w option tells Perl to warn you when it encounters something questionable in your code. The -n option tells Perl to apply the program to every line in the input.

The chmod utility is used to make the file executable:

The chmod utility is discussed in Section 6.17.

§ `chmod a+x cat2.pl` (RETURN)

How you run the program depends on whether the current working directory is included in the search path. If not, type the following at the command line:

§ `./cat2.pl < solar.system` (RETURN)

On the other hand, if the current directory is included in the search path, simply type the command line

§ `cat2.pl < solar.system` (RETURN)

To learn more about running Perl (including a list of command-line options) refer to the perlrun page:

§ `man perlrun` (RETURN)

35.4 Script Layout

Although Perl allows considerable flexibility in the layout of scripts, there are a few rules you must observe:

■ **Statements.** A Perl statement is terminated a semicolon. Although it is permissible to put several statements on the same line, it is generally more readable to put each statement on its own line.

■ **Allowable whitespace.** Whitespace—including blank lines, spaces, tabs, and newlines—is ignored by Perl except in quoted strings. Blank lines may be inserted before and after any statement. Spaces and tabs may be inserted around operators, after opening braces and parentheses, and before closing braces and parentheses.

■ **Continuation.** Because Perl treats the newline as whitespace, there is no need for a special line-continuation character.

■ **Identifiers.** The name of a variable or function may not contain spaces. (If a space is inserted into a variable name, Perl will interpret it as two variable names.)

■ **Parentheses.** Perl allows you to omit parentheses in many places. (However, it is a good idea to insert parentheses where they will help make the meaning clear.)

In general, you should use whitespace to enhance readability for the human reader. Indent statements within a block of code to show program structure.

35.5 Scalar Literals

A *literal* is a value written (almost) exactly as it is meant to be understood. In other words, the value of a literal should be obvious to any human reader of a program. Literals are also called *constants* because their values do not change during the execution of a program. Two kinds of literals occur in Perl: numbers and character strings. (The file `solar.system` contains both kinds of data.)

A Perl numeric constant may be written as an integer (such as `123`), as a decimal fraction (such as `-47.9`), or in *e-notation* (such as `6.02e+23`). The latter is a way of representing scientific notation without using superscripts. Hence,

The *e* may be capitalized: this is called *E-notation*.

`6.02e+23` and `6.02E+23` mean 6.02×10^{23}

`9.11e-31` and `9.11E-31` mean 9.11×10^{-31}

`-1.2e-09` and `-1.2E-09` mean -1.2×10^{-9}

Long integers may be written using underscores to separate multiples of 1000:

The population of New Mexico in 1990 was 1,819,046.

`1_819_046` is the same as `1819046`

Regardless of how it is written, every numeric quantity is stored by Perl as a floating point number. (Floating point may be considered as a variation of scientific notation for binary numbers.)

Perl has two kinds of string literals, single-quoted and double-quoted. We will most often use *double-quoted string literals*, which are written as plain (ASCII) text enclosed in double quotes:

`"This is a double-quoted string."`

`"So is this."`

`"123"`

`" "`

The null string contains no characters.

`""`

Table 35-1
Escape sequences.

Sequence	Meaning
\a	Alert (audible alarm)
\b	Backspace
\f	Form feed
\n	Newline
\r	Carriage return
\t	Horizontal tab
\v	Vertical tab
\\	Backslash (\)
\"	Double quote (")
\l	Lowercase (next letter)
\L	Lowercase (apply to all letters until the next \E)
\u	Uppercase (next letter)
\U	Uppercase (apply to all letters until the next \E)
\Q	Quote (insert backslashes) all letters until the next \E
\E	End previous \L, \U, or \Q

Note the difference between 123 and "123"; the former is a number, the latter a string. Also, " " is a string containing a single space (ASCII value 32), and "" is the *null string* containing no characters.

The double quotes surrounding a string constant are not considered part of the string. To include a double quote in a string, "quote" it with a leading backslash:

```
"\"Play it again,\" he said."
```

A double-quoted string may contain *escape sequences* to represent special characters. Table 35-1 lists the escape sequences recognized by Perl. Some of these—the alert (\a), backspace (\b), carriage return (\r), formfeed (\f), horizontal tab (\t), newline (\n), and vertical tab (\v)—are said to be *nonprinting* because they affect the spacing of text in the output, but otherwise do not cause anything to be printed.

Certain variable values also may be inserted into a double-quoted string. This is called interpolation, and will be described later.

A single-quoted string consists of ASCII text enclosed in single quotes:

```
'This is a single-quoted string.'
```

The single quotes are not part of the string. To include a single quote in the string, it must be quoted using a backslash; to include a backslash, it must be preceded by another backslash. Otherwise, none of the escape sequences listed in Table 35-1 has any special meaning in a single-quoted string. Thus, `'\n'` is interpreted as a backslash followed by the letter *n*, not as the newline character.

35.6   Scalar Variables

In Perl, as in most programming languages, a *variable* is a named storage location for data. Perl has three principal kinds of variables: scalars, arrays, and hashes. We discuss scalars in this section; we will discuss arrays and hashes later.

A *scalar variable* is one that can hold just one value at a time. The value may be a number or a string. Scalar variables are denoted by a dollar sign prefix ($).

In general, a declaration specifies the variable's name and other pertinent characteristics.

Perl does not require that variables be declared: to use a variable, you need only to write its name. However, it is a good idea to declare most variables, which you may do using the `my` operator. For example,

```
my $first_variable = 3.14159
```

The special value `undef` means "undefined."

creates the scalar variable `$first_variable` and gives it the initial value `3.14159`. If you do not give the variable an initial value, it starts out with the value `undef`, which is short for "undefined."

A valid name or identifier for a user-defined variable may include the following characters:

- Uppercase letters (A through Z)
- Lowercase letters (a through z)
- Numerals (0 through 9)
- The underscore character (_)

A variable name may not contain spaces or begin with a numeral.

A value can be put into a variable using the assignment operator. For example, the assignment

```
$first_variable =   3.14159
```

stores the constant value `3.14159` in the variable `first_variable`, overwriting any value that may already be stored there. Once this is done, the value can be assigned to another variable:

```
$second_variable =   $first_variable
```

This assignment copies the value `3.14159` from `first_variable` into `second_variable`. As a result, both variables contain the same value.

Listing 35-3 shows a script that uses several scalar variables.

```
#!/usr/bin/perl -w

① use strict;

   print "What is your name?  ";
② my $name;
③ $name = <STDIN>;
④ chomp($name);

   print("What is your mass in pounds?  ");
⑤ chomp(my $pounds = <STDIN>);

⑥ my $kilograms = $pounds/2.2046226;

⑦ print("Hello, $name; $pounds lb is $kilograms kg.\n");
```

Listing 35-3
The helloUser.pl
script.

This script introduces a number of new Perl features:

① use strict;

This is an example of a *pragma*, which is a special instruction to the Perl compiler. The strict pragma directs the compiler to enforce some good programming practices, such as requiring that all variables be declared using the my operator.

② my $name;

Here the my operator is used to declare the scalar variable $name. Because of the strict pragma, the compiler will issue a warning and stop compiling if you do not declare your variables this way.

③ $name = <STDIN>;

Filehandles
are discussed in Section
35.16 below.

This statement gets a line from the standard input and assigns it to the scalar variable $name. STDIN is a *filehandle* that refers to the standard input. The angle brackets (< >) are the line-input operator. Thus <STDIN> causes a line to be read from the standard input.

④ chomp($name);

The Perl chomp function
removes the record
separator (usually "\n")
from the end of a string.

The last key you press when entering a line of text at the keyboard is ⟨RETURN⟩, which generates a newline ("\n"). The line input operation <STDIN> then gets your input line, including the newline. In most cases, you do not want the newline, so you can use the chomp function to remove it.

⑤ chomp(my $pounds = <STDIN>);

This statement (1) declares the scalar variable $pounds; (2) reads a line from the standard input; (3) assigns the input line to $pounds; and (4) removes the newline from the stored string using chomp. We previously used three separate statements to do all this.

⑥ my $kilograms = $pounds/2.2046226;

This statement (1) declares the scalar variable $kilograms; (2) divides the value of $pounds by the literal 2.2046226; and (3) assigns the result to $kilograms. Note that the value of $pounds is not changed by either the division or the assignment operation, allowing us to use it again in the next statement.

⑦ `print("Hello, $name; $pounds lb is $kilograms kg.\n");`

The print function is used to print the results. Because the output string is double-quoted, the values of the variables $name, $pounds, and $kilograms are interpolated into the string when it is printed.

The parentheses around the argument to the `print` function could have been omitted:

```
print "Hello, $name; $pounds lb is $kilograms kg.\n";
```

However, we will generally include parentheses for clarity in function calls.

35.7   Built-in Scalar Functions

A *function* is a self-contained group of statements that may be called upon as needed to perform some task. Table 35-2 lists Perl's built-in functions for performing numeric calculations; Table 35-3 lists Perl's built-in string functions. Some points to note about these functions:

■ **Documentation.** You can learn about any Perl function by referring to the `perlfunc` man pages. At the shell prompt, type the command

§ `man perlfunc` ⟨RETURN⟩

■ **Arguments.** Most of the built-in mathematical functions take at least one *argument*, which is a numerical expression written immediately following the function name. Consider, for example, the cosine function `cos`:

`cos($x)`

Here, the argument is the scalar variable $x. Any constant, variable, or expression may be used as an argument in place of $x. Thus, if $z is a numerical variable, we may write

`cos(14.5+log($z))`

The argument in this example is the expression 14.5+log($z).

■ **Optional parentheses.** In many function calls, Perl allows you to omit the parentheses surrounding the argument list. Thus, the previous function calls could have been written as

In this chapter, we will always put parentheses around the argument list.

`cos $x`

`cos 14.5+log $z`

Table 35-2
Built-in Perl numeric
functions. The param-
eters $x and $y may be
numeric expressions.
Parentheses may be
placed around the
function arguments.

Function	Return Value
abs $x	Absolute value of $x
atan2 $y,$x	Arctangent of $y/$x, in radians
cos $x	Cosine of $x, where $x is in radians
exp $x	Exponential of $x, e^x, where $e = 2.7183...$
hex $x	Decimal [base-10] equivalent of hexadecimal [base-16] $x
int $x	Integer part of $x, truncating the fractional part
log $x	Natural or base-e logarithm of a positive number $x
oct $x	Decimal [base-10] equivalent of octal [base-8] string $x
rand $x	Uniform pseudo-random number between 0 and $x
rand	Uniform pseudo-random number between 0 and 1
sin $x	Sine of $x, where $x is in radians
sqrt $x	Square root of non-negative number $x

The $_ variable is discussed
in Section 35.15.

■ **Default argument.** Perl allows you to omit the argument entirely from some function calls. When this is done, Perl uses the current value of the default variable $_. Thus, the following calls have the same effect:

$y = cos;

$y = cos $_;

■ **Pseudo-random numbers.** The rand function behaves differently from the other numeric functions. When called with an argument $arg, rand returns a pseudo-random floating-point between 0 and $arg (including 0 but excluding $arg):

$y = rand($arg);   # Note: 0 ≤ $y < $arg

When called with no argument, rand returns a pseudo-random floating-point between 0 and 1 (including 0 but excluding 1):

$y = rand;   # Note: 0 ≤ $y < 1

Although rand is sometimes called a "random number generator," it really produces *pseudo-random* numbers. A sequence of pseudo-random numbers appears to be random, but is computed from a starting value—called a "seed"—using a well-defined formula. (The seed value for rand is set using the srand function. If you do not call srand explicitly, rand will call it for you.)

■ **Return value.** A mathematical function acts somewhat—but not exactly—like a variable that computes its own value. It may appear anywhere a variable may, except on the left side of an assignment. Thus you may write

Table 35-3
Built-in Perl string
functions. Parenthe-
ses may be written
around the function
arguments.

Function	Return Value (and Side Effects)
chomp $var	Number of characters deleted (removes trailing newline from a string in a variable $var)
chop $var	Character that was chopped (removes the last character from the string in $var)
chr number	Character represented by number in the character set, either ASCII or Unicode
crypt text salt	One-way hash computed from the plaintext text and the "salt" value salt—see perlfunc
index str sub off	Position of the first occurrence of the substring sub in the string str; optional offset off specifies how many characters to skip
lc str	Copy of the string str having all uppercase letters converted to lowercase
lcfirst str	Copy of the string str with the first character converted to lowercase
length str	Number of characters in the string str
ord str	ASCII, Latin-1, or Unicode value of the first character of str
rindex str sub pos	Position of the last occurrence of the substring sub in the string str; optional argument pos specifies the rightmost position that may be returned
sprintf fmt,ex1,….	String that printf would print using format fmt and data ex1, ….
uc str	Copy of the string str having all lowercase letters converted to uppercase
ucfirst str	Copy of the string str with the first character converted to uppercase

```
$y = cos($x)
```

but not

```
cos($x) = $y    # Error!
```

The value computed by a function is called its *return value*. This value does not persist; you must assign it to a variable if you want to use it later in the program.

■ **Side effects.** Each of the functions listed in Table 35-2 and Table 35-3 returns a scalar value that can be used in subsequent calculations. Some functions also produce *side effects*, meaning that they directly alter the contents of some variable.

For instance, the `chomp` function returns a value, but it is useful mostly for its side effect of removing a trailing newline. Consider the following statements:

```
$question = "Who, me?\n";
$n = chomp($question);
```

The result of these statements is that `$n` contains 1 and `$question` contains the string `"Who, me?"` (without the newline or double quotes).

35.8 Expressions and Operators

An *expression* is a formula for representing or computing some value. The simplest expression is a single constant, variable, or function. From such building blocks, more complicated expressions can be created using symbols called *operators*.

Table 35-4 lists the scalar operators available in Perl, along with examples of how they are used. Several points should be noted about the information in the table:

■ **Documentation.** Not all of Perl's operators are described in detail in Table 35-4. You can learn about any Perl operator by referring to the `perlop` man pages. At the shell prompt, type the command

§ `man perlop` (RETURN)

■ **Precedence.** Precedence refers to the order in which two operations are performed when they occur near each other in an expression. For example, multiplication and division have a higher precedence than addition and subtraction. Consequently, 3 + 9 * 2 equals 21, not 24. In Table 35-4, operators having the same precedence are grouped together between horizontal lines. Groups are listed in order of precedence, those near the top of the table having priority over those further down.

School children are taught the mnemonic "Please Excuse My Dear Aunt Sally" for the precedence of arithmetic operations: Parentheses, Exponents, Multiplication and Division, Addition and Subtraction

Use parentheses to enforce the precedence you want!

Precedence can be altered using parentheses: (3+9)*2 equals 24. Indeed, you should always use parentheses to indicate the desired order of operations; do not rely on your memory of the precedence rules.

■ **Side effects.** The primary effect of any operation is to obtain or compute a value. In addition, some operators also have the side effect of modifying a stored value. For instance, the primary effect of the increment operation ++$z is to add 1 to the value taken from the variable $z. The side effect is that the new value is put back into $z. (In the case of the assignment operator =, the "side effect" is what interests us.)

■ **Associativity.** The far right column in Table 35-4 is labeled "Assoc.", short for "Associativity." When two operations having the same precedence (such as addition and subtraction) occur near each other in an expression, the associativity rules determine which is to be performed first.

For example, addition and subtraction are left-associative, so $x + $y + $z is equivalent to ($x + $y) + $z. In contrast, exponentiation is right-associative, so $x**$y**$z is equivalent to $x**($y**$z).

■ **Increment and decrement.** The increment (++) and decrement (--) operators were borrowed from C, and work much as their C counterparts do. These operators may be written in *prefix* form to the left of the variable or in *postfix* form to the right of the variable. Thus, if $x contains a number, either ++$x or $x++ have the effect of adding 1 to the current value in $x. There is a difference, however:

```
$y = ++$x;   # Add 1 to $x, then assign to $y
$y = $x++;   # Assign $x to $y, then add 1 to $x
```

Similar remarks apply to the decrement operator:

```
$y = --$x;   # Subtract 1 from $x, then assign to $y
$y = $x--;   # Assign $x to $y, then subtract 1 from $x
```

■ **True and false.** The logical operators (!, &&, ||, ...), relational operators (>, >=, ==, !=, <=, <, ...), and conditional operator (?:) are used to make decisions depending on whether an expression is true or false. In Perl, any scalar expression that evaluates to the numeric value zero (0) or the null string ("") are considered "false," as is any undefined variable. A nonzero number (such as 1) or non-null string is considered "true."

> Zero, null, or undef is false; nonzero or non-null is true.

■ **Relational Operations.** Perl has two sets of relational operators, one for comparing numerical expressions (>, >=, ==, !=, <=, <), the other for comparing strings (gt, ge, eq, ne, le, lt). The numerical comparisons work much as you would expect. Comparison of two strings is more complicated. The strings are examined character by character, starting with their first (leftmost) characters. On most systems, characters are compared according to their places in the ASCII table:

"19" lt "2" is true (equals 1) because 1 precedes 2 in ASCII;

"ba" lt "wa" is true (equals 1) because b precedes w in ASCII;

"Aw" lt "aw" is true (equals 1) because A precedes a in ASCII;

"ab" lt "ax" is true (equals 1) because b precedes x in ASCII.

Table 35-4 Perl Operators

Operator and Name		Example	Value (and Side Effect)	Assoc.
Terms and leftward list operators —see `perlop`				None
`->`	Arrow—see `perlop`			Left
`++`	Increment	`++$x`	$x + 1$ (result stored in x)	None
`--`	Decrement	`--$x`	$x - 1$ (result stored in x)	None
`**`	Exponentiation	`$x**$y`	x raised to the power y	Right
`!`	Logical NOT	`!$x`	1 if x is false, 0 otherwise	Right
`~`	Bitwise negation—see `perlop`			Right
`\`	Backslash—see `perlop`			Right
`+`	Unary plus	`+$x`	x	Right
`-`	Unary minus	`-$x`	negative of x	Right
`=~`	Pattern binding	`str=~/pat/`	1 if `str` matches `pat`, 0 otherwise	Left
`!~`	Pattern non-binding	`str!~/pat/`	0 if `str` matches `pat`, 1 otherwise	Left
`*`	Multiplication	`$x * $y`	product of x and y	Left
`/`	Division	`$x / $y`	quotient of x and y	Left
`%`	Modulus	`$x % $y`	remainder from x / y	Left
`x`	Repetition	`"ab"x4`	`"abababab"`	Left
`+`	Addition	`$x + $y`	sum of x and y	Left
`-`	Subtraction	`$x - $y`	difference of x and y	Left
`.`	Concatenation	`"a"."z"`	`"az"`	Left
`>>`	Bit-shift—see `perlop`			Left
`<<`	Bit-shift—see `perlop`			Left
Named unary operators—see `perlop`				Right
`<`	Less than (numeric)	`$x < $y`	1 if x is less than y, 0 otherwise	None
`lt`	Less than (string)	`$x lt $y`	1 if x is less than y, 0 otherwise	None
`<=`	Less than or equal (num.)	`$x <= $y`	1 if x is not greater than y, 0 otherwise	None
`le`	Less than or equal (string)	`$x le $y`	1 if x is not greater than y, 0 otherwise	None
`>`	Greater than (num.)	`$x > $y`	1 if x is greater than y, 0 otherwise	None
`gt`	Greater than (string)	`$x gt $y`	1 if x is greater than y, 0 otherwise	None
`>=`	Greater than or equal (num.)	`$x >= $y`	1 if x is not less than y, 0 otherwise	None
`ge`	Greater than or equal (string)	`$x ge $y`	1 if x is not less than y, 0 otherwise	None

Table 35-4 Perl Operators (cont.)

Operator and Name		Example	Value (and Side Effect)	Assoc.
==	Equality (numeric)	$x == $y	1 if $x is equal to $y, 0 otherwise	None
eq	Equality (string)	$x eq $y	1 if $x is equal to $y, 0 otherwise	None
!=	Non-equality (numeric)	$x != $y	1 if $x does not equal $y, 0 otherwise	None
ne	Non-equality (string)	$x ne $y	1 if $x does not equal $y, 0 otherwise	None
<=>	Comparison (numeric)	$x <=> $y	−1 if $x is less than $y, 0 if $x equals $y, +1 if $x is greater than $y	None
cmp	Comparison (string)	$x cmp $y	−1 if $x is less than $y, 0 if $x equals $y, +1 if $x is greater than $y	None
&	Bitwise AND—see perlop			Left
|	Bitwise OR—see perlop			Left
^	Bitwise XOR—see perlop			Left
&&	Logical AND	$x && $y	1 if both $x and $y are true, 0 otherwise	Left
||	Logical OR	$x || $y	1 if either $x or $y is true, 0 otherwise	Left
..	Range	(1..5)	(1,2,3,4,5)	None
?:	Conditional	$x?$y:$z	$y if $x is true, $z otherwise	Right
=	Assignment	$y = $x	$x (result stored in $y)	Right
**=	Power-assignment	$y **= $x	power $y**$x (result stored in $y)	Right
+=	Add-assignment	$y += $x	sum $y+$x (result stored in $y)	Right
-=	Subtract-assignment	$y -= $x	difference $y−$x (result stored in $y)	Right
*=	Multiply-assignment	$y *= $x	product $y*$x (result stored in $y)	Right
/=	Divide-assignment	$y /= $x	quotient $y/$x (result stored in $y)	Right
%=	Modulus-assignment	$y %= $x	remainder of $y/$x (result stored in $y)	Right
.=	Concatenation-assignment	$y .= $x	concatenation $y.$x (result stored in $y)	Right
x=	Repetition-assignment	$y x= $n	$y repeated $n times (result stored in $y)	Right
Other compound-assignment operators (&=, |=, ^=, &&=, ||=, >>=, <<=)—see perlop				Right
,	Comma—see perlop			Left
=>	Comma arrow—see perlop			Left
Rightward list operators—see perlop				Right
not	Logical not	not $x	1 if $x is false, 0 otherwise	Right
and	Logical and	$x and $y	1 if both $x and $y are true, 0 otherwise	Left
or	Logical or	$x or $y	1 if $x or $y or both are true, 0 otherwise	Left
xor	Exclusive or	$x xor $y	1 if $x is true or $y is true, 0 otherwise	Left

35.9 Pattern Matching and Substitution

The operator m// may be written as //.

The binding operator (=~) and pattern matching operator m// are used to determine whether a string matches a specified pattern. Thus the expression

```
$this_string =~ m/Pattern/
```

is true (has value 1) if the value of $this_string matches the Pattern.

Regular expressions are summarized in Appendix D.

In Perl, patterns are written using regular expressions. A regular expression is a notation for describing text strings.

The matching operator m// can take one or more modifiers. For instance, the "global" (/g) modifier specifies that matching be done as many times as possible within the string:

```
$this_string =~ m/Pattern/g     # Global match
```

The "case-insensitive" (/i) modifier specifies that upper- and lowercase characters be treated the same:

```
$this_string =~ m/Pattern/i    # Case-insensitive match
```

Modifiers can be combined:

```
$this_string =~ m/Pattern/ig  # Case-insensitive global match
```

The matching operator only tests for a match between a string and a pattern, but does not actually alter the string. In contrast, the substitution operator s/// will substitute one string for another where there is a match. Thus, the statement

```
$this_string =~ s/Pattern/Substitute/;
```

causes Subsititute to be inserted into this_string where a pattern match occurs.

35.10 Code Blocks

Perl statements may be grouped together and enclosed in curly braces to form a *code block* or *compound statement*:

```
{
    statement1;
    statement2;
       ...
}
```

A block may be nested inside another block:

```
{
    statement1;
    statement2;
    {
        statement3;
        statement4;
```

```
    }
    statement5;
}
```

It is customary to indent the statements inside a block for clarity, as we have done here, although this is not required by Perl.

Any variable declared inside a block using the my operator exists only in that block. (We say that the variable has "block scope" or that it is "lexically scoped.") Variables declared outside a block exist throughout the file. (They are "global variables.") Thus it is possible for two different variables to have the same name. To see how this works, consider the following code snippet:

```
my $x = 1;    # Global $x
my $y = 2;
{
    my $x = 100;    # Local $x
    print("Inside the block: $x $y \n");
}
print("Outside the block: $x $y \n");
```

When executed, this code will produce the output

```
Inside the block: 100 2
Outside the block: 1 2
```

Compound statements are useful as building blocks for Perl's other control structures.

35.11 Selection Structures

Statements and blocks in a Perl script are executed from top to bottom, one after another. However, it is possible to change the normal order of execution according to conditions.

The simple if structure can be written in the form

The braces may not be omitted even when *BLOCK* contains just one statement.

```
if (condition) {
    BLOCK
}
```

where *condition* can be any expression, and the *BLOCK* consists of one or more Perl statements. (Unlike C or awk, Perl always requires the braces around the *BLOCK*.)

Nonzero numbers and non-null strings are "true."

The if structure follows the rule "Do if true." If the *condition* is true, the *BLOCK* statements are run in the order they are written; if the *condition* is false, the *BLOCK* is skipped entirely.

The if-else structure is used to make choices between two alternatives, one of which must be selected:

```
if (condition) {
    first BLOCK
}
else {
    alternative BLOCK
}
```

If the *condition* is true, the *first BLOCK* is chosen; if the *condition* is false, the *alternative BLOCK* is chosen.

Finally, an extended `if-else` structure allows a choice between multiple alternatives:

```
if (condition1) {
    BLOCK1
}
else if (condition2) {
    BLOCK2
}
else if (condition3) {
    BLOCK3
}


    ...


else {
    default BLOCK
}
```

Starting at the top of the `if` structure, *condition1* is examined first. If it is true, *BLOCK1* is run and the remaining alternatives are skipped. Otherwise, *condition2* is checked, then *condition3*, and so on. If a condition is found to be true, its block of code is run and the remaining conditions and blocks are skipped. No more than one of the structure's block may be run.

The very last `else` is not accompanied by an `if` or a condition. This is the *default case*, which is executed if none of the previous conditions is true. The default `else` and its block are optional and may be omitted.

The `unless` structure executes its block of statements unless its condition is true:

```
unless (condition) {
    BLOCK
}
```

In other words, the `unless` structure is like a reverse `if` structure. Whereas the `if` executes its block of statements if its *condition* is *true*, the `unless` executes its block if its *condition* is *false*.

35.12   Repetition Structures

Perl is able to perform tasks over and over using *looping or repetition structures*. Perl has three loops that are similar to their counterparts in the C language: the `while` loop, the `do-while` loop, and the `for` loop. Perl also has two looping structures that are not available in C: a `foreach` loop and an `until` loop.

■ **The `while` loop.** The `while` loop has the general form

```
while (condition) {
    BLOCK
}
```

The `while` loop behaves as an `if` structure that can be executed more than once. Like the `if` structure, the `while` loop follows the rule "Do if true." When the `while` statement is encountered, its *condition* is tested. If the *condition* is false, the *BLOCK* of the loop is skipped entirely. If the *condition* is true, the statements in the *BLOCK* are executed in the order they are written. Then the *condition* is checked again, and the process is repeated until the *condition* is no longer true.

■ **The `do-while` loop.** The `do-while` loop is similar to the `while` loop, except that `do-while`'s *condition* is checked after the loop's block of code is executed. Consequently, the *BLOCK* is executed at least once:

```
do {
    BLOCK
} while (condition)
```

■ **The `for` loop.** The `for` loop has the general form

```
for (Initialize; Test condition; Update the counter) {
    BLOCK
}
```

The operation of the `for` loop may be summarized this way:

1. *Initialize* the loop.

2. *Test condition*; if true, run the *BLOCK*; otherwise skip to Step 5.

3. *Update the counter.*

4. Repeat Steps 2 and 3.

5. Continue beyond the loop.

The `for` loop is sometimes called a *counter-controlled loop* because it is often used in situations in which we count the repetitions.

■ **The `foreach` loop.** The `foreach` loop is designed for processing Perl lists, arrays, and hashes. It has the general form

```
foreach $var (LIST) {
    BLOCK
}
```

Lists are described in Section 35.13.

Here, *LIST* repersents a list of scalar values. The loop assigns the first item of the *LIST* to the scalar variable $var and executes the *BLOCK*; it then assigns the second item of the *LIST* to $var and executes the *BLOCK* again. This is repeated until every item in the *LIST* has been processed.

■ **The** until **loop.** The until loop executes its block of statements until its condition is true:

```
until (condition) {
    BLOCK
}
```

Listing 35-4 shows the gcd.pl script, which uses a while loop to determine the greatest common divisor (gcd). Recall that the gcd of two positive integers p and q $(p \geq q)$ is the largest integer that will divide p and q evenly. The script applies Euclid's algorithm while $q \neq 0$:

1. Compute the remainder: $r = p \% q$;

2. Replace p by q: $p = q$;

3. Replace q by the remainder: $q = r$;

4. If $q = 0$, the gcd is p. Otherwise, repeat Steps 1 through 4.

```
#!/usr/bin/perl -w
# Compute the greatest common divisor of two integers
# using Euclid's algorithm

use strict;

print("Compute the g.c.d of two positive integers:\n");
print("Enter the first integer: ");
chomp(my $p = <STDIN>);

print("Enter the second integer: ");
chomp(my $q = <STDIN>);

① while ($q != 0) {
②    my $r = $p % $q;
     $p = $q;
③    $q = $r;
}

print("The g.c.d is $p.\n");
```

Listing 35-4
The gcd.pl script.

The `gcd.pl` script includes several statements of interest:

① `while ($q != 0) {`

So long as q does not contain the value 0, the `while` loop will continue applying the algorithm.

② `    my $r = $p % $q;`

The modulus operator is used to compute the remainder when p is divided by q.

③ `    $q = $r;`

The third step in the algorithm is to assign the value of the remainder `$r` to the variable `$q`. If this is not done, the algorithm will not work. Moreover, if `$q` never reaches 0, the looping will continue indefinitely. A loop that does not stop is called an *infinite loop*. You can stop an infinite loop from the keyboard using the interrupt command, which on most systems will be (Control)-(C) or (Delete).

35.13 List Literals

A *list literal* is a sequence of numbers or strings separated by commas and enclosed in parentheses:

```
("Fee", "Fie", "Foe", "Fum")
```

```
(2, 4, 6, 8, 'whom do we appreciate?')
```

```
(0, 1, 2, 3, 4, 5, 6, 7, 8, 9, 10)
```

The latter list may be written more compactly using the range operator (..), which creates a list of integers by specifying the first and last values in the list:

```
(0..10)
```

Lists of strings often occur in Perl programs. The qw ("quoted words") operator allows you to create a list without typing the quotation marks and commas. Thus, the qw operation

```
qw/ Fee Fie Foe Fum /
```

is the same as the list

```
('Fee', 'Fie', 'Foe', 'Fum')
```

35.14 Arrays

Arrays are the second of Perl's three principal variable types.

A list may be stored in an *array variable*, which is a collection of one or more scalar variables all sharing the same name. An "at" symbol (@) is used as a prefix to mark the name of an array. Thus, the statement

```perl
my @F_words = ("Fee", "Fie", "Foe", "Fum");
```

declares the array @F_words and assigns to it the list ("Fee", "Fie", "Foe", "Fum"). The individual scalar variables of an array—called *elements*—are distinguished from each other by an integer *index* written inside square brackets. Thus, the previous declaration and assignments could have been written as follows:

```perl
my @F_words;
$F_words[0] = "Fee";
$F_words[1] = "Fie";
$F_words[2] = "Foe";
$F_words[3] = "Fum";
```

Note that because the individual elements of the array are scalars, they carry the $ prefix. Also note that the array indices start at 0 rather than 1, a convention inherited from the C programming language. The last index in the array is stored in the special scalar variable $#F_words. Since array numbering starts at 0, the number of elements in the array is $#F_words + 1.

Perl arrays are *dynamic*, meaning that the arrays grow and shrink automatically as needed. In fact, any time you refer to an element beyond the last existing element of an array, the array grows.

Listing 35-5 shows the Perl script planets.pl which is designed to print the names and orbital distances of the planets listed in the file solar.system.

```perl
#!/usr/bin/perl

use strict;
① use warnings;

# List the planets and their orbital distances

my $line;
② my @field;

③ while (defined($line = <STDIN>)) {
④     @field = split(/\s+/, $line);
⑤     if ($field[2] eq 'Sun') {
⑥         print("$field[0] $field[3] \n");
       }
   }
```

Listing 35-5
The planets.pl script.

Let's examine the new features introduced by this script:

① use warnings;

The warnings pragma causes the Perl compiler to print a warning if it encounters certain questionable programming constructs. The warnings pragma may be used instead of the -w switch.

② my @field;

Here is how the my operator is used to declare an array variable @field. Because of the strict pragma, the compiler will issue a warning if you do not declare the variable this way.

③ while (defined($line = <STDIN>)) {

The expression $line = <STDIN> gets a line from the standard input and assigns it to the scalar variable $line. When there are no more lines left in the standard input, <STDIN> returns the "undefined value" (undef). The defined function checks $line, returning "true" if $line contains a defined value, and "false" otherwise. As we shall see, the defined function is not required.

④   @field = split(/\s+/, $line);

This call to the split function separates the input line into substrings using whitespace as the separator. Its first argument is the pattern that describes the separator; in this case, the Perl regular expression /\s+/ matches whitespace. The second argument is the variable that holds the original string. The substrings returned by split are assigned to the array @field.

⑤   if ($field[2] eq 'Sun') {

Selection structures may be included in the code block of a loop. If the third field contains the string Sun, the record refers to a planet. Note that $field[2] is the third element of the array because Perl array indices are numbered starting from 0 not 1.

⑥   print("$field[0] $field[3] \n");

Here is how we print the values of the first and fourth elements of the @field array. Once again, note that the individual elements of an array are scalars, and therefore carry the $ prefix.

Once the planets.pl file has been made executable using chmod, we can run the script the usual way:

§ ./planets.pl < solar.system (RETURN)

The planets.pl script lists the planets (in alphabetical order) and their distances from the Sun:

```
Earth 149600000
Jupiter 778330000
Mars 227940000
Mercury 57910000
Neptune 4504300000
```

```
Pluto 5913520000
Saturn 1429400000
Uranus 2870990000
Venus 108200000
```

35.15 The Default Variable

Let's examine once again the `while` loop used in the `planets.pl` script:

```
while (defined($line = <STDIN>)) {
    @field = split(/\s+/, $line);
    if ($field[2] eq 'Sun') {
        print("$field[0] $field[3] \n");
    }
}
```

Most Perl programmers would write this loop differently. Not only is it unnecessary to call the `defined` function to test the value of `$line`; it is also unnecessary to use the `$line` variable at all. We could have written the loop this way:

```
while (<STDIN>) {
    @field = split(/\s+/, $_);
    if ($field[2] eq 'Sun') {
        print("$field[0] $field[3] \n");
    }
}
```

When a line-input operation such as <STDIN> appears by itself as the condition of a `while` loop, each input line is automatically assigned to the special variable `$_`, which we will call the *default variable*.

Although `$_` is frequently useful, it is rarely seen. That is, it can be used without being written explicitly. Many functions will take their argument values from `$_` if no other argument is supplied. For example, if the `split` function is called without arguments, the function assumes that you want to split the contents of `$_` using whitespace as the field separator. Thus, the statement

```
    @field = split(/\s+/, $_);
```

could instead have been written

```
    @field = split;
```

While `$_` is not Perl's only special variable, it is the one that is used most often.

35.16 Filehandles and Line Input

You may be wondering whether it is possible for a script to read data from a file without using the redirection operator. The answer is yes, but it requires that you know about filehandles and the line-input operator.

A *filehandle* is a name for a connection between a Perl script and a data stream. The filehandle is not necessarily the name of a particular data file, but a name for the connection itself.

A number of special filehandles are predefined. We have already used one of these, the STDIN filehandle that refers to the standard input. You will not be surprised to learn that there is also a STDOUT filehandle that refers to the standard output.

As we have seen, writing <STDIN> causes a line to be read from the standard input. More generally, placing angle brackets (<>) around *any* filehandle causes a line to be read from that filehandle's data stream. Used this way, the angle brackets are called the *line-input operator*.

If the filehandle is omitted, the line-input operator reads from the files listed on the command line (or from the standard input if no files are listed). Suppose, for example, that the while loop in Listing 35-5 were revised to read as follows:

```perl
while (<>) {
   @field = split;
   if ($field[2] eq 'Sun') {
       print("$field[0] $field[3] \n");
   }
}
```

The script could then be run this way:

§ ./planets.pl solar.system (RETURN)

An "empty" line-input operator (<>) is sometimes called the "diamond" operator, for obvious reasons.

Listing 35-6 shows a Perl script named wc.pl that mimics the Unix wc (word-count) utility, which prints the number of lines, words, and characters in a file. The script uses the diamond operator to read lines from the standard input.

```perl
#!/usr/bin/perl
# Mimic the Unix wc (word count) utility

my $lines = 0;
my $words = 0;
my $chars = 0;

① while (<>) {
②     chomp;
③     $lines++;
④     my @fields = split(' ', $_);
⑤     $words = $words + $#fields + 1;
⑥     $chars = $chars + length($_);
   }

⑦ print("      $lines      $words      $chars $ARGV\n");
```

Listing 35-6
The wc.pl script.

This script introduces some important new features:

```
① while (<>) {
```

The diamond operator <> causes a line to be read from the file(s) specified on the standard input, storing the input in the default variable $_. While there is still input to be read, the loop will repeat.

```
②      chomp;
```

Here we use chomp to remove the newline from the input line. Without an argument, chomp works on the default variable $_.

```
③      $lines++;
```

Every time a line is read, the increment operator (++) adds 1 to the value of the scalar variable $lines.

```
④      my @fields = split(' ', $_);
```

This split function call separates the input line into fields, with spaces serving as the field separators. The fields are stored in the array variable @fields. The scalar variable $#fields is also updated to hold the index of the last element of @fields.

```
⑤      $words = $words + $#fields + 1;
```

The scalar variable $words contains the count of the words. The value $#fields is the index of the last element. This is added to the value of $words, and the result is put back into $words.

```
⑥      $chars = $chars + length($_);
```

The variable $chars contains the count of the characters in the file. The built-in string function length computes the number of characters in a string; this is added to the value of the $chars variable, and the result is put back into $chars.

```
⑦ print("      $lines      $words      $chars $ARGV\n");
```

The special scalar variable $ARGV contains the name of the current input data file.

After making the wc.pl script executable, we can run it on a text file. For instance,

```
§ ./wc.pl solar.system (RETURN)
```

The wc.pl script produces the output

```
        88      792      4593 solar.system
```

However, the Unix wc command produces a different result for the number of characters in the file:

        88   792   4681 solar.system

Why the discrepancy? Our wc.pl script uses chomp to discard the newlines, whereas the wc utility counts the newlines as characters. We can correct our script by removing the call to chomp. Alternatively, we can add 1 to account for the missing newline:

$chars = $chars + length($_) + 1;

35.17 Built-in Array Functions

Perl has a set of built-in functions for processing arrays, which are listed in Table 35-5. All of these functions have side effects: they add or remove one or more array elements.

Consider, for example, the array

my @primes = (7, 11, 13);

Elements can be added to the beginning of the array using the unshift function:

$length = unshift(@primes, 1, 2, 3, 5);

After this function call, @primes will contain (1, 2, 3, 5, 7, 11, 13) and $length will contain 7, the total number of elements in the array. Likewise, elements can be added to the end of the array using the push function:

Here $length *is a user-defined scalar variable, not to be confused with the* length *string function.*

$length = push(@primes, 17, 19);

Then @primes will contain (1, 2, 3, 5, 7, 11, 13, 17, 19) and $length will contain 9.

The pop function removes and returns the last value from @primes:

$value = pop(@primes);

As a result, @primes will contain (1, 2, 3, 5, 7, 11, 13, 17) and $value will contain 19. Similarly, the shift function removes and returns the first value from the array:

$value = shift(@primes);

After this function call, @primes will contain (2, 3, 5, 7, 11, 13, 17) and $value will contain 1.

The most versatile of the functions listed in Table 35-5 is splice. Taking an array as its first argument, splice removes and returns $*length* elements from the array starting at a position specified by $*offset*; it then replaces the missing elements by the optional *LIST*. If $*offset* is negative, the elements are counted backwards from the end of the array. Thus,

Table 35-5
Built-in Perl array
functions. Here, *@arr*
represents an array
variable and *LIST* is a
list. The arguments
may be surrounded by
parentheses.

Function	Return Value (and Side Effects)
pop @arr	Last value of @arr (the last value is removed from the end of @arr, shortening @arr by one element)
push @arr, LIST	New length of @arr (after values from LIST are appended to @arr)
shift @arr	First value of @arr (the first value is removed from @arr, shortening @arr by one element)
splice @arr, $offset, $length, LIST	
	Element(s) removed from @arr ($length elements starting at $offset are removed from @arr and replaced by an optional LIST)
unshift @arr, LIST	New length of @arr (after values from LIST are inserted at the beginning of @arr)

splice(@arr, 0, 0, LIST); *is the same as* unshift(@arr, LIST);

splice(@arr, @arr, 0, LIST); *is the same as* push(@arr, LIST);

splice(@arr, -1, 1); *is the same as* pop(@arr);

splice(@arr, 0, 1); *is the same as* shift(@arr);

35.18 Formatted Output

The print command is adequate for quick and simple output. For fancier output, Perl offers the printf ("print-formatted") command. It has the form

printf(*fmt*, *exp1*, *exp2*,)

where *fmt* is a string describing the format of the output, and *exp1*, *exp2*, … are expressions to be printed according to this format.

For example, assume that x contains the value 5. The printf statement

printf("The square root of %f is %f.\n", x, sqrt(x))

will produce the output

The square root of 5.000000 is 2.236068.

The formats used by printf are discussed in greater detail in Appendix E.

Listing 35-7 shows orbits.1.pl, a version of the planets.pl script (Listing 35-5) that uses printf to format the output. The new script also computes the orbital radii in Astronomical Units (1 AU = 1.496×10^8 km).

```
#!/usr/bin/perl

# List the planets and their oribital distances

use strict;

① print("\t     Orbital Radius\n");
  print "PLANET\t      (km)\t(AU)\n";

  while (<>) {
      my @field = split(' ', $_);
      if ($field[2] eq 'Sun') {
②         printf("%-9s %8.3e %8.3f \n",
                  $field[0], $field[3], $field[3]/1.496e+08);
      }
  }
```

Listing 35-7
The orbits.1.pl
script.

This script includes several interesting statements:

```
① print("\t     Orbital Radius\n");
  print "PLANET\t      (km)\t(AU)\n";
```

Here we have called print with and without parentheses to print column labels. When the parentheses are present, print is considered a function. When the parentheses are absent, print is considered a list operator. In this case, the effect is the same either way.

```
②         printf("%-9s %8.3e %8.3f \n",
                  $field[0], $field[3], $field[3]/1.496e+08);
```

The printf function call prints the name of the planet as a left-justified string (%-9s), the orbital radius in kilometers in e-notation (%8.3e), and the radius in Astronomical Units as a decimal fraction (%8.3f).

When run using solar.system as the data file, the output is

```
          Orbital Radius
PLANET       (km)        (AU)
Earth      1.496e+08    1.000
Jupiter    7.783e+08    5.203
Mars       2.279e+08    1.524
Mercury    5.791e+07    0.387
Neptune    4.504e+09   30.109
Pluto      5.914e+09   39.529
Saturn     1.429e+09    9.555
Uranus     2.871e+09   19.191
Venus      1.082e+08    0.723
```

35.19 Opening Files

As we have seen, a filehandle is a name for a connection between a Perl script and a data stream. The predefined filehandles STDIN and STDOUT refer to the standard input and standard output, respectively.

You can also name your own filehandles. The rules for choosing a filehandle are the same as for choosing a variable name, except a filehandle does not carry a prefix such as $ or @. It is customary to write filehandles entirely in uppercase letters.

A filehandle is connected to a particular data stream using the open function. For example, the statement

```
open(DATA_INPUT, "solar.system");
```

opens the file solar.system and gives it the filehandle DATA_INPUT. We will use filehandles later.

35.20 Pipes

The orbits.1.pl script shown in Listing 35-7 prints the orbital data in alphabetical order according to the name of the planet because that is how the data are listed in solar.system. We may prefer to have the data listed in order of distance from the Sun. One way to do this is to sort the file before piping it to the orbits.1.pl script:

```
§ sort -n +3 solar.system | orbits.pl ⏎RETURN
```

The Unix sort utility is described in Section 11.6.

Here we have used the Unix sort command to perform a numerical sort (-n) on the fourth field (+3) of the solar.system file. The output of the sort is then piped to the orbits.pl script for formatting and printing. The output is

```
          Orbital Radius
PLANET       (km)        (AU)
Mercury    5.791e+07     0.387
Venus      1.082e+08     0.723
Earth      1.496e+08     1.000
Mars       2.279e+08     1.524
Jupiter    7.783e+08     5.203
Saturn     1.429e+09     9.555
Uranus     2.871e+09    19.191
Neptune    4.504e+09    30.109
Pluto      5.914e+09    39.529
```

It is possible to accomplish the same thing from within the Perl script itself using an appropriate filehandle, as shown in Listing 35-8.

```
#!/usr/bin/perl

print "\t     Orbital Radius\n";
print("PLANET\t     (km)\t(AU)\n");

① open(SORT, '|sort -n +2');

while (<>) {
    my @field = split(' ', $_);
    if ($field[2] eq 'Sun') {
②       printf SORT ("%-9s %8.3e %8.3f \n",
                $field[0], $field[3], $field[3]/1.496e+08);
    }
}
```

Listing 35-8
The orbits.2.pl
script.

Two changes were made to the previous script:

```
① open(SORT, '|sort -n +2');
```

The sort will be done on the third field of the output from printf, not the third field of the input file.

The **open** function is used to open a data stream and give it a filehandle. In this case, the file handle is SORT. The data stream is not connected to a file but to a pipe (|) leading to the Unix **sort** utility. Note the arguments to the **sort** command: -n specifies a numerical sort, and +2 specifies that the sort be done on the third field. (In other words, +2 means skip the the first two fields.) The quotes around the **sort** call are required.

```
②       printf SORT ("%-9s %8.3e %8.3f \n",
                $field[0], $field[3], $field[3]/1.496e+08);
```

Here the **printf** function prints to the filehandle SORT. This causes the output to be piped through the Unix **sort** utility before printing.

35.21 Context

In a natural language such as English, the meaning of a word often depends on its *context*—that is, the words that surround it. Consider the wise proverb

"Time flies like the wind; fruit flies like bananas."

Here, *flies* is first used as a verb meaning "passes quickly," then as a noun meaning "small insects." (Similarly, *like* is first used as a preposition, then as a verb.) You can figure out what the word means by the words around it.

Likewise, a Perl expression may have different meanings depending on its context. Perl distinguishes between void, list, and scalar contexts:

■ **Void context.** A void context is a situation in which an expression is evaluated for its side effects rather than its value. The **chomp** function, for example, returns a value (the number of characters chomped), but this value is usually ignored. If the return value were saved for some reason, this would not be a void context:

```
chomp($line);       # Void context: return value ignored

$x = chomp($line); # Scalar context: return value saved
```

Hashes are discussed in
Section 35.22 below.
■ **List context.** A list context is a situation in which a list, array, or hash would be expected. For example, the assignment

```
my @copy = @array;   # List context: @array copied to @copy
```

occurs in a list context because there is an array on each side of the assignment. This works much as you would expect: the values of the array @array are copied in order into the array @copy.

■ **Scalar context.** A scalar context is a situation in which a scalar value would be expected. For example, the assignment

```
my $n = @array;   # Scalar context: n receives size of @array
```

occurs in a scalar context because a scalar occurs on the left side. A scalar variable can hold only one value; it generally cannot hold the contents of an entire array. Instead, the size of @array—that is, the number of elements in the array— is assigned to the scalar $n.

Scalar contexts can be further subdivided into numeric, string, and Boolean contexts:

■ **Numeric context.** A numeric context is a situation in which a number would normally be expected, such as in an arithmetic operation or as the argument to a mathematical function. When a string occurs in a numeric context, its "numeric value" is used. If the string begins with some combination of characters that resembles a number, this becomes the numeric value of the string. Otherwise, the string has the numeric value 0. Thus,

`"221B Baker Street"` has the numeric value 221;

`"3.048e-01meters/foot"` has the numeric value 3.048e-01;

`"Answer=47"` has the numeric value 0 (it does not begin with a number).

■ **String context.** A string context is a situation in which a string would be expected, such as in a concatenation operation or as the argument to a string function. When a number occurs in a string context, the "string value" of the number is used. This is normally just the number as it would be printed by printf using the "%.14g"format.

■ **Boolean context.** A Boolean context is a situation in which an expression is expected to be either true or false. Remember, an expression is considered "false" if it evaluates to the numeric value zero (0) or the null string (""). A nonzero number (such as 1) or non-null string is considered "true."

35.22 Hashes

Hashes are Perl's third
principal data type.

Hashes (also known as *associative arrays*, *maps*, *lookup tables*, or *dictionaries*) consist of pairs of *keys* and *values*, each key being associated with a particular value. The keys of a hash serve much the same purpose as the indices of an array. The difference is that hash keys need not be integers or even numbers at all.

The percent symbol (%) is used as a prefix to mark the name of a hash. Thus, the statement

```
my %CA_capital = ("Belize", "Belmopan", "Guatemala",
            "Guatemala City", "Honduras", "Tegulcigalpa",
            "Nicaragua", "Managua", "El Salvador",
            "San Salavador", "Costa Rica","San Jose",
            "Panama", "Panama City");
```

declares the hash %CA_capital and assigns to it the countries as keys and the capital cities as values. When the initialization is done this way, it can be difficult to see which key belongs to which value, so Perl offers an alternative notation using the "comma arrow" or "big arrow" operator (=>):

```
my %CA_capital = ("Belize"=>"Belmopan", "Guatemala"=>
            "Guatemala City", "Honduras"=>"Tegulcigalpa",
            "Nicaragua"=>"Managua", "El Salvador"=>
            "San Salavador", "Costa Rica"=>"San Jose",
            "Panama"=>"Panama City");
```

A particular value of a hash is specified by writing its key inside curly braces following the hash name. Thus, the previous declaration and assignments could have been written as follows:

```
my %CA_capital;
$CA_capital{"Belize"} = "Belmopan";
$CA_capital{"Guatemala"} = "Guatemala City";
$CA_capital{"Honduras"} = "Tegulcigalpa";
$CA_capital{"Nicaragua"} = "Managua";
$CA_capital{"El Salvador"} = "San Salvador";
$CA_capital{"Costa Rica"} = "San Jose";
$CA_capital{"Panama"} = "Panama City";
```

Because the individual elements of the hash are scalars, they carry the **$** prefix.

Perl has a set of built-in functions for processing hashes, which are listed in Table 35-6. Of these functions, only `delete` has side effects. It removes a key and its related value from a hash and returns them.

Note that the return values from the `each`, `keys`, and `values` functions depend on context.

Function	Return Value (and Side Effects)
delete $HASH{$KEY}	Deleted values (deletes the specified $KEY and its value from %HASH)
each %HASH	Next key and value from %HASH in list context Next key from %HASH in scalar context
exists $HASH{$KEY}	True if $KEY exists
keys %HASH	Keys from %HASH in list context Number of elements in %HASH in scalar context
values %HASH	Values from %HASH in list context Number of elements in %HASH in scalar context

Listing 35-9 shows a Perl script that uses a hash to count each word in a file and to print out a list of the words and their counts.

```
#!/usr/bin/perl
# Count the occurrence of each word in a file

use strict;

my $field;
my $word;
my %count;

① while (<>) {
②     s/[0-9.,!?:;(){}\[\]]//g;
③     foreach $field (split) {
④         $word = uc($field);
⑤         ++$count{$word};
      }
}

⑥ foreach $word ( keys(%count) ) {
      printf "%5d %s\n", $count{$word}, $word;
}
```

Listing 35-9
The word.count.pl
script.

Let's dissect this script:

① while (<>) {

This script is designed to read from files listed on the command line. For this, we use the diamond operator in the while loop.

②   `s/[0-9.,!?:;(){}\[\]]//g;`

Here we have used the `s///g` ("global substitution") operator to eliminate the punctuation and numbers from the default variable `$_`. It is necessary to "quote" some of the punctuation characters using backslashes. The substitution string is empty because we want to eliminate these characters.

③   `foreach $field (split) {`

A `foreach` loop is used to step through the input fields. The scalar variable `$field` serves as the control variable for the loop; `$field` takes on the values produced by the `split` function in the parentheses. By default, the `split` function separates the contents of `$_` into fields using whitespace as field separators.

④   `$word = uc($field);`

The `uc` function converts all letters to uppercase. This is to prevent "String" from being counted as distinct from "string." The result is assigned to `$word`.

⑤   `++$count{$word};`

The increment operator (++) is used here to update the counter. Because each individual element of a hash is a scalar, we write `++$count{$word}`, not `++@count{$word}`.

⑥ `foreach $word ( keys(%count) ) {`
     `printf "%5d %s\n", $count{$word}, $word;`

In list context, the `keys` function returns a list of the keys belonging to `count`. The `foreach` loop considers each key, assigning them one by one to the scalar variable `$word`. The `printf` function prints out each word and its count.

35.23 User-Defined Subroutines

Perl allows you to create your own functions. User-defined functions are called *subroutines* in Perl. Subroutines are defined using a statement of the general form

```
sub name
{
    BLOCK
}
```

where `sub` is short for "subroutine," *name* represents the subroutine's name, and *BLOCK* is a code block comprising one or more Perl statements.

To call a subroutine, write its name with an ampersand (&) as a prefix. If the subroutine takes arguments, these are written in parentheses following the subroutine's name:

```
&name($x,$y,$z);    # Call name with $x,$y,$z as arguments.
```

The ampersand may be omitted in some cases, such as when the subroutine call includes the parentheses. However, for clarity (and simplicity), we will always use the ampersand prefix when calling a user-defined subroutine.

Argument values that are passed to a subroutine are stored automatically in another of Perl's special variables, the argument array @_ (which is also called @ARG).

Listing 35-10 shows the code for a program `trig.table.pl` that prints a table of the sine and cosine functions for angles from 0° to 360° in increments of 10°. The program calls the two built-in functions `sin` and `cos`, and two user-defined subroutines named `toRadians` and `PI`.

Because the built-in trigonometric functions take their arguments in radians, the program must convert from degrees to radians. The `toRadians` function performs this conversion according to the formula

$$\text{radians} = \text{degrees} \cdot \frac{\pi \text{ radians}}{180 \text{ degrees}}$$

The PI function approximates the value of $\pi = 3.14158\ldots$ using the fact that the arctangent of unity is $\pi/4$.

```
#!/usr/bin/perl

# Print a table of trigonometric functions

use strict;

printf("Degrees    Radians      Sine    Cosine\n");

for (my $degrees = 0; $degrees <= 360; $degrees += 10) {
    my $radians   = &toRadians($degrees);
    printf("%7.1f    %7.4f %7.4f  %7.4f\n",
        $degrees, $radians, sin($radians), cos($radians));
}

sub PI
{
    4 * atan2(1,1);
}

sub toRadians
{
    my $degrees = $_[0];
    return ($degrees * &PI/180);
}
```

Listing 35-10
The `trig.table.pl`
script.

This program introduces a number of Perl features:

```
① for (my $degrees = 0; $degrees <= 360; $degrees += 10) {
```

We have used the addition-assignment operator (+=) to update the value of degrees.

```
②     my $radians   = &toRadians($degrees);
```

An argument may be any expression, including a constant, a variable, a formula or a function call.

The toRadians subroutine is called to convert from degrees to radians. The argument to the subroutine is the variable $degrees. The value of the argument is passed to the toRadians function, which calculates and returns its own value. The result is then assigned to the variable $radians. The argument $degrees is unchanged by the function call.

```
③ sub PI
  {
      4 * atan2(1,1);
  }
```

Here is the definition of the PI subroutine. No return statement is used; the return value is just the value of the last expression evaluated in the subroutine.

```
④ sub toRadians{
```

The first line of the subroutine definition names the routine.

```
⑤     my $degrees = $_[0];
```

The argument array @_ receives the values that are passed to the subprogram when it is called. The toRadians subroutine is designed to take only one argument, which is stored as the first element of @_. Here we have assigned the argument value to the local scalar variable $degrees. You are not required to do this, but it prevents the program from accidentally changing the value of the original arguments. (This imitates the call-by-value semantics of most other programming languages.) Keep in mind that any variable declared in a code block (including variables declared in a subroutine) exists only in that block, so that the other code blocks cannot see it or use it. Thus the variable $degrees in the toRadians subroutine is distinct from the variable $degrees appearing elsewhere in the script.

```
⑥     return ($degrees * &PI/180);
```

This statement converts degrees to radians, and returns the result to the place where the toRadians subroutine was called. One Perl function or subroutine may call another: thus, toRadians calls PI to compute the value of π.

35.24 Optional Arguments

A subroutine may take a different number of arguments each time it is called. For example, Listing 35-11 shows a function that computes the logarithm to an arbitrary base B. It may take as many as two arguments; however, the second argument is optional.

```
sub logB
{
①    my $x = shift @_;    # The @_ may be omitted
②    my $B = shift;       # The @_ has been omitted

③    if (!defined($B)){
          return log($x)/log(10);    #Common (base-10) log
      }
④    elsif ($B eq "e") {
          return log($x);
      }
⑤    else {
          return log($x)/log($B);
      }
}
```

Listing 35-11
The `logB.pl` subroutine.

Let's examine some of the more interesting parts of this subroutine:

```
①    my $x = shift @_;    # The @_ may be omitted
```

The array @_ receives the arguments that are passed to the subroutine. Here, we have used the shift function to take the first argument from the array; this is then assigned to the local scalar variable $x.

```
②    my $B = shift;       # The @_ has been omitted
```

Note that if no argument is supplied to `shift`, @_ is assumed. Here we have called `shift` to get the second argument from the @_ array.

```
③    if (!defined($B)){
          return log($x)/log(10);    #Common (base-10) log
      }
```

If the calling program does not provide a value for the base, B will contain the value `undef` (for "undefined"). The first clause of the `if` structure tests for this. If B is undefined, the subroutine computes and returns the common (base-10) logarithm.

```
④    elsif ($B eq "e") {
          return log($x);
      }
```

This alternative computes the natural (base-*e*) logarithm and returns the result.

```
⑤    else {
        return log($x)/log($B);
     }
```

The default case calculates the logarithm to an arbitrary base $B and returns the result.

35.25 Exercises

1. Write a Perl program to accomplish each of the following tasks for the data file `solar.system`:

a. Print all records that do not list a discoverer in the eighth field.

b. Print every record after erasing the second field.

c. Print the records for satellites that have negative orbital periods. (A negative orbital period simply means that the satellite orbits in a counterclockwise direction.)

d. Print the data for the objects discovered by the Voyager2 space probe.

e. Print each record with the orbital period given in seconds rather than days.

2. The *periapsis* is the point of closest approach between a satellite and the object around which it orbits; the *apoapsis* is the point of greatest separation between the two. The periapsis distance P and the apoapsis distance A can be computed from the formulas

$$P = a(1 - \varepsilon)$$

$$A = a(1 + \varepsilon)$$

where a is the *semimajor axis* and ε is the *eccentricity* of the orbit. For a perfect circle, $\varepsilon = 0$; for an ellipse, $0 < \varepsilon < 1$. Print each record from `solar.system` with the values of P and A inserted between the orbital radius and the orbital period.

3. Modify the `trig.table.pl` script shown in Listing 35-10 so that it also prints the value of the tangent. Write a subroutine named `tan` to compute the tangent of an argument given in radians.

4. Write a script to test the logarithm subroutine `logB` shown in Listing 35-11.

5. Perl has just one inverse trigonometric function, `atan2`. Use this function to write the other inverse trig functions according to the formulas

```
asin(x) = atan2(x, sqrt(1-x*x))

acos(x) = atan2(sqrt(1-x*x), x)

atan(x) = atan2(x, 1)
```

6. Write a Perl script named `test.regexp.pl` to determine whether a given string matches a regular expression. If the user types the command line

§ `test.regexp.pl /Ma/ Mars` (RETURN)

the script should print

`Match: /Ma/ matches "Mars"`

7. The `rand(x)` function computes pseudo-random numbers uniformly distributed between 0 and x (between 0 and 1 if no argument is supplied). Write a subroutine `rand2` that computes a pseudo-random number x evenly distributed between two limits `low` and `high`, according to the formula

`x = rand *(high - low) + low`

8. Write a subroutine `randint` that computes a pseudo-random integer x evenly distributed between two limits 1 and `high`, according to the formula

`x =  int(high * rand) + 1`

9. Write a Perl script `mygrade.pl` that computes a student's grade given a score between 0 and 100. Thus, the command line

§ `mygrade.pl 90.1` (RETURN)

should produce the output

`You have an A!`

Account for the following cases:

$100 < \text{score} \Rightarrow$ error message (scores may not exceed 100%)

$90 \leq \text{score} \leq 100 \Rightarrow A$

$80 \leq \text{score} < 90 \Rightarrow B$

$70 \leq \text{score} < 80 \Rightarrow C$

$60 \leq \text{score} < 70 \Rightarrow D$

$0 \leq \text{score} < 60 \Rightarrow F$

$\text{score} < 0 \Rightarrow$ error message (scores may not be less than 0%)

PART IX
PROGRAMMING LANGUAGES

# Chapter 36

PROGRAMMING LANGUAGES

UNIX was originally written by professional programmers for the use of other professional programmers. It is not surprising, therefore, that UNIX provides a number of excellent programming tools. Traditionally, UNIX systems have come equipped with the C programming language. (UNIX itself is written in C.) Many UNIX systems also offer C++, Fortran, Java, and other languages as well.

In this chapter, we will see how C, C++, and Java programs can be written and run under UNIX. These are what we have been calling *systems languages*, to distinguish them from scripting languages such as awk or Perl. The differences between scripting and systems languages are discussed in Chapter 32.

36.1 Programming Languages

Recall that a *computer program* is a set of coded instructions that tell the computer how to perform some task. A programming language is a systematic set of rules for writing programs. We will discuss several different kinds of languages:

■ **Machine language.** Computers "understand" *machine language*, in which everything is represented by binary numbers—combinations of *0*s and *1*s:

```
00000000110001100000000000011000
00000000000000000001110000010010
00000000111000100001000000100000
00100000110001100000000000000001
```

■ **Assembly language.** An *assembly language* represents each of the machine's binary instructions symbolically. For example, the previous four lines of binary code might be represented by the following four lines of assembly language:

```
mult $6, $6
mflo $7
add $2, $7, $2
addi $6, $6, 1
```

■ **High-level language.** *High-level languages* (HLLs) are designed to be easier for humans to write and read than assembly languages. Examples of HHLs include awk, Perl, C, C++, Fortran, and Java. Most HHLs have keywords, instructions, and statements that resemble human language or mathematical notation. For example, the previous four lines of assembly language might be represented in C this way:

```
sum = sum + i * i;
i = i + 1;
```

Program translation by compilers and interpreters is discussed in Chapter 32.

A program written in a high-level language must be translated into machine code for the computer to run. This translation can be done either by an interpreter or a compiler. Each high-level statement usually translates into more than one machine-language instruction.

36.2 Code

Code refers to a program written in a programming language. We will encounter several kinds of computer code:

■ **Pseudocode.** A common tool in program design, *pseudocode* is an outline of the program written in abbreviated English. Pseudocode is laid out to resemble the structure of the actual program.

■ **Source code.** A computer program written in a high-level language is called *source code*. Source code is stored in an ASCII text file.

■ **Assembly code.** A computer program written in assembly language is called, appropriately enough, *assembly code*.

■ **Object code.** When source code is translated by a compiler, the resulting machine language is called *object code*.

■ **Library code.** Some languages (such as C) provide libraries of pre-compiled functions and routines. This *library code* can be linked to object code to make a complete program.

■ **Executable code.** Binary code that can be run directly by the computer is called *executable code*. Depending on the language, executable code may consist of both object code and library code.

36.3 Program Design

The first step in creating a program is to design it. That is, you plan what the program is to do, and how. This is perhaps the most important and the most difficult part of programming. Entire volumes have been devoted to this topic; obviously, we can only scratch the surface in this short book.

Program design often begins with the definition of the problem to be solved. To illustrate, let's see how we would design a program to calculate the reciprocal of a number. The problem is simple to define:

Problem: Create a program to calculate the reciprocals of numbers entered by the user at the keyboard; display the results on the terminal screen.

The pseudocode for our reciprocal program might be:

```
prompt the user for a number x
read x
calculate 1/x
display the answer
```

36.4 Source Code

Once you are satisfied with your program design, you can begin to write the solution to the problem using a programming language. Listing 36-1 shows how the reciprocal program might appear when written in C.

Listing 36-1
C code for computing reciprocals.

```c
/* Compute reciprocals */

#include <stdio.h>

int main(void)
{
    double x, recip;
    printf("This program computes reciprocals.\n");
    printf("Enter a number: ");
    scanf("%lf", &x);
    recip = 1.0/x;
    printf("The reciprocal of %f is %f.\n", x, recip);
}
```

Typically, you will use a text editor such as vi to prepare a file containing the source code. You will follow the usual naming rules for this file, but with one additional rule: the names for files containing source code always have a suffix or *extension* that indicates the language in which they are written. The extension .c indicates C-language source code, the extension .cpp indicates C++ source code, the extension .f indicates Fortran code, and the extension .java indicates Java code.

Thus, if we were to write C, C++, Fortran, and Java versions of our program to compute reciprocals, the files might be named as follows:

recip.c   (C version)

recip.cpp   (C++ version)

recip.f   (Fortran version)

Recip.java   (Java version)

36.5 Compiling and Linking

Once you have finished the source code, you must translate it into machine language. This is called compiling the code, and the program that performs this task is called a compiler. If you are programming in C or C++, compilation is actually a three-step process:

Neither Fortran nor Java has a preprocessor.

1. Preprocessing. The *preprocessor* goes through your source code and makes certain changes to the code.

2. Compilation. The compiler translates your modified source code into machine language. The output from the compiler is called *object code*.

3. Linking. Although object code consists of machine language, it is not yet a complete program. The *linker* combines your object code with code from the system software libraries to produce *executable code*.

Compilation of a Fortran program is a similar process; in fact, some Fortran "compilers" first convert Fortran code to C code, which is then translated into executable code by the C compiler.

Java compilers work differently. The Java compiler does not translate Java programs directly into machine code; instead, it produces *bytecode*, an intermediate code which must be interpreted by another program called the *Java Virtual Machine* (Java VM).

36.6 Program Execution

An executable file produced by compiling a C, C++, or Fortran program is given the name a.out by the linker (unless you specify another name). If the current directory is included in your search path, you can execute the program by typing

§ a.out (Return)

If the current directory is not in the search path, you can run the program by typing

§ ./a.out (Return)

The Java compiler produces a *class file* instead of an a.out file. For instance, if you were to compile a Java source file named Recip.java, the compiler would create a class file named Recip.class to hold the bytecode. To run the program, you would type

Note that the file name extension is not entered.

§ java Recip (Return)

or

§ java ./Recip (Return)

The `java` command causes the Java Virtual Machine to interpret the bytecode, converting it into machine code that can be executed by the computer. (Some Java programs—called *applets*—are not designed as stand-alone programs, but can be loaded and run by other programs. Java applets can be included in HTML files that are sent across the Internet to be run by a Web browser.)

36.7 Errors

The easiest thing about programming is making errors. Programming errors come in several varieties:

The computer cannot think, so you have to do the thinking for it.

■ **Logic errors.** The computer does what you tell it to do, not what you want it to do. If you specify the wrong way to solve the problem—if you multiply when you should have divided, for instance—your program may run and produce output, but the output will not be correct. This is called a logic error.

■ **Syntax errors.** A *syntax error* results when you violate one of the rules of the programming language. Such errors are often called *compilation errors* because they will be detected by the compiler when you try to compile the program.

Runtime errors are more commonly called bugs.

■ **Runtime errors.** More insidious than syntax errors are those errors that escape detection by the compiler. These are called *runtime errors* because they usually are not discovered until you run the program a few times. (And perhaps not even then—many runtime errors are never tracked down.)

36.8 Debugging

A serious runtime error, such as dividing by zero or taking the square root of a negative number, may cause the program to crash. When this happens, the program quits running and the UNIX shell sends you an error message of some sort. Error messages are usually not very informative: they tell you that the program crashed, but they don't always tell you the reason.

When a program aborts because of a runtime error, the system produces a *core dump*, which is a file containing a "snapshot" of the main memory at the time the program failed. This is put into a file named `core`.

The `core` file contains machine code, so it is not something you would try to read directly yourself. However, most UNIX systems include special programs called *debuggers* that are designed to help you exterminate bugs in your programs. A debugger can use the information in the `core` file to determine what the bug was and where it occurred. One debugger found on many UNIX systems is called `dbx`; it is described in Appendix F.

36.9 The make Utility

You can learn about `make` by reading Appendix G.

When writing large programs, it is the usual practice to divide the source code up among several different files. This allows different programmers to work on different parts of the program. It is also more efficient to change and recompile one part of the program at a time, rather than having to compile the entire program whenever a small change is made. The `make` program is used to keep track of the files making up a large program and to recompile parts of the program as needed. Although `make` is most often used with programs, it can also be useful in updating any project consisting of multiple files.

36.10 Other Programming Tools

Most UNIX systems come equipped with a battery of programming utilities, most of which are designed for use in creating C programs. (See Table 36-1.)

Table 36-1
Programming utilities.

Utility	Description	Function
cb	C beautifier	Formats C source code
cflow	Flow analyzer	Shows flow of control in C programs
ctrace	Execution tracer	Traces execution of a C program
cxref	C tracer	Lists references to variables in C programs
lint	C verifier	Warns of potential bugs, portability problems
prof	Profiler	Tests efficiency
time	Program timer	Times program execution
timex	Program timer	Times program execution

36.11 Exercises

1. Be sure you can define the following terms:

computer program	machine language	assembly language
pseudocode	compiler	source code
preprocessor	object code	executable code
linker	logic error	syntax error
runtime error	core file	debugger
bytecode	library code	

2. Write pseudocode for a program to compute square roots.

TUTORIAL:
PROGRAMMING IN C

It is a good idea to keep a C book handy as you read through this chapter.

C is the "native language" of UNIX—most of the UNIX operating system is written in C. So it is not surprising that for many applications C is the preferred language of UNIX programmers. In this chapter, you will see how to take advantage of some of the features that make programming in C possible. This is not intended to teach you C; for that, you should consult a standard text on C.

37.1 The hello.c Program

We will begin with the program shown in Listing 37-1, which prints a message on the standard output.

```
① /* Traditional first C program. */

② #include <stdio.h>

③ int main(void)
④ {
⑤     printf("Hello, world!\n");
⑥     return 0;
⑦ }
```

Listing 37-1
The hello.c program.

Let's examine this program in more detail:

```
① /* Traditional first C program. */
```

Any text appearing between /* and */ is treated as a comment and is ignored by the compiler. Comments are included for the benefit of the programmer and anyone else who may read the program later.

```
② #include <stdio.h>
```

Lines that begin with a pound sign (#) in the first column are taken to be instructions to the preprocessor. These are usually called preprocessor directives or control lines. In this case, the directive tells the preprocessor to include the contents of the file stdio.h ("standard input/output header" file) in the program before it is compiled. The angle brackets < > tell the preprocessor to search for stdio.h in the "usual place," which for most UNIX systems will be the directory /usr/include. You can also tell the preprocessor to include files that you have written yourself, in which case you would surround the file's pathname by double quotes. Thus the line

```
#include "/home/mylogin/myfile.h"
```

would direct the preprocessor to include /home/mylogin/myfile.h in the program before it is compiled.

③ `int main(void)`

C programs consist of one or more units called *functions*. Every C program must include a function named main() where execution begins. Here, the keyword void indicates that main() takes no arguments; int indicates that main() returns an integer value to the operating system.

④ `{`

Each function body begins with a left brace. Braces are also used within the function body to group lines of code together.

⑤   `printf("Hello, world!\n");`

The printf() function is discussed in Appendix E, "Formatted Output."

printf() is a standard C library function used to "print" output on the standard output. The argument to the function is a group of characters enclosed by double quotes, which is called a *string constant* or *string literal*. At the end of the string (but inside the double quotes) are the two characters \n, which together stand for a NEWLINE or (Return). The entire line is terminated by a semicolon.

⑥   `return 0;`

The last statement in main() returns an *exit code* to the operating system. An exit code of 0 indicates "success."

⑦ `}`

The function body ends with a right brace, which matches the left brace at the beginning of the function body. The compiler will consider it an error if you omit either brace.

37.2   Creating and Running hello.c

1. Find the compiler. The traditional UNIX C compiler is called cc. On systems conforming to the Single UNIX Specification, the standard C compiler is called c99. The Gnu C Compiler, another popular compiler, is called gcc. You should check for each of these on your system:

You can also use `find`, `whereis`, or `locate`.

§ `which cc` (Return)

§ `which c99` (Return)

§ `which gcc` (Return)

Remember that the file name must end in *.c*.

2. Create a source file. Use a text editor to create a file named `hello.c` and enter the program exactly as shown in Listing 37-1. Save the file and quit the editor.

3. Compile the source code. To compile the file, simply type the name of the compiler followed by the name of the file. Thus, if you are using the `cc` compiler, type:

§ `cc hello.c` (Return)

4. If necessary, correct any compiler errors and repeat Step 2. If the compiler cannot compile your code because of syntax errors, it will try to tell you where the errors are located. Reopen the file and correct the errors.

5. Run the program. By default, the linker gives the name `a.out` to the executable file. To run the program, type

§ `a.out` (Return)

if the current directory is included in your search path; or

§ `./a.out` (Return)

if the current directory is not included in your search path.

You should see the message

`Hello, world!`
§

The shell prompt appears when the program finishes, indicating that the shell is ready for your next command.

37.3 Review of the Compilation Process

Recall the command you used to compile the `hello.c` program:

§ `cc hello.c` (Return)

The `cc` command appears simple, but it starts a fairly complicated chain of events involving three separate programs:

The preprocessor works on a copy of the code; it does not actually alter `hello.c`.

1. The C preprocessor goes through the file `hello.c` and looks for preprocessor directives, which are marked by a leading pound sign (#). The preprocessor makes the requested changes and passes the altered code to the compiler.

2. The compiler translates the C code into object code, which it places in a file named `hello.o`. (If there are syntax errors, the compiler will not produce object code; instead, it will try to tell you where the errors are to be found.)

3. The linker combines your object code with any code your program may need from the standard libraries to produce executable code. In this case, the program calls the library function `printf()`. The executable code is placed in a file named `a.out`. (In some cases, the object file `hello.o` is deleted automatically.)

37.4 Renaming the Executable File

Note that the file containing the executable code is given the name `a.out` by the linker. If you want to save the executable code, you must use the `mv` command to give this file another name—otherwise, it will be overwritten the next time you use the `cc` compiler.

1. Use the `mv` command to rename the executable file. It is common practice to give the executable code the same name as the source code, but without the `.c` suffix:

§ `mv a.out hello` (Return)

2. Run the program. Enter the new name of the executable file:

Use `./hello` if the current directory is not in your search path.

§ `hello` (Return)
`Hello, world!`
§

As we shall see, you can compile the source code and rename the executable file all at once using `cc` with the `-o` option:

§ `cc hello.c -o hello` (Return)

Note that the arguments can be written in a different order:

§ `cc -o hello hello.c` (Return)

37.5 The recip.c Program

Our next program calculates reciprocals of numbers entered by the user at the keyboard. A pseudocode outline for this program is

```
Print a brief message about what the program does
Prompt the user for an integer n
Read n
Calculate 1/n
Display the answer
```

The corresponding C code is shown in Listing 37-2.

```
/* Compute reciprocals */

#include <stdio.h>

int main(void)
{
①    int n, recip;
     printf("This program computes reciprocals.\n");
     printf("Enter a number: ");
②    scanf("%d", &n);
③    recip = 1/n;
④    printf("The reciprocal of %d is %d.\n", n, recip);
     return 0;
}
```

Listing 37-2
C code for the `recip.c`
program.

This program introduces a few features that were not in the previous program:

①   `int n, recip;`

This is a *declaration*. It tells the compiler to create two variables to hold integers (`int`) and to give them the names `n` and `recip`. C requires that you declare all variables before you use them.

②   `scanf("%d", &n);`

A common mistake is to omit the address operator &.

`scanf()` is a standard C library function that is used to get input from the standard input. In this example, the function takes two arguments, `"%d"` and `&n`. The first argument (`"%d"`) is called a *control string*; it tells the compiler about the format of the input. In this case, the format specification `%d` stands for a single decimal integer. The second argument (`&n`) tells `scanf()` to store the integer that it reads in the variable `n`. The ampersand (`&`) is the address operator; it is required in this context.

③   `recip = 1/n;`

This is how we compute the reciprocal. The computer first divides the integer 1 by the contents of the variable `n`, and then assigns the result to the variable `recip`. In C, `=` is called the *assignment operator*; it tells the computer to take the value of the expression on the right and assign it to the variable on the left.

④   `printf("The reciprocal of %d is %d.\n", n, recip);`

This is another `printf()` function call, with a difference. There are three arguments this time instead of one. The first argument is a string containing two formats (`%d` and `%d`). The other two arguments are variables (`n` and `recip`). The `printf()` function prints out the string, substituting the contents of `n` and `recip` for the two formats.

37.6 Creating and Running recip.c

1. Create a source file. Use a text editor to create a file named `recip.c`; enter the program exactly as shown in Listing 37-2.

2. Compile the source code. The default name for an executable file is `a.out`. You can specify another name using `cc` with the `-o` option. For the executable file, let's use the name `recip` (without the `.c` suffix):

§ `cc -o recip recip.c` (Return)

This tells `cc` to compile `recip.c` and put the executable in the file `recip`.

3. If necessary, correct any syntax errors and repeat Step 2.

4. Run the program. To run the program, enter the name of the executable file:

Use `./recip` if the current directory is not in your search path.

§ `recip` (Return)

You should see a message and a prompt:

```
This program computes reciprocals.
Enter a number:
```

5. Enter a number at the prompt. Try the number 2:

```
Enter a number: 2  (Return)
```

The program will respond:

```
The reciprocal of 2 is 0.
§
```

This is obviously wrong: the reciprocal of 2 is 1/2, not 0. In fact, `recip.c` gives the correct answer only when you enter –1 or 1 as an input. The reason has to do with the way that the computer stores and uses integers. To repair this defect, you should revise the program to use variables of type `float` or `double` rather than type `int`. (We leave this as an exercise.)

37.7 Arithmetic Exceptions and Core Dumps

How does the `recip.c` program handle division by zero?

1. Run the program.

Use `./recip` if the current directory is not in your search path.

§ `recip` (Return)

The program will print a message and a prompt:

```
This program computes reciprocals.
Enter a number:
```

2. Enter zero at the prompt.

```
Enter a number: 0 (Return)
```

You should receive an error message, something like this:

```
Arithmetic exception (core dumped)
```

What happened? It is not hard to figure out. Division by zero is an undefined operation that caused the program to crash.

3. Check for a core file. If you list the files in your directory, you should see a file named core:

§ ls (Return)

Since you cannot read the core file, and because it takes up so much room, you should delete it.

4. Remove the core file.

§ rm core (Return)

37.8   Setting up recip.c for Debugging

Although you cannot read a core file as you would a normal UNIX text file, you can use a debugger such as dbx to examine the file and determine what caused the program to crash.

■ **Compile the program using the debug option.** With most compilers, the -g option indicates "debug":

§ cc -g recip.c (Return)

This causes the compiler to include additional information in the compiled code that can be used by dbx. If you would like to see how dbx is used, refer to Appendix F.

37.9   The sqroot.c Program

Our next program calculates the square roots of numbers entered by the user at the keyboard. A pseudocode outline for this program is shown below, and the C code itself is shown in Listing 37-3.

```
Print a brief message about what the program does
Prompt the user for a number n
Read n
Compute the square root of n
Display the answer
```

```
/* Compute square roots */

  #include <stdio.h>
① #include <math.h>

  int main(void)
  {
②     double n, root;
      printf("This program computes square roots.\n");
      printf("Enter a number: ");
③     scanf("%lf", &n);
④     root = sqrt(n);
      printf("The square root of %f is %f.\n", n, root);
      return 0;
  }
```

Listing 37-3
C code for the
sqroot.c program.

This program introduces some interesting new elements:

① #include <math.h>

This control line tells the preprocessor to include the contents of the file math.h (standard math header file) in the program before it is compiled. This file should be included whenever a library function such as sqrt() is used. As before, the angle brackets < > tell the preprocessor to search for the file in the "usual place," most likely the directory /usr/include.

②   double n, root;

This declaration tells the compiler to create two variables to hold floating-point (double) values and to give them the names n and root.

③   scanf("%lf", &n);

The control string in this scanf() function call contains the format specification %lf, which stands for "long float," a synonym for double.

④   root = sqrt(n);

This statement calls the library function sqrt() to compute the square root of n, then assigns the result to the variable root.

37.10 Creating and Running sqroot.c

1. Create a source file. Use a text editor to create a file named sqroot.c; enter the program shown in Listing 37-3.

2. Compile the source code. The program sqroot.c uses the math library function `sqrt()`. The `-lm` option tells the linker to combine compiled code from the math library with your object code:

§ `cc -o sqroot sqroot.c -lm`(Return)

Note that the `-lm` option comes at the end of the command line because it is an instruction to the linker rather than the compiler.

3. **If necessary, correct any syntax errors and repeat Step 2.**

4. **Run the program.** To run the program, enter the name of the executable file:

Use `./sqroot` if the current directory is not in your search path.

§ `sqroot`(Return)

The program will print a message and the prompt:

```
This program computes square roots.
Enter a number:
```

5. **Test the program.** Enter a 4 at the prompt:

```
Enter a number: 4 (Return)
```

You should see something like this:

```
The square root of 4 is 2.
§
```

37.11 The Trip Program

Our next sample program illustrates the use of separate source files for putting together a large program. Large programs are often the work of more than one programmer; it is common for each programmer to work on his or her own files, which then are assembled to make a complete program.

It is convenient to group the source files for a program in the same directory.

1. **Create a directory to hold the program.** Use `mkdir` to create a directory named `Trip`:

§ `mkdir Trip`(Return)

2. **Move to the new directory.**

§ `cd Trip`(Return)

All of the files making up the `Trip` program will be put in the `Trip` directory.

37.12 The main.c Function

Every C program must have one `main()` function, where execution begins. As shown in Listing 37-4, `main()` is a simple function. All `main()` does is call two other functions, `indiana()` and `chicago()`.

```
/* Illustrate multiple source files */

① void chicago(void);
   void indiana(void);

   int main(void)
   {
       chicago();
       indiana();
       chicago();
       return 0;
   }
```

Listing 37-4
C code for the `main.c`
file.

There is a new feature to note here:

① `void chicago(void);`

This is a *function prototype* (also called a *function declaration*). It tells the compiler that the function `chicago()` takes no arguments and returns no value.

37.13 Creating and Compiling main.c

As we just saw, `main()` is a simple function. All it does is call two other functions, `indiana()` and `chicago()`. We have not yet written either of these two functions, so the program is not complete. Nevertheless, we can still run `main.c` through the compiler to check for syntax errors and produce an object file.

1. Use the text editor to create a new source file. Open a file named `main.c` and enter the code shown in Listing 37-4.

2. Compile the function without linking. Invoke `cc` with the `-c` ("compile only") option:

§ `cc -c main.c` (Return)

If the compilation is successful, this creates an object file named `main.o`. On the other hand, if the compiler detects an error in the file, it will give you an error message, and it will not create an object file.

3. If necessary, correct any errors in the file and repeat Step 2.

37.14 Creating and Compiling chicago.c

Listing 37-5 shows the source code for the `chicago()` function.

1. Create a source file. Use your text editor to create a file named `chicago.c` and enter the C code shown in Listing 37-5.

2. Compile without linking. Invoke `cc` with the `-c` ("compile only") option:

```
/* The chicago function */

void chicago(void)
{
    printf("\nI'm waiting at O'Hare International,\n");
    printf("once the busiest airport in the world.\n");
}
```

Listing 37-5
C code for the main.c
file.

§ cc -c chicago.c (Return)

3. If necessary, correct syntax errors and compile again.

4. Verify that the object file has been created. Listing the files should show the source and object files:

§ ls (Return)
chicago.c   chicago.o   main.c   main.o

37.15   Creating indiana.c and indy.c

We are not yet finished with the program. Listing 37-6 and Listing 37-7 show the C code for indiana() and indianapolis().

```
/* The indiana() function */

void indianapolis(void);
①
void indiana(void)
{
    printf("\nBack home again, Indiana.\n");
    indianapolis();
    printf("\nWander Indiana--come back soon.\n");
}
```

Listing 37-6
C code for the
indiana.c function.

```
/* The indianapolis() function */

① #define   POP2000   1.6      /* Population in millions */

void indianapolis(void)
{
    printf("\nWelcome to Indianapolis, Indiana.\n");
    printf("Population: %f million.\n", POP2000);
}
```

Listing 37-7
C code for the indy.c
file.

Perhaps the most interesting feature introduced in Listing 37-7 is the #define preprocessor directive:

```
① #define   POP2000   1.6      /* Population in millions */     |
```

This directive tells the preprocessor to search through the file and replace every occurrence of the string POP2000 with 1.6, the population (in millions) of the Indianapolis Consolidated Metropolitan Area according to the 2000 census.

1. Create the source files indiana.c **and** indy.c. Use your text editor as you have done before to enter the C code shown in Listing 37-6 and Listing 37-7.

2. Compile (but do not link) the files indiana.c **and** indy.c. If necessary, review the previous section to remind yourself of how this is done.

37.16 Linking and Running the Trip Program

If you have done everything correctly, you should now have four files of C source code and four files of object code in the directory Trip. In this section, you will see how to link the object files to create an executable file.

1. Verify that the object files exist. Enter the ls command:

§ ls (Return)

You should see something like this:

```
chicago.c  indiana.c  indy.c  main.c
chicago.o  indiana.o  indy.o  main.o
```

2. Link the object files to make an executable file. The cc command will do the trick:

§ cc *.o (Return)

This will create an executable file named a.out.

3. Run the program. Simply enter the name of the executable file:

Use ./a.out if the current directory is not in your search path.

§ a.out (Return)

The output will be something like this:

```
I'm waiting at O'Hare International,
once the busiest airport in the world.

Back home again, Indiana.

Welcome to Indianapolis, Indiana.
Population: 1.60000 million.

Wander Indiana--come back soon.

I'm waiting at O'Hare International,
once the busiest airport in the world.
```

TUTORIAL: PROGRAMMING IN C++

It is a good idea to keep a C++ book handy as you read through this chapter.

C++ is an object-oriented programming language created by Bjarne Stroustrup at the Bell Labs in the mid 1980s. C++ is a "superset" of C, meaning that C++ retains almost all of the features of standard C while adding many powerful features of its own. In this chapter, you will see how to write, compile, and run C++ programs. This is not intended to teach you C++; for that, you should consult a text on C++.

38.1 The hello.cpp Program

We will begin with the program shown in Listing 38-1, which prints a message on the standard output.

```
① // Traditional first program.

② #include <iostream>
③ using namespace std;

④ int main()
⑤ {
⑥     cout << "Hello, world!" << endl;
⑦ }
```

Listing 38-1
The hello.cpp program.

Let's examine this program in more detail:

```
① // Traditional first program.
```

Two slashes (//) mark the beginning of a *comment*. Any text following the slashes to the end of the line is ignored by the compiler. (The C++ compiler also recognizes the C comment delimiters /* and */.) Comments are included for the benefit of the programmer and anyone else who may read the program later.

```
② #include <iostream>
```

Lines that begin with a pound sign (#) in the first column are taken to be instructions to the preprocessor. These are usually called preprocessor directives or control lines. In this case, the directive tells the preprocessor to include the contents of the file `iostream` ("input/output stream header" file) in the program before it is compiled. The angle brackets < > tell the preprocessor to search for `iostream` in the "usual place," which for most UNIX systems will be the directory `/usr/include`. You can also tell the preprocessor to include files that you have written yourself, in which case you would surround the file's pathname by double quotes. Thus the line

```
#include "/home/mylogin/myfile.h"
```

would direct the preprocessor to include `/home/mylogin/myfile.h` in the program before it is compiled.

③ `using namespace std;`

This line specifies that the standard (`std`) namespace is to be used in the program. Namespaces are used to group global classes, objects, and functions. This is important when two different classes, objects, or functions have the same name. All of the standard C++ libraries are defined within the standard namespace.

④ `int main()`

Execution begins at a function named `main()`. Here, `int` indicates that `main()` returns an integer value to the operating system.

⑤ `{`

Each function body begins with a left brace. Braces are also used within the function body to group lines of code together.

⑥   `cout << "Hello, world!" << endl;`

The standard C++ stream `cout` sends data to the standard output (which is normally the monitor). The *insertion operator* (<<) puts output into the stream. In this case, the output is a *string constant* or *string literal*, a group of characters surrounded by double quotes (`"Hello, world!"`). Insertion of `endl` into the stream causes a NEWLINE or (Return) to be put into the output stream. The entire line is terminated by a semicolon.

⑦ `}`

The function body ends with a right brace, which matches the left brace at the beginning of the function body. The compiler will consider it an error if you omit either brace.

38.2 Creating and Running hello.cpp

1. Find the compiler. On some systems, the C++ compiler is called c++. The GNU C++ compiler is called g++. The standard C compiler on your system (cc or c99) may be able to compile C++ programs. Check for these on your system:

You can also use find, whereis, or locate.

§ which c++ (Return)

§ which g++ (Return)

§ which c99 (Return)

Remember that the file name should end in *.cpp*.

2. Create a source file. Use a text editor to create a file named hello.cpp. Enter the program exactly as shown in Listing 38-1.

3. Compile the source code. The GNU C++ compiler is invoked using the g++ command. To compile the file, simply type g++ followed by the name of the file:

§ g++ hello.cpp (Return)

4. If necessary, correct any compiler errors and repeat Step 2. If the compiler cannot compile your code because of syntax errors, it will try to tell you where the errors are located. Reopen the file and correct the errors.

5. Run the program. By default, the linker gives the name a.out to the executable file. To run the program, type

§ a.out (Return)

if the current directory is included in your search path; or

§ ./a.out (Return)

if the current directory is not included in your search path.

You should see the message

Hello, world!
§

The shell prompt appears when the program finishes, indicating that the shell is ready for your next command.

38.3 Review of the Compilation Process

Recall the command you used to compile the hello.cpp program:

§ g++ hello.cpp (Return)

The g++ command appears simple, but it starts a fairly complicated chain of events involving three separate programs:

The preprocessor works on
a copy of the code; it does
not actually alter
hello.cpp.

1. The C++ preprocessor goes through the file hello.cpp and looks for preprocessor directives, which are marked by a leading pound sign (#). The preprocessor
makes the requested changes and passes the altered code to the compiler.

2. The compiler translates the C++ code into object code, which it places in a file
named hello.o. (If there are syntax errors, the compiler will not produce object
code; instead, it will try to tell you where the errors are to be found.)

3. The linker combines your object code with any code your program may need
from the standard libraries to produce executable code. The executable code is
placed in a file named a.out. (In some cases, the object file hello.o is deleted
automatically.)

38.4 Renaming the Executable File

Note that the file containing the executable code is given the name a.out by the
linker. If you want to save the executable code, you must use the mv command to
give this file another name—otherwise, it will be overwritten the next time you use
the g++ compiler.

1. Use the mv command to rename the executable file. It is common practice to
give the executable code the same name as the source code, but without the .cpp
suffix:

§ mv a.out hello (Return)

2. Run the program. Enter the new name of the executable file:

Use ./hello if the current
directory is not in your
search path.

§ hello (Return)
Hello, world!
§

As we shall see, you can compile the source code and rename the executable file all
at once using g++ with the -o option:

§ g++ hello.cpp -o hello (Return)

Note that the arguments can be written in a different order:

§ g++ -o hello hello.cpp (Return)

38.5 The recip.cpp Program

Our next program calculates reciprocals of numbers entered by the user at the
keyboard. A pseudocode outline for this program is shown below:

```
Print a brief message about what the program does
Prompt the user for an integer n
Read n
Calculate 1/n
Display the answer
```

The corresponding C++ code is shown in Listing 38-2.

```
① /* Compute reciprocals */

  #include <iostream>
  using namespace std;

  int main()
  {
②     int n, recip;

③     cout << "This program computes reciprocals.\n";
       cout << "Enter a number: ";

④     cin >> n;
⑤     recip = 1/n;

⑥     cout << "The reciprocal of " << n;
       cout << " is " << recip << "\n";
  }
```

Listing 38-2
C++ code for the
recip.cpp program.

This program introduces a few features that were not in the previous program:

① /* Compute reciprocals */ |

Any text between /* and */ is treated as a comment, and is ignored by the compiler. (This is how comments are indicated in C.)

②   int n, recip; |

This is a *declaration*. It tells the compiler to create two variables to hold integers (int) and to give them the names n and recip. C++ requires that you declare all variables before you use them.

③   cout << "This program computes reciprocals.\n"; |

Note the character combination \n that appears at the end of the string. This combination has the same effect as endl: it causes a NEWLINE or (Return) to be put into the output stream.

④   cin >> n; |

The standard C++ stream cin obtains data from the standard input (normally the keyboard). The *extraction operator* (>>) takes data from cin and puts it into the variable n.

⑤   recip = 1/n; |

This is how we compute the reciprocal. The computer first divides the integer 1 by the contents of the variable n, and then assigns the result to the variable `recip`. In C++, the equals sign (=) is called the *assignment operator*; it tells the computer to take the value of the expression on the right and assign it to the variable on the left.

⑥   `cout << "The reciprocal of " << n;` |

This is another output stream, with a difference. The stream will consists of a string literal (`"The reciprocal of "`) followed by the value of the variable n.

38.6 Creating and Running recip.cpp

1. Create a source file. Use a text editor to create a file named `recip.cpp`; enter the code shown in Listing 38-2.

2. Compile the source code. The default name for an executable file is `a.out`. You can specify another name using g++ with the `-o` option. For the executable file, let's use the name `recip` (without the `.cpp` suffix):

§ `g++ -o recip recip.cpp` (Return)

This tells g++ to compile `recip.cpp` and put the executable in the file `recip`.

3. If necessary, correct any syntax errors and repeat Step 2.

4. Run the program. To run the program, enter the name of the executable file:

Use `./recip` if the current directory is not in your search path.

§ `recip` (Return)

You should see a message and a prompt:

```
This program computes reciprocals.
Enter a number:
```

5. Enter a number at the prompt. Try the number 2:

`Enter a number: 2` (Return)

The program will respond:

```
The reciprocal of 2 is 0
§
```

This is obviously wrong: the reciprocal of 2 is 1/2, not 0. In fact, `recip.cpp` gives the correct answer only when you enter –1 or 1 as an input. The reason has to do with the way that the computer stores and uses integers. To repair this defect, you should revise the program to use variables of type `float` or `double` rather than type `int`. (We leave this as an exercise.)

38.7 Arithmetic Exceptions and Core Dumps

How does your `recip.cpp` program handle division by zero?

1. Run the program.

Use `./recip` if the current directory is not in your search path.

§ `recip` (Return)

The program will print a message and a prompt:

```
This program computes reciprocals.
Enter a number:
```

2. Enter zero at the prompt.

```
Enter a number: 0 (Return)
```

You may receive an error message, something like this:

```
Arithmetic exception (core dumped)
```

What happened? It is not hard to figure out. Division by zero is an undefined operation that caused the program to crash.

3. Check for a `core` **file.** If you list the files in your directory, you should see a file named `core`:

§ `ls` (Return)

Since you cannot read the `core` file (and it takes up so much room), delete it.

4. Remove the `core` **file.**

§ `rm core` (Return)

38.8 Setting up recip.cpp for Debugging

Although you cannot read a `core` file as you would a normal UNIX text file, you can use a debugger such as `dbx` to examine the file and determine what caused the program to crash.

■ **Compile the program using the debug option.** With most compilers, the `-g` option indicates "debug":

§ `g++ -g recip.cpp` (Return)

This causes the compiler to include additional information in the compiled code that can be used by `dbx`. To see how `dbx` is used, refer to Appendix F.

38.9 The sqroot.cpp Program

Our next program calculates the square roots of numbers entered by the user at the keyboard. A pseudocode outline for this program is shown below:

```
Print a brief message about what the program does
Prompt the user for a number x
Read x
Compute the square root of x
Display the answer
```

The C++ code for this program is shown in Listing 38-3.

```
    /* Compute square roots */

    #include <iostream>
①   #include <cmath>
    using namespace std;

    int main()
    {
②       double x, root;

        cout << "This program computes square roots.\n";
        cout << "Enter a number: ";
        cin >> x;

③       root = sqrt(x);

        cout << "The square root of " << x << " is ";
        cout << root << "\n";
    }
```

Listing 38-3
The sqroot.cpp program.

This program introduces some interesting new elements:

① `#include <cmath>`

This control line tells the preprocessor to include the contents of the file `cmath` in the program before it is compiled. This file should be included whenever you use a mathematics library function such as `sqrt()`. As before, the angle brackets `< >` tell the preprocessor to search for the file in the "usual place," most likely the directory `/usr/include`.

② `    double x, root;`

This declaration tells the compiler to create two variables to hold floating-point (`double`) values and to give them the names `x` and `root`.

③ `    root = sqrt(x);`

This statement calls the library function `sqrt()` to compute the square root of `x`, then assigns the result to the variable `root`.

38.10 Creating and Running sqroot.cpp

1. Create a source file. Use a text editor to create a file named `sqroot.cpp`; enter the C++ program as shown in Listing 38-3. Be sure to save the file before you quit the editor.

2. Compile the source code. The program `sqroot.cpp` uses the math library function `sqrt()`. The `-lm` option tells the linker to combine compiled code from the math library with your object code:

§ g++ -o sqroot sqroot.cpp -lm (Return)

Note that the `-lm` option comes at the end of the command line because it is an instruction to the linker rather than the compiler.

3. If necessary, correct any syntax errors and repeat Step 2.

4. Run the program. To run the program, enter the name of the executable file:

Use `./sqroot` if the
current directory is not in
your search path.

§ sqroot (Return)

The program will print a message and the prompt:

This program computes square roots.
Enter a number:

5. Test the program. Enter a 4 at the prompt:

Enter a number: 4 (Return)

You should see something like this:

The square root of 4 is 2
§

38.11 The Trip Program

Our next sample program illustrates the use of separate source files for putting together a large program. Large programs are often the work of more than one programmer; it is common for each programmer to work on his or her own files, which then are assembled to make a complete program.

It is convenient to group the source files for a program in the same directory.

1. Create a directory to hold the program. Use `mkdir` to create a directory named `Trip`:

§ mkdir Trip (Return)

2.   Move to the new directory.

§ cd Trip (Return)

All of the files making up the `Trip` program will be put in the `Trip` directory.

38.12 The main.cpp Function

Every C++ program must have one `main()` function, where execution begins. As shown in Listing 38-4, `main()` is a simple function. All `main()` does is call two other functions, `indiana()` and `chicago()`.

```
// Illustrate multiple source files

① void chicago(void);
   void indiana(void);

   int main()
   {
       chicago();
       indiana();
       chicago();
   }
```

Listing 38-4
The `main.cpp` file.

There is a new feature to note here:

① `void chicago(void);` |

This is a *function prototype* (also called a *function declaration*). It tells the compiler that the function `chicago()` takes no arguments and returns no value.

38.13 Creating and Compiling main.cpp

As we just saw, `main()` is a simple function. All it does is call two other functions, `indiana()` and `chicago()`. We have not yet written either of these two functions, so the program is not complete. Nevertheless, we can still run `main.cpp` through the compiler to check for syntax errors and produce an object file.

1. Use the text editor to create a new source file. Open a file named `main.cpp` and enter the code shown in Listing 38-4.

2. Compile the function without linking. Invoke `g++` with the `-c` ("compile only") option:

§ `g++ -c main.cpp` (Return)

If the compilation is successful, this creates an object file named `main.o`. On the other hand, if the compiler detects an error in the file, it will give you an error message, and it will not create an object file.

3. If necessary, correct any errors in the file and repeat Step 2.

38.14 Creating and Compiling chicago.cpp

Listing 38-5 shows the source code for the `chicago()` function.

```
// The chicago() function

#include <iostream.h>

void chicago(void)
{
    cout << "\nI'm waiting at O'Hare International,\n";
    cout << "once the busiest airport in the world.\n";
}
```

Listing 38-5
C++ code for the
`chicago.cpp` file.

1. **Create a source file.** Use a text editor to create a file named `chicago.cpp` and enter the C++ code as shown in Listing 38-5.

2. **Compile without linking.** Invoke g++ with the `-c` ("compile only") option:

§ `g++ -c chicago.cpp` (Return)

3. **If necessary, correct syntax errors and compile again.**

4. **Verify that the object file has been created.** Listing the files should show the source and object files:

§ `ls` (Return)
`chicago.cpp   chicago.o   main.cpp   main.o`

38.15 Creating indiana.cpp and indy.cpp

We are not yet finished with the program. Listing 38-6 and Listing 38-7 show the C++ code for `indiana()` and `indianapolis()`.

```
// The indiana() function

#include <iostream>
using namespace std;

void indianapolis(void);
void indiana(void)
{
    cout << "\nBack home again, Indiana.\n";
    indianapolis();
    cout << "\nWander Indiana--come back soon.\n";
}
```

Listing 38-6
C++ code for the
`indiana.cpp` file.

```
/* The indianapolis() function */

#include <iostream>

using namespace std;

① #define  POP2000  1.6      // Population in millions

void indianapolis(void)
{
    cout << "\nWelcome to Indianapolis, Indiana.\n";
    cout << "Population: " << POP2000 << " million.\n";
}
```

Listing 38-7
C++ code for the
indy.cpp file.

Perhaps the most interesting feature introduced in Listing 38-7 is the `#define` preprocessor directive:

① `#define  POP2000  1.6      // Population in millions` |

This directive tells the preprocessor to search through the file and replace every occurrence of the string POP2000 with 1.6, the population (in millions) of the Indianapolis Consolidated Metropolitan Area according to the 2000 census.

1. Create the source files indiana.cpp **and** indy.cpp. Use your text editor as before to enter the C++ code shown in Listing 38-6 and Listing 38-7.

2. Compile (but do not link) the files indiana.cpp **and** indy.cpp. If necessary, review the previous section to remind yourself of how this is done.

38.16 Linking and Running the Trip Program

If you have done everything correctly, you should now have four files of C source code and four files of object code in the directory Trip. In this section, you will see how to link the object files to create an executable file.

1. Verify that the object files exist. Enter the ls command:

§ `ls` (Return)

You should see something like this:

```
chicago.cpp  indiana.cpp  indy.cpp  main.cpp
chicago.o  indiana.o  indy.o  main.o
```

2. Link the object files to make an executable file. The g++ command will do the trick:

§ `g++ *.o` (Return)

This will create an executable file named a.out.

3. Run the program. Simply enter the name of the executable file:

Use ./a.out if the current directory is not in your search path.

§ a.out (Return)

The output will be something like this:

```
I'm waiting at O'Hare International,
once the busiest airport in the world.

Back home again, Indiana.

Welcome to Indianapolis, Indiana.
Population: 1.6 million.

Wander Indiana--come back soon.

I'm waiting at O'Hare International,
once the busiest airport in the world.
```

38.17 Compiling and Linking in One Step

In the previous section you linked four files of object code that you had previously compiled. For large programs, debugging is often easier when the program is broken up into smaller units. However, it is not necessary to separate the compilation and linking steps. In this section, you will see how to compile and link multiple source files all at once.

1. Compile and link the source code. The g++ command will do this:

§ g++ *.cpp (Return)

This will create an executable file named a.out.

2. Run the program as before.

Use ./a.out if the current directory is not in your search path.

§ a.out (Return)

38.18 Maintaining a Program with make

One advantage to breaking up a large program into multiple source files is that it allows you to modify and recompile one source file without having to recompile the entire program. The UNIX make program is useful in keeping track of the changes you make in the program files. You can learn about make in Appendix G.

38.19 Command Summary

Each of these commands is entered at the shell prompt and is terminated by a
(Return).

g++ *file.cpp*	compile and link the source code in *file.cpp*
g++ −c *file.cpp*	compile but do not link; put output in *file.o*
g++ −g *file.cpp*	compile *file.cpp*; set up for the debugger
g++ −o *file file.cpp*	compile *file.cpp*; put executable code in *file*
g++ *file.cpp* −o *file*	same as previous
g++ *file.cpp* −lm	compile *file.cpp* and link with math library code

38.20 Exercises

1. The g++ compiler available on most systems takes a number of options. Refer
to the UNIX manual to determine what each of the following commands will do:

g++ −E *source.cpp*

g++ −O *source.cpp*

g++ −S *source.cpp*

g++ *source* −l*name*

2. Rewrite `recip.cpp` to employ `double` variables. Does the program work
correctly? What happens if you enter zero?

3. Even if you have rewritten `recip.cpp` to use `double` or `float` data, it may
still not handle an input of zero correctly. Read your C++ book about the `if-
else` statement, then rewrite the `recip.cpp` program so that it prints the mes-
sage "The reciprocal of 0 is not defined" if the user enters a zero.

4. The `time` utility measures the time required to execute a program or shell
script. You can time the execution of `a.out` with the command line

§ `time a.out` (Return)

Use the `man` command to learn how `time` works. Then try out this utility on one
of your source files.

# Chapter 39

TUTORIAL:
PROGRAMMING IN JAVA

It is a good idea to keep a
Java book handy as you read
through this chapter.

Java was developed by James Gosling and a team of programmers at Sun
Microsystems in the early 1990s. Java was originally intended for programming
digital devices such as cable televisions. However, it has since become one of the
most popular computer languages on the World Wide Web. Although Java is not
a standard part of UNIX, it is found on most UNIX systems.

In this chapter, you will see how to write, compile, and run Java programs. This is
not intended to teach you Java; for that, you should consult a Java text. Indeed, it
is a good idea to keep a Java book handy as you read through this chapter.

39.1 Objects, Classes, and Packages

Java is an *object-oriented programming* (OOP) language. This means that Java
programs model the real world in terms of *objects*. Like objects in the real world,
software objects are defined by their properties (also called *variables*) and their
behaviors (also called *methods*).

A Java *class* is the blueprint from which software objects are created. When
writing a class, the programmer specifies the variables that each object will have
and the methods that will work on those variables. One or more objects (or
instances) can be created from a given class.

Normally, the variables and methods belonging to a particular class are not visible
or accessible to other classes. Such variables and methods are said to be *private*. If
a variable or method is to be accessible to other classes, it must be declared as
public.

Related Java classes may be grouped together into collections called *packages*.
Any Java code in a particular package has access to all of the Java classes in the
same package (but not to a class belonging to another package, unless that class
has been declared to be a *public* class).

39.2 The HelloWorld.java Application

We will begin with the program shown in Listing 39-1, which prints a message on
the standard output.

```
① // Traditional first program.

② public class HelloWorld
③ {
④     public static void main(String[] args)
      {
⑤         System.out.println("Hello, world!");
⑥     }
  }
```

Listing 39-1
HelloWorld.java
program.

Let's examine this program in more detail:

① `// Traditional first program.`

Two slashes (//) mark the beginning of a *comment*. Any text following the slashes to the end of the line is ignored by the compiler. (The Java compiler also recognizes the C comment delimiters /* and */.) Comments are included for the benefit of the programmer and anyone else who may read the program later.

② `public class HelloWorld`

This is the beginning of a class definition. The keyword `public` means the `HelloWorld` class will be visible everywhere.

③ `{`

The body of a class or method definition opens with a left brace. Braces are also used within the class definition to group lines of code together.

④ `    public static void main(String[] args)`
`    {`

Every stand-alone Java application must include a method named `main()` where execution begins. The keyword `public` makes this method visible outside the class; the keyword `void` means that `main()` does not return a value. (Refer to your Java text for a discussion of the keyword `static`.) Inside the parentheses, the argument `arg` is declared to be of type `String`—that is, an array of characters.

⑤ `        System.out.println("Hello, world!");`

`println()` is a standard Java method used to "print" a line of output on the standard output. It is part of the `java.lang.System` class. The argument to the function is a group of characters enclosed by double quotes, which is called a *string constant* or *string literal*.

⑥   }
}

The body of a class or method definition closes with a right brace, which matches the left brace at the beginning of the body. The compiler will consider it an error if you omit any of the braces.

39.3 Creating, Compiling, and Running HelloWorld.java

Java requires a class file to have the same name as the class it contains except for the addition of the *.java* file extension. Common practice is to capitalize class names, so class file names are usually capitalized.

The file name must be the same as the class name plus the extension .java.

1. **Create a source file.** Use your favorite text editor to create a text file named `HelloWorld.java` and enter the program exactly as shown in Listing 39-1. Save the file and quit the editor.

2. **Compile the source code.** The java compiler is called `javac`. To compile the code, simply type `javac` followed by the name of the file:

§ `javac HelloWorld.java` (Return)

3. **If necessary, correct any compiler errors and repeat Step 2.** If the compiler cannot compile your code because of syntax errors, it will try to tell you where the errors are located. Open the file, correct the errors, and compile again.

4. **Run the program.** The Java compiler gives the name `HelloWorld.class` to the class file containing the bytecode. To have the Java Virtual Machine interpret the program, type

Do not type the .class extension.

§ `java HelloWorld` (Return)

You should see the message

```
Hello, world!
§
```

The shell prompt appears when the program finishes, indicating that the shell is ready for your next command.

39.4 The SimpleApplet.java Applet

The `HelloWorld.java` program shown in Listing 39-1 is an example of a stand-alone program or *application*. This is the kind of program created by traditional programming languages such as C or Fortran.

Java can also be used to create special programs called *applets* which can be included in HTML documents and distributed over the Internet. A Java-enabled Web browser can load such documents and run the Java code.

Listing 39-2 shows a Java applet that will print the message "Hello, world!" on the computer screen.

```
// A simple Java applet

① import java.applet*;
② import java.awt.*;

③ public class SimpleApplet extends Applet
   {
④      public void paint(Graphics g) {
⑤         g.drawString("Hello, world!", 100, 400);
        }
   }
```

This applet introduces some new features:

① `import java.applet*;`

The standard package `java.applet` contains the `Applet` class and several interfaces that are useful in creating applets. It is part of the Java Applications Programming Interface (API), a collection of standard packages that include hundreds of predefined classes. The `import` statement allows you to use the `java.applet` package in your code; the asterisk (*) means we are importing all of the classes in the package.

② `import java.awt.*;`

`java.awt` is the Abstract Windowing Toolkit (AWT), another package that is part of the Java API. As before, the asterisk (*) means we are importing all of the classes in the package.

③ `public class SimpleApplet extends Applet`

The keyword `extends` makes `SimpleApplet` a subclass of the standard Applet class. Consequently, `SimpleApplet` "inherits" many of the variables and methods of the `Applet` class.

④ `    public void paint(Graphics g) {`

The `paint()` method—a part of many classes in the AWT package—is used to display graphical output on the computer screen. The `paint()` method takes as its argument a `Graphics` object.

⑤ `        g.drawString("Hello, world!", 100, 400);`

The `Graphics` object g includes a method named `drawString()` which displays text strings on the screen. The first argument to `drawString()` is the string to be displayed (in this case, "Hello, world!"). The second and third arguments specify the location of the string relative to the upper left corner of the screen. In this example, the string is to be positioned 100 units from the left edge of the screen and 400 units down from the top edge of the screen. (The default unit is a *pixel*, which equals 1/72 of an inch.)

39.5 Creating and Compiling the Applet

The file name must be the same as the class name plus the extension .java.

1. Create a source file. Use your favorite text editor to create a text file named SimpleApplet.java and enter the program exactly as shown in Listing 39-2. Save the file and quit the editor.

2. Compile the source code. As before, type javac followed by the file name:

§ javac SimpleApplet.java (Return)

Unless there are syntax errors in the source code, the Java compiler will create a file named SimpleApplet.class containing bytecode.

3. If necessary, correct any compiler errors and repeat Step 2. If the compiler cannot compile your code because of syntax errors, it will try to tell you where the errors are located. Open the file and correct the errors, then recompile the applet.

39.6 Creating an HTML File

A Java applet is not designed to be run by the Java interpreter. Instead, the applet can be embedded in a web page that can be loaded into a Web browser. Listing 39-3 shows a simple HTML file that invokes the applet we created in the previous section.

Listing 39-3
The HTML file
WebPage.html.

```
① <html>
②     <applet
③         code="SimpleApplet.class"
④         width=500
⑤         height=500
⑥     >
⑦ </applet>
⑧ </html>
```

Let's examine this file line by line:

① <html>

The <html> tag marks the start of the HTML code.

②   <applet

The `<applet` tag specifies the applet that is to be run within a Web document. Note that there is no closing angle bracket (>) on this line.

③   `code="SimpleApplet.class"`

The `code` attribute specifies the class file containing the compiled applet code. Note that the file name is in double quotes and includes the *.class* extension.

④   `width=500`

The `width` attribute specifies the width (in pixels) of the space that the applet requires in the browser window.

⑤   `height=500`

The `height` attribute specifies the height (in pixels) of the space that the applet requires in the browser window.

⑥   `>`

This angle bracket closes the `<applet>` tag.

⑦ `</applet>`

The `</applet>` tag marks the end of the applet code.

⑧ `</html>`

The `</html>` tag marks the end of the HTML code.

Now use your text editor to create a file named `WebPage.html`, and enter the code shown in Listing 39-3.

39.7 Running the Applet

Once you have embedded your applet in an HTML file, you can open the file using a Java-enabled Web browser, or you can open it using a program called the `appletviewer`. Let's use the `appletviewer`:

1. **Run the applet using the** `appletviewer`**.** Type the command line

§ `appletviewer WebPage.html` (Return)

This opens an `appletviewer` window containing the output from the applet.

2. **Close the** `appletviewer` **window.** Select Close from the window menu.

We leave it as an exercise for you to open the file using your Web browser.

39.8 Command Summary

Each command is entered at the shell prompt and is terminated by a (Return).

`javac` *Application.java*	compile source code in *Application.java*
`java` *Application*	interpret bytecode in *Application.class*
`appletviewer` *page.html*	invoke applet embedded in *page.html*

39.9 Exercises

1. What happens when you use a Java-enabled Web browser to open the file `WebPage.html`? Try it. If you are using Netscape or a similar browser, pull down the File menu and select Open File, then choose the `WebPage.html` file to open.

2. Refer to your Java book to see how to obtain floating-point input from the keyboard. Then write a Java application `Recip.java` that computes and displays the reciprocal of a number.

TAMING YOUR TERMINAL

The `stty` ("set terminal") command allows you to set parameters that affect the operation of your terminal. In this appendix you will see how to use `stty` to perform the following tasks:

■ Set your terminal to handle lowercase input.

■ Define the erase key.

■ Ensure that the terminal echoes your input properly.

A.1 Correcting Uppercase-Only Output

Sometimes the system may behave as if your terminal can handle only uppercase letters. (This can occur if you accidentally press the "Caps Lock" key before logging in.) The following command will correct the problem:

§ STTY -LCASE (RETURN)

A.2 Defining the Erase Key

Most users expect the (BACKSPACE) key to erase characters on the command line. (Others prefer to use (DELETE) or (CONTROL)-(H) for this.) The following command will make (BACKSPACE) the character-erase key:

§ stty erase (BACKSPACE) (RETURN)

The following command will set (DELETE) as the character-erase key:

§ stty erase (DELETE) (RETURN)

To set the (CONTROL)-(H) key combination as the character-erase key, use the command line

§ stty erase ^h (RETURN)

Note that the caret (∧) is used to represent the (CONTROL) key.

A.3 Setting the Terminal Echo

As you type characters on the keyboard, the system is supposed to echo them back to you on the terminal screen (except when you are entering your password). If what you type does not appear on the screen, you can turn on the echo using the following command:

§ stty echo (RETURN)

On the other hand, if every character is being echoed **twice**, you should turn off the echo:

§ stty -echo (RETURN)

THE UNIX MANUAL

The UNIX system is described in detail in a massive document called the UNIX Programmer's Manual or User's Reference Manual, or simply the User's Manual. Your UNIX installation may have a printed (paper) copy of this manual, an on-line (electronic) version, or both.

The UNIX manual has the reputation of being difficult to read. It has been said that if you can read the manual, you do not need the manual. That is a bit of an exaggeration, but the manual is terse and takes some getting used to. Even so, it is a good idea to get familiar with the manual—it can be very useful.

B.1 Organization of the Manual

Most UNIX manuals have eight sections:

Section 1   User Commands

Section 2   UNIX and C System Calls

Section 3   Library Calls

Section 4   Device Drivers and Special Files

Section 5   File Formats and Conventions

Section 6   Games

Section 7   Miscellany

Section 8   System Administration Commands and Procedures

Your system's manuals may be arranged a bit differently. (For example, it is not uncommon to find that some spoilsport has deleted the games from the system.)

In addition to the usual eight manual sections, you may find supplementary articles and technical papers describing the UNIX system. These are usually grouped together and called something like "Documents for Use with the UNIX System," or "UNIX User's Supplement," or perhaps "UNIX Programmer's

Manual, Volume 2." We won't say much about this second part of the manual—if you happen to find a copy, you might want to browse through it to see if it contains anything of interest to you.

B.2 Using the man Command

If your system has an on-line manual, you can read it using the man command, which has the general form

§ man *command* (RETURN)

For example, to read the manual entry for the cal command, you would type

§ man cal (RETURN)

If your system has an on-line manual, this command will list a man page for cal, as shown in Listing B–1.

```
CAL(1)                    USER COMMANDS                    CAL(1)

NAME
      cal - display a calendar

SYNOPSIS
      cal [ [ month ] year ]

DESCRIPTION
      cal displays a calendar for the specified year. If
      a month is also specified, a calendar for that
      month only is displayed. If neither is specified,
      a calendar for the present month is displayed.

      year can be between 1 and 9999. Be aware that 'cal
      78' refers to the early Christian era, not the
      20th century. Also, the year is always considered
      to start in January, even though this is
      historically naive.

      month is a number between 1 and 12.

      The calendar produced is that for England and her
      colonies.


      Try September 1752.
```

Listing B-1
The manual page for the cal command.

B.3 Organization of a Manual Entry

All manual entries follow much the same format. Let's examine the various parts of the entry for the `cal` command:

- CAL(1)   USER COMMANDS   CAL(1)

The first line begins and ends with the name of the command, written entirely in caps (CAL). The number in parentheses (1) gives the section of the manual in which this entry is found.

- NAME
        cal - display a calendar

The name and a one-line description of the command are listed next.

- SYNOPSIS
        cal [[**month**] **year**]

This is probably the most useful part of the man page. It shows how the command is actually used. Anything shown in square brackets [] is optional. In this case, the brackets show that you can use the `cal` command either by itself, with the year only, or with the month and year. Thus, each of the following commands would be legal:

§ cal (RETURN)
§ cal 2001 (RETURN)
§ cal 5 2001 (RETURN)

Some commands take various options, which are typically preceded by a hyphen. The options will be shown here, along with the other arguments.

- DESCRIPTION

Next comes a written description of the command. This description may be as short as a paragraph, or it may go on for several pages, depending on the command.

B.4 Other Categories

The manual entry for the `cal` command is rather simple because the `cal` command itself is rather simple. Entries for other commands may contain still more headings. Depending on the command, you may see one or more of the following:

- FILES—Files used or created by the command are listed here under this heading.

- SEE ALSO—This entry will direct you to other entries in the manual that are related to the current topic.

■ DIAGNOSTICS—Some UNIX commands generate error messages. The more important or cryptic error messages will be described under this heading.

■ BUGS—Believe it or not, some UNIX commands contain minor errors—usually called "bugs"—that have been identified but yet not eliminated. If you are lucky, such bugs will be listed here.

B.5 Reading Longer Manual Pages

The manual entry for `cal` will probably fit entirely on your screen. Other manual entries are too long to be shown on the typical terminal screen all at once. For example, try reading the manual entry describing `man` itself:

§ man man (RETURN)

If the entire manual entry is too long to fit on the screen, you can pipe the output from the `man` command through the `more` or `pg` utility:

§ man man | more (RETURN)

or

§ man man | pg (RETURN)

The vertical line is called the *pipe symbol*.

STARTING X AND MOTIF

If your system does not have a display manager that starts the X server and window manager automatically, you will have to start them yourself. To do this, you should first log in according to the procedure presented in Chapter 3.

C.1 Starting X

1. Look for evidence of windows on your screen. If you see one or more windows, the X server is already running, and you can skip to Section C.2.

2. Start X. One of the following commands should work:

If none of these commands works, ask your system administrator for help.

§ xinit (RETURN)

§ startx (RETURN)

§ openwin (RETURN)

3. Wait for an xterm **window to appear.** See **Figure C-1**.

C.2 Starting the Motif Window Manager

1. If necessary, select the xterm **window.** Use the mouse to move the pointer to the xterm window.

2. Start the window manager. Enter the following command line:

§ mwm & (RETURN)

The ampersand (&) at the end of the command line causes mwm to be run "in the background." (Remember, UNIX is a multitasking OS.) This way, mwm will not interfere with any other programs you run.

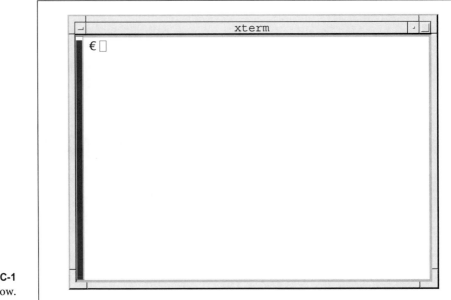

Figure C-1
An xterm window.

C.3 Logging Out

Some systems are configured to allow you to log out with a menu option. If your system does not offer such an option, logging out may be somewhat more complicated.

It is a good idea to ask your system administrator about the logout procedure.

1. Quit the window manager. There should be an option marked "Exit" or "Quit" on one of the pop-up menus. In some cases, this option will also stop X and log you out.

2. If necessary, stop X. Closing the original xterm window will do the trick.

3. If necessary, log out. One of the following commands should work:

§ logout (RETURN)

§ exit (RETURN)

§ (CONTROL)–(D)

REGULAR EXPRESSIONS

A *regular expression* (*regexp* or *regex* for short) is a notation for describing strings of characters. Regular expressions are used by many UNIX utilities (such as `vi` and `grep`) and scripting languages (such as the shell, `awk`, and Perl) to process text files.

D.1 Basic and Extended Regular Expressions

A number of regex dialects or "flavors" have been developed over the years. The differences between these flavors can sometimes be confusing. In an attempt to reduce the confusion, the 1986 POSIX standard defines two categories of regular expressions: Basic Regular Expressions (BRE) and Extended Regular Expressions (ERE). This appendix deals with both categories. Be warned that a particular utility or language may not follow the POSIX standards exactly.

D.2 Characters and Metacharacters

Regular expressions consist of *ordinary characters* and *metacharacters*. The ordinary characters include

- Uppercase and lowercase letters (A, B, C, …, a, b, c, …);

- Numerals (1, 2, 3, 4, 5, 6, 7, 8, 9);

- Spaces, underscores, commas, and other punctuation marks (except those used as metacharacters).

The metacharacters are

```
. [ ] ^ * ? + $ | \ ( ) { }
```

Each metacharacter has a special meaning in a regular expression—that is, it can represent characters other than itself. To use one of the metacharacters with its usual, literal meaning (representing only itself) you can quote it by writing a backslash (\) in front of it.

Metasymbol	Name	Meaning
.	Period	Any one character
[ ]	Character class	Any character listed in the brackets
[^]	Complement	Any character *not* listed in the brackets
*	Star	Zero or more of the preceding item
\{*min, max*\}	Range	As few as *min* or as many as *max* of the preceding item
^	Caret	Position at the start of a line
$	Dollar	Position at the end of a line
\<	Word boundary	Position at the start of a word
\>	Word boundary	Position at the end of a word
\(\)	Parentheses	Grouping
( )	Parentheses	Capturing
\1 *thru* \9	Backreferences	Reference to captured text
\	Backslash	Quote metacharacter
\\	Quoted backslash	Actual backslash
/	Delimiter	Beginning and end of a regular expression

Two or more metacharacters acting together are called a *metasequence*. We will use the term *metasymbol* to mean either a metacharacter or metasequence. Table D-1 lists the metasymbols used in Basic Regular Expressions (BRE); Table D-2 on page 541 lists the metasymbols used in Extended Regular Expressions (ERE).

D.3 Strings and Delimiters

The simplest regular expression is just a string of ordinary characters, not containing any metacharacters:

```
a
123_AbcdE
NCAA
armadillo
```

Programs such as awk, Perl, and sh (but not grep) recognize pattern *delimiters*, which enclose the regular expression but are not part of it. The usual delimiters are slashes (/). Hence,

```
/a/
/123_AbcdE/
/NCAA/
/armadillo/
```

Metasymbol	Name	Meaning
.	Period	Any one character
[ ]	Character class	Any character listed in the brackets
[^]	Complement	Any character *not* listed in the brackets
*	Star	Zero or more of the preceding item
?	Question	Zero or one of the preceding item
+	Plus	One or more of the preceding item
{*min, max*}	Range	As few as *min* or as many as *max* of the preceding item
^	Caret	Position at the start of a line
$	Dollar	Position at the end of a line
\<	Word boundary	Position at the start of a word
\>	Word boundary	Position at the end of a word
|	Bar	Alternation (or)
( )	Parentheses	Grouping
\	Backslash	Quote metacharacter
\\	Quoted backslash	Actual backslash
/	Delimiter	Beginning and end of a regular expression

Table D-2
Metasymbols used in POSIX Extended Regular Expressions (ERE).

Note that a slash that is part of a regular expression should be quoted (or "escaped") using a backslash:

1\/2 *matches the string* 1/2.

D.4 Matching

We will frequently talk about a regular expression "matching" a string of characters. What we mean is that the regular expression describes part of the string. Thus,

/at/ *matches* at, bat, battery, cat, catapult, *and so on.*

/a/ *matches any string containing the character* a.

We will omit the pattern delimiters in the examples that follow.

D.5 Single-Character Matches

There are three ways to specify a single character in a regular expression:

The period is similar to the ?
used in filename
completion.

■ **Period.** The period or dot (.) metacharacter matches any single character except (possibly) a newline or null character. Hence,

.at *matches* Aat, Bat, Cat, aat, bat, cat, 1at, 2at, *and so on.*

a.t *matches* aAt, aBt, aCt, aat, abt, act, a1t, a2t, *and so on.*

at. *matches* atA, atB, atC, ata, atb, atc, at1, at2, *and so on.*

To match a period, quote it using the backslash:

3\.14159\.\.\. *matches* 3.14159....

Be aware that some scripting languages allow the period to match a newline but most do not. Also many scripting languages allow a period to match a null character—that is, a character that has zero value.

■ **Character class.** Square brackets are used to match any one of a *class* of characters:

[aeiou] *matches any one of the letters* a, e, i, o, *or* u.

[br]at *matches* bat *or* rat.

...[aeiou] *matches any four-character string ending in a lowercase vowel.*

A hyphen may be used to specify a *range* of characters:

[A-Z] *matches any one of the uppercase letters* A *through* Z.

[1-5] *matches any single numeral from* 1 *to* 5.

[A-Za-z] *matches any single uppercase or lowercase letter.*

The hyphen is not special if it is the first character listed inside the brackets:

[-2468] *matches any one of the characters* -, 2, 4, 6, *or* 8.

■ **Complement class.** In a bracket expression, a caret (^) immediately following the open bracket means that none of the characters in the brackets is to be matched:

[^aeiou] *matches any single character except* a, e, i, o, *or* u.

...[^aeiou] *any four-character string not ending in a lowercase vowel.*

A caret is not special in a bracket expression if it does not immediately follow the open bracket:

[a^eiou] *matches any one of the characters* a, ^, e, i, o, *or* u.

As before, a hyphen may be used to specify a *range* of characters:

[^A-Z] *matches any single character that is not an uppercase letter.*

[^1-5] *matches any single character that is not 1, 2, 3, 4, or 5.*

[^A-Za-z] *matches any character except an uppercase or lowercase letter.*

[^br]at *matches a three-character string ending in* at *except* bat, *or* rat.

Within the square brackets, the only characters having a special meaning are the caret (^) when immediately following the open bracket, the hyphen (-) between two other characters, and other square brackets.

D.6 Quantifiers

The metacharacters discussed in the previous section match no more than one character at a time. You can modify this behavior by including one of the following quantifiers, which tell how many times a pattern is to be matched:

■ **Star.** The star or asterisk metacharacter (*) matches zero or more occurrences of the regular expression immediately preceding it. Hence,

c*at *matches* at, cat, ccat, cccat, *and so on.*

ca*t *matches* ct, cat, caat, caaat, *and so on.*

cat* *matches* ca, cat, catt, cattt, *and so on.*

[^1-9]* *matches any character sequence not beginning in a numeral.*

[a-zA-Z][a-zA-Z]* *matches any letter followed by zero or more letters.*

.* *matches any string (up to the next newline).*

Note that the last regular expression is similar to the asterisk wildcard (*) used in filename expansion, which matches any file name.

When multiple matches are possible, the asterisk tries to make the longest match possible.

[ERE]   ■ **Question mark.** The question mark metacharacter (?) matches zero or one occurrence of the regular expression immediately preceding it. In other words, the question mark indicates an optional item. Hence,

c?at *matches* at *or* cat.

ca?t *matches* ct *or* cat.

cat? *matches* ca *or* cat.

[^0-9]? *matches any character that is not a numeral*

[a-zA-Z][a-zA-Z]? *matches any letter followed by zero or one letters.*

.? *matches a null string or any character.*

[ERE]   ■ **Plus.** The plus sign metacharacter (+) matches one or more occurrences of the regular expression immediately preceding it. Hence,

c+at *matches* cat, ccat, cccat, *and so on, but not* at.

ca+t *matches* cat, caat, caaat, *and so on, but not* ct.

cat+ *matches* cat, catt, cattt, *and so on, but not* ca.

[^0-9]+ *matches one or more characters that are not numerals.*

[a-zA-Z][a-zA-Z]+ *matches any letter followed by one or more letters.*

When multiple matches are possible, the plus sign tries to make the longest match possible.

■ **Range quantifiers.** Both ERE and BRE allow you to specify the maximum and minimum number of times to match a pattern. The notation is slightly different:

[BRE]   c/{2,4/} *matches* cc, ccc, *and* cccc.

[ERE]   c{2,4} *matches* cc, ccc, *and* cccc.

D.7 Grouping

The quantifiers of the preceding section can be applied to groups of characters enclosed in parentheses. In a basic regular expression (BRE), the parentheses must be quoted by backslashes:

[BRE]   r\(at\)* *matches* r, rat, ratat, ratatat, *and so on.*

In an extended regular expression (ERE), no backslashes are used:

[ERE]   r(at)* *matches* r, rat, ratat, ratatat, *and so on.*

[ERE]   r(at)? *matches* r *and* rat.

[ERE]   r(at)+ *matches* rat, ratat, ratatat, *and so on.*

D.8 Anchors

The regular expressions discussed thus far will match strings that occur anywhere as part of other strings. Sometimes, it is required to specify where the match should occur. For this you need an anchor.

■ **Start of line.** When the caret (^) appears as the first character of a regular expression, it "anchors" the expression to the start of the line. In other words, a match is made only if the string is found at the beginning of a line:

^F *matches the character* F *occurring at the beginning of a line.*

^From *matches the string* From *occurring at the beginning of a line.*

^... *matches any three-character string at the beginning of a line.*

^cat* *matches* ca, cat, catt, cattt, *etc., at the beginning of a line.*

■ **End of line.** The dollar-sign metacharacter ($) anchors a regular expression to the end of a line. Hence,

F$ *matches the character* F *occurring at the end of a line.*

From$ *matches the string* From *occurring at the end of a line.*

...$ *matches any three-character string at the end of a line.*

cat*$ *matches* ca, cat, catt, cattt, *etc., at the end of a line.*

As the following examples show, both anchors may be used together:

^$ *matches blank lines.*

^.*$ *matches an entire line.*

You can cancel the special meaning of the anchors using the backslash (\):

\^$ *matches a caret appearing at the end of a line.*

^\$ *matches a dollar sign appearing at the start of a line.*

■ **Word boundary.** The word-boundary anchors \< and \> match the beginning and end of a word, respectively. A "word" is a sequence of "word characters" (usually alphanumeric characters such as a-z, A-Z, and 0-9).

\<hat *matches* hat, hate, hatter, *etc., but not* that, chat, chatter, *etc.*

hat\> *matches* that, chat, *etc.*

\<hat *matches the word* hat *only.*

...\> *matches any three-character string at the end of a word*

Some tools use different word-boundary anchors. For instance, Perl uses \b to match either the beginning or the end of a word.

D.9 Alternation

[ERE]
Extended regular expressions (ERE) allow the use of the alternation operator (|), which allows a choice between two or more alternatives:

(T|t)he *matches* The *or* the.

(Tom|Dick|Harry) *matches* Tom, Dick, *or* Harry.

D.10 Back-References

[BRE]
We have seen that parentheses can be used to group characters in a pattern. In a basic regular expression (BRE), parentheses also "capture" and store a substring matched by the pattern. A *back-reference* recalls the stored substring from memory to perform another match.

More than one pair of capturing parentheses may be used in a regular expression. Each pair of parentheses is associated with its own memory location. A back-reference consists of a backslash followed by a number corresponding to the set of parentheses. For example, \1 contains any matched string from the first pair of parentheses, \2 contains any matched string from the second pair of parentheses, and so on.

Instead of the backslash, Perl uses a dollar sign ($).

(.)\1 *matches any character followed by the same character* (aa, ! !, AA, *etc.*).

(the)\1 *matches* To the the top.

D.11 POSIX Character Classes

The POSIX standard introduced a set of special character classes that can be used inside bracket expressions. Some of these are listed in Table D-3. The exact list will vary by *locale*, which includes such considerations as the language and alphabet. Thus, in most English-speaking locales,

[[:upper:]] *matches any uppercase letter,* A *through* Z.

This is equivalent to the character class [A-Z]. In other locales, however, [[:upper:]] may include different characters (such as Å).

Table D-3
POSIX character classes.

Class	Meaning
[:alnum:]	Alphanumeric characters (letters and digits)
[:alpha:]	Alphabetic characters
[:blank:]	Blanks (space and tab)
[:cntrl]	Control characters
[:digit:]	Digits
[:graph:]	Printable and visible (non-blank) characters
[:lower:]	Lowercase alphabetic characters
[:print:]	Printable characters (not control characters)
[:punct:]	Punctuation
[:space:]	Spaces
[:upper:]	Uppercase alphabetic characters
[:xdigit:]	Characters allowed in hexadecimal numbers (0-9, a-f, A-F)

D.12 Class Shorthands

Many regexes (most notably Perl) recognize shorthand notation for certain character classes, as shown in Table D-4.

Table D-4

Class shorthand escape sequences.

Class	Meaning
\d	Digit—equivalent to [0-9]
\D	Not a digit—equivalent to [^0-9]
\n	Newline character
\r	Return character
\s	Whitespace (space, tab, newline, formfeed, etc.)
\S	Not whitespace
\t	Tab character
\w	"Word" character—equivalent to [a-zA-Z0-9_]
\W	Not a "word" character—equivalent to [^a-zA-Z0-9_]

Table D-4

Class shorthand escape sequences.

D.13 Regular Expression Flavors

Few utilities or scripting languages follow the POSIX regex syntax exactly. Most recognize a combination of basic regular expressions (BREs) and extended regular expressions (EREs), with a few extensions of their own. Table D-5 gives some idea of the differences that you may encounter.

Table D-5

Metasymbols used by various utilities and scripting languages.

	grep	egrep	sh	awk	Perl
Any character	.	.	.	.	.
Character class	[ ]	[ ]	[ ]	[ ]	[ ]
Complement	[^]	[^]	[^]	[^]	[^]
Zero or more	*	*	*	*	*
Zero or one	\?	?	?	?	?
One or more	\+	+	+	+	+
Range	\{n, m\}	{n, m}	{n, m}	{n, m}	{n, m}
Start of line	^	^	^	^	^
End of line	$	$	$	$	$
Word start	\<	\<	\<	\<	\b
Word end	\>	\>	\>	\>	\b
Alternation	|	|	|	|	|
Grouping	\(\)	( )	( )	( )	( )
Backreferences	\1 to \9		\1 to \9		$1 ...

FORMATTED OUTPUT

The C programming language introduced the `printf` ("print-formatted") library function for producing formatted output. Similar functions are available in C++, the Bourne family of shells, awk, and Perl.

A `printf` function call has the following form

printf(*format*, *expression1*, *expression2*, ...)

where *format* is a string describing the format of the output, and *expression1*, *expression2*, ... are expressions to be printed according to the format string.

For example, consider the following C statement, and suppose that x contains the value 5:

```
printf("The square root of %f is %f.\n", x, sqrt(x));
```

The call to `printf` will produce the output

```
The square root of 5.000000 is 2.236068.
```

The format string

```
"The square root of %f is %f.\n"
```

represents the output from `printf`, with placeholders (%f and %f) showing where the values x and `sqrt(x)` will appear.

The placeholders are called *conversion specifiers*. Table E-1 lists the most common `printf` conversion specifiers; Table E-2 shows how numbers are printed using various conversion specifiers. Keep in mind that a conversion specifier only affects how a number is printed; it does not change how the number is stored or used in calculations.

Specifier	Represents
%c	character
%d, %i	decimal (base-10) integer
%e	e-notation: one digit before, six digits after the decimal point; at least two digits in the exponent, lowercase e
%E	E-notation; one digit before, six digits after the decimal point; at least two digits in the exponent, uppercase E
%f	decimal fraction: six digits after decimal point
%g	%e or %f, whichever is shorter; trailing zeros after decimal point suppressed; no more than six digits printed
%G	%E or %f, whichever is shorter; trailing zeros after decimal point suppressed; no more than six digits printed
%o	unsigned octal (base-8) integer
%s	string
%u	unsigned decimal (base-10) integer
%x	unsigned hexadecimal (base-16) integer
%%	%

The %f specifier prints numbers as decimal fractions having six digits after the decimal point; if necessary, the number is padded with trailing zeros to fill out the six decimal digits.

The %e specifier also prints six digits after the decimal point (not including the digits in the exponent), and it pads the output with zeros if necessary. (The %E specification is similar, except that it prints an uppercase E for the exponent.)

The %g specifier is the most convenient for most numbers. For very large or very small magnitudes, it uses e-notation. Otherwise, it uses %f notation. The %g specifier also trims trailing zeros after the decimal point.

A printf conversion specifier can be modified to include a *field width*, which sets the minimum number of spaces to be reserved for the output. A minus sign preceding the field width causes the output to be left-justified. Hence,

%10f ⇒ right-justified, 10-space field, f-format

%10g ⇒ right-justified, 10-space field, g-format

%-4s ⇒ left-justified, 4-space field, string

	7.0×10^{-6}	5.69×10^{0}	1.066×10^{3}	9.87654321×10^{6}
%d	0	5	1066	9876543
%e	7.000000e-06	5.690000e+00	1.066000e+03	9.876543e+06
%E	7.000000E-06	5.690000E+00	1.066000E+03	9.876543E+06
%f	0.000007	5.690000	1066.000000	9876543.210000
%g	7e-06	5.69	1066	9.87654e+06
%G	7E-06	5.69	1066	9.87654E+06
%i	0	5	1066	9876543

Table E-2
Examples of conversion specifiers for numbers.

A specifier may include the *precision,* which tells how many characters or digits to print. For example,

%12.3f ⇒ right-justified, 12-space field, 3 digits after decimal point, f-format

%12.8s ⇒ right-justified, 12-space field, maximum 8 characters, string format

%-8.3g ⇒ left-justified, 8-space field, 3 significant digits, g-format

%10.8i ⇒ right-justified, 10-space field, at least 8 digits, integer

%.6g ⇒ 6 significant digits, g-format

Appendix

F

USING DBX

The standard UNIX debugger **dbx** can debug programs written in C, C++, Fortran, or Pascal. To use **dbx**, you must compile your program using the -g option. For example, consider the C program `recip.c` (Listing 37-2).

```
/* Compute reciprocals */

#include <stdio.h>

int main(void)
{
    int n, recip;
    printf("This program computes reciprocals.\n");
    printf("Enter a number: ");
    scanf("%d", &n);
    recip = 1/n;
    printf("The reciprocal of %d is %d.\n", n, recip);
    return 0;
}
```

Listing 37-2
C code for the `recip.c` program.

To prepare this program for debugging, you would use the command line

Note the "debugging option" -g.

§ cc -g recip.c (RETURN)

to compile the program using the **cc** compiler. (Other compilers behave similarly —see the **man** page for yours.) Once this is done, you can run **dbx** on the executable file:

§ dbx a.out (RETURN)

The computer will respond with a cryptic message (which you can ignore), something like

Reading symbolic information...

Then it will give you a prompt that shows you are inside **dbx**:

(dbx)

F.1 Getting Help with dbx

The first thing to try is the help command. At the dbx prompt type:

```
(dbx) help RETURN
```

The computer should respond with a listing of the various dbx commands:

```
Command Summary

Execution and Tracing
catch     clear     cont      delete    ignore
next      rerun     run       status    step
stop      trace     when
```

and so on. Take a moment to look over the entire list. You may notice a few UNIX shell commands (cd, pwd, setenv, sh), and some other commands whose purpose you can probably guess. (edit, for example, calls up the text editor so you can edit the source file from within dbx.) We will not try to go over all of the available commands; you can do quite a lot with just the following dozen commands:

```
cont    display   help    print  quit   rerun
run     sh        step    stop   trace  where
```

You can use the help command to find out more information on any of these commands. Try using help on itself:

```
(dbx) help help RETURN
```

You should see a brief synopsis of the help command. (Note that <cmd> stands for any dbx command, <topic> stands for any topic, and so forth.) Although the help command does not provide much information on any of the commands, it is better than nothing.

F.2 Running the Program

The command to run the program is, appropriately enough, run. Try this:

```
(dbx) run RETURN
```

Except for some additional information printed by dbx itself, your program should run as usual:

```
Running: a.out
(Access id 3431)
This program computes reciprocals.
Enter a number:
```

Enter the number 1 and press RETURN:

```
Enter a number: 1 RETURN
```

The output should resemble the following:

The output on your system may not be exactly like this.

```
The reciprocal of 1 is 1.
execution completed, exit code is 1
(dbx)
```

The message "exit code is 1" simply tells you that the program completed successfully.

Running a program from inside dbx doesn't seem too useful—after all, it is easier to run the program directly, without first calling up the debugger to do the job. What dbx allows you to do is step through the program, one line at a time, and examine the values of the variables and expressions as they change.

F.3 Listing the Source Code

The list command will show you the source code. Try it:

```
(dbx) list 1, 15 (RETURN)
```

This tells dbx that you wish to see the source code from line 1 to line 15. dbx will display the file, numbering the lines as it does so. (The line numbers are not actually added to the source file.)

F.4 Setting Breakpoints

A *breakpoint* is a place in the program where you want the execution to halt. Breakpoints may be set using the stop command. Let's set a breakpoint at line 8:

```
(dbx) stop at 8 (RETURN)
```

dbx will tell you that it has set the breakpoint:

```
stop at "recip.c":8
```

Now use the run command to begin execution:

```
(dbx) run (RETURN)
```

The program will run until it reaches line 8, where it will stop. dbx will then display line 8:

```
Running: a.out
stopped in main at line 8 in file "recip.c"
8    printf("This program calculates reciprocals.\n");
(dbx)
```

F.5 Stepping through the Program

At this point, you could resume execution of the program by using the `cont` ("continue") command, but it is more instructive to step through the program one line at a time. The `step` command allows you to do this:

```
(dbx) step (RETURN)
```

You should see something like this:

```
This program computes reciprocals.
stopped in main at line 9 in file "recip.c"
9   printf("Enter a number:");
(dbx)
```

Note that the first thing you see is the line that was printed out by the previous statement. Step again, but step two lines this time:

```
(dbx) step 2 (RETURN)
```

The prompt produced by line 9 now appears:

```
Enter a number:
```

Type in a 1 and press (RETURN):

```
Enter a number: 1 (RETURN)
```

The program reads the number (on line 10) as it would normally. Then it proceeds to the next line (line 11) of the program and stops:

```
stopped in main at line 11 in file "recip.c"
11   recip = 1/n;
(dbx)
```

F.6 Printing Expressions

The `print` command allows you to examine the values of variables. For example, to view the value of n, you would enter

```
(dbx) print n (RETURN)
```

dbx will respond with the current value of n:

```
n = 1
(dbx)
```

Step again:

```
(dbx) step
stopped in main at line 12 in file "recip.c"
12printf("The reciprocal of %d is %d.\n", n, recip);
```

Use `print` to check the values of both n and `recip`:

```
(dbx) print n, recip (RETURN)
n = 1
recip = 1
(dbx)
```

Use the cont command to continue execution of the program; this will run through the remaining lines without stopping:

```
(dbx) cont (RETURN)
```

You should see something like this:

```
The reciprocal of 1 is 1.
```

```
execution completed, exit code is 1
(dbx)
```

The program is now finished running, but you are still inside dbx. Leave dbx using the quit command:

```
(dbx) quit (RETURN)
§
```

F.7 Tracing Variables and Functions

The trace command prints the values of variables as they are changed, as well as the calls to functions in the program. Start up dbx:

```
§ dbx a.out (RETURN)
```

The dbx prompt tells you that you are in dbx:

```
Reading symbolic information...
(dbx)
```

We want to trace the value of n in the main() function:

```
(dbx) trace n in main (RETURN)
```

dbx will confirm that the trace is set up:

```
(2) trace n
(dbx)
```

We also want to trace the value of recip:

```
(dbx) trace recip in main (RETURN)
(3) trace recip
(dbx)
```

Let's trace calls to the main() function as well:

```
(dbx) trace main (RETURN)
(4) trace main
```

Now run the program:

```
(dbx) run (RETURN)
```

dbx will run the program, displaying the values of the variables and showing calls to the function:

```
Running: a.out
(process id 3558)
main called from function _start
initially (at line "recip_c":8): recip = -26843620
initially (at line "recip_c":8): n = 0
This program computes reciprocals.
Enter a number:
```

Enter the number 1 at the prompt and note how the values of the variables are printed as they change:

```
Enter a number: 1  (RETURN)
after line "recip.c":10: n = 1
after line "recip.c":11: recip = 1
The reciprocal of 1 is 1.
main returns 1

execution completed, exit code is 1
```

Enter the rerun command:

```
(dbx) rerun (RETURN)
```

dbx will run the program again:

```
Running: a.out
(process id 3565)
main called from function _start
initially (at line "recip_c":8): recip = -26843620
initially (at line "recip_c":8): n = 0
This program computes reciprocals.
Enter a number:
```

Enter zero to cause an error:

```
Enter a number: 0 (RETURN)
terminating signal 8 SIGFPE
```

Leave dbx:

```
(dbx) quit (RETURN)
```

Use the `ls` command to see that a `core` file was created:

§ `ls` (RETURN)

F.8 Using where

You cannot read a `core` file, but dbx can. In particular, the `where` command in dbx allows you to find out where in the program the error occurred. Start dbx on the `a.out` and `core` files:

§ `dbx a.out core` (RETURN)

You might expect to see a few warnings before the dbx prompt appears:

The output on your system may be different.

```
Reading symbolic information...
core header file read successfully.
Reading symbolic information...
Reading symbolic information...
Reading symbolic information...
program terminated by signal FPE (integer divide by zero)
Current function is main
   11        recip = 1/n;
(dbx)
```

This tells you that the `core` file was generated by a division by zero. It also shows that this occurred on line 11 in the `main()` function. Some versions of dbx require that you use the `where` command to determine where the error occurred:

```
(dbx) where (RETURN)
[1] .div(0x1, 0x0, 0x4, ...
[2] main(), line 11 in "recip.c"
(dbx)
```

The last line before the dbx prompt tells you that the error occurred on line 11 of the function `main()`.

For a short and simple program like `recip.c`, a debugger may not be a necessity. However, a debugger becomes very important when creating large or complicated programs.

F.9 Running Shell Commands in dbx

The `sh` command allows you to run shell commands while you are still inside dbx. Use this command with `rm` to delete the `core` file:

```
(dbx) sh rm core (RETURN)
```

Now use `sh` and `ls` to check that the `core` file has indeed been removed:

```
(dbx) sh ls (RETURN)
```

USING MAKE

The UNIX make program is designed to manage large, multifile projects by keeping track of any changes that are made in the source files. It allows you to modify and recompile one source file without having to recompile the entire program.

G.1 The makefile

The make program looks for its instructions in a file named either makefile or Makefile. For the C program in the Trip directory (Section 37.11), create a file named makefile, and enter the lines shown in Listing G–1.

```
① # Makefile for the Trip program

② trip: main.o chicago.o indiana.o indy.o
③ (TAB)cc -o trip main.o chicago.o indiana.o indy.o

   main.o: main.c
   (TAB)cc -c main.c

④ chicago.o: chicago.c
⑤ (TAB)cc -c chicago.c

   indiana.o: indiana.c
   (TAB)cc -c indiana.c

   indy.o: indy.c
   (TAB)cc -c indy.c

⑥ clean:
⑦ (TAB)rm *.o
```

Listing G—
Makefile for the Trip
program.

Let's consider some of the interesting features of this file:

① `# Makefile for the Trip program`

This is a *comment line*. `make` ignores anything that follows a pound sign (#).

② `trip: main.o chicago.o indiana.o indy.o`

This is a called a *dependency line*. It indicates that the file `trip` depends on the object files `main.o`, `chicago.o`, `indiana.o`, and `indy.o`. Note that the dependency line must begin in the first column.

③ (TAB)`cc -o trip main.o chicago.o indiana.o indy.o`

This is an *action line*. It follows the dependency line and shows how the file `trip` is created from the files `main.o`, `chicago.o`, `indiana.o`, and `indy.o`. In this case, `cc` links the object files and puts the executable into `trip`. Action lines must begin with a tab.

④ `chicago.o: chicago.c`

This is another dependency line, showing that `chicago.o` depends on the source file `chicago.c`.

⑤ (TAB)`cc -c chicago.c`

This is an *action line*, showing that `chicago.o` is produced by compiling `chicago.c` using `cc` with the `-c` option.

⑥ `clean:`

This dependency line indicates that "clean" does not depend on any file. It is an example of an *empty dependency*. In this case, "clean" is not the name of a file, but rather a command, which you would run by typing

§ `make clean` (RETURN)

`make` will then look through `makefile`, find the empty dependency "clean," and run the command on the next action line.

⑦ (TAB)`rm *.o`

This action line will remove any files ending in `.o`—in other words, the object files. This is the action that `make` will perform when you type

§ `make clean` (RETURN)

G.2 Running make

The first thing to do with make is to remove the executable and object files that were produced when you compiled the Trip program the first time. Try the ls command to see the files in Trip:

§ ls (RETURN)

You should see something like this:

```
a.out         indiana.c    indy.o      main.o
chicago.c     indiana.o    main.c      makefile
chicago.o     indy.c
```

Now get rid of the old object files:

§ make clean (RETURN)

The "clean" dependency line in makefile causes the following command line to run:

```
rm *.o
```

Use the ls command now to list the files remaining in Trip:

§ ls (RETURN)

You should see:

```
a.out         indiana.c    main.c
chicago.c     indy.c       makefile
```

Note that make did nothing to the old executable file a.out, because it was not instructed to do so.

Next, use make to compile the program. Simply type make and press (RETURN):

§ make (RETURN)

make then follows the instructions in makefile to compile the program:

```
cc -c main.c
cc -c chicago.c
cc -c indiana.c
cc -c indy.c
cc -o trip main.o chicago.o indiana.o indy.o
```

Note that the files are not necessarily compiled in exactly the same order as they appear in makefile; instead, make figures out which files should be compiled first. Try the ls command to see the files in Trip:

§ ls (RETURN)

You should see something like this:

```
a.out      indiana.c    indy.o     makefile
chicago.c  indiana.o    main.c     trip
chicago.o  indy.c       main.o
```

trip contains the new executable code, which you can run simply by typing trip, followed by (RETURN):

§ trip (RETURN)

The advantage of using make to compile the files becomes apparent when you begin making alterations in any of the source files. When you are finished, all you have to do is type make, and make will automatically recompile only those files that need it. And if you have not made any changes in the program, make will take no action. To see how this works, try running make again:

§ make (RETURN)

Assuming you have not made any changes in the files, you should see a message such as

'trip' is up to date. (RETURN)

WRITE AND TALK

The `write` and `talk` utilities are similar to each other in that both allow you to communicate directly with a user who is logged into the system. Whatever either of you types on your keyboard appears simultaneously on both screens. Of the two utilities, `write` is less convenient because the messages can become garbled if both of you try to type at the same time. `talk` separates the messages, even if both of you type simultaneously.

H.1 Sending and Receiving Messages

Using either `write` or `talk` is a five-step process:

1. The first user requests a session with the second user. Suppose, for example, that the user `george` wishes to communicate with `martha`. To do this, he would type

§ talk martha ⟨RETURN⟩

or

§ write martha ⟨RETURN⟩

2. The second user is notified. Thus, if `martha` is logged in and receiving messages, she will be alerted:

Message from george...

3. The second user agrees to answer. `martha` would have to type

§ talk george ⟨RETURN⟩

or

§ write george ⟨RETURN⟩

4. The two users exchange messages. Anything that either user types will be displayed on both terminals. Most people using `write` work out a convention whereby only one types at a time, signaling the end of a thought with an `o` (for "over").

5. When finished, they break off communication. To quit `talk`, one of the parties has to type (CONTROL)-(C). To quit `write`, however, both users must type (CONTROL)-(D).

H.2 Refusing and Accepting Messages

You can refuse to accept `write` or `talk` messages with the command

§ mesg n

which is short for "messages—no." Anyone trying to establish contact with you using `write` or `talk` will get the message:

Your party is refusing messages.

(Electronic mail will still get through, however.) To accept messages again, you would use the command

§ mesg y

INDEX

Symbols

A